W9-AQL-038

FOURTH EDITION
Reader's Choice

Sandra Silberstein
University of Washington

Barbara K. Dobson
University of Michigan

Mark A. Clarke
University of Colorado at Denver

Ann Arbor

THE UNIVERSITY OF MICHIGAN PRESS

808
.0427
Read

Acknowledgments

These are tender times. As we enter the new millennium, we are increasingly grateful for the love and support of those who live and work beside us and mindful of friends who are no longer here. This edition owes much to the leadership of Mary Erwin, who created an environment that permitted us to bear down on long-postponed tasks, and to Kelly Sippell, whose insightful contributions and personal commitment often reached the level of co-authorship.

Ann Arbor, Denver, Seattle, September 2001

As we enter our third decade of collaboration, we would like to thank spouses and children who have endured countless hours of conference calls and overnight-mail runs. Thanks are also due Sue Hodes and Sharon Tsutsui for thoughtful comments on this edition. And we are especially fortunate to have had the skilled and enthusiastic support of the University of Michigan Press: Associate Editor Chris Milton has been correcting us for as long as we can remember; Executive Editor LeAnn Fields first persuaded us that our sanity could withstand revision; Assistant Director Mary Erwin erased our memories of the first revision; and Director Colin Day has paid the bills.

Ann Arbor, Denver, Seattle, February 1994

We thank the many teachers who, over the years, have provided insights and suggestions for revision. To the roll call from the previous edition, we add the following names and apologize for any omissions: Sally Alexander, Kathryn Allahyari, Carol Deselams, Patricia A. Carrell, Joan Eisterhold, Pat Grogan, Liz Hamp-Lyons, Linda Hillman, Sara Klinghammer, Cherie Lenz-Hackett, Ellen Lipp, Daphne Mackey, Sharon Myers, Marnie Ramker, Sam Shepherd, Jerry Stanfield, Marianne Wieferich, Kay Winfield. We are grateful to our colleagues and to the dynamic context of TESOL reading pedagogy and research. Similarly, we continue to benefit from the contributions of our coauthors on the first edition, Margaret Baudoin Metzinger and Ellen Bober.

Special thanks to research assistants Elisabeth Mitchell, University of Washington, and Kathy Riley, University of Colorado at Denver, and to our colleagues at the University of Michigan Press.

Finally, we once again thank our families for continued support and patience toward a task that, no doubt, they hoped they had seen the last of.

Denver, Detroit, Seattle, June 1987

The successful completion of *Reader's Choice* is the result of the cooperation, confidence, and endurance of many people. The authors greatly appreciate the contributions of the individuals listed below. It is impossible to overestimate the importance of their efforts in helping us meet deadlines, their insights during classroom testing, and their encouragement through critique and rewrite sessions.

Heartfelt thanks, therefore to:

H. Douglas Brown, director of the English Language Institute (ELI), University of Michigan, whose assistance ranged from personal and professional advice to administrative and financial support. Professor Brown has consistently encouraged creativity and innovation at the ELI. His continued support of *Reader's Choice* ensured its successful completion.

Eleanor Foster, ELI administrative assistant and her capable secretarial and production staff: Elaine Allen, Ginny Barnett, Shelly Cole, Gail Curtis, Lynne Davis, Sue Feldstein, Martha Graham, Donna Head, Barbara Kerwin, Debbie Milly, Lisa Neff, Cathy Pappas, and Louisa Plyler.

George E. Luther and Roderick D. Fraser, ELI administrators, whose efforts made possible financial support and the classroom testing of *Reader's Choice*.

David P. Harris, director of the American Language Institute, Georgetown University; ELI authors Joan Morley and Mary Lawrence; Betsy Soden, ELI lecturer and reading coordinator; Carlos A. Yorio, professor of Linguistics, Toronto University—colleagues in English as a second language (ESL) whose critiques of early drafts proved invaluable.

ESL teachers whose patient and skillful use of the materials through numerous stages of development made detailed revisions and improvements possible—Honor Griffith and Lynne Kurylo of the University of Toronto; Betsy Berriman, Cristin Carpenter, Eve Daniels, Susan Dycus, Adelaide Heyde, Wayne Lord, Michele McCullough, Nancy Morrison, Syd Rand, and John Schafer of the English Language Institute.

And finally, thank you to Mario, Patricia, Tom, and Doug, friends and family for their patience and support; our parents and children, for whose pride and enthusiasm we are grateful; our students, whose insightful suggestions made revisions possible; and all the teachers and staff of the English Language Institute for providing an atmosphere which nurtures innovative teaching and creative materials development.

The authors wish to gratefully acknowledge grants from the English Language Institute and *Language Learning,* which provided funds for released time for several of the authors, and for secretarial and production assistance.

Ann Arbor, June 1977

Contents

Introduction

To:	Students
From:	Sandra Silberstein, Barbara K. Dobson, Mark A. Clarke
Re:	Getting acquainted with *Reader's Choice*

Welcome to the fourth edition of *Reader's Choice*. This book has been written to meet the needs of teachers and students in a rapidly changing world. The purpose of this introduction is to acquaint you with the book and with our approach to teaching reading in English as a second or foreign language.

We believe that reading is an active process in which effective readers bring their understanding of the world to bear on text. Whether reading a book or an article, an advertisement or a chart, or surfing the World Wide Web—regardless of the content or form of the material—successful readers rely on an attitude of independence and the coordination of a number of skills and strategies. Efficient readers approach material with goals in mind, and they adjust their behavior accordingly. They develop expectations, and they read to confirm, reject, or adjust those expectations. Most of this is done without conscious attention to the process. The material in *Reader's Choice* gives you practice in this kind of independent, efficient, and critical reading.

We believe *Reader's Choice* is most effective when it is used in situations where curiosity and active participation are encouraged. It is a tool that will help you and your teachers develop a partnership for learning. You will see that we speak directly to students in the directions, exercises, and answer key. To the extent possible, we have tried to permit you to get to know us and our approach to teaching and learning—and to living. We encourage you to take a playful approach to the readings and exercises in this book and to interact with the book and each other in ways that permit you, as individuals, to develop your own attitude and approach to learning.

When you look at the Contents page you will notice that there are three kinds of units in *Reader's Choice*. The odd-numbered units (1 through 11) contain language skills work. These exercises give you intensive practice in using word-, sentence-, and discourse-level reading strategies. The even-numbered units (2 through 12) contain reading selections that give you the opportunity to use the skills you have learned to interact with and evaluate the ideas of texts. Finally, Units 13 and 14 consist of longer, more complex reading selections.

Basic language and reading skills are introduced in early units and reinforced throughout the book. The large number of exercises provides opportunities for repeated practice. Do not be discouraged if you do not finish each exercise, if you have trouble answering specific questions, or if you do not understand everything in a particular reading. The purpose of the tasks in *Reader's Choice* is to help improve your problem-solving skills. For this reason, the process of attempting to answer a question is often as important as the answer itself.

Reader's Choice contains exercises that provide practice in both language and reading skills. In this Introduction we will first provide a description of language skills exercises followed by a description of the reading skills work contained in the book.

Language Skills Exercises

Word Study Exercises

Upon encountering an unfamiliar vocabulary item in a passage there are several strategies available to readers. First, you can continue reading, realizing that often a single word will not prevent understanding of the general meaning of a selection. If further reading does not solve the problem, you can use one or more of three basic skills to arrive at an understanding of the unfamiliar word. You can use context clues to see if surrounding words and grammatical structures provide information about the unknown word. You can use word analysis to see if understanding the parts of the word leads to an understanding of the word. Or, you can use a dictionary to find an appropriate definition. *Reader's Choice* contains numerous exercises that provide practice in these three skills.

Word Study: Context Clues

Guessing the meaning of an unfamiliar word from **Context Clues** involves using the following kinds of information:
  a. knowledge of the topic about which you are reading
  b. knowledge of the meanings of the other words in the sentence (or paragraph) in which the word occurs
  c. knowledge of the grammatical structure of the sentences in which the word occurs

When these exercises appear in skills units, their purpose is to provide practice in guessing the meanings of unfamiliar words using context clues. Students should not necessarily try to learn the meanings of the vocabulary items in these exercises. The **Vocabulary from Context** exercises that accompany reading selections have a different purpose. Generally these exercises should be done before a reading selection is begun and used as an introduction to the reading. The vocabulary items have been chosen for three reasons:
  a. because they are fairly common and therefore useful for students to learn
  b. because they are important for an understanding of the passage
  c. because their meanings are not easily available from the context in the selection

Word Study: Stems and Affixes

Another way to discover the meanings of unfamiliar vocabulary items is to use word analysis, that is, to use knowledge of the meanings of the parts of a word. Many English words have been formed by combining parts of older English, Greek, and Latin words. For instance, the word *bicycle* is formed from the parts *bi,* meaning two, and *cycle,* meaning round or wheel. Often knowledge of the meanings of these word parts (along with context) can help the reader to guess the meaning of an unfamiliar word. Exercises in **Word Study: Stems and Affixes** provide practice in this skill at regular intervals throughout the book. The **Appendix** lists all of the stems and affixes that appear in these exercises.

Word Study: Dictionary Use

Sometimes the meaning of a single word is essential to an understanding of the total meaning of a selection. If context clues and word analysis do not provide enough information, it will be necessary to use a dictionary. The **Word Study: Dictionary Use** exercises in the skills units provide students with a review of the information available from dictionaries and practice in using a dictionary to obtain that information. The **Dictionary Study** exercises that accompany some of the reading selections require students to use the context of an unfamiliar vocabulary item to find an appropriate definition of the items from the dictionary entries provided.

Sentence Study Exercises

Sometimes comprehension of an entire passage requires the understanding of a single sentence. **Sentence Study** exercises give students practice in analyzing the structure of sentences to determine the relationships of ideas within a sentence. You will be presented with a complicated sentence followed by tasks that require analyzing the sentence for its meaning. Often you will be required to use the available information to draw inferences about the author's message.

Paragraph Reading and Paragraph Analysis Exercises

These exercises give you practice at the paragraph level. Some of the paragraph exercises are designed to provide practice in discovering the general message. You will be asked to determine the main idea of a passage: that is, the idea that is the most important, around which the paragraph is organized. Other paragraph exercises are meant to provide practice in careful, detailed reading. You will be required not only to find the main idea of a passage but also to guess vocabulary from context, to answer questions about specific details in the paragraph, and to draw conclusions based on an understanding of the passage.

Discourse Focus

Effective reading requires the ability to select skills and strategies appropriate to a specific reading task. The reading process involves using information from the full text and knowledge of the world in order to interpret a passage. Readers use this information to make predictions about what they will find in a text and to decide how they will read. Sometimes we need to read quickly to obtain only a general idea of a text; at other times we read carefully, drawing inferences about the intent of the author. Discourse-level exercises introduce these various approaches to reading, which are then reinforced throughout the book. These reading skills are described in more detail in the discussion that follows.

Nonprose Reading

Throughout *Reader's Choice,* nonprose selections (such as a menu, bus schedule, road map, etc.) provide practice reading material that is not primarily arranged in sentences and paragraphs. It is important to remember that the same problem-solving skills are used to read both prose and nonprose material.

Reading Skills Exercises

Students will need to use all of their language skills in order to understand the reading selections in *Reader's Choice.* The book contains many types of selections on a wide variety of topics. These selections provide practice in using different reading strategies to comprehend texts. They also give practice in four basic reading skills: **skimming, scanning, reading for thorough comprehension,** and **critical reading.** An introduction to each of these is presented, with exercises, in Unit 1, and practiced throughout the even-numbered units.

Skimming

Skimming is quick reading for the general idea(s) of a passage. This kind of rapid reading is appropriate when trying to decide if careful reading would be desirable or when there is not time to read something carefully.

Scanning

Like skimming, scanning is also quick reading. However, in this case the search is more focused. To scan is to read quickly in order to locate specific information. When you read to find a particular date, name, or number, you are scanning.

Reading for Thorough Comprehension

Reading for thorough comprehension is careful reading in order to understand the total meaning of the passage. At this level of comprehension, the reader is able to summarize the author's ideas but has not yet made a critical evaluation of those ideas.

Critical Reading

Critical reading demands that readers make judgments about what they read. This kind of reading requires posing and answering questions such as *Does my own experience support that of the author? Do I share the author's point of view? Am I convinced by the author's arguments and evidence?*

Systematic use of the exercises and readings in *Reader's Choice* will give you practice in the basic language and reading skills necessary to become a proficient reader. Additional suggestions for the use of *Reader's Choice* in a classroom setting are included in the **Teacher** section.

To:	**The Teacher**
From:	**Sandra Silberstein, Barbara K. Dobson, Mark A. Clarke**
Re:	**Using *Reader's Choice***

Welcome to the fourth edition of *Reader's Choice*. In this section we present our perspective on teaching and learning, and we provide tips for using the book. We do not intend this as prescription; there are as many ways to use a text as there are teachers and classrooms. In fact, the book is designed to encourage teacher flexibility, both in sequencing and in presentation. At the same time, we do have opinions about teaching and learning that have shaped the development of these materials. We have been influenced by our own classroom experiences and by the feedback of scores of teachers and students who have used the book.

We would like you to benefit from these experiences. In the pages that follow, we outline general guidelines for creating an environment conducive for language and literacy development. First, we outline our view of teaching; second, we provide hints for using specific exercises and readings in the book; and finally, we present a narrative of classroom practice that we hope will give you a sense of how we use the book.

General Guidelines

We view learning as change over time through engagement in activity. We believe that students learn a great deal in the course of classroom activity in addition to the content of the curriculum. Among the most important things learned are those that have to do with students' identities as language users and literate human beings. For this reason, we are concerned about the atmosphere in the classroom and about our stance as teachers toward the material and toward students. We work toward classrooms that embrace diversity and encourage students to express themselves freely.

In contrast to traditional wisdom, we do not view good teaching as virtuoso performance of method. The primary task is not to cover the material or keep up with the curriculum, nor is it to assure that students score well on tests, although all of these are by-products of effective teaching. Rather, we view teaching as creating an environment in which the students can learn (in this case, to be effective readers), as a function of communication in the context of authentic relationships. We will be effective teachers, we believe, to the extent that we are able to forge meaningful connections with students and move them toward common goals.

We recognize that you may be teaching in a situation that does not give you total discretion in how you use materials or how you approach classroom management or lesson planning. We also know that some students are not prepared for the sort of democratic approach to instruction that we attempt to achieve. However, we will present our approach to using the book as clearly as possible, in the hopes that you will be able to adapt it to your own situation.

We believe *Reader's Choice* can be an important resource in the process of developing independent, critical readers. We have selected a wide variety of readings in an attempt to appeal to a broad range of interests and needs. The activities have been developed to encourage the students to explore ideas while developing and improving reading and language skills and strategies.

We use *Reader's Choice* as a foundation and framework for interaction with students around important topics; we hope to provoke thoughtful conversations and insightful exploration of ideas. In general, we use students' experiences as the departure point for reading the selections and working the exercises. We attempt to provoke students to bring their own experience to bear on the topics presented in the text, and to weigh the knowledge and perspectives of the author, their teacher, and their classmates against their own. In most cases, the process is more important than the product; that is, we care less about the answers to questions than we do the students' reasoning in arriving at the answers.

The ultimate goal of *Reader's Choice* is to produce independent readers who are able to determine their own goals for a reading task and then use the appropriate skills and strategies to reach those goals. For this reason, we believe the best learning environment is one in which all individuals—students and teachers—participate in the process of setting and achieving goals. A certain portion of class time is therefore profitably spent in discussing reading tasks before they are begun. If the topic is a new one for the students, teachers are encouraged to provide and/or access background information for the students, adapting the activities under **Before You Begin** to specific teaching contexts. When confronted with a specific passage, students should become accustomed to the practice of skimming quickly, taking note of titles and subheadings, pictures, graphs, etc., in an attempt to determine the most efficient approach to the task. In the process, they should develop expectations about the content of the passage and the amount of time and effort needed to accomplish their goals. In this type of setting students are encouraged to offer their opinions and ask for advice, to teach each other and to learn from their errors.

Reader's Choice was written to encourage maximum flexibility in classroom use. Because of the large variety of exercises and reading selections, the teacher can plan several tasks for each class and hold in reserve a number of appropriate exercises to use as the situation demands. In addition, the exercises have been developed to make possible variety in classroom dynamics. The teacher can encourage the independence of students by providing opportunities for work in small groups, pairs, or individually. Small group work in which students self-correct homework assignments has also been successful.

Exercises do not have to be done in the order in which they are presented. In fact, we suggest interspersing skills work with reading selections. One way to vary tasks is to plan lessons around pairs of units, alternating skills exercises with the reading selections. In the process, the teacher can show students how focused skills work transfers to the reading of longer passages. For example, **Sentence Study** exercises provide intensive practice in analyzing grammatical structures to understand sentences; this same skill should be used by students in working through reading selections. When communication breaks down, the teacher can pull sentences from readings for intensive classroom analysis, thereby demonstrating the value of this skill.

It is important to *teach before testing*. Tasks should be introduced, modeled, and practiced before students are expected to perform on their own. Although we advocate rapid-paced, demanding class sessions, we believe it is extremely important to provide students with a thorough introduction to each new exercise. At least for the first example of each type of exercise, some oral work is necessary. The teacher can demonstrate the skill using the example item and work through the first few items with the class as a whole. Students can then work individually or in small groups.

Specific Suggestions

Reader's Choice has been organized so that specific skills can be practiced before students use those skills to tackle reading selections. Although exercises and readings are generally graded according to difficulty, it is not necessary to use the material in the order in which it is presented. Teachers are encouraged

a. to intersperse skills work with reading selections
b. to skip exercises that are too easy or irrelevant to students' interests
c. to do several exercises of a specific type at one time if students require intensive practice in that skill
d. to jump from unit to unit, selecting reading passages that satisfy students' interests and needs
e. to sequence longer readings as appropriate for their students either by interspersing them among other readings and skills work or by presenting them at the end of the course

Language Skills Exercises

Nonprose Reading

For students who expect to read only prose material, teachers can point out that nonprose reading provides more than an enjoyable change of pace. These exercises provide legitimate reading practice. The same problem-solving skills can be used for both prose and nonprose material. Just as one can skim a textbook for general ideas, it is possible to skim a menu for a general idea of the type of food offered, the price range of a restaurant, etc. Students may claim that they can't skim or scan; working with nonprose items shows them that they can.

Nonprose exercises are good for breaking the ice with new students, for beginning or ending class sessions, for role playing, or for those Monday blues and Friday blahs. Because they are short, rapid-paced exercises, they can be kept in reserve to provide variety or to fill a time gap at the end of class.

The **Menu, Newspaper Advertisements, Bus Schedule,** and **Road Map** exercises present students with realistic language problems they might encounter in an English-speaking environment. The teacher can set up simulations to achieve a realistic atmosphere. Since the focus is on following directions, students usually work individually.

With poetry, students' problem-solving skills are challenged by the economy of poetic writing. **Poetry** is especially good for reinforcing vocabulary from context skills, for comprehending through syntax clues, and for drawing inferences.

Word Study

These exercises can be profitably done in class either in rapid-paced group work or by alternating individual work with class discussion. Like nonprose work, **Word Study** exercises can be used to fill unexpected time gaps.

Context Clues exercises appear frequently throughout the book, both in skills units and accompanying reading selections. Students should learn to be content with a general meaning of a word and to recognize situations in which it is not necessary to know a word's meaning. In skills units, these exercises should be done in class to ensure that students do not look for exact definitions in the dictionary. When **Vocabulary from Context** exercises appear with reading selections, in addition to providing practice in this skill, they are intended as tools for learning new vocabulary items and often for introducing ideas that will be encountered in the reading. In this case they can be done at home as well as in class.

Stems and Affixes exercises appear in five skills units and must be done in the order in which they are presented. The exercises are cumulative: each exercise makes use of word parts presented in previous units. All stems and affixes taught in *Reader's Choice* are listed with their definitions in the **Appendix.** These exercises serve as an important foundation in vocabulary skills work for students whose native language does not contain a large number of words derived from Latin or Greek. Students should focus on improving their ability to analyze word parts as they work with the words presented in the exercises. During the introduction to each exercise students should be encouraged to volunteer other examples of words containing the stems and affixes presented. Exercises 1 and 2 can be done as homework; the matching exercise can be used as a quiz.

    Dictionary Study exercises provide review of information available in English/English dictionaries. **Dictionary Use** exercise 1 in Unit 1 requires a substantial amount of class discussion to introduce information necessary for dictionary work.

Sentence Study

Students should not be concerned about unfamiliar vocabulary in these exercises; grammatical clues should provide enough information to allow them to complete the tasks. In addition, questions are syntax based; errors indicate structures that students have trouble reading, thus providing the teacher with a diagnostic tool for grammar instruction.

Paragraph Reading and Paragraph Analysis

If **Main Idea** paragraphs are read in class, they may be timed. If the exercises are done at home, students can be asked to come to class prepared to defend their answers in group discussion. One way to stimulate discussion is to ask students to identify incorrect responses as too broad, too narrow, or false.

    Restatement and Inference and **Paragraph Analysis** exercises are short enough to allow sentence-by-sentence analysis. These exercises provide intensive practice in syntax and vocabulary work. In the **Paragraph Analysis** exercises the lines are numbered to facilitate discussion.

Discourse Focus

In Units 1 and 3, **Web Work** sections use Internet Web pages to introduce students to a range of approaches to reading. Web pages are reproduced in the text, but if students are online, they may complete these exercises by using the *Reader's Choice* Web site: <u>**<http://www.press.umich.edu/esl/readerschoice>**</u>.

    Throughout the book, skimming and scanning activities should be done quickly in order to demonstrate to students the utility of these approaches for some tasks. Critical reading activities introduce the kinds of decisions students will need to make in their own research. In addition to these, the short mysteries benefit from group work, as students use specific elements of the text to defend inferences. Prediction activities are designed to have students focus on the discourse signals that allow them to predict and sample texts. The diversity of student responses that emerges during group work can reinforce the notion that there is not a single correct answer, that all predictions are, by definition, only working hypotheses to be constantly revised.

Reading Selections

Readings represent a wide variety of topics and styles. The exercises have been written to focus on the most obvious characteristic of each reading.

    Teachers have found it valuable to introduce readings in terms of ideas and vocabulary before students are asked to work on their own. **Before You Begin** introduces the concepts and issues encountered in reading selections. Several types of classroom dynamics have been successful with reading selections after an introduction to the passage.

1. *In class*—teacher reads entire selection orally; or teacher reads part, students finish selection individually; or students read selection individually (perhaps under time constraint).
2. *In class and at home*—part of selection is read in class, followed by discussion; students finish reading at home.
3. *At home*—students read entire selection at home.

Comprehension questions are usually discussed in class with the class as a whole, in small groups, or in pairs. The paragraphs in the selections are numbered to facilitate discussion.

The teacher can pull out difficult vocabulary and/or sentences for intensive analysis and discussion.

The **Web Work** activities that accompany some reading selections point students to additional Web-based research. This gives you the opportunity to extend reading activities if the technology is avilable.

Longer Readings

These readings can be presented in basically the same manner as other selections in the book. Longer readings can be read either at the end of the course or at different points throughout the term. A typical schedule for working with longer readings is roughly as follows.

a. Readings are introduced by vocabulary exercises, discussion of the topic, reading and discussion of selected paragraphs.
b. Students read the selection at home and answer the comprehension questions. Students are allowed at least two days to complete the assignment.
c. In-class discussion of comprehension questions proceeds with students referring to the passage to support their answers.
d. The vocabulary review can be done either at home or in class.
e. Vocabulary questions raised on the off day between the assignment and the due day may be resolved with items from **Vocabulary from Context** exercises and **Figurative Language and Idioms** exercises.

"The Milgram Experiment" requires students to confront their own attitudes toward authority. The unit begins with a questionnaire that asks students to predict their behavior in particular situations and to compare their behavior with that of fellow natives of their culture and of U.S. natives. Psychologist Stanley Milgram was concerned with the extent to which people would follow commands even when they thought they were hurting someone else. Because the results of the study are surprising and because most people have strong feelings about their own allegiance to authority and their commitment to independence, small group discussions and debriefing from the teacher will be important in this lesson.

"The Dusty Drawer" is a suspense story whose success as a teaching tool depends on students understanding the conflict between the two main characters. Teachers have found that a preliminary reading and discussion of the first eleven paragraphs serves as an introduction to the most important elements of the story. The discussion questions can be integrated into the discussion of comprehension questions.

Answer Key

Because the exercises in *Reader's Choice* are designed to provide students with the opportunity to practice and improve their reading skills, the processes involved in arriving at an answer are often more important than the answer itself. It is expected that students will not use the **Answer Key** until they have completed the exercises and are prepared to defend their answers. If a student's answer does not agree with the Key, it is important for the student to return to the exercise to discover the source of the discrepancy. In a classroom setting, students should view the **Answer Key** as a last resort, to be used only when they cannot agree on an answer. The **Answer Key** also makes it possible for students engaged in independent study to use *Reader's Choice*. You will find that the **Answer Key** also provides insight into our approach to teaching reading. It can be used as another opportunity to coach students in comprehension and critical reading.

Teaching Narrative: Glimpses of a *Reader's Choice* Teacher

The story that follows provides a glimpse into how we have used *Reader's Choice* in our classes. It is a fictional account of a single teacher, a composite of experiences we have had over the years. Our goal in presenting it is to give you a sense of the pace and rhythm of our teaching using *Reader's Choice*. We do not want to imply that this is the correct way of teaching the text; we see the story as suggestive rather than prescriptive.

The narrative takes place in an urban setting, at an intensive English language center where the students attend five 50-minute classes a day, five days a week. What follows is a narrative of the first five days of the course. You will need to flip back and forth between the narrative and the activities discussed in the text to fully understand the suggestions we are making.

Monday

I enjoy teaching advanced reading at the Intensive English Center. The students tend to be serious about their studies, and they are operating with high enough English language proficiency and reading skills that I am able to involve them in active decision making about the content and the dynamics of the class. The text, *Reader's Choice,* provides just the right amount of structure and flexibility—a good supply of interesting readings and a wide variety of exercises.

I arrive a few minutes before the first class and arrange the desks in a circle. I push the teacher's table against the wall and arrange the handouts where they will be handy when I need them later. I decide to sit in one of the student desks near the board, in case I want to use it during class, and I put blank name tags on all the desk tops. I peruse the class list as I wait for the students to arrive.

Fifteen students are in Reading VI this term. A good number, even considering that the highest levels have been hit less by the decline in international students. My class roster lists country of origin and native language: four students each from Japan, Mexico, and the Arab Emirates, one student each from Russia, China, and Argentina.

Japan: Shinya, Shoko, Yuko, Mina
Mexico: Carlos, Ana, Hector, Maria
UAE: Jassim, Mohamed, Mahmoud, Jamal
Russia: Svetlana
China: Pyk
Argentina: Rachel

I know Shinya and Jassim from previous semesters. I will be able to count on them to help me introduce activities and approaches that might be new for some of the students. I notice that I have four students who are here on immigrant visas—Svetlana, Carlos, Hector, and Maria. The rest are on student visas.

As the students enter I ask them to take a seat and fill out their name tags. I pass out an information sheet that solicits basic information—living situation (whether they live with their own family, with a host family, or with other students), hobbies, contact information, etc. I ask about their university and career interests and their goals for this class. One item is a request for them to give their email address and to describe their familiarity with the World Wide Web, including an estimate of the amount of time they spend surfing the Web, how often they check email, and so on. Another item is a request for them to list the kinds of reading they do and titles of recent books or journals they have read. The last item is a request for suggestions on making the class work for them.

I tell the class to browse through *Reader's Choice,* and to begin reading the student section of the Introduction when they have finished with the information sheet. Maria asks if I want to collect the information sheets, and I tell them to hang on to them in case they think of additional things they want to mention in the course of the class session.

It is time for introductions. We begin with the syllabus for the course, which doesn't take long. Basically, all I expect of them is that they do the reading and participate in class discussions. I have built in some encouragements—tests and the "assignments" so that if they become distracted I can get their attention. But my intent is to orchestrate events in such a way that they become active, thoughtful participants in literate conversations. I tell them that the only certain requirement is that they read and write every day.

Next, I tell them we need to become acquainted. I have organized an icebreaker that will give them a chance to talk to each other and provide me with a sense of who they are and what their interests are. I tell them that we are going to be working together this term and that we will need to get to know each other well. I lead off with the introductions, telling a little about me and my family, our travels and interests, my education and my hobbies. I turn to Rachel, who is seated to my left, and we proceed around the circle with brief introductions. I take notes as they talk and interrupt only to remind them to speak up or to ask for more information if their introduction seems too brief.

When we have finished, I tell them to take out a piece of paper and make a seating chart that includes everyone's first and last names, and one fact or piece of interesting information about each person. This is something of a surprise for them, I think. They are used to doing quick introductions and then not worrying about remembering anybody's name, much less details about each other's lives.

This is the first hint they have that in this class they will not be able to coast along in neutral when other students are speaking. I give them time to work, and after a few minutes, tell them all to stand up, move about the room talking to each other as if they were at an art reception or party, and to complete the task in ten minutes.

I remain seated and take notes. I am interested to see how they interact with each other. I try to watch them all, but I am especially mindful of the quiet ones. Luckily, all goes well on this first excursion into communicative language learning; no one hangs back, no one offends anyone else, and there are no political blowups. I ask them to return to their seats. They are to put the seating charts in their notebooks; if they did not finish getting all the information, they need to do this before class tomorrow.

The next task is to become familiar with the textbook. I initiate a session of "Say Something," a round-robin reading technique that I use a lot in my classes. I begin, to give them a model to follow. I read a paragraph or two aloud while they read silently. When I stop, I say something about what I've just read (hence the name for the technique). I might summarize it, I might ask a question about a concept or vocabulary item, or I might disagree or elaborate on a point in the text. Then the floor is open to the rest of the class for comment or question.

Next, I ask Jassim to begin because he is familiar with the technique; he was in my Grammar IV class last term. Today there is not much discussion because the technique is new to most of the students, so I prod and prompt after Jassim finishes reading, before I ask Shinya to read. We continue in this fashion until we have completed the student section of the Introduction.

I like this technique for balancing control and initiative in a reading lesson. It gives everyone a chance to participate with minimal risk, and it gives me a chance to assess their oral reading and to probe their comprehension. It also often leads to class discussion that otherwise would not surface. It is a regular feature of my classes. Today the activity goes reasonably well. The students seem to have sufficient language and reading skills for the kind of class I want to teach, and they seem amenable to interactive classroom activities.

I give them a few minutes to identify the type of exercise they expect to find most helpful and to locate an example of that type in the text. For most of them, in spite of their advanced language proficiency, the idea of approaching reading selections from a variety of angles is a new idea. As they begin flipping through the book, I walk around and talk quietly with individual students. Pyk, whose language does not have Greek or Latin roots, has focused on the **Stems and Affixes** exercises. Mina, it turns out, likes poetry; we discuss the differences between haiku and the poems in the text.

I get their attention, and we go around the room. The students identify the exercise types they think they will find the most helpful this term. As questions arise about the different types of exercises, we turn to examples in the book and discuss why it is important to approach different kinds of reading tasks differently. I have them flip out the menu in Unit 1 and simultaneously find the article on the genome in Unit 6 (p. 164). It has been my experience that some students view realia like the menu to be a waste of time, while others are intimidated by technical reading such as the genome article. I decide to nip these objections in the bud by making explicit the importance of being able to shift gears depending on the nature of the reading.

"How do you read these two types of text?" I ask. "Where would you be reading them? What would be your purpose?" The conversation turns to their preferences and reading habits. I encourage them to voice their opinions about the type of reading they want to do in the class and the kind of classroom dynamics they believe to be the most important. I tell them that my goal is to make sure that we accommodate everyone's preferences, and I point out that this will require them to speak up, and that it will also require a certain amount of tolerance for differences of opinion and style.

My goal here is to get them thinking analytically about how we spend our time together in the class. I want them to see that they have choices and that I am interested in shaping the class to meet their needs. This is just the first example of the pattern of interaction that I will use to connect the work we do in class with their lives outside of school.

Time is running out; we have about ten minutes left in the period. I ask them to take out a piece of paper and make a journal entry for the day. The journal is a way of encouraging reflection and extending comprehension. It is also a way of helping them consolidate lessons learned during the class period. Some days I ask them to reflect on what they have read or to respond to comprehension or composition questions. Today, I keep it simple, suggesting that they jot down new words they have encountered, perhaps with brief definitions and sample sentences. I also suggest that they indicate aspects of the class that they like and that they provide suggestions for future classes. I tell them that I will collect approximately a third of the journals each Friday to read over the weekend. I use the journals as a way of monitoring students' learning and their attitude toward the class. They are graded only on the number of entries; I encourage them to be frank in their assessments.

I collect the information sheets as they leave for their next class.

Tuesday

I begin the day with the first exercise in the book: **Discourse Focus: Reading for Different Goals—Web Work.** I write the following words on the board: *skim, scan, thorough comprehension, critical reading,* and ask people to volunteer definitions. We talked on Monday about choosing the best strategy for different kinds of readings, so this is not new, but I want to give them a chance to review the different terms and to become comfortable with the notion that we will use different strategies depending on the reading task that we are focused on.

Using excerpts from Web sites will spark some interesting discussion, I think. I know from the information sheets that the class is divided almost equally between individuals who are comfortable with computers and people who rarely use them, so I have them pair up for this exercise. I explain that next week we will be going to the computer lab to do some Web surfing and that I want to use this exercise as a way of making sure that everyone knows what the Web is and how to use it. I make it clear that I have paired them up so that they can teach each other as we go, and I encourage them to ask questions, no matter how foolish they may think they will appear.

I have them look at the Web page, and I read the questions aloud. They confer with their partners and arrive at conclusions together. I stroll among the desks and monitor their conversations, asking and answering questions as I go. As the partners finish with a set of questions, I open up the discussion for the whole class, encouraging them to respond to each other and express their own opinions.

We proceed section by section. They bend to the task, and the room is filled with the pleasant buzz of collaboration. We proceed through the four types of reading, and I am pleased with the camaraderie, but I know that the range of learning is broad. Some are accomplished computer users, but several of the non-computer users are only vaguely aware of what "dot com" means and what is involved in "clicking." It turns out that Pyk is going to be a multimedia major; she is clearly the most knowledgeable computer user in the class and will be an important resource for me and the students as the term proceeds.

We turn next to what is, in my opinion, one of the most important skills students will acquire in my class—learning to read with only an approximate understanding of unfamiliar vocabulary. I begin by asking them what they find most difficult in their study of English and, predictably, they say "vocabulary." I ask what they do when they come to words they do not understand, and a lively discussion breaks out as they all brandish their favorite dictionaries. Several have state-of-the art hand held PDAs (Personal Digital Assistants) with bilingual dictionaries and mini speakers for hearing the pronunciation of words and phrases.

I amaze them with an ostentatious yawn at their electronic wizardry and assert that the most important skill they will learn in my class is to make wild guesses about the meanings of unfamiliar words. I tell them that I am proud of my ability to travel in a wide variety of countries without the benefit of dictionaries. (I do confess, under some pressure, that my partner is an inveterate dictionary user, however, so I am not totally a free spirit.)

I have them open their books to page 7, and Word Study: Context Clues. I read the introduction aloud while they follow along, and after a brief exchange to make sure they are tracking the argument being made, I ask them to turn to the example exercise. I read the directions to them and give them three minutes to fill in the blanks on their own. When they have a guess for each blank, we go around the room, reading the sentences and volunteering answers. I keep this light, encouraging all guesses and refusing to arbitrate or give answers. It is the spirit of guessing, I tell them, that will serve them in this enterprise. After we have finished the seven items, I have them turn the page and read the explanation silently. When they have finished, we work through it together, comparing their answers with the ones offered in the book. I underscore the strategies and the linguistic clues, encouraging them to use the whole range of textual supports for gleaning the meaning of the text.

I ask them to continue with Exercise 1. They work on their own for about five minutes and then I have them compare answers with their neighbors. I walk around the room eavesdropping on the conversations and encouraging them to guess, guess, guess—to write down whatever word comes to mind.

"To require perfection is the greatest imperfection," I proclaim. I work hard during this portion of the class. I want them to become comfortable with ambiguity and to grow in their confidence that guessing is, in fact, a productive strategy. With about five minutes left in the class I convene the group to hear each other's answers. We go in order around the room, each student in turn reading an item aloud and giving the answer and the rationale. Because I am interested more in the strategy than the definitions, we do not finish the exercise before time is up.

I say we will finish the exercise on Wednesday, and I remind them to make journal entries tonight. Next week I'll spend portions of several class sessions working on the journal entries. For now, it is sufficient to remind them that I expect them to write something in their journals every day.

Wednesday

We begin the day by finishing up with the Vocabulary from Context exercise, and then I tell them we are going out to eat.

"Turn to page 5, and fold out the menu," I instruct. "Have any of you eaten at Denny's?" I ask. "What do you think of it?" We spend a few minutes talking about eating habits, the benefits and demerits of fast food, their favorite restaurants, and so on. I ask them what reading skills and strategies are required for reading menus. We answer the **Before You Begin** questions during this conversation, as I worked them into the exchange.

I read the directions to **Scanning** to them as they follow along. Then, as they scan the menu for the answers, I read questions 1 through 13 item by item, encouraging them to shout out the answers, calling on students who have not spoken, promoting as rambunctious a session as possible.

I announce that they have seven minutes to work individually on the questions in Exercises 2 and 3. As they work I circulate and discuss items with individuals, asking questions, providing scaffolding for their efforts, encouraging them to work quickly.

I tell them to confer in small groups if they have finished working. When everyone has finished, we discuss the answers using what will become a familiar format: A student reads the question and gives an answer. If no one disagrees, we move on. I keep moving around the classroom, and if I suspect that students disagree but haven't spoken up, I encourage them to voice their opinions. If there is disagreement, I choreograph discussion and encourage all points of view. In the event that the class cannot agree, I call for a vote. On occasion, I leave the issue hanging without a definitive answer, telling them that this is just like life—there are no final answers out there.

We finish the menu work and I shift gears slightly, asking them what goals they had put on their information sheet for the study of English. They take out their sheets, and we hear excerpts from a few students; most have merely indicated that they want to use English to get into a university or to get a job.

I intend to move on to "Can English Be Dethroned?" on page 44, but I want to approach the text through their own words. I ask, "Do you believe you have to lose your native language to become proficient in English? What about the languages you speak? Are they in danger of becoming extinct?" Silence. I leave the questions hanging, waiting for the students to warm up to the topic. It doesn't appear that they have thought about it before, or maybe it is too early in the day for serious discussion, because no one speaks. I wait quietly, as if I had nothing better to do than watch the chalk dust settle in the room.

Finally, someone comments, someone responds—a question, an opinion, a counteropinion—and we gradually attain the rhythm of a conversation. I let them do most of the talking, nodding and rephrasing, asking questions, prompting and encouraging, asking for clarification, holding the floor as a student searches for the right word, but basically indicating by word and gesture that this discussion is their responsibility.

I work the **Before You Begin** questions on page 44 into the exchange as things proceed, and then ask them to turn to the article. I read the title aloud.

"What does 'dethrone' mean," I ask. "Is English the royalty of languages?" Then I read the author line aloud and ask them what they think *geolinguist* means. Several students offer definitions, and I tell them to hold those ideas in mind as we work on the essay. I move deliberately here, pausing to permit them to muse about the topic, to let their eyes wander over the page.

I have them turn to **Vocabulary from Context**, Exercise 1 (p. 48), and we do the first paragraph together. I read the paragraph and solicit guesses as to the meanings of *trend* and *imperialism*. Someone offers, "idea." Another says, "power." I nod in what I hope is seen as encouragement without confirmation. I point to the phrase, "gradually over time." I ask for other examples of trends. No answer. I didn't expect one because I don't think they know what the word means yet, or at least, they can't quite articulate their understanding. I walk slowly toward the board, not speaking, so that they can think without my hovering over them. A few minutes pass. I am comfortable with the silence; most of them will become more comfortable with it as the term unfolds. I speak finally. "What about pierced noses?" Is that a trend? "Or tattoos? Brightly colored hair?" I see a glimmer of understanding. Shinya asks if espresso coffee is a trend. "Maybe in this country," Maria says. "In my country we have had it for a long time." They seem to be getting the idea, so I push on. "What about *imperialism*," I ask. Rachel knows this one, and she does a good job of explaining it to everyone's satisfaction. "So, do you get the idea?" I ask. Heads nod. I tell them to work the remaining items as quickly as possible. I watch for signs that most of the students have managed to complete the exercise and then convene the class to go over the answers. As they volunteer answers and debate meanings of words, I work on making them aware of both vocabulary skills and the argument being developed about the role and status of English.

Svetlana and Carlos, apparently, have thought about this topic before, because they speak right up, but for most of the students this doesn't appear to be a burning issue.

I have them turn to the article and I read paragraph 1 aloud as they follow along. We discuss the assertions Breton makes there. I demonstrate a technique I adopted in my college years when faced with a particularly challenging text: I read the first sentence of each paragraph as I attempt to get an idea of the author's argument.

We have about ten minutes left, so I give them the remainder of the period to use as they wish. They can write in their journals or continue reading the passage. I ask them to arrive tomorrow with the article read and the **Comprehension** questions answered.

Thursday

I begin promptly at the appointed hour with **Stems and Affixes** on page 14. I read the introduction aloud as they follow along. I know that the Spanish speakers will find this easier than the students whose native languages do not have as many Latin and Greek roots, so I am alert to ways of using them as experts in the lesson. I tell them to get into five groups with a Spanish speaker in each group, and as we proceed I encourage them to talk among themselves. I remind them to not jump in too quickly with answers—to give each other time to guess. We go through the chart and Exercise 1 in a rambunctious whole-group conversation with the smaller groups conferring as we go. My main goal is to make sure that everyone understands the answers.

I then give them ten minutes to complete Exercise 2 individually. I tell them when they have finished to work within their groups to confirm the answers. I circulate to monitor progress and respond to questions, usually by deferring to others in the group or by opening the conversation to the floor.

We spend the rest of the lesson on "Can English Be Dethroned?" (p. 44). Here is what happens.

I ask students to get into five clusters based primarily on a goal of mixing native languages.

Shinya (J)	Shoko (J)	Yuko (J)	Mina (J)	Carlos (Sp)
Jassim (A)	Mohamed (A)	Mahmoud (A)	Jamal (A)	Svetlana (R)
Maria (Sp)	Pyk (Ch)	Ana (Sp)	Hector (Sp)	Rachel (H/Sp)

I tell them that they are to compare their responses to the **Comprehension** questions on pages 45–46, and to arrive at agreement on the best answer. As often happens, some students have done a more careful job of preparing than others, and it turns out that many students need to read the selection more carefully to arrive at an understanding of the author's point of view. I see that it is slow going, so I decide to approach the task from the direction of the vocabulary.

I interrupt their work to tell them that I have changed my mind, that we will do Exercises 2 and 3 together (p. 50). I had planned to do these after the **Comprehension** exercise, but they are helpful for working on comprehension through vocabulary clarification. The questions require students to find the meanings of words in the paragraph. They give students a focused vocabulary task, but at the same time require them to read the paragraph and understand the context. I cue the paragraph and ask the question while they search for the answer. I ask them to hold up their hands when they think they have the answer. I wait until most have their hands up and then call on someone to respond. We discuss each item briefly, and I use the opportunity to extend their understanding of the article. We continue with **Figurative Language and Idioms** in the same way.

When we have finished with the vocabulary work, I have them return to their small groups and finish answering the **Comprehension** questions. Things proceed much more smoothly this time, and within a few minutes all of the groups have finished. We check the answers together, going around the room—different students reading an item and giving their answer, followed by discussion and clarification.

We do **Stems and Affixes** (p. 51) together, quickly, to round out the discussion. I think we are wrapping it up, but Carlos and Svetlana have been having an intense conversation in hushed tones at the back of the room. I finally decide it isn't going to end any time soon, so I ask them to let the rest of the class in on their discussion. It turns out that they have discovered common ground with the author, and they agree entirely with him about the importance of minority languages. They are both from remote regions of their countries and their grandparents were speakers of minority languages before Spanish and Russian were imposed on them. They believe that English poses a threat to all the world's languages.

A discussion breaks out in full force. Carlos and Svetlana lead the way, playing off each other's points with energy tinged with indignation. They want international laws and money to support minority languages. And they want the nations with the most widely used languages to curtail their economic and cultural imperialism.

A few students look at me with questioning expressions, and I encourage them to jump in. Jassim and Mohamed join forces with Carlos and Svetlana, who are happy to have allies in the debate. Yuko takes the opposite point of view. Japan, he says, is often accused of such imperialism by its neighbors. These are complex issues, he argues. Culture cannot be controlled by laws and regulations.

Emotions are running high, and most of the class has not spoken, but I like the energy and I am loathe to lose the opportunity for spirited exchanges. On the other hand, it is only the first week of the term, and I don't want this to escalate into a full-fledged schism in the class. I tell the students that I am very pleased with the discussion and that I would like them to record their opinion on the debate in their journals tonight. I tell them that we will return to the topic, pointing out that there are several related articles in *Reader's Choice* and that there is undoubtedly a lot more that we can find on the Web. I ask Carlos, Svetlana, Jassim, and Mohamed to see me after class; perhaps we can organize some sort of class project out of this.

I bid them good day and remind my language rights group of our meeting as the students file out.

Friday

We begin Friday with a quizlike presentation of **Stems and Affixes,** Exercise 3 (p. 17). I tell them that I hope they will take time every night to review vocabulary they have learned, and that they will arrive each day ready for brief comprehension checks of this sort. I give them five minutes to complete the exercise and then check their answers with the person sitting next to them. I ask if there are questions, but everyone seems to have answered whatever questions they had, so we push on.

I want to wrap up the introduction to the Word Study work, so I have them open their books to page 10, and **Dictionary Use.** I ask them to compare the entry for *prefix* in their dictionaries with the one on that page. I tell them they have five minutes to answer the eight questions in Exercise 1 and to discuss their answers with a friend. We go over their answers together and clear up confusions. I have them work in pairs on Exercise 2, with one person reading the questions and the other finding the answers. I wander around and monitor their progress. When they have all finished, we go through the answers quickly.

We have about half the period left, just enough time to launch the project that I have cooked up with the four language rights activists. I give the floor to Svetlana. She asks the group if they would be interested in exploring this issue of globalization, perhaps having a debate. This is a dream for a language teacher—a student taking over the class, proposing an authentic activity, modeling curiosity and mature pursuit of knowledge. I bask in the glow of my good fortune. Svetlana is a bit older than most of the students, late thirties, early forties, perhaps, and she has seen some tough times en route to her current position at a university hospital lab. The other students respond well to her serious demeanor and precise speech.

She briefly explains the plan. There are six selections in Unit 2 that address the issue, one of which we have already read—"Can English Be Dethroned?" She proposes that they divide up responsibility for reading the remaining five selections and that they develop a position statement on globalization that reflects all the points of view in the class. This is what we decided yesterday in our meeting. I had described the Jigsaw Procedure, a technique I often use in situations where there are many interests around a theme. It involves individuals or small groups reading different selections and then creating opportunities for people to inform each other about what they have found. It is particularly valuable when there are a variety of interests and a range of language proficiencies in the group.

Svetlana has the class open their books to the table of contents, and she identifies the five stories that relate to the topic (Reading Selections 1A, 1B, and 1C, concerning tourism; and Reading Selections 3B and 3C, which continue the theme of minority languages).

"What do you think?" she asks. "Should we take a few minutes to look at these and decide if they are of interest?"

The class seems amenable to her leadership, and all that can be heard for the next few minutes is the shuffling of pages. After a bit, I become concerned about the time, and ask Svetlana if I may step in and do a bit of previewing. I ask if they have found selections they want to read, but no one seems to be ready to commit, so I volunteer to go through the five and briefly summarize them.

I read the introductory paragraphs and give quick sketches of the content and intent of each selection. "The Globalization of Tourism" (selection 1A, p. 25) is a summary report with graphics, which might appeal to the more technically inclined reader. Selection 1B, "The Politics of Travel," (p. 29) is a densely argued essay that calls into question the whole idea of recreational travel; it will be of interest to the ecologically and politically sensitive reader. Selection 1C, "Learning Holidays" (p. 38), is essentially a public service advertisement for different types of travel, including service learning. Selections 3B and 3C (pp. 53 and 57) provide quantitative demographic information about the world's languages—their distribution, the number of speakers, and whether they are in danger of dying out. Taken together, the five articles can be seen as providing differing views of issues of concern to everyone, examples of globalization.

I want to work Web work into the mix, but for the time being, I leave the choices as they are. Some students want clarification about procedures, and I explain that the ideal thing would be for everyone to choose a selection of interest to him or her, and then read it and teach it to the rest of the class. If more than one person chooses the same selection, then they would work on it together.

This seems to have been the question several students were wanting to ask, because there is an audible sigh as heads bow and thumbs feather pages again. Svetlana has put the titles of the selections on the board for people to sign up, and in short order there are names under all of the titles. I suggest that the groups convene and discuss how to proceed.

The rest of the period is spent in groups, reading and discussing the selections. I am pleased at the level of engagement, but we are running out of time. I tell them that we will spend time on Monday discussing next steps and preparing ways of teaching their selection to the rest of the class.

I ask them to make two entries in their journals: first, to jot down ideas for teaching their readings to others, and second, to collect their thoughts about the possibility of maintaining a cultural identity in today's complex world.

The first week ends with serious conversation about matters of importance.

Discussion

This is a fictionalized (and somewhat idealized) narrative, of course, but it represents the spirit in which we have written *Reader's Choice,* and it illustrates the approach we take to teaching and learning. Let us examine some of the attributes of the classroom just described.

Creating connections. The teacher has provided a safe environment for authentic relationships, in which everyone is encouraged to make connections with each other, with the readings, and with the authors of pieces they read. There is a respect for diversity of experience and opinion, and there is an opportunity for people to thoughtfully develop the identity they present to others. Everyone—teacher and students—is encouraged to learn from everyone else.

Reflection and decision making. Literacy is presented here as an active, problem-posing and problem-solving process, one in which there is a variety of answers to every situation. The reading task shapes the approach that teacher and students take. The menu is treated as a tool for getting a meal, and Web pages as tools for getting information; the article on language policy is used as an opportunity for exploring issues and values. Vocabulary and grammar work are treated as tools for comprehension, rather than solely as ends in themselves.

Teamwork and collaborative problem solving. Reading and writing are explored as an interactional process, one in which individual decision making is negotiated with others, and in which meaning is emergent in the discourse, rather than existing "out there" to be discovered. Classroom dynamics change to fit the task, and everyone is assumed to bring something to the table. That is, the teacher may be the most proficient English speaker in the room most of the time, but everyone is an expert on something, and everyone has areas of ignorance. Literacy is treated as a social as well as a psychological phenomenon, one that occurs inside individuals' heads but is mediated by interpersonal interaction. Meaning is emergent in the process, always being constructed, rather than lurking beneath the words to be discovered.

Student choice and engagement. The class is presented as an opportunity for people to bring their interests and concerns to the table, a place where everyone has a say in tasks and topics. Comprehension occurs when individuals bring their knowledge and experience to bear on the task at hand.

Shifting roles and responsibilities. Teaching and learning in this class are responsibilities, not roles. Everyone is an expert on something, and everyone is ignorant and willing to learn about something else. As teachers, it is our responsibility to organize time and orchestrate interaction. Sometimes the best role for this is the one of teacher as conventionally understood—standing at the head of the class explaining a language point at the board. As facilitators, we make possible a range of interaction and learning. At other times, we make an important contribution to our students' learning when we assume the role of participant, contributing our two cents' worth along with everyone else. And there are times when we put ourselves in the position of learner, submitting to students' superior knowledge on matters where they have more experience.

Textbook as tool. The text is a tool for learning—sometimes a lens for looking at the world, sometimes a lever for getting something done. We shift from focused language skills to reading skill development utilizing the exercises that are most appropriate for each. If we see that a particular selection does not seem to be going anywhere, we drop it and go on to something else. We keep our eye on the progress students are making and adjust our work accordingly. The book lends itself to mixing and matching readings and language exercises. With the exception of the **Stems and Affix** work in the skills units, we do not worry about doing exercises in order; we jump around according to what kinds of skills and strategies seem to be required by the classroom context. We integrate skills exercises and readings, working back and forth between units to vary the pace and maintain interest.

What's New in This Edition?

Visual Literacy. The fourth edition of *Reader's Choice* looks different. This is not simply marketing. Students in the twenty-first century are confronted with a dizzying array and combination of print and graphics. The average commercial Web page, for example, contains more links to information than does the table of contents of the average ESOL textbook. Throughout this edition are activities that develop strategies for gleaning information from combinations of text and graphics. This is especially true in the **Web Work.**

Web Work. Web Work appears in two skills units. While both of these introduce students to some of the intricacies of the World Wide Web, their primary purpose is broader: to introduce and provide practice in decision-making strategies for effective reading. In all cases students must decide how to read and then must skim, scan, read thoroughly and/or critically, depending on the task at hand. The ability of students to evaluate information sources is nowhere more crucial than on the Internet, and these activities highlight critical reading skills. Additional Web-based activities accompany several of the reading selections.

New Readings. Sixteen of the twenty-nine reading selections are new, often arranged in thematically linked sets of passages. Again, these respond to the changing environment faced by our students. Topics range from genetic engineering to globalization to stereotyping in a multicultural, multigenerational world. Our new fiction passages, under "Family Narratives," expand the range of cultural experiences reflected in the text.

Additional Vocabulary. The new reading selections bring with them extensive additional vocabulary work. New lexical items are often topically related across a series of linked readings. Items are introduced and practiced in a variety of formats, as always reinforcing both the given item and more general literacy and acquisition skills.

Updating. Virtually all of the remaining skills work and reading selection units have been updated. Throughout the text are new items along with expanded and updated introductions and activities.

What Hasn't Changed?

Language Work. The odd-numbered skills units continue to provide the intensive language-based reading practice that teachers and students have come to rely on.

Authentic Reading. The text continues to provide authentic reading passages and tasks. From the menu to the Web to textbooks to science reporting to fiction, the fourth edition of *Reader's Choice* continues to provide realistic literacy tasks.

Integrated Skills. The activities in *Reader's Choice* encourage integrated skills work with a focus on reading. The text provides thoroughgoing opportunities for speaking, listening, and writing in the context of the issues raised in the readings. At the core are literate activities that afford opportunities for task-based work.

Respect for the Students. Throughout *Reader's Choice,* students are addressed as intelligent language users who bring to their tasks a great deal of knowledge about learning and about the world. Instructions explain to students the rationale for activities and provide options for productive ways to approach the task at hand.

High-Quality Work. In all activities, students are stretched to interact with texts in challenging and meaningful ways. The book assumes intelligent, engaged students who will be stimulated to do their best work.

Humor and Whimsy. Throughout the text we continue to provide light-hearted moments. In the fourth edition, we have sprinkled the Internet convention of the winking face to key some of those moments. ;-)

Discourse Focus
Reading for Different Goals—Web Work

Would you read a menu in the same way as you would a textbook? Efficient readers read differently depending on what they are reading and their goals. There are four basic types of reading behaviors or skills: **skimming, scanning, reading for thorough comprehension,** and **critical reading.** Each is explained below, and exercises are provided to give you practice in each of these. The exercises below are also designed to introduce reading on the World Wide Web. To work on these activities, you may either use the Web pages reproduced below or, if you are online, your teacher may want you to use the *Reader's Choice* Web site to work on the exercises in this section: <u><http://www.press.umich.edu/esl/readerschoice></u>.

Skimming

Skimming is quick reading for general ideas. When you skim, you move your eyes quickly to acquire a basic understanding of the text. You do not read everything, and you do not read carefully. You read, quickly, such things as the title and subtitles and topic sentences. You also look at pictures, charts, graphs, icons, etc., for clues to what the text is about.

Use the Web page from <u>CNN.com</u> (p. 2) to answer the following questions. Move quickly from the questions to the Web page. Do not write out your answers completely; just make notes that will help you remember your answers. Your teacher may want to read the questions aloud as you skim to find the answers.

1. Have you ever visited this Web site before? What kind of information would you expect to find here?

2. Would you use this page to shop online?

3. How is the page organized? For example, what kind of information do you find in the columns on the sides of the page? What else is on the page?

4. Are there topics here that interest you? Where would you click to learn more?

Scanning

Scanning is also quick reading, but when you scan, you are looking for information about a question you want to answer. You are usually looking for a number or a word or the name of something. When you scan, you usually take the steps listed on page 3.

CNN Sites

MAINPAGE
WORLD
U.S.
WEATHER
BUSINESS
SPORTS
POLITICS
LAW

SCI-TECH

SPACE
HEALTH
ENTERTAINMENT
TRAVEL
EDUCATION
CAREER
LOCAL
IN-DEPTH

EDITIONS:
CNN.com Asia
CNN.com Europe
set default edition

MULTIMEDIA:
video
audio
multimedia showcase
more services

E-MAIL:
Subscribe to one of our
news e-mail lists.
Enter your address:

[   ] go

free address

DISCUSSION:
message boards
chat
feedback

CNN WEB SITES:
myCNN.com   CNNSI
allpolitics   CNNfn
Quick News
CNNfyi.com
CNN.com Europe
CNN.com Asia
Spanish
Portuguese

Airline travelers to go online while en route

January 23, 2001
Web posted at: 5:38 p.m. EST (2238 GMT)

In this story:

Still not widely available

RELATED STORIES, SITES ↓

By Marsha Walton
CNN Technology Producer

MONTREAL, Quebec (CNN) -- Ladies and gentlemen, start your laptops.

Just seconds after the flight crew of Air Canada 413 announced that it was OK to use approved electronic devices, 16 people did things they'd never been able to do before in the air: They sent and received e-mails, and surfed the Internet.

"It's not exactly like being in your office but we've tried to make it as close as we possibly could given the constraints of technology on an aircraft," said Alan Pellegrini from his first class seat.

Pellegrini is chief operating officer of Tenzing, the company that's developing the onboard Internet service for Air Canada and Cathay Pacific Airlines.

During the 54-minute flight from Montreal's Dorval airport to Toronto, the first class cabin was filled with reporters and photographers testing the still-evolving technology.

QUICKVOTE

Is access to the Internet while flying important to you?

Yes   ○
No   ○

View Results   [vote]

"I was pretty impressed," said Annalise Bomenblit, one of the reporters who logged on. Bomenblit is the editor of the Corporate Travel Newsletter.

"Road warriors are really an important market for the airlines and the most lucrative customers. They want the comfort and familiarity of Internet access," she said after the flight.

"Anyone familiar with dial-up access at home or in a hotel would be comfortable using this service," said Pellegrini. "We simply plug a connector in like a phone socket at home, but instead of dialing up your Internet service provider, you're dialing into an ISP on the aircraft, essentially, it's the Tenzing ISP."

1. Decide exactly what information you are looking for and what form it is likely to take. For example, if you wanted to know how much something cost, you would be looking for a number. If you wanted to know when something will start, you would be scanning for a date or a time. If you wanted to know who did something, you would be looking for a name.

2. Next, decide where you need to look to find the information. You would turn to the sports section of the newspaper to discover who won a baseball game, and you would scan the "C" section of the phone book for the phone number of Steven Cary.

3. Move your eyes quickly down the page until you find what you want. Read to get the information.

4. When you find what you need, you usually stop reading.

The following questions give you practice in scanning. Use the Web page from **CNN.com** (p. 2) to answer the questions. Your teacher may want you to do this orally or by circling answers on the Web page.

1. If you wanted to return to the main CNN site, where would you click?

2. If you were preparing for a trip to Montreal and you wanted to know what the weather would be, where could you click?

3. If you wanted to read news in Spanish, what would you do?

4. If you wanted to read about sports after finishing this story, where would you click?

Reading for Thorough Comprehension

When you read for thorough comprehension, you try to understand the full meaning of the reading. You want to know the details as well as the general meaning of the selection. When you have thoroughly comprehended a text, you have done the following things.

1. You have understood the main ideas and the author's point of view.

2. You have understood the relationships of ideas in the text, including how they relate to the author's purpose.

3. You have understood most of the concepts in the passages as well as the vocabulary. This may require you to guess the meanings of unfamiliar words from context or to look up words in the dictionary.

4. You have begun to note that some of the ideas and points of view that were not mentioned were, however, implied by the author. This is called "drawing inferences." It is the beginning of "critical reading," which will be the focus of the next activity.

The following questions give you practice in reading for thorough comprehension. Answer the questions according to your understanding of the Web page from **CNN.com**. Your teacher may want you to work on these individually, in small groups, or in pairs. True/False items are indicated by a T / F before the statement. Some questions may have more than one correct answer. Others require an opinion. Choose the answer you like best; be prepared to defend your choices.

Look at the headline in the middle of the page and the photo just under it.

1. What is this story about?

2. T / F   Air Canada flight 413 was en route from Montreal to Cathay.

3. T / F   Air Canada has remodeled its first class compartment into office space for travelers.

4. T / F   Air Canada is the only airline that is developing online Internet access.

Critical Reading

When we read critically, we draw conclusions and make judgments about the reading. We ask questions such as, "What inferences can be drawn from this? Do I agree with this point of view?" We often do this when we read, but in some cases it is more important than others, as, for example, when authors give opinions about important issues or when you are trying to make a decision.

Use the Web page from **CNN.com** (p. 2) to answer the following examples of critical reading questions. For statements preceded by T / F / N, circle T if the statement is true, F if the statement is false, and N if there is not enough information for us to know if the statement is true or false. There is no single correct answer; readers' opinions will vary according to their experiences.

1. Who would be likely to use this Web site? Would you bookmark this site on your own computer?

2. Would you come to this site if you were interested in buying or selling a used car?

3. T / F / N   This Web site contains only news stories.

4. Near the bottom of the left column you can subscribe to CNN email lists. Would you do this? What would be the benefits? What would be reasons not to subscribe?

5. Look again at "Airline Travelers to Go Online While en Route" to answer the following questions.

   a. T / F/ N   If you want to surf the Internet while in flight, you must provide your own computer.

   b. T / F / N   At the time this story was written, air travelers were generally not able to use the Internet during flights.

      • Has the situation changed since then?
      • What about the airlines you have used? Are computers available for surfing the Net? Have you used them?

   c. T / F / N   Marsha Walton was impressed by the demonstration.

   d. T / F / N   This story is an advertisement for Tenzing.

   e. T / F / N   Access to the Internet is available only in first class.

   f. Note the *QUICKVOTE* insert in the story. How would you vote? Why? How do you think the rest of the world voted? How would you find out?

Nonprose Reading
Menu

Nonprose writing consists of disconnected words and numbers instead of the sentences and paragraphs you usually learn to read. Each time you need information from a train schedule, a graph, a menu, an ad, or the like, you must read nonprose material. This exercise and similar exercises that begin subsequent units will help you practice the problem-solving skills you will need in order to read nonprose material.

Between pages 6 and 7 is a menu such as you might find in a restaurant in the U.S. or Canada.

Before You Begin
1. What are your impressions of this restaurant? Is it similar or different from restaurants with which you are familiar?

2. Is this the kind of restaurant you would go to for a fancy, formal dinner? Why or why not?

Scanning

The questions below are designed to help you quickly become more acquainted with this menu so that you would be able to order a meal. They are the kind of questions that you might have when you look at a restaurant's menu for the first time. Scan the menu to answer the questions in exercise 1. You will notice that this restaurant, like many others, has given unusual names to many of the menu items. Don't let that slow you down. You do not need to understand every word on the page. Note: not all questions have a single correct answer. The answer to some questions may be "We don't know; the menu doesn't give this information." Other questions may have more than one answer. Do not go on to exercise 2 until you have checked your answers to exercise 1.

1. Does this restaurant serve alcoholic drinks? How do you know?

2. Does this restaurant serve desserts? How do you know?

3. Does this restaurant serve buffalo meat?

4. If you don't want to eat pork, list some entries you would avoid.

5. If you don't eat meat, what are some items you could order at this restaurant?

6. If you don't eat meat, what Breakfast Favorite could you order?

7. Scan to find the headings *Select Sides, Breakfast Sides,* and *Choose Your Sides.* What does *sides* mean?

8. If you want fruit for breakfast, what could you order?

9. It's six o'clock on a Sunday evening. Can you order eggs and pancakes?

10. Is tax included in the prices on this menu?

11. Is a tip for the server included in the prices on this menu?

12. a. How much does a Classic Burger with french fries and a salad cost?
    b. How much does it cost if you also want to have soup?

13. How much does a piece of pie cost?

Reading for Details

Indicate if each statement is true (T) or false (F).

1. _____ Shrimp is the only seafood served in this restaurant.

2. _____ Bread always comes with the Classic Dinners.

3. _____ There is no extra cost for salad if you order a Classic Dinner.

4. _____ This restaurant has special menu items for children.

5. _____ You have $6.00. You can afford a Grilled Chicken dinner with rice and a vegetable.

6. _____ The Breakfast Favorites include your choice of a Breakfast Side.

7. _____ You can order a baked potato with your Classic Dinner any time before 10 P.M.

8. _____ If you order a Ham and Cheddar Omelette, potatoes and bread come with it.

9. _____ This restaurant will prepare food for you to take home to eat.

Critical Reading

The following questions require drawing inferences and giving your own opinion.

1. You have $10.00 to spend. What would you order? (Make sure to save enough for tax and tip.)

2. Do you think many vegetarians eat at this restaurant? Why or why not?

3. Do you think you would like to eat at this restaurant? Why or why not?

4. Many restaurants give unusual names to their menu items. Sometimes these names have a theme; they're related to each other in some way. Several items on the Denny's menu include the word *slam,* which is a sports term. Which four items on the menu include the word *slam*? Which of these four items do you think Denny's has been serving for the longest time? *Grand slam* is a baseball term. Do you know what it means? If not, ask someone who knows sports.

Going Beyond the Text: Web Work

You may have heard of the chain of Denny's restaurants with more than a thousand locations across the United States and Canada. In the 1990s, Denny's was the subject of many television, radio, and newspaper stories. First, the publicity was terrible. Denny's was found guilty of racial discrimination. By the end of the decade, though, the situation was very different. Denny's was honored by national organizations as one of the best companies in the United States for minorities and women.

1. Find out more about what happened. Some places you can go for information are the Denny's Web site (**www.dennys.com**), or a book published in 2000 about Denny's (*The Denny's Story: How a Company in Crisis Resurrected Its Good Name,* by Jim Adamson); or you can use your favorite search engine to find other Web sites related to this story. Report your findings to your classmates.

2. The Denny's story is now used in many business schools as a case study in responding to racial and ethnic discrimination, improving corporate diversity policies, and managing a corporate crisis.

   • What lessons can business leaders learn from Denny's?
   • What lessons can the general public learn from Denny's?

Word Study
Context Clues

Efficient reading requires the use of various problem-solving skills. For example, it is impossible for you to know the exact meaning of every word you read, but by developing your guessing ability, you will often be able to understand enough to arrive at the total meaning of a sentence, a paragraph, or an essay. Context Clues exercises are designed to help you improve your ability to guess the meaning of unfamiliar words by using context clues. (Context refers to the sentence and paragraph in which a word occurs.) In using the context to decide the meaning of a word, you have to use your knowledge of grammar and your understanding of the author's ideas. Although there is no formula that you can memorize to improve your ability to guess the meanings of unfamiliar words, you should keep the following points in mind.

1. Use the meanings of the other words in the sentence (or paragraph) and the meaning of the sentence as a whole to reduce the number of possible meanings.

2. Use grammar and punctuation clues that point to the relationships among the various parts of the sentence.

3. Be content with a general idea about the unfamiliar word; the exact definition or synonym is not always necessary.

4. Learn to recognize situations in which it is not necessary to know the meaning of the word.

The explanation on page 8 for each sentence in the example exercise shows how context clues can be used to guess the meaning of unfamiliar words.

Example

Each of the sentences in this exercise contains a blank in order to encourage you to look only at the context provided as you attempt to determine the possible meanings of the missing word. Read each sentence quickly and supply a word for each blank. There is no single correct answer. You are to use context clues to help you provide a word that is appropriate in terms of grammar and meaning.

1. I removed the _____ from the shelf and began to read.

2. Harvey is a thief; he would _____ the gold from his grandmother's teeth and not feel guilty.

3. Our uncle was a _____, an incurable wanderer who never could stay in one place.

4. Unlike his brother, who is truly a handsome person, Hogartty is quite _____.

5. The Asian _____, like other apes, is specially adapted for life in trees.

6. But surely everyone knows that if you step on an egg, it will _____.

7. Mary got a new _____ for her birthday. It is a sports model, red, with white interior and bucket seats.

Explanation

1. I removed the _____ from the shelf and began to read.

   book
   magazine
   paper
   newspaper

   The number of things that can be taken from a shelf and read is so few that the word *book* probably jumped into your mind at once. Here, the association between the object and the purpose for which it is used is so close that you have very little difficulty guessing the right word.

2. Harvey is a thief; he would _____ the gold from his grandmother's teeth and not feel guilty.

   steal
   take
   rob

   Harvey is a thief. A thief steals. The semicolon (;) indicates that the sentence that follows contains an explanation of the first statement. Further, you know that the definition of *thief* is: a person who steals.

3. Our uncle was a _____, an incurable wanderer who never could stay in one place.

   nomad
   roamer
   traveler
   drifter

   The comma (,) following the blank indicates a phrase in apposition, that is, a word or group of words that could be used as a synonym of the unfamiliar word. The words at the left are all synonyms of *wanderer*.

4. Unlike his brother, who is truly a handsome person, Hogartty is quite _____.

   ugly
   homely
   plain

   Hogartty is the opposite of his brother, and since his brother is handsome, Hogartty must be ugly. The word *unlike* signals the relationship between Hogartty and his brother.

5. The Asian _____, like other apes, is specially adapted for life in trees.

   gibbon
   monkey
   chimp
   ape

   You probably didn't write *gibbon,* which is the word the author used. Most native speakers wouldn't be familiar with this word either. But since you know that the word is the name of a type of ape, you don't need to know anything else. This is an example of how context can teach you the meanings of unfamiliar words.

6. But surely everyone knows that if you step on an egg, it will _____.

   break

   You recognized the cause and effect relationship in this sentence. There is only one thing that can happen to an egg when it is stepped on.

7. Mary got a new _____ for her birthday. It is a sports model, red, with white interior and bucket seats.

   car

   The description in the second sentence gave you all the information you needed to guess the word *car.*

In the following exercise, do NOT try to learn the italicized words. Concentrate on developing your ability to guess the meanings of unfamiliar words using context clues. Read each sentence carefully and write a definition, synonym, or description of the italicized word on the line provided.

1. _____ We watched as the cat came quietly through the grass toward the bird. When it was just a few feet from the victim, it gathered its legs under itself and *pounced*.

2. _____ Some people have no difficulty making the necessary changes in their way of life when they move to a foreign country; others are not able to *adapt* as easily to a new environment.

3. _____ In spite of the fact that the beautiful *egret* is in danger of dying out completely, many clothing manufacturers still offer handsome prices for their long, elegant tail feathers, which are used as decorations on ladies' hats.

4. _____ When he learned that the club was planning to admit women, the colonel began to *inveigh against* all forms of liberalism; his shouting attack began with universal voting and ended with a protest against divorce.

5. _____ The snake *slithered* through the grass.

6. _____ The man thought that the children were defenseless, so he walked boldly up to the oldest and demanded money. Imagine his surprise when they began to *pelt* him with rocks.

7. _____ Experts in *kinesics*, in their study of body motion as related to speech, hope to discover new methods of communication.

8. _____ Unlike her *gregarious* sister, Jane is a shy, unsociable person who does not like to go to parties or to make new friends.

9. _____ After a day of skiing, Harold is *ravenous*. Yesterday, for example, he ate two bowls of soup, salad, a large chicken, and a piece of chocolate cake before he was finally satisfied.

10. _____ After the accident, the ship went down so fast that we weren't able to *salvage* any of our personal belongings.

Word Study
Dictionary Use

Before You Begin

1. When do you use a dictionary?

2. What kind of information does it give you?

3. When reading English, do you use a monolingual (English-English) or bilingual dictionary?

4. What are the advantages and disadvantages of a bilingual dictionary? Of a monolingual dictionary?

5. Are there times when you do not know what a word means and you do not use a dictionary?

The dictionary provides many kinds of information about words. Below is an excerpt from an English language dictionary. Study the entry carefully; notice how much information the dictionary presents under the word *prefix*.

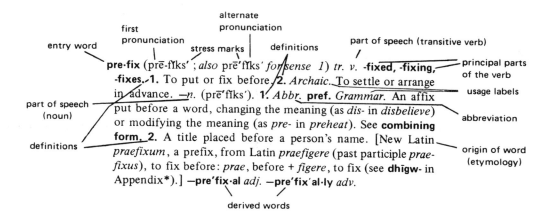

Your dictionary may use a different system of abbreviations or different pronunciation symbols. It is important for you to become familiar with your English dictionary and with the symbols it uses. Look up *prefix* in your dictionary and compare the entry to the entry shown above. Discuss any differences that you find.

Exercise 1

Use the sample entry above, the dictionary page (p. 13), and your own dictionary to discuss this exercise. Your teacher may want you to work alone, in pairs, or in small groups.

1. When a dictionary gives more than one spelling or pronunciation of a word, which one should you use?

From *The American Heritage Dictionary of the English Language* (Boston: Houghton Mifflin).

2. Look at the sample entry.

   a. How many syllables are in *prefix*?

   b. What symbol does the dictionary use to separate the syllables?

   c. Why would you need to know where a word is divided into syllables?

3. *Prefix* can be pronounced with the stress on either syllable when used as a verb.

   a. Which syllable is stressed in the first pronunciation of the verb *prefix*?

   b. Which syllable is stressed when *prefix* is used as a noun?

   c. Practice pronouncing *prefix* with the stress on the first and on the second syllable.

4. a. Where is the pronunciation guide on page 13?

   b. Where is it in your dictionary?

   c. What is the key word in the pronunciation guide on page 13 that shows you how to pronounce the *e* in the first pronunciation of *prefix*?

5. a. How many different meanings are given for the verb *prefix*?

   b. How many are there for the noun *prefix*?

6. What are *derived words*?

7. What is the meaning of the Latin root from which *pre-* has developed?

8. Dictionary entries sometimes include usage labels such as *archaic, obsolete, slang, colloquial, poetic, regional,* and *informal*. Why are these labels useful?

Exercise 2

In this exercise you will scan a page of a dictionary (on p. 13) to find answers to specific questions. Read each question, find the answer as quickly as possible, and then write it in the space provided. These questions will introduce you to several kinds of information to be found in a dictionary.

1. Would you find the word *glory* on this page? _____

2. How many syllables are there in *glossolalia*? _____

3. Which syllable is stressed in the word *glutamic*? _____

4. What are the key words that tell you how to pronounce the *o* in the first pronunciation shown for *glycerol*? _____

5. What is the first way shown to spell the plural of *glottis*? _____

6. What is the past tense of *to glue*? _____

7. What is the adverb derived from *glower*? _____

8. What word must you look up to find *glossographer*? _____

9. For whom was *gloxinia* named? _____

10. From what two languages has *glucose* developed? _____

11. Is the intransitive verb *gloze* commonly used today? _____

12. How many synonyms are listed for the word *glum*? Why are these words

    defined here? _____

13. When was Christoph Willibald Gluck born? _____

14. What is the population of Gloucester, Massachusetts? _____

15. List five different kinds of information you can find in a dictionary.

    _____

    _____

    _____

Dictionary page from *The American Heritage Dictionary of the English Language* (Boston: Houghton Mifflin).

in the margin or between lines of a text or manuscript. **2.** An expanded version of such notes; a glossary. **3.** A purposefully misleading interpretation or explanation. **4.** An extensive commentary, often accompanying a text or publication. —*v.* **glossed, glossing, glosses.** —*tr.* **1.** To provide (a text) with glosses. **2.** To give a false interpretation to. —*intr.* To make glosses. [Middle English *glose,* from Old French, from Medieval Latin *glōsa,* from Latin *glōssa,* word that needs explanation, from Greek *glōssa,* tongue, language. See **glōgh-** in Appendix.*] —**gloss'er** *n.*

gloss. glossary.

glos·sal (glôs'əl, glŏs'-) *adj.* Of or pertaining to the tongue. [From Greek *glōssa,* tongue. See **gloss** (explanation).]

glos·sa·ry (glôs'ə-rē, glŏs'-) *n., pl.* **-ries.** *Abbr.* **gloss.** A collection of glosses, such as a vocabulary of specialized terms with accompanying definitions. [Latin *glossārium,* from *glōssa,* GLOSS (explanation).] —**glos·sar'i·al** (glô-sâr'ē-əl, glŏ-) *adj.* —**glos·sar'i·al·ly** *adv.* —**glos'sa·rist** *n.*

glos·sog·ra·phy (glô-sŏg'rə-fē, glŏ-) *n.* The writing and compilation of glosses or glossaries. [Greek *glōssa,* tongue, language, GLOSS (explanation) + -GRAPHY.] —**glos·sog'ra·pher** *n.*

glos·so·la·li·a (glôs'ō-lā'lē-ə, glŏs'-) *n.* **1.** Fabricated nonmeaningful speech, especially as associated with certain schizophrenic syndromes. **2.** The **gift of tongues** *(see).* [New Latin *glossolalia,* from (New Testament) Greek *glōssais lalein,* "to speak with tongues" : *glossa,* tongue (see **glōgh-** in Appendix*) + *lalein,* to talk, babble (see **la-** in Appendix*).]

glos·sol·o·gy (glô-sŏl'ə-jē, glŏ-) *n.* *Obsolete.* Linguistics. [Greek *glōssa,* tongue, language, GLOSS (explanation) + -LOGY.] —**glos·sol'o·gist** *n.*

gloss·y (glôs'ē, glŏs'ē) *adj.* **-ier, -iest.** **1.** Having a smooth, shiny, lustrous surface. **2.** Superficially attractive; specious. —*n., pl.* **glossies.** *Photography.* A print on smooth, shiny paper. Also called "glossy print." —**gloss'i·ly** *adv.* —**gloss'i·ness** *n.*

glost (glôst, glŏst) *n.* **1.** A lead glaze used for pottery. **2.** Glazed pottery. [Variation of GLOSS (sheen).]

glot·tal (glŏt'l) *adj.* **1.** Of or relating to the glottis. **2.** *Phonetics.* Articulated in the glottis. [From GLOTTIS.]

glottal stop. *Phonetics.* A speech sound produced by a momentary complete closure of the glottis, followed by an explosive release.

glot·tis (glŏt'ĭs) *n., pl.* **-tises** or **glottides** (glŏt'ə-dēz') **1.** The space between the vocal cords at the upper part of the larynx. **2.** The vocal structures of the larynx. [New Latin, from Greek *glōttis,* from *glōtta, glōssa,* tongue, language. See **glōgh-** in Appendix.*]

Glouces·ter (glôs'tər, glŏs'-). **1.** Also **Glouces·ter·shire** (-shîr, -shər). *Abbr.* **Glos.** A county of south-central England, 1,257 square miles in area. Population, 1,034,000. **2.** The county seat of this county. Population, 72,000. **3.** A city, resort center, and fishing port of Massachusetts, 27 miles northeast of Boston. Population, 26,000.

glove (glŭv) *n.* **1. a.** A fitted covering for the hand, usually made of leather, wool, or cloth, having a separate sheath for each finger and the thumb. **b.** A gauntlet. **2. a.** *Baseball.* An oversized padded leather covering for the hand, used in catching balls; especially, one with more finger sheathes than the catcher's or first baseman's mitt. **b.** A **boxing glove** *(see).* —**hand in glove.** In a close or harmonious relationship. —*tr.v.* **gloved, gloving, gloves.** **1.** To furnish with gloves. **2.** To cover with or as if with a glove. [Middle English *glove,* Old English *glōf.* See **lep-[2]** in Appendix.*]

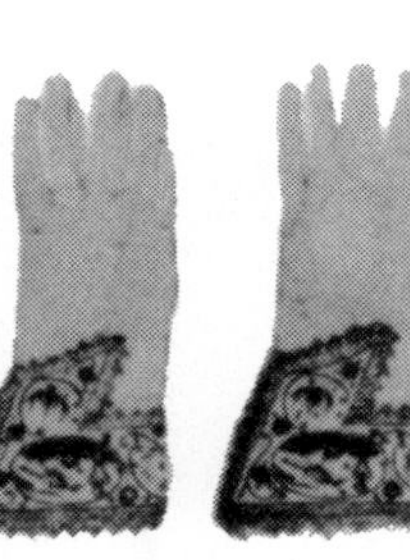

glove
Pair of 17th-century English leather gloves with embroidered cuffs

glove compartment. A small storage container in the dashboard of an automobile.

glov·er (glŭv'ər) *n.* One who makes or sells gloves.

glow (glō) *intr.v.* **glowed, glowing, glows.** **1.** To shine brightly and steadily, especially without a flame: *"a red bed of embers glowing in the furnace"* (Richard Wright). **2.** To have a bright, warm color, usually reddish. **3. a.** To have a healthful, ruddy coloration. **b.** To flush; to blush. **4.** To be exuberant or radiant, as with pride. —*n.* **1.** A light produced by a body heated to luminosity; incandescence. **2.** Brilliance or warmth of color, especially redness: *"the evening glow of the city streets when the sun has gone behind the tallest houses"* (Sean O'Faolain). **3.** A sensation of physical warmth. **4.** A warm feeling of passion or emotion; ardor. —See Synonyms at **blaze.** [Middle English *glowen,* Old English *glōwan.* See **ghel-[2]** in Appendix.*]

glow·er (glou'ər) *intr.v.* **-ered, -ering, -ers.** To look or stare angrily or sullenly; to frown. —*n.* An angry, sullen, or threatening stare. [Middle English *glo(u)ren,* to shine, stare, probably from Scandinavian, akin to Norwegian dialectal *glora.* See **ghel-[2]** in Appendix.*] —**glow'er·ing·ly** *adv.*

glow·ing (glō'ĭng) *adj.* **1.** Incandescent; luminous. **2.** Characterized by rich, warm coloration; especially, having a ruddy, healthy complexion. **3.** Ardently enthusiastic or favorable.

glow plug. A small heating element in a diesel engine cylinder used to facilitate starting.

glow·worm (glō'wûrm') *n.* A firefly; especially, the luminous larva or wingless, grublike female of a firefly.

glox·in·i·a (glŏk-sĭn'ē-ə) *n.* Any of several tropical South American plants of the genus *Sinningia;* especially, *S. speciosa,* cultivated as a house plant for its showy, variously colored flowers. [New Latin, after Benjamin Peter *Gloxin,* 18th-century German botanist and physician.]

gloxinia
Sinningia speciosa

gloze (glōz) *v.* **glozed, glozing, glozes.** —*tr.* To minimize or underplay; to gloss. Used with *over.* —*intr. Archaic.* To use flattery or cajolery. [Middle English *glosen,* to gloss, falsify, flatter, from Old French *glosser,* from *glose,* GLOSS (explanation).]

Gluck (glo͝ok), **Christoph Willibald.** 1714–1787. German composer of operas.

glu·cose (glo͞o'kōs') *n.* **1.** A sugar, **dextrose** *(see).* **2.** A colorless to yellowish syrupy mixture of dextrose, maltose, and dextrins with about 20 per cent water, used in confectionery, alcoholic fermentation, tanning, and treating tobacco. [French, from Greek *gleukos,* sweet new wine, must. See **dlku-** in Appendix.*]

glu·co·side (glo͞o'kə-sīd') *n.* A **glycoside** *(see),* the sugar component of which is glucose. —**glu'co·sid'ic** (-sĭd'ĭk) *adj.*

glue (glo͞o) *n.* **1.** An adhesive substance or solution; a viscous substance used to join or bond. **2.** An adhesive obtained by boiling animal **collagen** *(see)* and drying the residue. In this sense, also called "animal glue." —*tr.v.* **glued, gluing, glues.** To stick or fasten together with or as if with glue. [Middle English *gleu,* glue, birdlime, gum, from Old French *glu,* from Late Latin *glūs* (stem *glūt-*), from Latin *glūten.* See **gel-[1]** in Appendix.*]

glum (glŭm) *adj.* **glummer, glummest.** **1.** In low spirits; dejected. **2.** Gloomy; dismal. [From Middle English *glomen, gloumen,* to look sullen, GLOOM.] —**glum'ly** *adv.* —**glum'ness** *n.*

Synonyms: *glum, gloomy, morose, dour, saturnine.* These adjectives mean having a cheerless or repugnant aspect or disposition. *Glum* implies dejection and silence, and more often than the other terms refers to a mood or temporary condition rather than to a person's characteristic state. *Gloomy* differs little except in being more applicable to a person given to somberness or depression by nature. *Morose* implies sourness of temper and a tendency to be uncommunicative. *Dour* especially suggests a grim or humorless exterior and sometimes an unyielding nature. *Saturnine* suggests severity of aspect, extreme gravity of nature, and often a tendency to be bitter or sardonic.

glu·ma·ceous (glo͞o-mā'shəs) *adj.* Having or resembling a glume or glumes.

glume (glo͞om) *n. Botany.* A chaffy basal bract on the spikelet of a grass. [New Latin *gluma,* from Latin *glūma,* husk. See **gleubh-** in Appendix.*]

glut (glŭt) *v.* **glutted, glutting, gluts.** —*tr.* **1.** To fill beyond capacity; satiate. **2.** To flood (a market) with an excess of goods so that supply exceeds demand. —*intr.* To eat excessively. —See Synonyms at **satiate.** —*n.* **1.** An oversupply. **2.** The act or process of glutting. [Middle English *glotten, glouten,* probably from Old French *gloutir,* to swallow, from Latin *gluttīre.* See **gwel-[5]** in Appendix.*]

glu·tam·ic acid (glo͞o-tăm'ĭk) *n.* An amino acid present in all complete proteins, found widely in plant and animal tissue, and having a salt, sodium glutamate, that is used as a flavor-intensifying seasoning. [GLUT(EN) + AM(IDE) + -IC.]

glu·ta·mine (glo͞o'tə-mēn', -mĭn) *n.* A white crystalline amino acid, $C_5H_{10}N_2O_3$, occurring in plant and animal tissue and produced commercially for use in medicine and biochemical research. [GLUT(EN) + AMINE.]

glu·ten (glo͞ot'n) *n.* A mixture of plant proteins occurring in cereal grains, chiefly corn and wheat, and used as an adhesive and as a flour substitute. [Latin *glūten,* glue. See **gel-[1]** in Appendix.*] —**glu'te·nous** *adj.*

gluten bread. Bread made from flour with a high gluten content and low starch content.

glu·te·us (glo͞o'tē-əs, glo͞o-tē'-) *n., pl.* **-tei** (-tē-ī', -tē'ī'). Any of three large muscles of the buttocks: **a.** *gluteus maximus,* which extends the thigh; **b.** *gluteus medius,* which rotates and abducts the thigh; **c.** *gluteus minimus,* which abducts the thigh. [New Latin, from Greek *gloutos,* buttock. See **gel-[1]** in Appendix.*] —**glu'te·al** *adj.*

glu·ti·nous (glo͞ot'n-əs) *adj.* Resembling or of the nature of glue; sticky; adhesive. [Latin *glūtinōsus,* from *glūten,* glue. See **gel-[1]** in Appendix.*] —**glu'ti·nous·ly** *adv.* —**glu'ti·nous·ness, glu'ti·nos'i·ty** (-ŏs'ə-tē) *n.*

glut·ton[1] (glŭt'n) *n.* **1.** One that eats or consumes immoderately. **2.** One that has inordinate capacity to receive or withstand something: *a glutton for punishment.* [Middle English *glotoun,* from Old French *gluton, gloton,* from Latin *gluttō.* See **gwel-[5]** in Appendix.*] —**glut'ton·ous** *adj.* —**glut'ton·ous·ly** *adv.*

glut·ton[2] (glŭt'n) *n.* A mammal, the **wolverine** *(see).* [From GLUTTON (eater), translation of German *Vielfrass,* "great eater."]

glut·ton·y (glŭt'n-ē) *n.* Excess in eating or drinking.

glyc·er·ic acid (glĭ-sĕr'ĭk, glĭs'ər-). A syrupy, colorless compound, $C_3H_6O_4$. [From GLYCERIN.]

glyc·er·ide (glĭs'ə-rīd') *n.* An ester of glycerol and fatty acids. [GLYCER(IN) + -IDE.]

glyc·er·in (glĭs'ər-ĭn) *n.* Glycerol. [French, from Greek *glukeros,* sweet. See **dlku-** in Appendix.*]

glyc·er·ol (glĭs'ə-rôl', -rōl', -rŏl') *n.* A syrupy, sweet, colorless or yellowish liquid, $C_3H_8O_3$, obtained from fats and oils as a by-product of the manufacture of soaps and fatty acids, and used as a solvent, antifreeze and antifrost fluid, plasticizer, and sweetener, and in the manufacture of dynamite, cosmetics, liquid soaps, inks, and lubricants. [GLYCER(IN) + -OL.]

glyc·er·yl (glĭs'ər-əl) *n.* The trivalent glycerol radical CH_2CHCH_2. [GLYCER(IN) + -YL.]

gly·cin (glī'sĭn) *n.* Also **gly·cine** (-sēn', -sĭn). A poisonous compound, $C_8H_9NO_3$, used as a photographic developer. [From GLYCINE.]

gly·cine (glī'sēn', -sən) *n.* **1.** A white, very sweet crystalline amino acid, $C_2H_5NO_2$, the principal amino acid occurring in sugar cane, derived by alkaline hydrolysis of gelatin, and used in biochemical research and medicine. **2.** Variant of **glycin.** [GLYC(O)- + -INE.]

ă pat/ā pay/âr care/ä father/b bib/ch church/d deed/ĕ pet/ē be/f fife/g gag/h hat/hw which/ĭ pit/ī pie/îr pier/j judge/k kick/l lid, needle/m mum/n no, sudden/ng thing/ŏ pot/ō toe/ô paw, for/oi noise/ou out/o͝o took/o͞o boot/p pop/r roar/s sauce/sh ship, dish/

Word Study
Stems and Affixes

Using context clues is one way to discover the meaning of an unfamiliar word. Another way is word analysis, that is, looking at the meanings of parts of words. Many English words have been formed by combining parts of older English, Greek, and Latin words. If you know the meanings of some of these word parts, you can often guess the meaning of an unfamiliar English word, particularly in context.

For example, *report* is formed from *re-*, which means *back,* and *-port*, which means *carry. Scientist* is derived from *sci-*, which means *know,* and *-ist*, which means *one who. Port* and *sci* are called stems. A stem is the basic part on which groups of related words are built. *Re* and *ist* are called affixes, that is, word parts that are attached to stems. Affixes like *re*, which are attached to the beginnings of stems, are called prefixes. Affixes attached to the end, like *ist*, are called suffixes. Generally, prefixes change the meaning of a word, and suffixes change its part of speech. Here is an example.

Stem	Prefix	Suffix
pay (verb)	*re*pay (verb)	repay*ment* (noun)
honest (adjective)	*dis*honest (adjective)	dishonest*ly* (adverb)

Word analysis is not enough to give you the precise definition of a word you encounter in a reading passage, but often along with context it will help you to understand the general meaning of the word so that you can continue reading without stopping to use a dictionary.

Below is a list of some commonly occurring stems and affixes. Study their meanings. Your teacher may ask you to give examples of other words you know that are derived from these stems and affixes. Then do the exercises that follow.

Prefixes		
com-, con-, col-, cor-, co-	together, with	cooperate, connect
in-, im-, il-, ir-	in, into, on	invade, insert
in-, im-, il, ir-	not	impolite, illegal
micro-	small	microscope, microcomputer
pre-	before	prepare, prehistoric
re-, retro-	back, again	return, retrorocket

Stems		
-audi-, -audit-	hear	auditorium, auditor
-chron-	time	chronology, chronological
-dic-, -dict-	say, speak	dictator, dictation
-graph-, -gram-	write, writing	telegraph, telegram
-log-, ology-	speech, word, study	biology
-phon-	sound	telephone

-scrib-, -script-	write	describe, script
-spect-	look at	inspect, spectator
-vid-, -vis-	see	video, vision
Suffixes		
-er, -or	one who	worker, spectator
-ist	one who	typist, biologist
-tion, -ation	condition, the act of	action, celebration

Exercise 1

1. For each item, select the best definition of the italicized word.

   a. He lost his *spectacles*.

   _____ 1. glasses   _____ 3. pants

   _____ 2. gloves   _____ 4. shoes

   b. He drew *concentric* circles.

   _____ 1. OO   _____ 3. ∞

   _____ 2. ◎   _____ 4. ⊖⊖

   c. He *inspected* their work.

   _____ 1. spoke highly of   _____ 3. examined closely

   _____ 2. did not examine   _____ 4. did not like

2. Circle the words where *in-* means *not*. Watch out; there are false negatives in this list.

   inject   inside   insane   inspect

   invaluable   inflammable   inactive   invisible

3. In current usage, the prefix *co-* is frequently used to form new words (for example, *co-* + *editors* becomes *coeditors*). Give another example of a word that uses *co-* in this way.

   _____

4. The prefix *re-* (meaning *again*) often combines with simple verbs to create new verbs (for example, *re-* + *do* becomes *redo*). List three words familiar to you that use *re-* in this way.

   _____

Word analysis can help you to guess the meanings of unfamiliar words. Using context clues and what you know about word parts, write a synonym, description, or definition of the italicized word or phrase.

1. _____ The doctor asked Martin to *inhale* deeply and hold his breath for 10 seconds.

2. _____ Many countries *import* most of the oil they use.

3. _____ Three newspaper reporters *collaborated* in writing this series of articles.

4. _____ Calling my professor by her first name seems too *informal* to me.

5. _____ It is Joe's *prediction* that by the year 2012 there will be a female president of the United States.

6. _____ Historians use the *inscriptions* on the walls of ancient temples to guide them in their studies.

7. _____ You cannot sign up for a class the first day it meets in September; you must *preregister* in August.

8. _____ After his long illness, he didn't recognize his own *reflection* in the mirror.

9. _____ I *dictated* the letter to my assistant over the phone.

10. _____ I'm sending a sample of my handwriting to a *graphologist* who says he can use it to analyze my personality.

11. _____ The university has a very good *microbiology* department.

12. _____ *Phonograph recordings* of early jazz musicians are very valuable now.

13. _____ At the drugstore, the pharmacist refused to give me my medicine because she could not read the doctor's *prescription*.

14. _____ He should see a doctor about his *chronic* cough.

15. _____ Maureen was not admitted to graduate school this year, but she *reapplied* and was admitted for next year.

16. _____ I recognize his face, but I can't *recall* his name.

17. _____ Ten years ago, I decided not to complete high school; *in retrospect*, I believe that was a bad decision.

18. _____ She uses *audiovisual* aids to make her speeches more interesting.

19. _____ Some people believe it is *immoral* to fight in any war.

20. _____ Babies are born healthier when their mothers have good *prenatal* care.

Exercise 3

Following is a list of words containing some of the stems and affixes introduced in this unit. Definitions of these words appear on the right. Put the letter of the appropriate definition next to each word.

1. _____ microbe

2. _____ phonology

3. _____ audience

4. _____ chronicler

5. _____ chronology

6. _____ irregular

7. _____ microphone

8. _____ invisible

a. an instrument used to make soft sounds louder

b. not able to be seen

c. a group of listeners

d. the study of speech sounds

e. not normal

f. a historian; one who records events in the order in which they occur

g. an organism too small to be seen with the naked eye

h. a listing of events arranged in order of their occurrence

Paragraph Reading
Main Idea

In this exercise, you will practice finding the main idea of a paragraph. Being able to determine the main idea of a passage is one of the most useful reading skills you can develop. It is a skill you can apply to any kind of reading. For example, when you read for enjoyment or to obtain general information, it is probably not important to remember all the details of a selection. Instead, you want to quickly discover the general message—the main idea of the passage. For other kinds of reading, such as reading textbooks or articles in your own field, you need both to determine the main ideas and to understand the way in which these are developed.

The main idea of a passage is the thought that is present from the beginning to the end. In a well-written paragraph, most of the sentences support, describe, or explain the main idea. It is sometimes stated in the first or last sentence of the paragraph. Sometimes the main idea is only implied. In a poem, the main idea is often implied rather than stated explicitly.

In order to determine the main idea of a piece of writing, you should ask yourself what idea is common to most of the text. What is the idea that relates the parts to the whole? What opinion do all the parts support? What idea do they all explain or describe?

Read the following paragraphs and poem quickly. Concentrate on discovering the main idea. Remember, don't worry about the details in the selections. You only want to determine the general message.

After each of the first five paragraphs, select the statement that best expresses the main idea. After paragraphs 6 and 7 and the poem, you will not see the multiple choice format. Instead, you will write a sentence that expresses the main idea in your own words.

When you have finished, your teacher may want to divide the class into small groups for discussion. Study the example paragraph carefully before you begin.

Example | By the time the first European travelers on the American continent began to record some of their observations about Native Americans, the Cherokee people had developed an advanced culture that probably was exceeded only by the civilized tribes of the Southwest: Mayan and Aztec groups. The social structures of the Cherokee people consisted of a form of clan kinship in which there were seven recognized clans. All members of a clan were considered blood brothers and sisters and were bound by honor to defend any member of that clan from wrong. Each clan, the Bird, Paint, Deer, Wolf, Blue, Long Hair, and Wild Potato, was represented in the civil council by a councillor or councillors. The chief of the tribe was selected from one of these clans and did not inherit his office from his kinsmen. Actually there were two chiefs, a Peace chief and a War chief. The Peace chief served when the tribe was at peace, but the minute war was declared, the War chief was in command.

From Tim B. Underwood, *The Story of the Cherokee People* (S.B. Newman Printing Co.).

Select the statement that best expresses the main idea of the paragraph.

_____ a. The Cherokee chief was different in wartime than in peacetime.

_____ b. Before the arrival of the Europeans, the Cherokees had developed a well-organized society.

_____ c. The Mayans and the Aztecs were part of the Cherokee tribe.

_____ d. Several Native American cultures had developed advanced civilizations before Europeans arrived.

Explanation

_____ a. This is not the main idea. Rather, it is one of the several examples the author uses to support his statement that the Cherokee people had developed an advanced culture.

✔ b. This statement expresses the main idea of the paragraph. All other sentences in the paragraph are examples supporting the idea that the Cherokees had developed an advanced culture by the time Europeans arrived on the continent.

_____ c. This statement is false, so it cannot be the main idea.

_____ d. This statement is too general. The paragraph describes the social structure of the Cherokee people only. Although the author names other advanced Native American cultures, he does this only to strengthen his argument that the Cherokees had developed an advanced culture.

Paragraph 1 | A remarkable feature of Australian English is its comparative uniformity. Australia, a continent roughly the size of Europe, has almost no regional variation of accent. A citizen of Perth can sound much like a citizen of Adelaide or Sydney, or like a station hand in Alice Springs or Broken Hill. In Britain or the United States, by contrast, even the outsider can probably decide from the local accent whether he or she is in Scotland or Dorset, New England or Louisiana.

Select the statement that best expresses the main idea of the paragraph.

_____ a. Regional accents are remarkably useful in deciding where someone is from.

_____ b. In Britain or the United States, there are different accents in different regions.

_____ c. English spoken across Australia is not very different from that spoken in Britain and in the United States.

_____ d. There are surprisingly few regional differences in Australian English.

Paragraph 1 from *The Story of English* by Robert McCrum, William Cran, and Robert MacNeil (New York: Penguin, 1986).

Paragraph 2 | At the University of Kansas art museum, investigators tested the effects of different colored walls on two groups of visitors to an exhibit of paintings. For the first group the room was painted white; for the second, dark brown. Movement of each group was followed by an electrical system under the carpet. The experiment revealed that those who entered the dark brown room walked more quickly, covered more area, and spent less time in the room than the people in the white environment. Dark brown stimulated more activity, but the activity ended sooner. Not only the choice of colors but also the general appearance of a room communicates and influences those inside. Another experiment presented subjects with photographs of faces that were to be rated in terms of energy and well-being. Three groups of subjects were used; each was shown the same photos, but each group was in a different kind of room. One group was in an "ugly" room that resembled a messy storeroom. Another group was in an average room—a nice office. The third group was in a tastefully designed living room with carpeting and drapes. Results showed that the subjects in the beautiful room tended to give higher ratings to the faces than did those in the ugly room. Other studies suggest that students do better on tests taken in comfortable, attractive rooms than they do in ordinary-looking or ugly rooms.

Select the statement that best expresses the main idea of the paragraph.

_____ a. People in beautiful rooms tend to give higher ratings to photographs of faces than do people in ugly rooms.

_____ b. The color and general appearance of a room influence the behavior and attitudes of the people in it.

_____ c. The University of Kansas has studied the effects of the color of a room on people's behavior.

_____ d. Beautifully decorated, light-colored rooms make people more comfortable than ugly, dark rooms.

Paragraph 3 | Teaching is supposed to be a professional activity requiring long and complicated training as well as official certification. The act of teaching is looked upon as a flow of knowledge from a higher source to an empty container. The student's role is one of receiving information; the teacher's role is one of sending it. There is a clear distinction assumed between one

Paragraph 2 from Jeffrey Schrank, *Deception Detection* (Boston: Beacon Press).
Paragraph 3 from Herbert Kohl, *Reading: How To* (New York: Bantam Books).

who is supposed to know (and therefore not capable of being wrong) and another, usually younger person, who is supposed not to know. However, teaching need not be the province of a special group of people nor need it be looked upon as a technical skill. Teaching can be more like guiding and assisting than forcing information into a supposedly empty head. If you have a certain skill you should be able to share it with someone. You do not have to get certified to convey what you know to others or to help them in their attempt to teach themselves. All of us, from the very youngest children to the oldest members of our cultures, should come to realize our own potential as teachers. We can share what we know, however little it might be, with someone who has need of that knowledge or skill.

Select the statement that best expresses the main idea of the paragraph.

_____ a. The author believes that it is not difficult to be a good teacher.

_____ b. The author believes that every person has the potential to be a teacher.

_____ c. The author believes that teaching is a professional activity requiring special training.

_____ d. The author believes that teaching is the flow of knowledge from a higher source to an empty container.

Paragraph 4 | "The artist," Alberto Giacometti once told his boarding school classmates, "must portray things as he sees them, not as others show them." He was just 16, but those words would define and haunt him for the rest of his life. Born just 100 years ago, he became one of the titans of twentieth century sculpture and painting, an artist who gave Picasso advice on sculpting and was picked to draw Matisse's portrait for a medallion honoring the painter's career. Yet to his last days, Giacometti was still trying to live up to those boyhood words, and claiming that he'd failed.

Select the statement that best expresses the main idea of the paragraph.

_____ a. Giacometti believed he had failed to give Picasso good advice.

_____ b. Giacometti was a major artist of the twentieth century.

_____ c. Giacometti was a better sculptor than Picasso.

_____ d. Throughout his life, Giacometti was not convinced he was a true artist.

Adapted from Paul Trachtman, "Magnificent Obsession," *Smithsonian*, November 2001, 56.

Paragraph 5 | Some tribes in Africa speak to each other with a vocabulary that includes sharp clicking sounds. Genetic comparison of two such tribes suggests that the click languages, known as Khoisan languages, could resemble the ancestral tongue of all human kind. These tongues are most prevalent in southwestern Africa where many tribes, including the San and !Kung tribes (the ! represents a click sound) speak them. The Hadzabe people and several other tribes in the East African country of Tanzania also talk with clicks. The geographical and genetic diversity of Khoisan speakers and Africa's apparent role as the birthplace of humanity have led some scientists to propose that all living humans descended from speakers of a click language.

Select the statement that best expresses the main idea of the paragraph.

_____ a. Several different African tribes speak languages with clicks.

_____ b. Africa is the place where humans probably originated.

_____ c. The earliest humans may have spoken a click language.

_____ d. Click languages appear to be Khoisan languages.

Adapted from *Science News*, October 27, 2000.

Paragraph 6   There is widespread fear among policymakers and the public today that the family is disintegrating. Much of that anxiety stems from a basic misunderstanding of the nature of the family in the past and a lack of appreciation for its resiliency in response to broad social and economic changes. The general view of the family is that it has been a stable and relatively unchanging institution through history and is only now undergoing changes; in fact, change has always been characteristic of it.

Write a sentence that expresses the main idea of the paragraph. _____

_____

Paragraph 7   Enough is known about the ancient Maya—those sophisticated artists and architects, astronomers and calendar keepers of South America—to realize that much remains to be learned before all the mysteries can be unraveled. Once considered peaceful stargazers, they are now suspected of being bloodthirsty and warlike. Dogged and brilliant scholars have wrestled with the problems for a century and a half. There has been a steady revision of ideas, regular expansion of the boundaries of knowledge, and there is certain to be more.

Write a sentence that expresses the main idea of the paragraph. _____

_____

Paragraph 6 adapted from Maris Vinovskis, "Historical Perspectives on the Development of the Family and Parent-Child Interactions," in *Parenting Across the Life Span*, ed. Jane B. Lancaster, Jeanne Altman, Alice S. Rossi, and Lonni R. Sherrod (New York: Aldine de Gruyter).

Paragraph 7 adapted from William Weber Johnson, "Two New Exhibitions Explore the Dark Mysteries of the Maya," *Smithsonian*.

Poem

Fueled

Fueled
by a million
man-made
wings of fire—
the rocket tore a tunnel
through the sky—
and everybody cheered.
Fueled
only by a thought from God—
the seedling
urged its way
through the thickness of black—
and as it pierced
the heavy ceiling of the soil—
and launched itself
up into outer space—
no
one
even
clapped.

Marcie Hans

Write a sentence that expresses the main idea of the poem. _____

_____

Marcie Hans, "Fueled," from *Serve Me a Slice of Moon*, by Marcie Hans (New York: Harcourt Brace Jovanovich).

 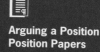

2

Reading Selections 1A–1C
International Agency Reports and Essay

Selection 1A Journal Graphic

Before You Begin   Have you been a tourist? Where did you go? How did you choose your destination?

The article that follows, from a United Nations publication, was written at the turn of the twenty-first century. It reports on the globalization of tourism. See if you can predict some of the findings in this article.

1. Which country do you predict received the most visitors at the turn of the twenty-first century? Which were the top 10 destinations?

2. Which country do you predict will receive the most visitors in 2020? Which do you predict will be among the top 10 tourist destinations in 2020?

3. Where do you think most tourists will come from in 2020?

Comprehension

Read "The Globalization of Tourism" quickly to see if your predictions are confirmed, and then answer the questions that follow. True/False items are indicated by a T / F preceding the statement.

1. T / F   The purpose of the pair of bar graphs at the top of page 27 is to compare spending on tourism in different years.

2. T / F   The purpose of the bar graphs at the bottom of page 27 is to show changes in where tourists will be traveling to in the future.

3. T / F   Tourism was the world's leading industry when this article was written.

4. What does the author say is an effect of electronic technology (the World Wide Web) on

   tourism? _____

_____

"The Globalization of Tourism" is from *UNESCO Courier,* July/August 1999.

25

The **globalization** of tourism

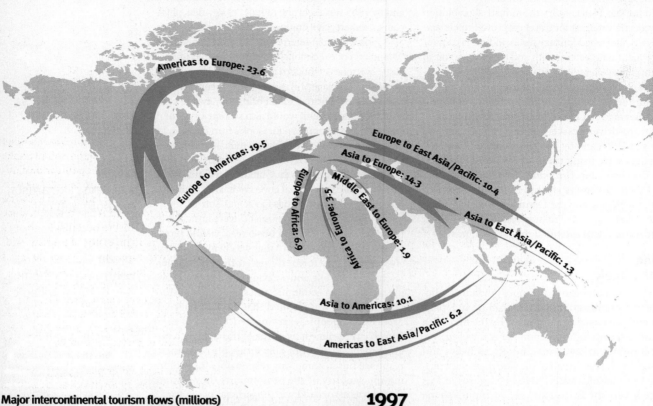

Americas to Europe: 23.6

Europe to Americas: 19.5

Europe to East Asia/Pacific: 10.4

Asia to Europe: 14.3

Europe to Africa: 6.9

Middle East to Europe: 1.9

Africa to Europe: 3.5

Asia to East Asia/Pacific: 1.3

Asia to Americas: 10.1

Americas to East Asia/Pacific: 6.2

Major intercontinental tourism flows (millions)

1997

2020

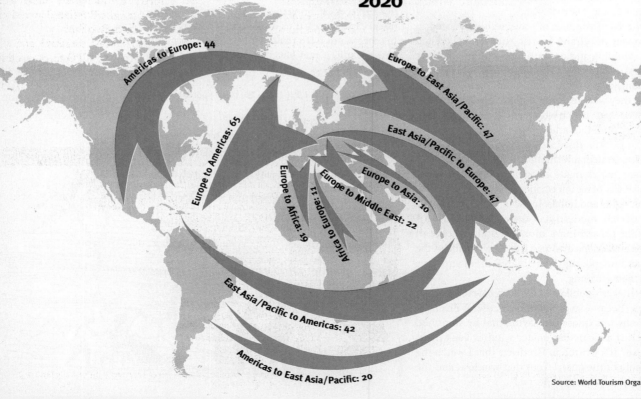

Americas to Europe: 44

Europe to East Asia/Pacific: 47

Europe to Americas: 65

East Asia/Pacific to Europe: 47

Europe to Asia: 10

Europe to Africa: 19

Europe to Middle East: 22

Africa to Europe: 11

East Asia/Pacific to Americas: 42

Americas to East Asia/Pacific: 20

Source: World Tourism Organizati

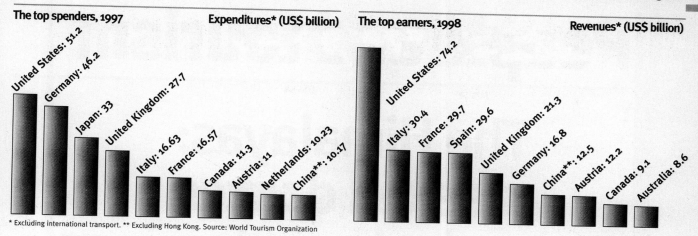

The top spenders, 1997   Expenditures* (US$ billion)

United States: 51.2
Germany: 46.2
Japan: 33
United Kingdom: 27.7
Italy: 16.63
France: 16.57
Canada: 11.3
Austria: 11
Netherlands: 10.23
China**: 10.17

The top earners, 1998   Revenues* (US$ billion)

United States: 74.2
Italy: 30.4
France: 29.7
Spain: 29.6
United Kingdom: 21.3
Germany: 16.8
China**: 12.5
Austria: 12.2
Canada: 9.1
Australia: 8.6

* Excluding international transport. ** Excluding Hong Kong. Source: World Tourism Organization

1 If the World Tourism Organization's forecasts are on target, international tourist arrivals will climb from the present 625 million a year to 1.6 billion in 2020. By this date, travellers will spend over US$2 trillion, (against US$44.5 billion today), making tourism the world's leading industry.

2 Electronic technology is facilitating this growth by offering access to fare and hotel information and online reservation services. Despite a modest annual growth rate (3.1%), Europe will remain, by far, the most popular destination (it can expect 717 million international arrivals in 2020, double the 1998 figure), though its market share will decline from 59 to 45%. Growth on the continent will be led by Central and Eastern European countries, where arrivals are expected to increase by 4.8% per year. At the same time, almost half the world's tourists will be coming from Europe. Given this dominance, it is not surprising to find that six European countries count among the top ten tourism earners and spenders. The United States holds first place in both categories.

3 With a 7% per annum growth in international arrivals, the East Asia/Pacific region will overtake the Americas as the second most popular destination, holding a 27% market share in 2020 against 18% by the Americas. But the industry will also be doing its utmost to court the Asian traveller, since East Asia/Pacific is forecast to become the world's second most important generator of tourists, with a 7% annual growth rate, pushing the Americas into third position. China is expected to become the fourth largest source of tourists on the world market, while it is not even among the first twenty today. Both arrivals to and departures from Africa (and especially Southern Africa), the Middle East and South Asia are expected to grow by above 5% per year.

4 While France has held its place as the top destination throughout the 1990s, it will be dethroned in the next decades, with China (excluding Hong Kong) expected to top the list by 2020 even though it is not even featured on it today. Also making an entry into the top ten are the Russian Federation, Hong Kong, and the Czech Republic.

5 Despite this growth forecast, tourism is and will remain the privilege of a few: WTO forecasts that only 7% of the world population will travel abroad by 2020.

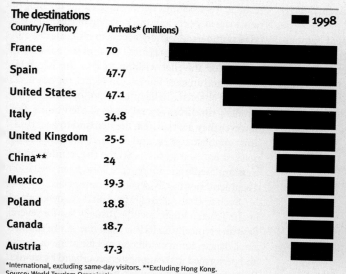

The destinations

Country/Territory	Arrivals* (millions)
France	70
Spain	47.7
United States	47.1
Italy	34.8
United Kingdom	25.5
China**	24
Mexico	19.3
Poland	18.8
Canada	18.7
Austria	17.3

*International, excluding same-day visitors. **Excluding Hong Kong.
Source: World Tourism Organization

■ 1998   ■ 2020

Country/Territory	Arrivals* (millions)
China*	137.1
United States	102.4
France	93.3
Spain	71
Hong Kong, China**	59.3
Italy	52.9
United Kingdom	52.8
Mexico	48.9
Russian Fed.	47.1
Czech Rep.	44

*Excluding Hong Kong. **Hong Kong has been a Special Administrative Region of China since 1997.
Source: World Tourism Organization

5. According to the bar graphs, in what did the United States lead the world in 1998? _____

6. T / F   The number of travelers to Europe is predicted to decline 45 percent by 2020.

7. Which continent both spends the most on tourism and earns the most from tourism?

_____

8. T / F   Germany spends more on tourism than it earns from tourism.

9. T / F   The United States is predicted to be the most popular tourist destination in 2020.

10. What changes related to tourism are predicted for China by 2020? _____

_____

11. T / F   The arrows on the maps on page 26 show all international tourism in 1997 and all international tourism predicted for 2020.

12. T / F   According to the maps on page 26, fewer tourists from Asia will visit the East Asia/Pacific region in 2020 than visited in 1997.

Critical Reading

1. In what ways do world events (for example, economic cycles, international meetings, political unrest, or terrorist attacks) affect tourism? Are there predictions made in this article that you believe no longer hold true because of recent world events?

2. a. It is sometimes the case that the text and the graphics in technical reports aren't completely consistent. Below are two claims made in the text of "The Globalization of Tourism." Does the information in the bar graphs support these statements?

   • (Paragraph 3): "the East Asia/Pacific region will overtake the Americas as the second most popular destination."

   • (Paragraph 4): China is "expected to top the list [of tourist destinations] by 2020 even though it is not even featured on it today."

   b. When you do research, if you are faced with a discrepancy (difference) in information between the text and graphics in an article, you will probably need to do further study. How might you find additional information that would make you more confident of the claims made in "The Globalization of Tourism"?

Discussion/Composition

1. From which areas do most tourists come to your home country or region? If you were developing an advertising brochure designed to encourage tourists to visit your home country or region, what kinds of information would you include? What physical and cultural sights should tourists be sure to see? What cultural and historical information would they need? Are there common things that you would want to explain to tourists? Would you mention these in your brochure? After discussing these issues, write a brochure to advertise your locality.

2. If tourism to your home country or region were to double in the next 20 years, would this be a good thing or a bad thing? Write a letter to your local newspaper arguing your point of view.

The previous article in this section, "The Globalization of Tourism," predicts that the number of people traveling the globe will increase dramatically. In fact, tourism is predicted to become the world's leading industry. The author of the next article, "The Politics of Travel," argues that this is a mixed blessing since tourism brings problems as well as profits.

Before You Begin   1. What are advantages to regions that become popular tourist attractions?

2. What are problems brought on by tourism?

3. Why do people become tourists? What are the attractions of travel?

Read "The Politics of Travel" to discover the author's perspective, and then answer the questions that follow. Do not be concerned if you don't know the meaning of every word. Your teacher may want you to do Vocabulary from Context exercise 1 on pages 32–33 before you begin reading.

Comprehension

Indicate if each statement below is true (T) or false (F) according to your understanding of the author's point of view.

1. T / F Tourism threatens the environment.

2. T / F Taking a shower in the Himalayas can lead to global warming.

3. T / F Taking an airplane contributes to climate change.

4. T / F The "Golf Wars" took place between Iraq and Kuwait.

5. T / F There is no good side to tourism.

6. T / F If you kill a lion in Kenya, you can sell it for $7,000.

7. T / F The author is disappointed that whale watching is now a bigger business than whaling.

8. T / F The author believes that tourism can strengthen local culture.

9. T / F Tourism changes tradition.

10. T / F The author believes that by writing articles such as this he can persuade people to stop taking vacations.

11. T / F Working holidays will not help the environment.

12. T / F A major concern of the author is the environment.

Critical Reading

1. Why do you think the author talks about "consumers" instead of "tourists" in paragraph 1?

2. Why do you think this article is titled "The Politics of Travel"? How is travel political?

Excerpt from THE POLITICS OF TRAVEL

by David Nicholson-Lord

1 Tourism has seriously damaged fragile ecosytems like the Alps—the winter skiing playground of Europe—and the trekking areas of the Himalayas. Worldwide, it poses a serious threat to coastal habitats like dunes, mangrove forests and coral reefs. It fuels a booming and usually illegal trade in the products of threatened wildlife, from tortoiseshell and coral to ivory. Its "consumers" inevitably bring their habits and expectations with them—whether it's hot showers and flush toilets or well-watered greens for golfers. In the Himalayas, showers for trekkers often mean firewood, which means deforestation. In Hawaii and Barbados, it was found that each tourist used between six and ten times as much water and electricity as a local. In Goa, villagers forced to walk to wells for their water had to watch as a pipeline to a new luxury hotel was built through their land. Over the past decade golf, because of its appetite for land, water and herbicides, has emerged as one of the biggest culprits, so much so that "golf wars" have broken out in parts of Southeast Asia; campaigners in Japan, one of the chief exponents of golf tourism, have launched an annual World No Golf Day.

2 This is not to say tourism can't do some good—but the cost-benefit equation is complex. Historic monuments, houses and gardens thrive on visitors. Throughout much of the world, but notably in southern and eastern Africa, tourism underpins the survival of wildlife. Why else would small farmers put up with elephants trampling their crops? Whale watching is now a bigger business than whaling. In the uplands of Rwanda, known to millions through the film *Gorillas in the Mist,* the mountain gorilla's salvation lies partly in the income and interest generated by tourists visiting in small groups. In Kenya a lion's worth is estimated at $7,000 a year in tourist income—for an elephant herd the figure is $610,000. And if large animals, with large ranges, are protected, then so are their habitats—the national parks.

3 Yet none of these gains is unqualified. To get to see your whales and your gorillas, for example, you have to travel, by car, coach or plane. Each time you do so you're effectively setting fire to a small reservoir of gasoline—and releasing several roomfuls of carbon dioxide into the atmosphere. Transport is the world's fastest growing source of carbon dioxide emissions; leisure travel accounts for half of all transport. The cumulative result of such activity is one of the biggest disruptions in the Earth's history—global warming, climate change and rising seas.

4 Some observers now argue that tourism can strengthen local cultures by encouraging an awareness of tradition and the ceremonies and festivals that go with it. But what's the value of tradition if it's kept alive self-consciously, for profit, and bears little relation to real life—which, today, across the world, grows ever more uniform? The pressures of tourism breed a phenomenon often referred to as "Disneyfication," in which culture and history are transformed, the authentic giving way to Disney-like replicas. What's undeniable is that tourism, in one way or another, changes tradition.

5 In truth, there are no easy answers to the dilemmas posed by mass tourism. Awareness, certainly, is a step forward—the knowledge of what it means to be a tourist. With that comes the ability to make better choices, where and how and even whether to travel. An increasing number of nonprofit organizations offer working holidays, in which the economic and social asymmetries that lie at the heart of the holiday industry are somewhat redressed: The tourist takes but also gives. Among the best-known is the research organization Earthwatch.

To read more about working holidays, see "Learning Holidays: A Thumbnail Guide," pages 39–40.

6 Such initiatives are undoubtedly one of the ways forward for tourism. The world, clearly, is not going to stop taking holidays—but equally clearly we can no longer afford to ignore the consequences. And if one of the major culprits has been the industrialization of travel, a genuinely postindustrial tourism, with the emphasis on people and places rather than product and profits, could turn out to be significantly more planet-friendly.

David Nicholson-Lord, who lives in England, is former environment editor of The Independent on Sunday *and author of* The Greening of the Cities *(Routledge).*

From *The Nation,* October 6, 1997.

Discussion/Composition

1. *Simulation:* You and your classmates are government officials in a nation that very much needs tourist money. However, the beautiful natural and cultural sights that bring tourists will also be threatened if too many people visit. You will have to develop a reasonable tourist policy.

   a. Break up into groups representing various government groups.
      - Ministry of the Treasury
        ○ This is the group that must worry about the financial state of the government.
      - Ministry of the Interior
        ○ This group protects natural and cultural sites.
      - Ministry of Education
        ○ This group needs money from tourism but also worries about the effects on the younger generation of so many visitors from other cultures.
      - Ministry of Transportation
        ○ On the one hand, this group hopes that tourist money will help fund new roads, but its members are worried that they can't build roads fast enough to accommodate large numbers of tourists.
      - Ministry of Health
        ○ This group, too, needs tourist money, but its members also worry that they don't have the resources to take care of tourist health needs.

   Your teacher may decide to have fewer groups, but you must have the final one:

      - Ministry of Tourism
        ○ This is the group that will be deciding on a final tourist policy for your country.

   b. In groups, prepare statements. First, brainstorm (additional) concerns and desires of your ministry. What do you want to see in the tourism policy? What do you want to avoid happening? Now work on preparing a two- to three-minute presentation to representatives from the Ministry of Tourism arguing for a specific tourist policy. You may use your time however you wish; you may have one speaker or more. The following are examples of issues you might want to address.

      – Why should/shouldn't your country encourage tourism?
      – Should there be unlimited tourism into your country? If not, how many tourists should you aim for?
      – Should there be a high cost for a tourist visa? Should there be no tourist visas required?
      – Should you focus your tourist advertising on certain countries?
      – Should some sites be closed to visitors all the time or during some periods of the year?
      – Should some sites limit the number of visitors?
      – Should you increase the cost of admission to cultural sites?
      – How will you protect your environment?
      – How should your tourist dollars be spent?

   During this time, the Ministry of Tourism will be meeting to decide what criteria they will be using to make decisions and to see if there are specific questions they would like to ask of the other ministries.

   c. Government hearings. Sometimes when governments make policy, they hold public "hearings," at which groups make presentations and provide information in an effort to influence government policy. Each group will make its presentation to the Ministry of Tourism.

    d. Rebuttals. Groups may have one minute to rebut (argue against) statements made by other ministries. Groups may then have one minute to respond to the rebuttals.

    e. Government policy is made. The Ministry of Tourism will meet and deliver its policy.

    f. Written statements. Your teacher may ask each group for a written statement. The Ministry of Tourism would present a tourism policy. The other ministries would present written statements arguing their positions.

2. In the Before You Begin section, you considered why people travel. The author addresses this question, too, in a longer version of this article. He argues that people travel to escape their lives. He quotes a Swiss academic, Jost Krippendorf, who believes that people travel because "they no longer feel happy where they are—where they work, where they live. They feel the monotony of the daily routine." The author says that "we need the unknown, what historians of religion call 'otherness', to lend our lives significance." Do you think this is why people travel? Support your position orally or in writing by presenting reasons and examples.

3. Should you feel guilty when you travel? By and large, is travel a positive or a negative thing for travelers and the places they visit? After reading this article, will you make any different travel decisions?

Vocabulary from Context

Exercise 1

Both the ideas and the vocabulary in the following exercise are taken from "The Politics of Travel." Use the context provided to determine the meanings of the italicized words or phrases. Write a definition, synonym, or description of each of the italicized vocabulary items in the space provided.

1. _____

2. _____

3. _____

4. _____

5. _____

6. _____

To attract tourism to one's country was once thought of as an *unqualified* success; there seemed to be no negative aspects to it. However, today we are coming to realize that tourism is a mixed blessing: it has advantages and disadvantages. On the one hand, it can bring money to parts of the world that very much need it. People can earn a great deal through tourism. And this *income* can help to preserve the environment. Anything that helps to protect the *ecosystem,* the interrelated community of plants and animals that makes up the Earth, is, of course, positive.

A recent worry, however, is the fact that tourists can cause serious damage to the *fragile* environments they love to visit. Ecosystems are delicate and easily damaged. Around the world, areas are endangered by the large numbers of tourists who visit them. On every continent, tourism *threatens* the environment. Even *trekkers* who take difficult journeys on foot can cause damage.

7. _____

8. _____

9. _____

10. _____

11. _____

12. _____

13. _____

14. _____

15. _____

16. _____

17. _____

18. _____

19. _____

There are, then, serious dangers that come with the promise of tourism. Every advantage brings with it real disadvantages and vice versa. This *dilemma* makes planning difficult for nations trying to decide what to do. Countries can make a good deal more money from the tourist industry than they need to put into attracting tourists. This financial *profit* can help nations protect *habitats* where endangered animals (and plants) live. These efforts can assure the *survival* of wildlife that otherwise would not continue to exist. It also may be that tourism can help strengthen local cultures by encouraging awareness of traditions and ceremonies. Historic buildings *thrive on* tourism. These cultural locations enjoy great success with the money and attention and respect brought by tourism.

But there is a downside to all this. Because cultural sites are becoming too crowded, Disneyland-like reproductions are being created. These are not *authentic* cultural sites but copies of something that may or may not have ever really existed. The author says, "what's the value of tradition if it's kept alive for profit, and bears little relation to real life?"

Taken together, the negative effects of tourism grow larger over time. The *cumulative* effects of tourism are great because every time we use cars or planes to travel we contribute to one of the greatest *disruptions* in the history of the planet: global warming and climate change are interrupting what has been the normal climate pattern for centuries.

As people understand the problems of tourism, some are beginning to organize against it through planned actions with particular goals. *Campaigns* in Japan have been *launched* against the sport of golf. Japan is one of the chief *exponents* of golf tourism. Because golf uses so much land and water, campaigners have introduced an annual World No Golf Day.

New approaches to the problem are also being developed. One *initiative* has been the development of tourist opportunities in which the tourists both give and receive through working and studying vacations. This kind of personal, small-scale tourism is meant to be a positive response to the kind of *industrialization* of tourism that has become typical with its large-scale organizing. Working tourism may not be for everyone, but the hope is that some kinds of travel can become more planet friendly.

Exercise 2

This exercise should be done after you have finished reading "The Politics of Travel." The exercise is designed to give you practice using context clues to guess the meaning of unfamiliar vocabulary. Give a definition, synonym, or description of each of the words below. The number in parentheses indicates the paragraph in which the word can be found. Your teacher may want you to do these orally or in writing.

1. (1) local _____

2. (1) culprits _____

3. (2) monuments _____

4. (2) notably _____

5. (2) trampling _____

6. (4) replicas _____

7. (4) awareness _____

8. (5) redressed _____

9. (6) postindustrial _____

Figurative Language and Idioms

In the paragraph indicated by the number in parentheses, find the word or phrase that best fits the meaning given. Your teacher may want to read these aloud as you quickly scan* the paragraph to find the answer.

1. (1) What phrase means *creates a significant danger*?

2. (1) What phrase means *hunger for; need for*?

3. (2) What phrase means *relation of advantages to disadvantages, of costs to benefits*?

4. (2) What phrase means *rescue/recovery/saving/survival depends on*?

5. (4) What word means *create*?

---

*For an introduction to scanning, see Unit 1.

Stems and Affixes

The sentences below were adapted from "The Politics of Travel." Use your knowledge of stems and affixes* and the context to guess the meanings of the italicized terms in the sentences below. Your teacher may want you to do this orally or in writing.

1. In the Himalayas, showers for tourists often mean cutting down firewood to make warm water, which leads to *deforestation.* _____

2. Because of golf's appetite for land, water, and *herbicides,* people worried about the ecosystem have launched an annual World No Golf Day. _____

3. Because tourism brings in money, in southern and eastern Africa, tourism *underpins* the survival of *wildlife.* _____

   _____

4. Each time we travel by car, bus, train, we're effectively setting fire to a small *reservoir* of gasoline.

   _____

5. Through the Disneyfication of culture, what we think of as "tradition" around the world can come to look more and more *uniform.* _____

6. Through Disneyfication, authentic culture and history are *transformed* into Disney-like replicas.

   _____

7. To give people better travel choices, *nonprofit* organizations offer working holidays that address the economic and social *asymmetries* that are characteristic of many tourist experiences.

   _____

   _____

*For a list of all stems and affixes taught in *Reader's Choice,* see the Appendix.

Dictionary Study

Many words have more than one meaning. When you use a dictionary to discover the meaning of an unfamiliar word or phrase, you need to use the context to determine which definition is appropriate. The sentences below are based on "The Politics of Travel." Use the portions of the dictionary provided to select the best definition for each of the italicized words. Write the number of the definition in the space provided.

_____ 1. Tourism *fuels* a *booming* trade in buying and selling products made from threatened

_____ 2. wildlife, such as the illegal sale of ivory from elephants' tusks.

_____ 3. If large animals, with large *ranges,* are protected, then so are their habitats—the national parks.

fu·el (fyo͞o′əl) *n.* **1.** Something consumed to produce energy, esp.: **a.** A material such as coal, gas, or oil burned to produce heat or power. **b.** Fissionable material used in a nuclear reactor. **c.** Nutritive material metabolized by a living organism; food. **2.** Something that maintains or stimulates an activity or emotion. — *v.* **-eled, -el·ing, -els** also **-elled, -el·ling, -els.** — *tr.* **1.** To provide with fuel. **2.** To support or stimulate the activity or existence of. — *intr.* To take in fuel. [ME *feuel* < OFr. *feuaile* < VLat. **focālia,* neut. pl. of **focālis,* of the hearth < Lat. *focus,* hearth.] — **fu′el·er** *n.*

boom¹ (bo͞om) *v.* **boomed, boom·ing, booms.** — *intr.* **1.** To make a deep resonant sound. **2.** To grow or develop rapidly; flourish. — *tr.* **1.** To utter or give forth a boom. **2.** To cause to boom; boost. — *n.* **1.** A deep resonant sound, as of an explosion. **2.** A time of economic prosperity. **3.** A sudden increase. [ME *bomben,* imit. of a loud noise.]
boom² (bo͞om) *n.* **1.** *Naut.* A spar extending from a mast to hold or extend the foot of a sail. **2.** A long pole extending upward from the mast of a derrick to support or guide objects being lifted or suspended. **3.a.** A barrier composed of a chain of floating logs enclosing other free-floating logs. **b.** A floating barrier serving to contain an oil spill. **4.** A long movable arm used to support a microphone. **5.** A spar connecting the tail surfaces and the main structure of an airplane. [Du., tree, pole < MDu. See **bheuə-*.**]

range (rānj) *n.* **1.a.** Extent of perception, knowledge, experience, or ability. **b.** The area or sphere in which an activity takes place. **c.** The full extent covered: *the range of possibilities.* **2.a.** An amount or extent of variation. **b.** *Mus.* The gamut of tones that a voice or an instrument is capable of producing. **3.a.** The maximum extent or distance limiting operation, action, or effectiveness, as of an aircraft or a sound. **b.** The maximum distance that can be covered by a vehicle with a specified payload before its fuel supply is exhausted. **c.** The distance between a projectile weapon and its target. **4.** A place equipped for practice in shooting at targets. **5.** *Aerospace.* A testing area for rockets and missiles. **6.** An extensive area of open land for livestock. **7.** The geographic region in which a plant or an animal normally lives or grows. **8.** The act of wandering or roaming over a large area. **9.** *Math.* The set of all values a given function may take on. **10.** *Statistics.* The difference or interval between the smallest and largest values in a frequency distribution. **11.** A class, a rank, or an order. **12.** An extended group or series, esp. a row or chain of mountains. **13.** One of a series of double-faced bookcases in a library stack room. **14.** A north-south strip of townships, each six miles square, numbered east and west from a specified meridian in a U.S. public land survey. **15.** A stove with spaces for cooking a number of things at the same time. — *v.* **ranged, rang·ing, rang·es.** — *tr.* **1.** To arrange or dispose in a particular order, esp. in rows or lines. **2.** To assign to a particular category; classify. **3.** To align (a gun, for example) with a target. **4.a.** To determine the distance of (a target). **b.** To be capable of reaching (a maximum distance). **5.** To pass over or through (an area or a region). **6.** To turn (livestock) onto an extensive area of open land for grazing. **7.** *Naut.* To uncoil (a line or rode) along the deck so that it will pay out smoothly. — *intr.* **1.** To vary within specified limits. **2.** To extend in a particular direction. **3.** To extend or lie in the same direction. **4.** To pass over or through an area or a region in or as if in exploration. See Syns at **wander.** **5.** To wander freely; roam. **6.** To live or grow within a particular region. [ME, row, rank < OFr. < *rangier,* to put in a row < *rang, reng,* line, of Gmc. orig. See **sker-²*.**]

From *The American Heritage College Dictionary,* 3d ed. (Boston: Houghton Mifflin, 2000).

Vocabulary Review

Two of the words in each line below are similar or related in meaning. Circle the word that does not belong.

1. ecosystem   asymmetry   habitat

2. survival   profit   salvation

3. campaign   initiative   inevitable

4. consumer   campaigner   exponent

5. thriving   fragile   threatened

In the previous selection, "The Politics of Travel," the author suggests that working holidays are more planet friendly than typical tourism. If you were trying to locate such trips, you might try guides such as the one on pages 38–39. "Learning Holidays: A Thumbnail Guide" includes a variety of options. Skim* the guide first to get a general sense of its contents. Then do the Comprehension exercise following.

Learning holidays: a thumbnail guide

Garry Marchant

People wanting to spend their vacations in pursuit of culture have a fairly wide choice of options that go beyond mere sightseeing. Numerous companies organize tours for lovers of architecture or art. Those who don't mind roughing it can do volunteer project work, join archaeological digs or help with cultural studies. Though not an endorsement of any tour organization or programme, the following sample includes just a few of the many options available.

ART AND ARCHITECTURE

• Instituto per l'Arte e il Restauro Palazzo Spinelli offers throughout the summer two- to four-week courses on Italian art including fresco, painting, ceramics, stone, archaeological, paper, glass, carpet, textile and wood restoration; study of the antique trade; drawing and painting; graphic design; computer graphics; interior design; garden design and planning; and Italian language. **Website www.spinelli.It**

• The Instituto Allende in San Miguel de Allende, Mexico, has short-term courses in painting, silver work, drawing, lithography and etching, silk screening, ceramics, multi-media sculpture, traditional Mexican weaving, Mexican art history, Spanish language classes and iron sculpture. **E-mail iallende@institutoallende.edu.com**

• Wisconsin, USA-based Adventures in Perspective brings together Mayan, Mexican and American artists to teach painting, ceramics, batik making, drumming, cooking and story-telling from their respective cultures. Week-long courses take place at the Sian Ka'an Biosphere Reserve, on Mexico's Yucatan Peninsula. **E-mail advenper@win.bright.net**

• Sua Bali offers two-week and longer courses in batik painting, local music, cookery, herbal medicine and the Indonesian language. Classes take place at a mini-resort of seven traditional guest houses in a rural setting south of the village of Ubud, renowned for its painting. **E-mail suabail@indosat.net.id**

ARCHAEOLOGICAL SITE WORK

• There are numerous opportunities to take part in archaeological digs. For example, every spring, *Current Archaeology* magazine publishes the Directory of British Archaeology, listing more than 700 societies, universities and professional units. A small number of these open their archaeological fieldwork to outsiders on weekends, or for several weeks in the summer. **Website www.currentarchaeology.com**

• Aberdeen University Centre for Continuing Education runs a "field school" in archaeology at three sites in Scotland during July and August. **E-mail cce-aberdeen @abdn.ac.uk**

• In Antigua, West Indies, Betty's Hope, a 350-year-old sugar plantation, is undergoing a multi-year restoration programme. Volunteers take part in archaeological excavations and archival research, and learn surveying and excavation techniques, processing and cataloguing of artefacts, conservation methods, archival record research and report preparation. **Website www.interimpact.com/ expedition**

• In Ecuador, weekend archaeologists unearth artefacts from pre-Hispanic chiefdoms in the Guayllabamba valley. They learn labeling and washing artefacts in the lab. **E-mail jvogel @earthwatch.org (See below Earthwatch entry in Further Information.)**

• Amateur archaeologists learn about one of the original North American civilizations, the Hopis, in Arizona. Crews of four (with a graduate student supervisor) photo-

---

*For an introduction to skimming, see Unit 1.
From the *UNESCO Courier,* July/August 2000.

graph and map artefacts, draw stratigraphy, excavate and wash, sort and catalogue artefacts. **(See Earthwatch in Further Information.)**

CULTURE
• Educational programmes relating to a specific culture can often be found through a country's official tourism board. **(www.towd.com has the address of every tourist board in the world, along with all of their branches.)**

LANGUAGE
• A language stay of two or three weeks arranged through Eurocentres combines a summer holiday with serious language learning, for adults, ages 16 and over. Students stay with a host family and participate in sports, culture and other entertainment. They can learn Japanese in Kanazawa, on Honshu, Japan's main island, French in Paris, Amboise, La Rochelle and Lausanne, Russian at the Moscow Linguistic University and Italian in the Scuola Leonardo da Vinci, Siena. English schools in North America are in Washington, DC; New York; East Lansing, Michigan; San Diego, California; Toronto, Ontario; and Vancouver, British Columbia. **Website www.eurocentres.com**

LIVING IN
• Asian Overland Services operates a five-day tropical adventure tour in various parts of Malaysia. Students live with local tribes to learn how indigenous people hunt, trap, fish and gather edible plants and medicinal herbs. Aborigines give practical lessons on how to build shelters and make traps. **E-mail aos@aostt.po**
• Wind, Sand & Stars, a British tour company, runs eight-day camel treks through the Sinai desert in which tourists travel and live with local Bedouin. Also eight-day Biblical tours. **E-mail office @windsandstars.co.uk**

MUSIC
• Amateur musicologists can help document Irish musical communities, video-taping and photographing music performances and interviewing audiences about their attitudes toward Irish traditional and Celtic music. Volunteers document festivals as well as private and pub sessions. Accommodation is in bed and breakfasts, university dorm rooms, and vacation cottages. **E-mail jvogel @earthwatch.org (See Earthwatch in Further Information.)**
• A Sound of Northern Moments music tour of Finland, Denmark, Norway and Sweden includes classic, choir, opera or jazz programmes. The Shaman's Drum folklore tour of Finland and Sweden focuses on cultural life, folk music festivals, domestic and international music, dance and theatre, both classical and modern. **E-mail sslnml@planet.net**

FURTHER INFORMATION
• US-based Earthwatch Institute funds scientific research by charging members of the public, aged 16-85, to help on some 130 projects world-wide. Many projects are based on cultural themes, including, for example, documenting Africa's musical traditions and excavating Mayan ruins. Teams are small and no previous research skills are required. Participants pay their air fare to the site, room and board and a fee to join the project. **Website www.earthwatch.org**
• The Specialty Travel Guide lists tour operators around the world offering a variety of commercial special interest tours and courses–although these can be expensive. **Website www.infohub.com**
• The Educated Traveler newsletter also provides information on specialty travel. **E-mail edtravel@aol.com; www.educated-traveler.com**
• Tourism Concern, a London, UK-based NGO which campaigns for responsible tourism, lists travel agents around the world offering home stays and opportunities of "real human exchange." **Website www.gn.apc.org/ tourismconcern**

Comprehension

Answer the following questions. Your teacher may want you to answer the questions orally, in writing, or by underlining parts of the text. True/False items are indicated by a T / F preceding the statement. Some questions may have more than one right answer.

1. T / F   This magazine recommends these particular tours and programs.

2. T / F   You can get college credit for taking courses offered in these learning holidays.

3. If you wanted to take courses on your vacation to learn Italian, which two holidays listed might interest you?

4. T / F   If you wanted to spend your vacation relaxing in a warm, faraway location, you would probably like the "Living In" tours.

5. How would you describe the types of holidays that are listed under the heading "Living In"? Would you enjoy them?

6. T / F   If you wanted to join a traveling choir, you could do that on one of the Music tours.

7. If you were interested in the culture of the native tribes of the Americas, name two holidays that might interest you.

8. If you wanted to live with local people instead of just with other tourists, which holidays listed might interest you?

9. T / F   You should be an experienced archaeologist to sign up for one of the archaeology holidays.

10. In which section would you look to find out about other learning holidays and special interest tours that are not described in this article?

11. Which of these trips is most interesting to you? Why? Which one would be your least favorite? Why?

Reading Selection 2
Mystery

Mystery stories are written to involve readers in solving a problem. The problem is presented early in the passage, and the tension grows gradually until it is solved.

In this story, a man named Ausable will certainly die unless he can outsmart his enemy. Read the story carefully. You should be able to solve the problem before the end of the story.

The Midnight Visitor

Robert Arthur

1   Ausable did not fit the description of any secret agent Fowler had ever read about. Following him down the musty corridor of the gloomy French hotel where Ausable had a room, Fowler felt disappointed. It was a small room, on the sixth and top floor, and scarcely a setting for a romantic figure.

2   "You are disappointed," Ausable said wheezily over his shoulder. "You were told that I was a secret agent, a spy, dealing in espionage and danger. You wished to meet me because you are a writer, young and romantic. You envisioned mysterious figures in the night, the crack of pistols, drugs in the wine.

3   "Instead, you have spent a dull evening in a French music hall with a sloppy man who, instead of having messages slipped into his hand by dark-eyed beauties, gets only an ordinary telephone call making an appointment in his room. You have been bored!" The man chuckled to himself as he unlocked the door of his room and stood aside to let his frustrated guest enter.

4   "You are disillusioned," Ausable told him. "But take cheer, my young friend. Presently you will see a paper, a quite important paper for which several men and women have risked their lives, come to me in the next-to-last step of its journey into official hands. Some day soon that paper may well affect the course of history. In that thought is drama, is there not?" As he spoke, Ausable closed the door behind him. Then he switched on the light.

5   And as the light came on, Fowler had his first authentic thrill of the day. For halfway across the room, a small automatic pistol in his hand, stood a man. Ausable blinked a few times. "Max," he wheezed, "you gave me quite a start. I thought you were in Berlin. What are you doing in my room?"

6   Max was slender, not tall, and with a face that suggested the look of a fox. Except for the gun, he did not look very dangerous. "The report," he murmured. "The report that is being brought to you tonight concerning some new

Adapted from "The Midnight Visitor" from *Mystery and More Mystery,* by Robert Arthur (New York: Random House).

missiles. I thought I would take it from you. It will be safer in my hands than in yours."

7   Ausable moved to an armchair and sat down heavily. "I'm going to raise the devil with the management this time; I am angry," he said grimly. "This is the second time in a month that somebody has gotten into my room off that confounded balcony!" Fowler's eyes went to the single window of the room. It was an ordinary window, against which now the night was pressing blackly.

8   "Balcony?" Max asked curiously. "No, I had a passkey. I did not know about the balcony. It might have saved me some trouble had I known about it."

9   "It's not my balcony," explained Ausable angrily. "It belongs to the next apartment." He glanced explanatorily at Fowler. "You see," he said, "this room used to be part of a large unit, and the next room—through that door there—used to be the living room. *It* had the balcony, which extends under *my* window now. You can get onto it from the empty room next door, and somebody did, last month. The management promised to block it off. But they haven't."

10   Max glanced at Fowler, who was standing stiffly a few feet from Ausable, and waved the gun with a commanding gesture. "Please sit down," he said. "We have a wait of a half an hour, I think." "Thirty-one minutes," Ausable said moodily. "The appointment was for twelve-thirty. I wish I knew how you learned about the report, Max."

11   The little spy smiled evilly. "And we wish we knew how your people got the report. But, no harm has been done. I will get it back tonight. What is that? Who is at the door?"

12   Fowler jumped at the sudden knocking at the door. Ausable just smiled, "That will be the police," he said. "I thought that such an important paper as the one we are waiting for should have a little extra protection. I told them to check on me to make sure everything was all right."

13   Max bit his lip nervously. The knocking was repeated. "What will you do now, Max?" Ausable asked. "If I do not answer the door, they will enter anyway. The door is unlocked. And they will not hesitate to shoot."

14   Max's face was black with anger as he backed swiftly toward the window; with his hand behind him, he opened the window and put his leg out into the night. "Send them away!" he warned. "I will wait on the balcony. Send them away or I'll shoot and take my chances!"

What will happen now? How will Ausable escape? Do you think he has a plan? In a few words, tell how you think the story will end.

_____

_____

Now continue reading.

15   The knocking at the door became louder and a voice was raised. "Mr. Ausable! Mr. Ausable!"

Keeping his body twisted so that his gun still covered the fat man and his guest, the man at the window grasped the frame with his free hand to support himself as he rested his weight on one thigh. Then he swung his other leg up and over the window sill.

16   The doorknob turned. Swiftly Max pushed with his left hand to free himself and drop to the balcony. And then as he dropped, he screamed once, shrilly.

17   The door opened and a waiter stood there with a tray, a bottle and two glasses. "Here is the drink you ordered, sir." He set the tray on the table, deftly uncorked the bottle, and left the room.

18   White faced and shaking, Fowler stared after him. "But . . . but . . . what about . . . the police?" he stammered.

"There never were any police," Ausable sighed. "Only Henry, whom I was expecting."

"But what about the man on the balcony . . . ?" Fowler began.

"No," said Ausable, "he won't return."

Why won't Max return? _____

Comprehension Clues

If you were not able to write an ending to the story, perhaps answering the following questions will help you. Mark each of the following statements true (T) or false (F).

1. _____ Max had never been to Ausable's room before.

2. _____ Max knew about the balcony because he had used it to enter the apartment.

3. _____ Ausable knew that someone would knock on the door.

4. _____ The apartment was on the sixth floor of the building.

5. _____ Max knew about the balcony because Ausable told him about it.

Now: Why won't Max return? _____

Discussion /Composition

Prepare alternative ending(s) to this story. Your endings might require that you add or change elements of the story.

Reading Selections 3A–3C
Essay and International Agency Reports

Selection 3A   Essay

Before You Begin
1. How many languages do you speak?

2. What do you consider to be your native language(s)?

3. Do you think it would be a good thing or a bad thing if everyone in the world studied English in school?

4. What would you expect to read about in an article entitled "Can English Be Dethroned?"?

What better place to think about the role of English than in an English class! "Can English Be Dethroned?" (taken from a UNESCO publication) raises issues concerning the spread of English. Read the article, and see what you think. Your teacher may want you to do Vocabulary from Context exercise 1 on pages 48–49 before you begin reading.

Can English be dethroned?

Ronald J.-L. Breton
Geolinguist and emeritus professor at the University of Paris

Major languages other than English are spoken by over half the people on the planet. What can be done to give them more clout in international bodies?

1 Back in 1919, U.S. President Woodrow Wilson managed to have the Treaty of Versailles, which ended the First World War between Germany and the Allies, written in English as well as French. Since then, English has taken root in diplomacy and gradually economic relations and the media. The language now seems set to have a monopoly as the worldwide medium of communication.

2 In the beginning of the 21st century, faster economic globalization is going hand in hand with the growing use of English. More and more people are being encouraged to use or send messages in English rather than in their own language. Many do not mind. They see this as part of the unavoidable trend towards worldwide uniformity and a means whereby a growing number of people can communicate directly with each other.

3 From this point of view, the spread of English may be seen as a positive development which saves resources and makes cultural exchanges easier. After all, it might be said, the advance of English is not aimed at killing off local languages but is simply a means of reaching a wider audience.

4 Perhaps. But accepting that as the last word ignores the deep-rooted ties between individual freedom and political power, between the linguistic, social and economic mechanisms which in every society underpin relations between people and groups and between culture and communities. A person makes a mark through his or her ability to use the most useful language or languages. And over several generations, the most useful languages eliminate the others.

5 Cultural imperialism is much more subtle than economic imperialism, which is itself less tangible than political and military imperial-

From the *UNESCO Courier,* April 2000.

ism, whose excesses are obvious and easy to denounce. It would be wrong to say that the world domination of English is something deliberately organized and supported by Anglo-Saxon powers, hand in glove with political initiatives or the penetration of the world economy by their transnational firms. The "language war" has very seldom been regarded as a war and has never, anywhere, been declared.

6   The military, diplomatic, political and economic strategies of the major powers can be studied and criticized, but linguistic strategies seem to be inconspicuous and tacit, even innocent or nonexistent. Will countries stand up to domination by a single language?

7   Many years after the founding in 1945 of the Arab League, whose current 22 member states have 250 million people, the countries which share a French linguistic heritage broke new ground by circulating a joint policy. In order to promote linguistic, economic and political cooperation, they set up the International Organization of French-Speaking Countries, which (like the British Commonwealth) embraces more than 50 countries with over 500 million inhabitants.

8   Since 1991, there have been conferences of Dutch speakers from eight or more communities representing some 40 million people, as well as Ibero-American summits, which every two years bring together more than 20 Spanish-speaking countries (350 million inhabitants). Turkish-speaking summits have been held biennially since 1992, with delegates from six independent countries (120 million people) of Europe, Central Asia and small ethnic communities elsewhere. Since 1996, the Association of Portuguese-speaking countries has brought together people from seven countries (200 million people).

Pockets of Resistance

9   Will uncoordinated resistance by the world's most widely-used languages be enough to cope with the threat of cultural uniformity? Perhaps not, since each language has its own geographical sphere in which it is used with varying degrees of competence. If you add up the number of speakers of the world's dozen most-used languages, you come up with a figure of more than three billion–half of humanity–which easily surpasses the two billion for whom English is more or less the official language (the Commonwealth and the United States). Backed by a concerted strategy, these major languages would surely make headway in international institutions.

10   It is not just the future of the world's major languages that is at stake. Further down the scale are 100 or so tongues officially recognized by governments or subnational regions, such as the constitutional languages of India and the languages of the Russian nationalities. These languages have their place and a right to defend it. At the bottom of the scale are thousands of sometimes struggling languages variously called native, minority, communal or ethnic tongues. Most are in danger of disappearing. They are spoken by some 300 million people.

11   Will minor languages die out, as some predict? Yes, because the best way to kill off a language is to teach another one. The monopoly that about 100 national languages have on education makes it inevitable that languages not taught in schools will be confined to the home and to folklore and eventually be pushed out of nurturing cultural environments.

12   Language murder or "linguicide," whether it is carried out intentionally or not, is one of the basic tools of ethnocide, of the deculturation of peoples which has always been perpetuated by colonization and is still the semi-official aim of governments which do not recognize the rights of their native ethnic minorities. As local languages are increasingly excluded from education systems, "linguicide" is speeding up.

13   The language issue in the 21st century raises two questions. How can widely-used national languages resist the encroachment of English? And how can minority languages in danger of extinction be saved and gain access to development?

Comprehension

Answer the following questions based on your understanding of the author's point of view. True/False items are indicated by a T / F preceding the statement.

1. T / F   The growing use of English makes cultural and economic exchanges easier.

2. T / F   Over time the most useful language eliminates other languages.

3. T / F   Whether or not a language is taught in school has no impact on its use in the community.

4. T / F   The growing importance of English is part of a plan by English-speaking nations for global economic domination.

5. T / F   Economic policies are more obvious than language policies.

6. T / F   The creation of language-based organizations such as the International Organization of French-Speaking Countries has solved the problem of the spread of English.

7. T / F   More people speak English than speak the world's next dozen most-used languages combined.

8. T / F   Deculturation is a result of linguicide.

9. T / F   The spread of English and other world languages is a threat to minority languages.

10. T / F   Minority languages can be helped by using the same strategies used by speakers of major languages.

11. In what sense do you think the author uses the terms *major* and *minor* languages? The author of another article in this series uses the term *small* instead of *minority* languages. Which term do you prefer, or can you suggest an alternative? _____

_____

_____

Critical Reading

1. a. How are minority languages endangered by the spread of English and other "world languages"?

   b. How would you answer the author's final question, "How can minority languages in danger of extinction be saved?" Below is a list of actions that speakers of "minority" languages might take. Check (✔) those that you think might be effective in protecting endangered languages. You may want to work with your classmates or compare your answers after you are finished.

    _____ Write down oral languages
    _____ Have linguists learn and teach the languages to other nonnative speakers
    _____ Make tapes of native speakers
    _____ Teach minority languages in school
    _____ Teach schools in minority languages
    _____ Pass laws requiring the use of minority languages in government and business
    _____ Require public signs to be in minority languages
    _____ Take steps to increase the use of minority languages on the World Wide Web
    _____ Encourage writers to publish in minority languages
    _____ Translate classic books into minority languages
    _____ Translate popular writing into minority languages
    _____ Have TV programs in minority languages
    _____ Use subtitles or "dub" international movies in minority languages
    _____ Translate all instructions for imported appliances into minority languages ;-)
    _____ Other? _____

2. In paragraphs 3–4, the author says that to accept the idea that English is "simply a means of reaching a wider audience . . . ignores the deep-rooted ties between individual freedom and political power, between the linguistic, social and economic mechanisms which in every society underpin relations between people and groups and between culture and communities." What are the "ties" (connections) the author is talking about? According to the author, how does understanding these connections make the use of English seem to be a problem? Work on this question with other classmates.

3. For this international publication, the author wrote in English about the dangers of English. Do you think he would have been more or less effective if he'd written in another language?

Discussion/Composition

1. Some people argue that English is no longer associated with British or American culture or with its colonial past. Instead, they argue that English has become a culturally neutral medium of communication. As evidence they point out that most people studying English today have as their goal communicating with *non*native speakers. And many different varieties of "World Englishes" are spoken as native languages today—for example, in India and Africa. Do you think English has become culturally neutral for second-language speakers? What are arguments for and against this point of view?

2. a. Below is a list of reasons why someone might study English. How would the author of "Can English Be Dethroned?" see each of these in terms of cultural imperialism? This question allows you to explore how the author might think about these things. There is no single correct answer; do not be concerned if you have trouble coming up with an answer for each item. As an example, we've given our thinking for the first one.

   • To publish scientific papers

     The need to publish in English shows the breakdown of local research communities. It also gives an unfair advantage to English-speaking researchers.

   • To read scientific papers
   • To get a job in the tourist industry in your country
   • To talk to nonnative-speaking businesspeople
   • To do business in the United States or Britain
   • To get a job in a multinational corporation
   • To study in an English-speaking country
   • To get a job teaching English
   • To marry an English-speaking person
   • To immigrate to an English-speaking country
   • Other? _____

b. On the basis of your answers, do you see the use of English more as a convenience or as contributing to cultural imperialism?

c. Write a position paper that begins "English is/is not an instrument of cultural imperialism." Support your position with your own knowledge as well as information from "Can English Be Dethroned?"

3. Worldwide, governments make "language policies." These policies can include what languages are used in government, schools, and courts and even what language workers may use among themselves. In general terms, nations have two very different positions available to them: they can encourage uniformity, or they may encourage diversity. Which approach do you think is best for your country? Support your position orally or in writing by presenting reasons and examples.

4. Over the next 10 years, do you think the use of major languages other than English will increase or decrease on the World Wide Web? Support your position orally or in writing by presenting reasons and examples.

Vocabulary from Context

Note: Because "Can English Be Dethroned?" is especially rich in unfamiliar vocabulary, the following sections include quite a few vocabulary activities. After you do exercise 1, your teacher may ask you to complete only some of the activities that follow.

Exercise 1

Use the context provided to determine the meanings of the italicized words. Write a definition, synonym, or description of each of the italicized vocabulary items in the space provided.

1. _____

2. _____

3. _____

4. _____

5. _____

English has become the dominant language for worldwide communication and business. For many people this is a convenience. Increased use of English is seen as a *trend* that simply developed gradually over time. Others see the use of English quite differently. For them, it is a form of economic, social, and political domination and control. It is, they argue, a form of cultural *imperialism*. This is the point of view the author of "Can English Be Dethroned?" examines.

If English were used only for *diplomacy,* he argues, probably few would complain. But it is used for more than international relations. Because the use of English and other world languages is so widespread, especially in schools, the worry is that languages with fewer speakers will die out. Over several generations, the most useful language *eliminates* the others.

It's difficult to criticize cultural imperialism, such as the use of English on the Internet. How do you *denounce* something whose negative effects are so hard to see? They are, indeed,

6. _____

7. _____

8. _____

9. _____

10. _____

11. _____

12. _____

13. _____

14. _____

15. _____

16. _____

17. _____

18. _____

19. _____

20. _____

quite *inconspicuous* compared to other, more obvious forms of imperialism. Economic imperialism is more *tangible;* people can touch and see the results. And certainly political and military imperialism are not at all *subtle*. Their extreme actions are quite obvious. And their *excesses* are easy to denounce.

And it's not that English-speaking governments have had a conscious, explicit plan to support the growing importance of English, says the author. It has not been a *deliberate policy* on their parts. There have not been *intentional initiatives* to spread English as their corporations have entered the world economy, *penetrating* world markets. Linguistic strategies are not explicit. Rather they are *tacit* and unspoken.

Are there ways for speakers of other languages, particularly "minor" languages, to oppose the domination of "major" world languages if they so choose? One kind of *resistance* is to work with others to see that local languages are taught in schools. Perhaps there can be meetings of speakers in the same way that there have been *summits* for major languages such as Arabic, French, Spanish, and Dutch. In order to *promote* linguistic, economic, and political cooperation, the French-speaking countries set up an international organization, much like the British Commonwealth. These are all ways to deal with a perceived threat of cultural uniformity. Groups *cope with* this threat by working together.

However, the difficulties faced by minority languages are quite different from those faced by languages such as French. French is a major language that is losing speakers, but minority languages are in danger of disappearing completely. Linguicide, some people argue, is the equivalent of ethnocide, the death of a culture, and that has typically been a tool of *colonization*. The loss of a minority language can make a community feel like it's been taken over by others. The dangers to minor languages do not come from English alone. Around the world minority languages are endangered by both local and international events.

Exercise 2

This exercise is designed to give you additional clues to determine the meanings of unfamiliar vocabulary items in context. In the paragraph of "Can English Be Dethroned?" indicated by the number in parentheses, find the word or phrase that best fits the meaning given. Your teacher may want to read these aloud as you quickly scan* the paragraph to find the answer.

1. (2) What phrase means *don't care; aren't bothered by this*?

2. (9) What word means *circle*?

3. (11) What word means *unavoidable; certain; definite*?

4. (11) What word means *traditional customs*?

5. (13) What word means *spread; intrusion; advance beyond the usual limits*?

6. (13) What word means *disappearance; death; loss*?

Exercise 3

This exercise should be done after you have finished reading "Can English Be Dethroned?" The exercise is designed to give you practice using context clues to guess the meaning of unfamiliar vocabulary in the article. Give a definition, synonym, or description of each of the words below. The number in parentheses indicates the paragraph in which the word can be found. Your teacher may want you to do these orally or in writing.

1. (4) mechanisms _____

2. (7) embraces _____

3. (9) surpasses _____

4. (10) tongues _____

Figurative Language and Idioms

In the paragraph indicated by the number in parentheses, find the phrase that best fits the meaning given. Your teacher may want to read these aloud as you quickly scan the paragraph to find the answer.

1. (1) What phrase means *has become established*?

2. (4) What phrase means *the truth; the final judgment; all there is to say on a subject*?

3. (4) What phrase means *firmly established; strong*?

4. (4) What phrase means *has influence; creates an impression*?

---

*For an introduction to scanning, see Unit 1.

5. (5) What phrase means *together with*? (You can find a synonymous phrase in paragraph 2.)

6. (7) What phrase means *did something new*?

7. (9) What phrase means *an action taken together; a joint action; an organized approach or plan*?

8. (9) What phrase means *make progress*?

9. (10) What phrase means *at issue; at risk; in danger*?

Stems and Affixes

The sentences below are adapted from "Can English Be Dethroned?" Use your knowledge of stems and affixes* and the context to guess the meanings of the italicized terms in the sentences below. Your teacher may want you to do this orally or in writing.

1. English now seems *to have a monopoly* as the worldwide medium of communication.

2. In the beginning of the twenty-first century, faster economic *globalization* is going hand in hand with the growing use of English.

3. Many people see the use of English as part of the *unavoidable* trend toward worldwide uniformity.

4. To see the spread of English as being innocent is to ignore the relations between linguistic, social, and economic mechanisms that *underpin* relations between culture and communication.

5. It would be wrong to say that the world domination of English is deliberately organized by the Anglo-Saxon powers to help the penetration into other countries by their *transnational* firms.

6. Turkish-speaking summits have been held *biennially* since 1992, with delegates from six independent countries.

7. Further down the scale are 100 or so tongues officially recognized by governments or *subnational* regions, such as the constitutional languages of India and the languages of the Russian nationalities.

8. Language murder, or *linguicide,* whether it is carried out intentionally or not, is one of the basic tools of *ethnocide,* of the *deculturation* of peoples which has always been perpetrated by colonization and is still the *semi-official* aim of governments which do not recognize the rights of their native ethnic minorities.

    linguicide: _____

    ethnocide: _____

    deculturation: _____

    semi-official: _____

---

*For a list of all stems and affixes taught in *Reader's Choice,* see the Appendix.

Vocabulary Review

Two of the words in each line below are similar or related in meaning. Circle the word that does not belong.

1. excess   inevitable   unavoidable

2. intentionally   subtly   deliberately

3. colonialism   imperialism   monopoly

4. inevitable   inconspicuous   subtle

Selection 3B Journal Graphic

The previous article discusses the spread of English. The remaining two articles in this section report on the situation for the rest of the world's languages. The first selection, "Winners and Losers" (pp. 54–55), presents information on patterns of language density. When writing about technical subjects, authors sometimes include graphics (such as maps and graphs) because visual aids can present information clearly and concisely. You will need to use information from both the graphics and the text in the article to complete the exercises.

Before You Begin   In terms of geography and number of speakers, the distribution of the world's 6,000 languages is very uneven. Before looking at the article and graphics of "Winners and Losers" make a few guesses. Your teacher may want you to work in groups or pairs. Be sure to write down your guesses.

1. What percentage of the world's languages would you guess are spoken in Europe?

2. What geographic area has the most languages?

3. "Can English Be Dethroned?" discusses the dangers to languages with only a few speakers. How many speakers do you think a language has to have to survive?

4. How many languages do you imagine die out every year?

5. Can you guess which eight languages have the most speakers?

Getting Oriented

Look at the graphics that accompany "Winners and Losers" to understand how the information is organized, and then answer the questions below.

1. What do the colors on the map represent?

2. Are these colors similar in meaning on the pie chart? Are they the same?

3. The bar graph is titled "The World's Top Ten Languages by Number of Speakers." Why does it list more than 10 languages? What would be a better title for the chart?

Winners and losers

Half the world's population uses a total of eight languages in daily life, while one sixth of the world's languages are spoken in New Guinea alone.

1   The linguistic heritage is very unevenly distributed. According to estimates made by the Summer Institute of Linguistics (SIL), which campaigns for the preservation of the least-known tongues, only three percent of the world's 6,000 languages are used in Europe, whereas half of them are spoken in the Asia-Pacific region, with the top prize going to New Guinea (the Indonesian territory of Irian Jaya plus Papua New Guinea), which is home to one sixth of the world's languages.

2   Linguistic diversity does not match population density: 96 percent of languages are spoken by only four percent of the world's population and over 80 percent are endemic, i.e., confined to one country. Only about 20 languages are spoken by hundreds of millions of people in several countries.

3   Although the figures vary according to the method of counting, it is estimated that around half the people in the world use in everyday life one of the planet's eight most widely spoken languages: Chinese (1.2 billion speakers), English (478 million), Hindi (437 million), Spanish (392 million), Russian (284 million), Arabic (225 million), Portuguese (184 million) and French (125 million). SIL and Linguasphere Observatory provide comparable figures, by adding to those who speak a language as a mother tongue those for whom it is a "second language."

Ten languages die out every year

4   The imbalance leads specialists to forecast that 95 percent of all living languages will die out during the next century. At present, 10 languages disappear every year somewhere in the world. Some go so far as to claim that a language dies out every two weeks. The rate of disappearance is especially high in areas where linguistic diversity is greatest.

5   In Africa, more than 200 languages have fewer than 500 speakers each and may soon die out. The minimum number of speakers to ensure survival is put at 100,000.

6   In North America, the biggest threats are to indigenous and Creole languages. With the exceptions of Navajo, Cree and Ojibwa, the 200 Amerindian tongues which have survived until now in the United States and Canada are endangered.

7   Between a third and a half of Latin America's 500 Amerindian languages are in danger, with the highest rate of extinction predicted in Brazil, where most languages are spoken by very small communities.

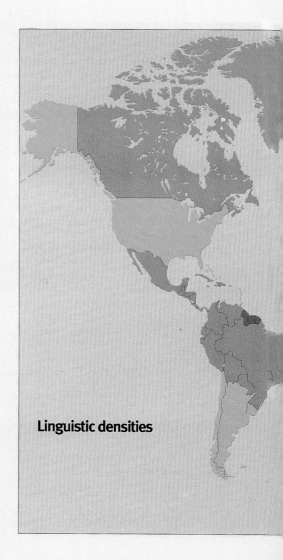

Linguistic densities

8   The languages of Southeast Asia are each spoken by relatively large numbers of people, and the future of about 40 of the 600 to 700 languages there will depend largely on government policies.

9   On the other hand, only six languages out of north-east Asia's 47 have any real chance of survival in the face of Russian. Twenty are "nearly extinct," eight are "seriously endangered" and 13 are "endangered." The first group are spoken by only a dozen people at most. The second group are more widely used but are not being passed down to children. The third category includes tongues spoken by some children but fewer and fewer, according to the forthcoming UNESCO *Red Book on Endangered Languages: Europe and North-east Asia*.

10   In Europe, where the number of languages varies by a factor of two according to the criteria used to define them, 123 languages are spoken, including nine which are nearly extinct, 26 seriously endangered and 38 endangered, according to the UNESCO book.

From the *UNESCO Courier,* April, 2000.

Exceptional density (over 100 languages per million inhabitants)

Very high density (from 10 to 100 languages per million inhabitants)

High density (from 1 to 10 languages per million inhabitants)

Medium density (from 1 to 10 million speakers by linguistic group)

Low density (over 10 million speakers per linguistic group)

Source: R. J. L. Breton

The world's top ten languages by number of speakers*

Source: Linguasphere Observatory/Observatoire linguistique , 2000

(millions)

English, Mandarin Chinese	1 000
Hindi (with Urdu)	900
Spanish	450
Russian	320
Arabic, Bengali	250
Portuguese	200
Malay+Indonesian	160
Japanese	130
French, German	125
Punjabi, Yue Chinese	85

* Primary (mother tongue) and alternate (second) language

Geographical distribution of the world's languages

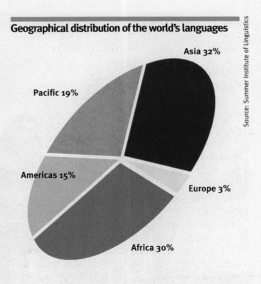

Asia 32%

Pacific 19%

Americas 15%

Europe 3%

Africa 30%

Source: Summer Institute of Linguistics

Skimming and Scanning

Skim "Winners and Losers" to get a general understanding of the information contained in the text and the graphics. Your teacher may want to set a time limit to encourage you to read quickly. Then scan to answer the following questions.* True/False items are indicated by a T / F preceding the statement.

1. First, quickly check the text and graphics to see how accurate your guesses were on the Before You Begin questions. Write the correct answers next to your guesses.

2. T / F   Africa is the continent with the highest number of languages.

3. Which territory has the highest density of languages?

4. Which continent has a "very high density" of languages?

5. T / F   Eighty percent of languages are spoken in more than one country.

6. T / F   Predictions are that during the next century most of the world's languages will die out.

7. Navajo, Cree, and Ojibwa are examples of the 200 Amerindian languages that are endangered.

8. T / F   Counting native and nonnative speakers, English and Mandarin Chinese have approximately the same number of speakers.

9. What are the three levels of endangerment for languages cited in paragraph 9? How are they defined?

Critical Reading

1. Compare the bar graph to the list in paragraph 3. What is the eighth most commonly spoken language? What is your best guess to explain this discrepancy (difference) between the graph and the text?

2. In paragraph 8, the author states that the future of 40 languages of Southeast Asia "will depend largely on government policies." What do you think this means: what government policies could affect the future of these languages?

3. Consider the title "Winners and Losers." In what sense is a language considered a "loser" in this article? In what ways is this a useful descriptor? Do you see any problems in using the term *loser*?

*For an introduction to skimming and scanning, see Unit 1.

The previous articles in this section discuss the threats to languages spoken by only a small number of people. The final article in this series, "6,000 Languages: An Embattled Heritage," explores causes and effects of the current situation.

Before You Begin

1. Language loss is not new. Can you think of languages that have disappeared? Can you think of languages that have survived for more than 2,000 years?

2. What do you think are major causes for the loss of so many languages over the last 300 years?

3. Should we be concerned about widespread language loss?

Skimming

Skim* "6,000 Languages: An Embattled Heritage" (p. 58) to discover the causes and effects of widespread language loss. Then answer the following questions.

1. What causes are given to explain widespread language loss over the past 300 years?

2. What effects of widespread language loss are given?

Critical Reading

The author states that the destruction of multilingualism will inevitably lead to the loss of multi-culturalism. In what ways are language and culture interdependent? Is it possible for cultures to survive without their native language?

Discussion/Composition

The author states that the preservation of languages is an urgent matter. Do you agree or disagree? Support your position orally or in writing by presenting reasons and examples.

---

*For an introduction to skimming, see Unit 1.
"6,000 Languages: An Embattled Heritage," from the *UNESCO Courier,* April 2000.

6,000 languages: an embattled heritage

Ranka Bjeljac-Babic

1 **A**re the vast majority of languages doomed to die out in the near future? Specialists reckon that no language can survive unless 100,000 people speak it. Half of the 6,000 or so languages in the world today are spoken by fewer than 10,000 people and a quarter by less than 1,000. Only a score are spoken by hundreds of millions of people.

2 The death of languages is not a new phenomenon. Languages usually have a relatively short life span as well as a very high death rate. Only a few, including Basque, Egyptian, Chinese, Greek, Hebrew, Latin, Persian, Sanskrit and Tamil, have lasted more than 2,000 years.

Minority languages sidelined

3 What is new, however, is the speed at which they are dying out. Europe's colonial conquests caused a sharp decline in linguistic diversity, eliminating at least 15 percent of all languages spoken at the time. Over the last 300 years, Europe has lost a dozen, and Australia has only 20 left of the 250 spoken at the end of the 18th century. In Brazil, about 540 (three-quarters of the total) have died out since Portuguese colonization began in 1530.

4 The rise of nation-states, whose territorial unity was closely linked to their linguistic homogeneity, has also been decisive in selecting and consolidating national languages and sidelining others. By making great efforts to establish an official language in education, the media and the civil service, national governments have deliberately tried to eliminate minority languages.

5 This process of linguistic standardization has been boosted by industrialization and scientific progress, which have imposed new methods of communication that are swift, straightforward and practical. Language diversity came to be seen as an obstacle to trade and the spread of knowledge. Monolingualism became an ideal.

6 More recently, the internationalization of financial markets, the dissemination of information by electronic media and other aspects of globalization have intensified the threat to "small" languages. A language not on the Internet is a language that "no longer exists" in the modern world. It is out of the game. It is not even used in business.

7 The effects of the death of languages are serious for several reasons. First of all, it is possible that if we all ended up speaking the same language, our brains would lose some of their natural capacity for linguistic inventiveness. We would never be able to plumb the origins of human language or resolve the mystery of "the first language." As each language dies, a chapter of human history closes.

8 Multilingualism is the most accurate reflection of multiculturalism. The destruction of the first will inevitably lead to the loss of the second. Imposing a language without any links to a people's culture and way of life stifles the expression of their collective genius. A language is not only used for the main instrument of human communication. It also expresses the world vision of those who speak it, their imagination and their ways of using knowledge. The preservation of languages is an urgent matter. ■

> Nothing stays longer in our souls
> than the language we inherit.
> It liberates our thoughts
> unfolds our mind
> and softens our life.
>
> **From a poem in the Sami language (Sweden)**

Ranka Bjeljac-Babic is a lecturer and specialist in the psychology of language at the University of Poitiers (France).

Nonprose Reading
Newspaper Advertisements

Classified advertisements, or "want ads," like the ones on pages 60–61 appear in most newspapers.

Before You Begin   1. Have you ever tried to use this kind of advertisement? For what purpose(s)?

2. In what ways does the writing differ from normal prose writing?*

The ads on pages 60–61 come from a university newspaper called *The Daily*. If you were living in this community, you might use the ads in this newspaper to find a job or to rent an apartment.

Overview

Skim the classified ads on pages 60–61 to get a general layout of the pages. Then scan for the answers to the following questions.** Your teacher may want to read these aloud as you scan for the answers.

1. If you needed to earn money, under which section(s) would you look?

2. If you were looking for an apartment, under which sections(s) would you look?

3. If you were looking for someone to share housing with, under which section(s) would you look?

_____

4. If you were willing to pay to have a parking place close to campus, under which section would you look? _____

5. Where would you look for jobs that prepare you for professional positions? _____

_____

---

*For an explanation of nonprose reading, see Unit 1.
**For an introduction to skimming and scanning, see Unit 1.

CLASSIFIED ADS

Help Wanted

PART-TIME PIZZA DELIVERY driver, base pay + tips. Our vehicle. Must be over 26 for insurance purposes. Dellino's Pizzeria, University Village, 555-3466.

PART-TIME RECEPTIONIST. PRESTIGIOUS real estate firm seeks customer service oriented receptionist for 20-30 hours per week and occasional weekends. FAX resume to (206)555-0368 or call Lisa at (206)555-5462.

PART-TIME WORK = FULL-TIME PAY
The Seattle Times newspaper is currently hiring people to sell subscriptions door-to-door. No experience is necessary; top-notch training is provided. Qualified applicants must be enthusiastic, outgoing, and at least 16 years of age. College students encouraged. Call the office nearest you today.
Lynnwood: (425)555-7822
Seattle area: (206)555-6247
Eastside: (425)555-3411
$$$$$$$$$$$$$$$$

RESTAURANT–SUMMER JOB in Alaska! Experienced, presentable waitresses and cooks needed for busy restaurant in Valdez, Alaska. Fax resume/application to 907-555-2877, att: Mike.

SAT TUTORS NEEDED! SCORE! Prep is currently hiring for positions starting in June, August and September. Make your own schedule, reliable transportation required. Graduate students preferred. $13-$22/hour. Call 1-800-555-7182 for more information.

NWSS
NORTHWEST SECURITY SERVICES

SECURITY OFFICERS
WANTED
-IMMEDIATE OPENINGS-
Full-time/Part-time
Seattle and Bellevue Sites
$8.57/Hour Minimum
Plus Benefits &
Tuition Reimbursement Plan
$9.00/Hour
in 6 months
Check the Competition
Then See us
We Value our Employees!
Guaranteed Interviews
8am-4pm Monday-Friday
Other Times By Appointment
Uniforms and Training Provided
We promote from within!
NORTHWEST SECURITY SERVICES
555-8142

SMART, ENERGETIC, CREATIVE help needed for daycare. Part-time/full-time positions available, $8/hour. Paid vacations. 206-555-1767.

SUMMER JOB IN Seattle! $8- $12/hour. Work outside & get a tan! Hard work = good pay. Jon 555-0432.

SUMMER JOBS
FOOD PROCESSING:
DARK SWEET CHERRIES. SEASON APPROXIMATELY JUNE 22ND TO AUGUST 5TH FULL-TIME POSITIONS. DAY AND NIGHT SHIFT. PAY SCALE $7 TO $9 per hour, plus Season bonus.
Call Penny Wykes (206)555-1730
Georgetown area of Seattle
Tree Fruit Packers, Inc.

TEACHER AND ASSISTANT positions open in early childhood program. Downtown and UW locations. Beautiful environments. Great staff. Ed Psych or Sociology students or graduates preferred. For interview call (206)555-6878 or (206)555-9850.

TEACHER/TUTORS. ESL Secondary English/ Math part-time, summer full-time. 425-555-0120.

TELEMARKETER/APPOINTMENT SETTER. $10/hour, part-time. No experience necessary. 1-800-555-5198.

TREKLEADER
Lead small groups of world travelers on adventure camping tours during the summer in the USA, Canada, Alaska, Mexico, Belize, and Hawaii. Must be available until mid-September. Please call 1-800-555-8735.

WANTED! PART-TIME TELEMARKETER. Make up to $12/hour setting up appointments. Monday-Thursday evenings. Call from office or home. Call 253-555-1200.

WASHINGTON ATHLETIC CLUB, a private hotel and athletic club in downtown Seattle, has openings for part-time lifeguards and swim instructors. Please call Stuart at 206-555-3067.

Help Wanted Over 18

EVENING CASHIER OVER 21. Part-time, good pay, some benefits. Apply Northlake Tavern and Pizza House, 660 NE Northlake Way between 2:00-4:00 pm, Monday-Thursday.

FOOD SERVER FULL- OR PART-TIME. OVER 21. EXPERIENCE PREFERRED, BUT NOT NECESSARY. APPLY NORTHLAKE PIZZA, 660 NE NORTHLAKE WAY BETWEEN 2-4 PM, MONDAY-THURSDAY.

VALET PARKING POSITION. Perfect student part-time job. Evenings and weekends. Good driving record. Must be 21 or older. Excellent pay. Call (206)555-3754, leave message.

Business Opportunities

The Daily makes every effort to ensure you are responding to a reputable and legitimate job opportunity. REMEMBER: Legitimate employers do not ask for money as part of the application process. Do not send money, especially out of state, or give any credit card information. The majority of our Business Opportunities are at least in part commission-based, as well as multi-level marketing and self-employment opportunities. A small investment MAY be required, and you may be asked to work from your home. If you have responded to an ad that seems deceptive, please call the Daily at 555-2390.

#1 HOME-BASED BUSINESS
Famous Millionaire Maker Reveals
How to Earn Multiple Streams of $$$.
For Info + Free Tape Call
1-877-555-8948

EARN NEW COMPUTER and make money at the same time. $2000 in your first two weeks with unlimited income potential. This offer is going fast. Call and get the facts. 1-800-555-9758.

US GOVERNMENT JOBS hiring now all levels. Paid training, benefits. $11-$33/hour. Call free, 1-800-555-1680, ext. 801.

Internships

STUDENT INTERN - Summer intern position in DNA Sequencing department for Eastside biotech. Responsibilities include various duties in sequencing lab. Requires undergrad molecular biology experience and experience using micropipetor. $8-$10/hr DOE. For more info call Holly at 425-555-8140.

VOLUNTEER INTERNSHIP IN CRIMINAL DEFENSE INVESTIGATION with King County Public Defender. Training and supervision provided. 20 hour per week commitment required. June 9th deadline for applications. Training begins June 21st. Call 555-3900, ext. 692 for application packet.

Child Care

BABYSITTER WANTED: CARING and responsible babysitter for adorable good natured 21 month old boy. 15 hours/week. Days/times negotiable. Experience preferred. 555-1293

CHILD CARE NEEDED during summer in Wallingford for three great children: 6, 10, 13. 25-30 hours/ week, Monday, Wednesday, Friday. $9/hour. Begins 6/28. Own car/references required. (206) 555-2375.

From *The Daily,* University of Washington, May 20, 1999.

LAURELHURST FAMILY SEEKS Nanny/ Mother's Helper approximately 25 hours/ week in non-smoking home. Great opportunity for student taking time off, 1 or 2 classes, or recent grad. Some flexibility with days/times. Must be fun, loving, energetic, reliable, and swimmer with references. Competitive wages and fun travel opportunities. Need reliable car and WSDL. No full-time students or bring-along children. Approximate start date: 8/1. Please call 555-7355.

NANNY/ MOTHER'S HELPER needed immediately for Eastside family. Full time/live-out. 2 boys. Experience and references necessary. Must have own car. One year commitment. Benefits, vacation negotiable. Great pay, great family.

SEATTLE ATHLETIC CLUB/Northgate Childcare is looking for a part-time helper. Monday-Friday, and occasional Saturdays. Fun atmosphere with membership benefits. Salary DOE. Call (206)555-7664 for information.

Volunteers

INTERESTED IN A HEALTH CARE CAREER, BUT DON'T KNOW WHERE TO START? TRY VOLUNTEERING! VOLUNTEER OPPORTUNITIES AVAILABLE ON CAMPUS AT UNIVERSITY OF WASHINGTON MEDICAL CENTER. CALL 555-4218.

Tutoring

HIGH-SCHOOL FRESHMAN NEEDS math tutoring in advanced trigonometry/algebra. Math major and teaching experience required. 555-1471 (evenings).

Rooms

$425, NEW BUILDING. Studio room with private full bath, fridge, intercom and built-ins. Quiet building. No smoking, no musical instruments or pets. (206)555-6608.

1-1/2 BLOCKS TO UW—Clean, quiet, nonsmoking room, private refrigerator. Month to month agreement. $375 includes all utilities. Also, daylight basement room, $345.
555-2488

1/2 BLOCK TO UW
HUSKY COURT
Newer Building
Rooms with private bath
555-5544

BRAND NEW BUILDING close to UW. Furnished rooms with private baths and deck. Starting at $455. 5608 15th Ave. NE (206)555-1435.

CLEAN SPACIOUS 2 bed/1 bath house, large deck, w/d in Ballard. $450/month + utilities (about $30) deposit needed. Nice neighborhood near Golden Gardens. Roommate is male 20 yr. Student/waiter/outdoors person.
Call 555-8346

FROM $260 - $280. Rooms, 1-1/2 blocks north of UW. Clean and quiet, studious residence. No smoking, no musical instruments. (206) 555-6608.

LARGE BEDROOM, FURNISHED, phone. Shared kitchen, etc. Nice family home, safe neighborhood, two miles to campus, near bus. Seeking mature female student, non-smoking. $340 plus utilities. (206) 555-9754.

TWO BEDROOMS AVAILABLE in ten bedroom house. June 10th - August 31st. Free laundry, cool roommates. 52nd/16th. Call for details! 555-8065.

Furnished Apartments

STUDIO APARTMENTS AVAILABLE starting June 10th-20th, walking distance to campus, washer/dryer on site. $525/month. Call Monika (425)-555-8330, ext. 434.

WALK TO UW. Attractive, fully furnished apartment. Kitchenware, linens. All utilities. Studio $775. 1 bedroom $945. 2 bedroom $985. 1 month minimum possible. Call 555-9009, cell 555-2544.

Unfurnished Houses

2 HOUSES: 4 rooms, 1 bath or 5 rooms, 1 bath. Both with washer, dryer. Walk to UW. $1440 or $1800. 425-555-3788, 6-9 pm.

Duplex - Newly Remodeled for FALL!!
2 BLOCKS FROM CAMPUS!!
Available September 9th

7 bedrooms, 2 bath, large, $2800/month

3 bedrooms, 1 bath, large, $1350/month

OPEN HOUSE- 4728 18th Avenue NE, Sunday, May 23rd, 1:30-3:30 pm. (206)555-0358.

HEY DORMIES! Get a real house, one left– 9+ Bedrooms, near UW. (206)555-5306.

Parking

COVERED PARKING. CLOSE TO UW, Secure garage, $65 per month, 5608 15th AVE. NE, 206-555-1435.

PARKING NEAR UW. 3 locations, $58/ month. Secured Garage, $85/ month. (206) 555-2944.

Shared Housing

FEMALE ROOMMATE WANTED for coed housing. Large room on bus route. Ravenna $410. 555-5411.

FEMALE ROOMMATE WANTED to share 3 bedroom U-District house with two females for summer, $350, utilities included. 555-7293.

SHARE 3 BEDROOM apartment with easy-going guy, 6/15 (negotiable) through 8/31. $387/ month. 555-8661.

Unfurnished Apartments

SUMMER RENTALS
ONE STOP SHOPPING!

Locations on 8th
1 Bedroom 1 bath $570
1 Bedroom w/den $700
2 Bedroom 1 bath $720
3 Bedroom 1 bath $ 890
4 Bedroom 1 bath $1000
Call managers at
555-8885, 555-6899 and 555-4824.

Locations on 12th
1 Bedroom w/den $730
2 Bedroom 1 bath $770
2 Bedroom 2 bath $855
3 Bedroom 1 bath $965
4 Bedroom 2 bath $1040

Call managers at
555-1320, 555-0832 and 555-0424.

Guaranteed lowest prices or we'll match. Newer units, well-managed, secured entrances, parking, decks, skylights, microwaves and dishwashers. No smoking and no pets. Apartments available mid June.
Customer Service Line 555-0424

0 BLOCKS TO UW
OPEN HOUSE, 1:00-5:00 pm every day, 2-bedroom, $860-$900; 3-bedroom, $1050-$1400; Washington Square Apartments, 4504 16th NE, A101-Office. Also showing Brooklyn Plaza Apartments, 4106 Brooklyn, by appointment only after May 10, 1:00-5:00pm. (206)555-2829, 555-9988.

APARTMENTS FOR RENT fall and sublease this summer. 1, 3, 5 and 6 bedroom units located at 4233 7th Ave NE. Mondays and Wednesdays 2-6pm and Saturdays 1-4pm. Phone 555-5240 or 555-7613. Leave message if no answer.

LAKE CITY, HIGH-end apartment. Washer/ dryer, New, security. 2-bedroom, 2-bath: $765. 2-bedroom, 1-bath: $755. Studio: $485. 11038 Lake City Way NE. 555-6495.

ONE AND TWO bedroom apartments. Walk to campus. Very spacious, lots of light. Very quiet. 555-0810.

WALK TO UW. 2-bedroom, $860; 5-bedroom/ 2-bath, $1750. Intercom, modern kitchen, laundry, on-site manager, rooftop deck. Garage parking available. (206)555-2974.

Comprehension

Now that you have a general sense of the layout of the ads, scan for the answers to the following questions. True/False items are indicated by a T / F preceding the statement. *Note:* because there are so many ads, just put the number of the question that you are answering next to appropriate ads.

1. If you were looking for a job and liked to teach adolescents and adults, find three job ads you could answer.

2. If you wanted to work with young children but didn't want to work in someone's home, find three ads you could answer.

3. If you were looking for a job only for the summer, which ad(s) would you answer? We found six ads. Which three look interesting to you?

4. Which ad(s) could you answer if you had good telephone skills?

5. Do you have the qualifications necessary to apply for the valet job? Do you have to be a perfect student?

6. T / F   *The Daily* ensures that the companies who advertise in the Business Opportunities section are lawful and trustworthy businesses.

7. If you were interested in a health care career and needed to earn money this summer, would you answer the ad for health care volunteers?

8. T / F   The student intern position in DNA is a volunteer position.

9. T / F   If you are a smoker, you probably shouldn't apply for the Laurelhurst nanny job.

10. If you're looking for a place to live and are allergic to cigarette smoke, circle two ads you would answer.

11. If you like a quiet environment, would you answer the Two Bedrooms Available ad?

12. Which apartment is closest to UW?

13. Your sister is moving to town and wants to share housing for less than $400 per month. Which ads would you tell her about?

14. If you have access to the World Wide Web, can you read *Daily* ads online?

Critical Reading

1. If you needed a new computer, would you answer Earn New Computer in the Business Opportunities section? Why or why not?

2. Under Business Opportunities what do you think is the opportunity offered by the famous millionaire maker? Would you answer this ad? Why or why not?

3. If you are familiar with Mexico but have no camping experience, would you answer the Trekleader ad?

4. Are there any job ads that you would want to answer?

Web Activity

If you have access to the World Wide Web, you can also check classified ads online. On page 64 you will find an index for the online classified ads for *The Daily*. (Note that if an online classified ad page is updated daily, the index will also change daily.)

1. Which numbers would you click on to look for apartments?

2. Which number would you click on to find someone to type your school papers?

3. What kinds of ads are found under the "personals"? Why might you need to be cautious about meeting someone this way?

4. You want to submit an ad for the Online *Daily*.

    a. How much will it cost to run a 10-word ad for three days?

    b. Can you get a refund if you don't want to run the ad for the full three days?

    c. What day will your ad appear if you submit it electronically at 2:00 P.M. on Thursday?

5. You need a roommate to share your apartment close to campus. Write a 10-word ad in the box "Enter Your Ad."

  NEW DAWG **NEW STUFF** **NEW SITE** www.bookstore.washington.edu Check It Out!

THE DAILY *online*

Articles
- Front Page
- Arts/Entertainment
- Newsroom Specials
- Features
- News
- Opinion
- Sports

Web Features
- Campus Calendar
- Classifieds
- Comics
- Online Articles
- Intramural Sports
- Slate.com
- Soundboard / Radio

Services
- Advertising
- Business Directory
- Career Directory
- Contact Us
- Archives

Recent Issues:

Classifieds updated daily

Submit a Classified Ad

- RATE: 20¢ per word, $4.00 minimum. Pay for four days, get the fifth day free.
- DEADLINE: 2:00 pm the weekday before publication. 12:00 noon the day before publication for ads sent via e-mail.
- NO REFUNDS for cancellation once ad has begun.
- NO CHANGES in ad text once ad has begun.
- The Daily must be notified of errors before 2:00 pm on the first day of publication. The Daily is not responsible for errors past the first day.
- **Before your ad appears in the Daily you must arrange payment.** Please CONTACT:

> The Daily Classified Advertising
> 144 Communications
> PO Box 353720
> Seattle, WA 98195
> (206) 543-2335
> E-mail: dailycls@u.washington.edu

Enter your Ad:

Classified Ads

040 Announcements
050 Special Notices
080 Adoptions
090 Personals
100 Automobiles For Sale
110 Motorcycles
150 Automotive Repair
270 Entertainment
360 Typing/Word Processing
400 Work-Study
410 Help Wanted
420 Help Wanted Over 18
440 Business Opportunities
450 Volunteers
460 Internships
530 Child Care
620 Music
630 Tutoring
720 Garage/Yard Sales
770 Sporting Goods/Supplies
800 Miscellaneous For Sale
810 Rooms
835 Furnished Apartments
840 Unfurnished Houses
845 Unfurnished Apartments
850 Parking
900 Shared Housing
910 Housesitting
920 Homes For Sale

Word Study
Stems and Affixes

Below is a list of some commonly occurring stems and affixes.* Study their meanings and then do the exercises that follow. Your teacher may ask you to give examples of other words you know that are derived from these stems and affixes.

Prefixes		
ante-	before	anterior, ante meridiem (A.M.)
circum-	around	circumference
contra-, anti-	against	anti-war, contrast
inter-	between	international, intervene
intro-, intra-	within	introduce, intravenous
post-,	after	post-game, post-graduate
sub-, suc-, suf-, sug-, sup-, sus-	under	subway, support
super-	above, greater, better	superior, supermarket
trans-	across	trans-Atlantic, transportation

Stems		
-ced-	go, move, yield	precede
-duc-	lead	introduce
-flect-	bend	reflect, flexible
-mit-, -miss-	send	remit, missionary
-pon-, -pos-	put, place	postpone, position
-port-	carry	portable
-sequ-, -secut-	follow	consequence, consecutive
-spir-	breathe	inspiration, conspiracy
-tele-	far	telegraph, telephone
-ven-, -vene-	come	convene, convention
-voc-, -vok-	call	vocal, revoke

Suffixes		
-able-, ible-, -ble	capable of, fit for	trainable, defensible
-ous, -ious, -ose	full of, having the qualities of	poisonous, anxious, verbose

*For a list of all stems and affixes taught in *Reader's Choice*, see the Appendix.

Exercise 1

For each item, select the best definition of the italicized word or phrase, or answer the question.

1. The first thing Jim did when he arrived at the airport was look for a *porter*.

   _____ a. person who sells tickets   _____ c. person who carries luggage

   _____ b. taxi cab   _____ d. door to the luggage room

2. No matter what Fred said, Noam *contradicted him*.

   _____ a. said the opposite   _____ c. laughed at him

   _____ b. yelled at him   _____ d. didn't listen to him

3. The doctor is a specialist in the human *respiratory* system. She is an expert on _____

   _____ a. bones.   _____ c. nerves.

   _____ b. lungs.   _____ d. the stomach.

4. He *circumvented* the problem.

   _____ a. described   _____ c. went around, avoided

   _____ b. solved   _____ d. wrote down, copied

5. Which is a postscript?

6. Use what you know about stems and affixes to explain how the following words were derived.

   a. telephone _____

   b. telegram _____

   c. television _____

7. When would a photographer use a telephoto lens for her camera? _____

   _____

8. Use word analysis to explain what *support* means. _____

   _____

9. What is the difference between interstate commerce and intrastate commerce? _____

_____

10. At one time, many European towns depended on the system of aqueducts built by the Romans for their water supply. What is an aqueduct? _____

_____

11. If a person has a *receding* hairline, what does he look like? _____

_____

12. The abbreviation *A.M.* (as in 10:30 A.M.) stands for *ante meridiem*. What do you think *P.M.* (as in 10:30 P.M.) stands for? _____

_____

13. Consider these sentences.

    a. She *subscribes* to *Time* magazine.

    b. She *subscribes* to the theory that the moon is made of green cheese.

    Explain how these meanings of *subscribe* developed from the meanings of *sub* and *scribe*.

    _____

    _____

    _____

    _____

    _____

Exercise 2

Word analysis can help you to guess the meanings of unfamiliar words. Using context clues and what you know about word parts, write a synonym, description, or definition of the italicized word or phrase.

1. _____   Despite evidence *to the contrary*, Mark really believes that he can pass an exam without studying.

2. _____   I haven't finished the report you asked for yet; let's *postpone* our meeting until next Tuesday.

3. _____   Ask your *supervisor* if you can take your vacation next month.

4. _____   Please *remit* your payment in the enclosed envelope.

5. _____ Something must be wrong with this machine. It doesn't always type *superscripts* correctly: $\frac{2}{x}$ x2 x_2 x^2

6. _____ *Antibiotics,* such as penicillin, help the body fight bacterial but not viral infections.

7. _____ Nowadays, very little mail is *transported* by train.

8. _____ Don't invite Frank again; his behavior tonight was *inexcusable*.

9. _____ Scientists study the *interaction* between parents and their babies to better understand how infants learn.

10. _____ After the plane crash, the pilot had to fix his radio before he could *transmit* his location.

11. _____ The committee decided to stop working at noon and to *reconvene* at 1:30.

12. _____ The state of Texas *revoked* his driver's license because he had had too many accidents.

13. _____ This material is very useful because it is strong yet *flexible*.

14. _____ Barbara wanted to buy a *portable* CD player.

15. _____ The Portuguese sailor Magellan set out to *circumnavigate* the world.

16. _____ The king *imposed* a heavy tax on his people to pay for his foreign wars.

Exercise 3

Following is a list of words containing some of the stems and affixes introduced in this unit and the previous one. Definitions of these words appear on the right. Put the letter of the appropriate definition next to each word.

1. _____ anteroom   a. characterized by a noisy outcry or shouting

2. _____ antecedent   b. a room forming an entrance to another one

3. _____ vociferous   c. the career one believes oneself called to; one's occupation or profession

4. _____ vocation   d. something that happened or existed before another thing

5. _____ subsequent   e. following in time, order, or place

6. _____ subscript   a. the observation or examination of one's own thought processes

7. _____ superscript   b. a letter or symbol written immediately below and to the right of another symbol

8. _____ intervene   c. a logical result or conclusion; the relation of effect to cause

9. _____ introspection   d. a letter or symbol written immediately above and to the right of another symbol

10. _____ convene   e. to come between people or points in time

11. _____ consequence   f. to come together as a group

Word Study
Dictionary Use

In Unit 1, you were introduced to the types of information that a dictionary can provide. In this exercise, you will again scan* for information from a dictionary page, but here you will concentrate only on the definition of words. Read the questions, and then scan the dictionary page (p. 72) to find the answers.

1. In the following sentences, first determine the part of speech of the italicized word, and then use the dictionary page to find a synonym for the word.

    a. Because of her all-night study sessions, Sandy is *run-down*.

        1. noun, verb, adjective, adverb

        2. synonym: _____

    b. José's telephone call to Peter caused a *rupture* in their four-year friendship.

        1. noun, verb, adjective, adverb

        2. synonym: _____

2. Find a synonym for *running* as it is used in the following sentence.

    We have won the contest four years *running*. _____

3. Check all the following words that are synonyms of *rural*.

    _____ a. rustic   _____ b. rubric   _____ c. pastoral

4. Under which word would you find synonyms of *run-of-the-mill*?

    _____ a. mill   _____ b. average   _____ c. run

5. Which word must you look up to find a description of a running knot?

    _____ a. slipknot   _____ b. running   _____ c. knot

6. According to this dictionary, a running mate can be either _____

    _____ a. a horse or a person.

    _____ b. a horse or a machine.

    _____ c. a person or a machine.

Dictionary page from *The American Heritage Dictionary of the English Language* (Boston: Houghton Mifflin).
*For an introduction to scanning, see Unit 1.

7. Which word must you look up to find the definition of *rung* as used in the following sentence?

   I would have rung you earlier but I didn't have time.

   _____ a. ring   _____ b. rang   _____ c. rung

8. From the dictionary definitions give the number of the appropriate definition for each of the italicized words in the following sentences.

   a. We put a *runner* in the hall from the front door to the kitchen. _____

   b. The singer walked onto the *runway* in order to get closer to the audience. _____

   c. There were 24 *runes* in the Germanic alphabet. _____

9. Which of the following runes is a modern *m*?

   _____ a. ᛉ

   _____ b. ᛗ

   _____ c. ᛘ

10. What is the meaning of the italicized word in the following sentence?

    John complained that *Ruse* was dangerous.

    _____ a. a misleading action

    _____ b. a city

    _____ c. an artifice

11. Complete the following sentence with the appropriate form of the word *rural*.

    Because of his anti-urban feelings Kenworthy Piker is known as the leading

    _____ of his time.

12. Choose the word that correctly completes the following sentences.

    a. Let me give you a brief _____ of what we talked about before you arrived.

       1. run-off
       2. rundown

    b. We must have a _____ in order to decide which person will be the new president.

       1. run-off
       2. run off

Dictionary page from *The American Heritage Dictionary of the English Language* (Boston: Houghton Mifflin).

runcinate
Runcinate leaf of dandelion

rune

f u th a r k
g w h n i j e
p z s t b e
m l ng o d

basic Germanic runic alphabet

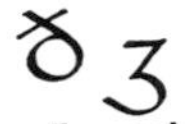

edh yogh

two later runes used in English

run·a·gate (rŭn′ə-gāt′) *n. Archaic.* **1.** A renegade or deserter. **2.** A vagabond. [Variant of RENEGADE (influenced by RUN).]
run·a·round (rŭn′ə-round′) *n.* Also **run·round** (rŭn′round′). **1.** Deception, usually in the form of evasive excuses. **2.** *Printing.* Type set in a column narrower than the body of the text, as on either side of a picture.
run·a·way (rŭn′ə-wā′) *n.* **1.** One that runs away. **2.** An act of running away. **3.** *Informal.* An easy victory. —*adj.* **1.** Escaping or having escaped from captivity or control. **2.** Of or done by running away. **3.** Easily won, as a race. **4.** Of or pertaining to a rapid price rise.
run·back (rŭn′băk′) *n.* **1.** The act of returning a kickoff, punt, or intercepted forward pass. **2.** The distance so covered.
run·ci·ble spoon (rŭn′sə-bəl). A three-pronged fork, as a pickle fork, curved like a spoon and having a cutting edge. [*Runcible,* a nonsense word coined by Edward Lear.]
run·ci·nate (rŭn′sə-nāt′, -nĭt) *adj. Botany.* Having saw-toothed divisions directed backward: *runcinate leaves.* [Latin *runcinātus,* past participle of *runcināre,* to plane, from *runcina,* carpenter's plane (formerly taken also to mean a saw), from Greek *rhukanē*†.]
run down. **1. a.** To slow down and stop, as a machine. **b.** To exhaust or wear out. **c.** To lessen in value. **2.** To pursue and capture. **3.** To hit with a moving vehicle. **4.** To disparage; decry. **5.** To give a brief or summary account of. **6.** *Baseball.* To put out a runner after trapping him between two bases.
run-down (rŭn′doun′) *n.* **1.** A summary or résumé. **2.** *Baseball.* A play in which a runner is put out when he is trapped between bases. —*adj.* **1.** In poor physical condition; weak or exhausted. **2.** Unwound and not running.
rune (ro͞on) *n.* **1.** One of the letters of an alphabet used by ancient Germanic peoples, especially by the Scandinavians and Anglo-Saxons. **2.** Any poem, riddle, or the like written in runic characters. **3.** Any occult characters. **4.** A Finnish poem or canto. [In sense 4, from Finnish *runo.* In other senses, Middle English *roun, rune,* secret writing, rune, from Old Norse *rūn* (unattested). See **rūno-** in Appendix.*] —**run′ic** *adj.*
rung[1] (rŭng) *n.* **1.** A rod or bar forming a step of a ladder. **2.** A crosspiece supporting the legs or back of a chair. **3.** The spoke in a wheel. **4.** *Nautical.* One of the spokes or handles on a ship's steering wheel. [Middle English *rung, rong,* Old English *hrung,* akin to Old High German *runga,* Gothic *hruggat*†.]
rung[2]. Past tense and past participle of **ring.** See Usage note at **ring.**
run in. **1.** To insert or include as something extra. **2.** *Printing.* To make a solid body of text without a paragraph or other break. **3.** *Slang.* To take into legal custody.
run-in (rŭn′ĭn′) *n.* **1.** A quarrel; an argument; a fight. **2.** *Printing.* Matter added to a text. —*adj.* Added or inserted in text.
run·let (rŭn′lĭt) *n.* A rivulet. [Diminutive of RUN (stream).]
run·nel (rŭn′əl) *n.* **1.** A rivulet; a brook. **2.** A narrow channel or course, as for water. [Middle English *rynel,* Old English *rynel,* from *rinnan,* to run, flow. See **er-**[1] in Appendix.*]
run·ner (rŭn′ər) *n.* **1.** One who or that which runs, as: **a.** One that competes in a race. **b.** A fugitive. **c.** A messenger or errand boy. **2.** An agent or collector, as for a bank or brokerage house. **3.** One who solicits business, as for a hotel or store. **4.** A smuggler. **5.** A vessel engaged in smuggling. **6.** One who operates or manages something. **7.** A device in or on which a mechanism slides or moves, as: **a.** The blade of a skate. **b.** The supports on which a drawer slides. **8.** A long narrow carpet. **9.** A long narrow tablecloth. **10.** A roller towel. **11.** *Metallurgy.* A channel along which molten metal is poured into a mold; gate. **12.** *Botany.* **a.** A slender, creeping stem that puts forth roots from nodes spaced at intervals along its length. **b.** A plant, such as the strawberry, having such a stem. **c.** A twining vine, such as the **scarlet runner** *(see).* **13.** Any of several marine fishes of the family Carangidae, such as the blue runner, *Caranx crysos,* of temperate waters of the American Atlantic coast.
run·ner-up (rŭn′ər-ŭp′) *n.* One that takes second place.
run·ning (rŭn′ĭng) *n.* **1.** The act of one that runs. **2.** The power or ability to run. **3.** Competition: *in the running.* **4.** An operating: *the running of a machine.* **5. a.** That which runs or flows. **b.** The amount that runs. —*adj.* Continuous: *a running commentary.* —*adv.* Consecutively: *four years running.*
running board. A narrow footboard extending under and beside the doors of some automobiles and other conveyances.
running gear. **1.** The working parts of an automobile, locomotive, or other vehicle. **2.** **Running rigging** *(see).*
running hand. Writing done rapidly without lifting the pen from the paper.
running head. *Printing.* A title printed at the top of every page or every other page. Also called "running title."
running knot. A **slipknot** *(see).*
running light. **1.** One of several lights on a boat or ship kept lighted between dusk and dawn. **2.** One of several similar lights on an aircraft; a navigation light.
running mate. **1.** A horse used to set the pace in a race for another horse. **2.** The candidate or nominee for the lesser of two closely associated political offices.
running rigging. The part of a ship's rigging that comprises the ropes with which sails are raised, lowered, or trimmed, booms and gaffs are operated, etc. Also called "running gear."
running stitch. One of a series of small, even stitches.
run·ny (rŭn′ē) *adj.* **-nier, -niest.** Inclined to run or flow.
Run·ny·mede (rŭn′ĭ-mēd). A meadow on the Thames, 19 miles west of London, where King John is thought to have signed the Magna Carta in 1215. [Middle English *Runimede,* "meadow on the council island" : Old English *Rūnīeg,* council island : *rūn,* secret, secret council (see **rūno-** in Appendix*) + *īeg, īg,* island (see **akwā-** in Appendix*) + *mede,* MEAD (meadow).]
run off. **1.** To print, duplicate, or copy. **2.** To run away; elope. **3.** To spill over; to overflow. **4.** To decide a contest or competition by a run-off.
run-off (rŭn′ôf′, -ŏf′) *n.* **1. a.** The overflow of a fluid from a container. **b.** Rainfall that is not absorbed by the soil. **2.** Eliminated waste products from manufacturing processes. **3.** An extra competition held to break a tie.
run-of-the-mill (rŭn′əv-*thə*-mĭl′) *adj.* Ordinary; not special; average. See Synonyms at **average.** [From *run of (the) mill,* products of a mill that are not graded for quality.]
run on. **1.** To continue on and on. **2.** *Printing.* To continue a text without a formal break.
run-on (rŭn′ŏn′, -ôn′) *n. Printing.* Matter that is appended or added without a formal break. —*adj.* Being run on.
run·round. Variant of **run-around.**
runt (rŭnt) *n.* **1.** An undersized animal; especially, the smallest animal of a litter. **2.** A person of small stature. Often used disparagingly. [Possibly from Dutch *rund,* small ox. See **ker-**[1] in Appendix.*] —**runt′i·ness** *n.* —**runt·y** *adj.*
run through. **1.** To pierce. **2.** To use up (money, for example) quickly. **3.** To examine or rehearse quickly.
run-through (rŭn′thro͞o′) *n.* A complete but rapid review or rehearsal of something, such as a theatrical work.
run·way (rŭn′wā′) *n.* **1.** A path, channel, or track over which something runs. **2.** The bed of a water course. **3.** A chute down which logs are skidded. **4.** *Bowling.* A narrow track on which balls are returned after they are bowled. **5.** A smooth ramp for wheeled vehicles. **6.** A narrow walkway extending from a stage into an auditorium. **7.** A strip of level ground, usually paved, on which aircraft take off and land.
Run·yon (rŭn′yən), **(Alfred) Damon.** 1884–1946. American journalist and author of short stories.
ru·pee (ro͞o-pē′, ro͞o′pē) *n. Abbr.* **Re., r., R.** **1. a.** The basic monetary unit of Ceylon and Mauritius, equal to 100 cents. **b.** The basic monetary unit of India, equal to 100 paise. **c.** The basic monetary unit of Nepal, equal to 100 pice. **d.** The basic monetary unit of Pakistan, equal to 100 paisas. See table of exchange rates at **currency.** **2.** A coin worth one rupee. [Hindi *rupaīyā,* from Sanskrit *rūpya,* wrought silver, from *rūpa*†, shape, image.]
Ru·pert (ro͞o′pərt). A river of Quebec, Canada, flowing 380 miles westward from Mistassini Lake to James Bay.
Ru·pert (ro͞o′pərt), **Prince.** 1619–1682. German-born English military, naval, and political leader; supporter of Charles I; inventor.
Ru·pert's Land (ro͞o′pərts). The Canadian territory granted the Hudson's Bay Company in 1670, most of which was incorporated in The Northwest Territories after its purchase by Canada in 1870.
ru·pi·ah (ro͞o-pē′ä) *n., pl.* **rupiah** or **-ahs.** **1.** The basic monetary unit of Indonesia, equal to 100 sen. See table of exchange rates at **currency.** **2.** A note worth one rupiah. [Hindi *rupaīyā,* RUPEE.]
rup·ture (rŭp′chər) *n.* **1. a.** The act of breaking open or bursting. **b.** The state of being broken open or burst. **2.** A break in friendly relations between individuals or nations. **3.** *Pathology.* **a.** A **hernia** *(see),* especially of the groin or intestines. **b.** A tear in bodily tissue. —*v.* **ruptured, -turing, -tures.** —*tr.* To break open; burst. —*intr.* To undergo or suffer a rupture. —See Synonyms at **break.** [Middle English *ruptur,* from Old French *rupture,* from Latin *ruptūra,* from *rumpere* (past participle *ruptus*), to break. See **reup-** in Appendix.*] —**rup′tur·a·ble** *adj.*
ru·ral (ro͝or′əl) *adj.* **1.** Of or pertaining to the country as opposed to the city; rustic. **2.** Of or pertaining to people who live in the country. **3.** Of or relating to farming; agricultural. Compare **urban.** [Middle English, from Old French, from Latin *rūrālis,* from *rūs* (stem *rūr-*), country. See **rewe-** in Appendix.*] —**ru′ral·ism′** *n.* —**ru′ral·ist** *n.* —**ru′ral·ly** *adv.*
Synonyms: *rural, arcadian, bucolic, rustic, pastoral, sylvan.* These adjectives are all descriptive of existence or environment which is close to nature; those with a literary flavor are often used facetiously. *Rural* applies to sparsely settled or agricultural country, as distinct from settled communities. *Arcadian* implies ideal or simple country living. *Bucolic* is often used derisively of country people or manners. *Rustic,* sometimes uncomplimentary, applies to country people who seem unsophisticated, but may also apply favorably to living conditions or to natural environments which are pleasingly primitive. *Pastoral* implies the supposed peace of rural living and the shepherd's life, with a suggestion of artificiality. *Sylvan* refers to wooded as opposed to cultivated country, and carries the sense of unspoiled beauty.
rural free delivery. *Abbr.* **R.F.D., RFD** Free government delivery of mail in rural areas.
ru·ral·i·ty (ro͝o-răl′ə-tē) *n., pl.* **-ties.** **1.** The state or quality of being rural. **2.** A rural trait or characteristic.
ru·ral·ize (ro͝or′əl-īz′) *v.* **-ized, -izing, -izes.** —*tr.* To make rural. —*intr.* To live or visit in the country. —**ru′ral·i·za′tion** *n.*
rural route. *Abbr.* **R.R.** A rural mail route.
Ru·rik (ro͞o′rĭk). Died A.D. 879. Scandinavian warrior; founder of the dynasty that ruled Russia until 1598.
Rus. Russia; Russian.
Ru·se (ro͞o′sā). *Turkish* **Rus·chuk** (ro͞os′cho͝ok). A Danubian port in northeastern Bulgaria. Population, 118,000.
ruse (ro͞oz) *n.* An action or device meant to confuse or mislead. See Synonyms at **artifice.** [Middle English, detour of a hunted animal, from Old French, from *ruser,* to repulse, detour. See **rush** (to dash off).]

ă pat/ā pay/âr care/ä father/b bib/ch church/d deed/ĕ pet/ē be/f fife/g gag/h hat/hw which/ĭ pit/ī pie/îr pier/j judge/k kick/l lid, needle/m mum/n no, sudden/ng thing/ŏ pot/ō toe/ô paw, for/oi noise/ou out/o͝o took/o͞o boot/p pop/r roar/s sauce/sh ship, dish/

Sentence Study
Introduction

The exercises in this book provide you with practice in using a number of reading skills and strategies to understand a reading passage. Context Clues, Stems and Affixes, and Dictionary Use exercises provide you with practice in quickly finding specific pieces of information in a passage. Skimming, introduced in Unit 1, focuses on reading a passage quickly for a general idea of its meaning.

When you have difficulty understanding a passage, just reading further will often make the passage clearer. Sometimes, however, comprehension of an entire passage depends on your being able to understand a single sentence. Sentences that are very long and sentences that contain difficult vocabulary or difficult grammatical patterns often cause comprehension problems for readers. The sentence study exercise that follows as well as similar ones in later units gives you the opportunity to develop strategies for understanding complicated sentences.

Although there is no easy formula that will help you to arrive at an understanding of a difficult sentence, you should keep the following points in mind.

1. Try to determine what makes the sentence difficult:

   a. If the sentence contains a lot of difficult vocabulary, it may be that the sentence can be understood without knowing the meaning of every word. Try crossing out unfamiliar items.

      > The West had sent armies to capture and hold Jerusalem; instead they themselves fell victim to a host of new ideas and subtle influences which left their mark on the development of European literature, chivalry, warfare, sanitation, commerce, political institutions, medicine, and the papacy itself.

   b. If the sentence is very long, try to break it up into smaller parts:

      > The West had sent armies to capture and hold Jerusalem. The West fell victim to a host of new ideas and subtle influences. These ideas and influences left their mark on the development of European literature, chivalry, warfare, sanitation, commerce, political institutions, medicine, and the papacy.

   c. Also, if the sentence is very long, try to determine which parts of the sentence express specific details supporting the main idea. Often clauses which are set off by commas, or introduced by words such as *which, who, and that,* are used to introduce extra information or to provide supporting details. Try crossing out the supporting details in order to determine the main idea:

      > These ideas, which left their mark on the development of European literature, chivalry, warfare, sanitation, commerce, political institutions, medicine, and the papacy, greatly changed Western culture.

Be careful! A good reader reads quickly but accurately!

2. Learn to recognize the important grammatical and punctuation clues that can change the meaning of a sentence:

a. Look for single words and affixes* that can change the entire meaning of a sentence.

> Summery weather is *not un*common.
> The *average* daytime *high* temperature is *approximately* 56°.

b. Look for punctuation clues:

> Wally ⁀sings⁀ at all of his friends' parties.
> Barry said, "George has been elected president⑦"

Note that all of the italicized words or affixes and the circled punctuation above are essential to the meaning of the sentences; if any of these are omitted, the meaning of the sentences changes significantly.

c. Look for key words that tell you of relationships within a sentence:

> The school has grown *from* a small building holding 200 students *to* a large institute that educates 4,000 students a year.

> *From . . . to* indicates the beginning and end points of a period of change.

> Many critics have proclaimed Doris Lessing as *not only* the best writer of the postwar generation, *but also* a penetrating analyst of human affairs.

> *Not only . . . but also* indicates that both parts of the sentence are of equal importance.

> *In order to* graduate on time, you will need to take five courses each semester.

> *In order to* is like *if;* it indicates that some event must occur before another event can take place.

> The West had sent armies to capture and hold Jerusalem; *instead* they themselves fell victim to new ideas and subtle influences.

> *Instead* indicates that something happened contrary to expectations.

> *As a result of* three books, a television documentary, and a special exposition at the Library of Congress, the mystery has aroused considerable public interest.

> *As a result of* indicates a cause and effect relationship. The clause that follows *as a result of* is the cause of some event. The three books, television program, and exposition are the *cause;* the arousal of public interest is the *effect.*

> *Because of* the impact of these ideas, *which* had been introduced originally to Europe by soldiers returning from the East, the West was greatly changed.

> *Because of* indicates a cause and effect relationship. The West was changed as a result of these ideas. The information between the word *which* and the final comma (,) refers to *these ideas.*

---

*For a list of all stems and affixes taught in *Reader's Choice,* see the Appendix.

Sentence Study
Comprehension

Read the following sentences carefully. The questions that follow are designed to test your comprehension of complex grammatical structures. Select the *best* answer.

Example | The student revolt is not only a thorn in the side of the president's newly established government, but it has international implications as well.

Whom or what does the revolt affect?

_____ a. the students

_____ b. the side of the president's body

_____ c. only the national government

_____ d. national and international affairs

Explanation

_____ a. According to the sentence, the students are the cause of certain events, not among those affected.

_____ b. Although you may not have been familiar with the idiom *a thorn in someone's side*, context clues should have told you that this phrase means *a problem* and does not actually refer to the side of the president's body.

_____ c. National government is an incomplete answer. The construction *not only . . . but . . . as well* should tell you that more than one element is involved. The president's newly established government (the national government) is not the only area affected by the revolt.

__✓__ d. The revolt affects both national and international affairs.

1. I disagreed then as now with many of John Smith's judgments, but always respected him, and this book is a welcome reminder of his big, honest, friendly, stubborn personality.

   How does the author of this sentence feel about John Smith?

   _____ a. He dislikes him but agrees with his ideas.

   _____ b. He considers him to be a disagreeable person.

   _____ c. He disagrees with his ideas but respects him.

   _____ d. He disagreed with him then but agrees with him now.

2. Concepts like *passivity*, *dependence*, and *aggression* may need further research if they are to continue to be useful ways of thinking about human personalities.

   What might require more research?

   _____ a. human thought processes   _____ c. human personalities

   _____ b. certain concepts   _____ d. useful ways of thinking

3. In order for you to follow the schedule set by the publisher, your paper must be looked over over the weekend, revised, and handed in in its final form on Monday.

What must you do on Saturday and Sunday?

_____ a. meet the publisher

_____ b. examine your paper

_____ c. hand in a paper

_____ d. look over the weekend

4. The real reason why prices were, and still are, too high is complicated, and no short discussion can satisfactorily explain this problem.

What word or phrase best describes prices?

_____ a. complicated

_____ b. adequately explained

_____ c. too high in the past, but low now

_____ d. too high in the past and in the present

5. This is not just a sad-but-true story; the boy's experience is horrible and damaging, yet a sense of love shines through every word.

How does the author of this sentence feel about the story?

_____ a. It transmits a sense of love.

_____ b. It is just sad

_____ c. It is not true

_____ d. It is horrible and damaging.

6. In the past five years the movement has grown from unorganized groups of poorly armed individuals to a comparatively well-armed, well-trained army of anywhere from 10,000 to 16,000 members.

What is the present condition of this movement?

_____ a. The members are poorly armed.

_____ b. There are only a few poor individuals.

_____ c. There are over 16,000 members.

_____ d. The members are organized and well armed.

7. The financial situation isn't bad yet, but we believe that we have some vital information and, if it is correct, unemployment will soon become a serious problem.

What do we know about the financial situation?

_____ a. It won't change.

_____ b. It will become a serious problem.

_____ c. It is not bad now.

_____ d. It will improve.

8. The general then added, "The only reasonable solution to the sort of problems caused by the current unstable political situation is one of diplomacy and economic measures and not the use of military force."

What type of solution does the general support?

_____ a. economic and diplomatic action

_____ b. diplomatic and economic action if military force fails

_____ c. only diplomatic action

_____ d. military actions in response to political problems

9. Because the supply of natural gas was plentiful in comparison to other choices like coal and fuel oil, and because it burns cleaner, many people changed their heating systems to natural gas, thereby creating shortages.

Why did people prefer natural gas?

_____ a. It was natural.

_____ b. There were no other choices.

_____ c. The other fuels were dirtier and less plentiful.

_____ d. There is, even today, a plentiful supply of it.

Paragraph Reading
Main Idea

This exercise is similar to the one you did in Unit 1. Read the following paragraphs and poem quickly. Concentrate on discovering the main idea. Remember, don't worry about details in the selections. You only want to determine the general message.

After each of the first five paragraphs, select the statement that best expresses the main idea. After paragraphs 6 and 7 and the poem, write a sentence that expresses the main idea in your own words. When you have finished, your teacher may want to divide the class into small groups for discussion.

Paragraph 1 | John Cabot was the first Englishman to land in North America. However, this man who legitimized England's claim to everything from Labrador to Florida left no sea journal, no diary or log, not even a portrait or a signature. Until 1956 most learned encyclopedias and histories indicated that Cabot's first landfall in America was Cape Breton, Nova Scotia. Then a letter was discovered in the Spanish archives, making it almost certain that he had touched first at the northernmost tip of Newfoundland, within five miles of the site of Leif Ericsson's ill-fated settlement at L'Anse-aux-Meadows. Researchers studying the voyages of Columbus, Cartier, Frobisher, and other early explorers had a wealth of firsthand material with which to work. Those who seek to recreate the life and routes used by Cabot must make do with thirdhand accounts, the disloyal and untruthful boasts of his son, Sebastian, and a few hard dates in the maritime records of Bristol, England.

Select the statement that best expresses the main idea of the paragraph.

_____ a. John Cabot claimed all the land from Labrador to Florida for England.

_____ b. Much of what is known about Cabot is based on the words of his son, Sebastian, and on records in Bristol, England.

_____ c. The lack of firsthand accounts of Cabot's voyage has left historians confused about his voyages to North America.

_____ d. Historians interested in the life and routes used by Cabot recently discovered an error they made in describing his discovery of North America.

From Allan Keller, "The Silent Explorer: John Cabot in North America," *American History Illustrated.*

Paragraph 2 | The Bible, while mainly a theological document, is secondarily a book of history and geography. Selected historical materials were included in the text for the purpose of illustrating and underlining the religious teaching of the Bible. Historians and archaeologists have learned to rely upon the amazing accuracy of historical memory in the Bible. The smallest references to persons and places and events contained in the accounts of the Exodus, for instance, or the biographies of such Biblical heroes as Abraham and Moses and David, can lead, if properly considered and pursued, to extremely important historical discoveries. The archaeologists' efforts are not directed at "proving" the correctness of the Bible, which is neither necessary nor possible, any more than belief in God can be scientifically demonstrated. It is quite the opposite, in fact. The historical clues in the Bible can lead the archaeologist to a knowledge of the civilizations of the ancient world in which the Bible developed and with whose religious concepts and practices the Bible so radically differed. It can be considered as an almost unfailing indicator, revealing to the experts the locations and characteristics of lost cities and civilizations.

Select the statement that best expresses the main idea of the paragraph.

_____ a. The Bible can provide valuable geographical information.

_____ b. The Bible is primarily a religious document.

_____ c. The Bible was intended by its authors to be a record of the history of the ancient world.

_____ d. The Bible, though primarily a religious text, is a valuable tool for people interested in history.

From Nelson Glueck, "The Bible as Divining Rod," *Horizon.*

Paragraph 3 | At one time it was the most important city in the region—a bustling commercial center known for its massive monuments, its crowded streets and commercial districts, and its cultural and religious institutions. Then, suddenly, it was abandoned. Within a generation most of its population departed and the once magnificent city became a ghost town. This is the history of a pre-Columbian city called Teotihuacán (the Aztec Indians' word for "the place the gods call home"), once a metropolis of as many as 200,000 inhabitants 33 miles northeast of present-day Mexico City and the focus of a far-flung empire that stretched from the arid plains of central

Mexico to the mountains of Guatemala. Why did this city die? Researchers have found no signs of epidemic disease or destructive invasions. But they have found signs that suggest the Teotihuacanos themselves burned their temples and some of their other buildings. Excavations revealed that piles of wood had been placed around these structures and set afire. Some speculate that Teotihuacán's inhabitants may have abandoned the city because it had become "a clumsy giant . . . too unwieldy to change with the times." But other archaeologists think that the ancient urbanites may have destroyed their temples and abandoned their city in rage against their gods for permitting a long famine.

Select the statement that best expresses the main idea of the paragraph.

_____ a. Teotihuacán, once the home of 200,000 people, was the center of a large empire.

_____ b. Many archaeologists are fascinated by the ruins of a pre-Columbian city called Teotihuacán.

_____ c. Teotihuacán, once a major metropolitan area, was destroyed by an invasion.

_____ d. A still unsolved mystery is why the people of Teotihuacán suddenly abandoned their city.

Paragraph 3 from "Twilight of the Gods," *Time.* Photograph © Philip Baird **www.anthroarcheart.org**.

Paragraph 4 | In any archaeological study that includes a dig, the procedures are basically the same: (1) selecting a site (2) hiring local workers (3) surveying the site and dividing it into sections (4) digging trenches to locate levels and places to excavate (5) mapping architectural features (6) developing a coding system that shows the exact spot where an object is found (7) and recording, tagging, cleaning and storing excavated materials. Neilson C. Debevoise, writing on an expedition to Iraq in the early 1930s, described the typical "route" of excavated pottery. Workers reported an object to staff members before removing it from the ground. The date, level, location and other important information were written on a piece of paper and placed with the object. At noon the objects were brought in from the field to the registry room where they were given a preliminary cleaning. Registry numbers were written with waterproof India ink on a portion of the object previously painted with shellac. The shellac prevented the ink from soaking into the object, furnished a good writing surface, and made it possible to remove the number in a moment. From the registry room objects were sent to the drafting department. If a clay pot, for example, was of a new type, a scale drawing was made on graph paper. Measurements of the top, greatest diameter, base, height, color of the glaze, if any, the quality and texture of the body, and the quality of the workmanship were recorded on paper with the drawing. When the drafting department had completed its work, the materials were placed on the storage shelves, grouped according to type for division with the Iraq government, and eventually shipped to museums. Today, the steps of a dig remain basically the same, although specific techniques vary.

Select the statement that best expresses the main idea of the paragraph.

_____ a. For a number of years, archaeologists have used basically the same procedure when conducting a dig.

_____ b. Neilson C. Debevoise developed the commonly accepted procedure for organizing a dig.

_____ c. Archaeologists take great care to assure that all excavated objects are properly identified.

_____ d. A great deal of important historical and archaeological information can be provided by a dig.

From "Unearthing the Past," *Research News.*

Paragraph 5

The unprecedented expansion of Modern architecture throughout the world must be considered one of the great events in the history of art. Within the space of a single generation, the contemporary movement became the dominant style of serious building not only in the United States and Europe, where pioneers had been at work since the late nineteenth century, but also in nations such as Brazil and India, where almost no Modern architecture existed until much later. Only the Gothic perhaps, among all styles of the past, gained popular acceptance with anything like the speed of the Modern. And like the Gothic—which required a full seventy-five years of experimentation before it produced the cathedral of Chartres—the Modern continually improved its structural techniques, gained in scale, and revised its aesthetics as it attempted to meet the full range of people's civilized needs.

Select the statement that best expresses the main idea of the paragraph.

_____ a. Gothic architecture gained popular acceptance faster than Modern architecture did.

_____ b. Modern architecture has not changed fast enough to meet the needs of civilization.

_____ c. The rapid growth and development of Modern architecture (as an art form) is nearly unequaled in the history of art.

_____ d. If architectural styles are to endure, they must develop and improve in an attempt to meet society's needs.

Paragraph 6

A summit is not any old meeting between two heads of state. Potentates have been visiting each other since the beginning of time. The Queen of Sheba came to visit King Solomon and exchanged riddles with him. Mark Antony came to visit Cleopatra and stayed on. Royalty, presidents and prime ministers of allied nations have sometimes gotten together after a victorious war to divide the spoils, as they did at the Congress of Vienna in 1814 and then at Paris after World War I. But a summit, in the sense in which Winston Churchill introduced the word into the language when he called for one in 1950, is something quite different and quite specific: it is a meeting between the leaders of two or more rival enemy Great Powers trying to satisfy their mutual demands and head off future conflict.

Write a sentence that expresses the main idea of the paragraph.

_____

Paragraph 5 adapted from Allan Temko, "The Dawn of the 'High Modern'," *Horizon*.
Paragraph 6 from Robert Wernick, "Summits of Yore: Promises, Promises and a Deal or Two," *Smithsonian*.

Paragraph 7 | Through most of the time we are growing from infancy to adulthood, we are told that we have to do certain things: "You have to go to school," "You have to go to bed now." Most people seem to spend the rest of their lives thinking that they "have to" do the things that they do: "I have to go to work," "I have to go to the dentist." Initially, it may seem like mere rhetoric, but you don't *have* to do anything. Next time you find yourself on the verge of saying "I have to . . . ," try replacing it by "I choose to . . . ," "I want to . . . ," "I've decided to . . . ." It's incredibly liberating! Reminding yourself that you do things by choice gives you the sense that you are in control of your life.

Write a sentence that expresses the main idea of the paragraph. _____

_____

Adapted from *Wordplay: Ambigrams and Reflections on the Art of Ambigrams* by John Langdon (New York: Harcourt Brace, 1992).

Poem

Looking in the Album

Here the formal times are surrendered
to the camera's indifferent gaze: weddings,
graduations, births and official portraits taken
every ten years to falsify appearances.
Even snapshots meant to gather afternoons
with casual ease are rigid. Smiles
are too buoyant. Tinny laughter echoes
from the staged scene on an artificial
beach. And yet we want to believe
this is how it was: That children's hair
always bore the recent marks of combs;
that trousers, even at picnics, were always
creased and we traveled years with the light
but earnest intimacy of linked hands or arms
arranged over shoulders. This is the record
of our desired life: Pleasant, leisurely on vacations,
wryly comic before local landmarks, competent
auditors of commencement speakers, showing
in our poses that we believed what we were told.
But this history contains no evidence
of aimless nights when the wilderness of ourselves
sprang up to swallow the outposts of what
we thought we were. Nowhere can we see
tears provoked by anything but joy. There
are no pictures of our brittle, lost intentions.
We burned the negatives that we felt did not give a true
account and with others made this abridgement of our lives.

Vern Rutsala

Write a sentence that expresses the main idea of the poem. _____

_____

Vern Rutsala, "Looking in the Album," in *The Window* by Vern Rutsala (Middletown: Wesleyan University Press).

Discourse Focus

Reading for Different Goals—Web Work

Effective readers use all the clues available to make decisions about what they read and how they read. Web surfing is particularly demanding in this regard because of the amount and variety of information that vie for your attention. In order to find the information you want, you must skim to discover if you are at an appropriate Web site, scan to discover what information is relevant, and read thoroughly and critically to decide if the information is accurate and trustworthy.*

> *Web surfing* refers to moving from site to site on the World Wide Web, often without a specific purpose.
>
> Using a *Search engine* allows you to search the Web for specific topics.

This exercise is designed to give you practice in Web-based research. We provide the following Web pages to serve as examples in conducting a search. If you are online, your teacher may want you to use the *Reader's Choice* Web site to work on the exercises in this section: **<http://www.press.umich.edu/esl/readerschoice>**. Imagine that you are taking a trip to St. Louis, Missouri, and that you intend to use this opportunity to visit the Expressionist Museum to view an exhibit of paintings by van Gogh and the St. Louis Science Center. You decide to get organized before you go by using the Web to book your flight and your hotel and to get information about the exhibit.

GetAways.com | The first site you visit is **GetAways.com**. It was one of many sites that popped up when you entered "airline ticket" in your search engine. Your goal is to book a flight and a hotel room.

1. The first question you might ask yourself is whether you can buy a ticket here. Circle three locations on the Web page where you could start your search.

---

*For an introduction to reading for different goals, see Unit 1.
Photograph from St. Louis Convention and Visitors Commission.

GetAways.com

Welcome, GetAways members!
Sign in <u>here</u>.
Not a member? <u>Register today</u> and earn
1,000 BONUS MILES.

 Flights Car Rentals Trains Lodging Cruises Tours

Need help planning your trip? Our agents are available **24 hours.** **Call: 1 (800) GET - AWAY.**

Today's Specials

- NYC to Chicago
- LA to Santa Fe
- Las Vegas: 20% off!

This Weekend

Deals on Cruises

Business Travel

Mid-week Specials

Fare Finder

Enter info for your next trip, and we'll show you the **LOWEST** fares around!

From:

To:

Departing on:

Returning on:

[Search!] [Clear]

Family GetAways

Take the family to WaterWorld!
Stay four nights and get the fifth FREE. Restrictions apply.
Group must include two adults and two children.

Destination Highlights

Kick off to Kauai

Honeymoon in Bali

Caribbean Cruises

Customer Service

We're here 24/7. Contact us for help planning your next trip. We'll help you put together a package in your budget.

TRAVELERS' CENTER

<u>Weather</u>   <u>Maps</u>   <u>Currency Converter</u>   <u>Restaurants</u>   <u>Travel Tips & Advice</u>

2. Circle the place where you will click to begin your hotel search.

3. If you are interested in entering information to learn about the lowest fares for your trip, which two cities will you enter?

4. If you click **Travel Tips & Advice** you will see the following

> **Air Travel**
> - **Booking a flight**
> - **On the plane**
> - **At the airport**
>
> **Car Travel**
> - **Planning a car trip**
> - **Things to bring**
> - **Taking the scenic route**
>
> **Rail Travel**
> **Cruises**
> **Finding the Right Accommodations**
> **Traveling with Children**
> **Traveling with Pets**

Which link(s) would you click on

a. to find out how to get from the airport to your hotel?
b. to learn if you can store baggage at the airport?
c. to discover how much to tip the pilot of your flight?

5. What is your opinion of this Web site? Will you bookmark it for future use? What are the things you like about it? What do you dislike?

MapIt.com | You have purchased your tickets and decided to stay at a hotel near the St. Louis Science Center. You do a search in **MapIt.com** and come up with the map shown on page 88. Answer the questions below using the Web site.

1. Circle the approximate location of your hotel on the map.

    a. Do you think you might be able to walk from your hotel area to any of the museums on the map?

    b. Where would you click to find out if there is bus service near your hotel?

    c. Where would you click to get the exact address and phone number of the museum you want to visit?

2. Where would you click to find out about travel problems caused by road construction?

3. Where would you click to get directions from your hotel to the museum?

4. How will you find out about restaurants located near your hotel?

5. Where will you go to get more information on how to use the site?

YOUR CHOICE FOR TRIP PLANNING

I Directions TO this address I Directions FROM this address I

I Printer Friendly Map I Download to PDA I Save this map / route I

- DRIVING DIRECTIONS
- FIND A MAP
- MY MAPS & ROUTES
- TRIP PLANNER

⬡ CITY GUIDE ⬡
- CHAMBER OF COMMERCE
- LODGING
- MUSEUMS
- RESTAURANTS
- ENTERTAINMENT
- SHOPPING
- CONSTRUCTION UPDATE
- PUBLIC TRANSPORTATION

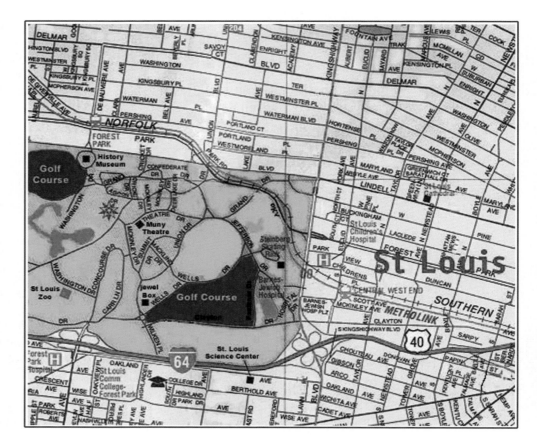

The Expres-
sionist
Museum

In your search for information about the van Gogh exhibit, you have found the exhibition Web page on the museum Web site (see p. 90). Answer the following questions using the Web site.

1. Will this site provide information about van Gogh's life and his career as a painter?

2. Where would you click to discover if the site has detailed information about the painter?

3. Where would you click to learn if the museum offers lectures on van Gogh?

ArtLive

After looking at the museum Web site, you decide you want to know more about van Gogh. Your search engine turns up the **ArtLive** Web site on pages 91 and 92. Use this Web site to answer the following questions. For statements preceded by T / F / N, circle T if the statement is true, F if the statement is false, and N if there is not enough information to know if the statement is true or false.

1. Skim* the Web pages to see how they are organized and answer the following questions.

   a. Does the summary on page 91 give more information about the artist's life than did the museum's Web site?

   b. T / F / N   The links on page 91 (**books**, **articles**, **online resources**) represent the table of contents of the Web site.

   c. Where would you click for more information on van Gogh?

2. Scan** the **ArtLive** Web pages for the following pieces of information.

   a. When was the artist born?

   b. When did he die?

   c. Where could you find more information about van Gogh's famous painting *The Starry Night*?

   d. Is there a book about van Gogh's self-portraits?

3. According to this Web site, what are the four periods of the artist's life?

4. T / F / N   *The Letters of Vincent Van Gogh* were edited by the artist's brother after the artist's death.

5. T / F / N   The Web site author does not have a high opinion of the online resource **Vincent van Gogh Information Gallery**.

6. T / F / N   If you click on the articles, you will find the complete texts.

7. T / F / N   Van Gogh committed suicide.

8. How would you become a patron of **ArtLive**? What do you think the benefits would be? What are some reasons not to subscribe?

---

*For an introduction to skimming, see Unit 1.
**For an introduction to scanning, see Unit 1.

The Expressionist Museum 🖋

The Collection | Special Exhibits | Education | Membership | Visitor Info

Special Exhibits

 The Expressionist Museum is the proud host of ***van Gogh, Gauguin, and Seurat: Tres Amis du Petit Boulevard.*** The exhibit features more than 120 paintings and works on paper by these three artists, who met and were associated with the various avant-garde movements in Paris (1886-1888). Van Gogh considered many artists of his time and place (e.g., <u>Pissarro</u> and <u>Toulouse-Lautrec</u>) to be the painters of the "petit boulevard," which reflected their desire to distinguish themselves from the Impressionists (painters of the "grand boulevard"). One of the exhibits explores, through photos, maps, and letters, the intense but clearly productive relationship between van Gogh and <u>Gauguin</u>, during which they shared van Gogh's studio space in Arles for nine weeks. This culminated in the famous "break-up" of the two artists, and ultimately, in van Gogh's death. Notwithstanding their modesty, the painters of the petit boulevard came to shape European modern art.

<u>Artists' Biographies</u> | <u>Tours & Lectures</u> | <u>Links</u>

<u>H o m e</u>

Vincent van Gogh

Early work *(1881-February 1888)*
Arles *(February 1888-May 1889)*
Saint Rémy *(May 1889-May 1890)*
Auvers-sur-Oise *(May 1890-July 1890)*

Books   Articles   Online Resources

Biography

"Vincent van Gogh was born near Brabant, the son of a minister. In 1869, he got a position at the art dealers, Goupil and Co. in The Hague, through his uncle, and worked with them until he was dismissed from the London office in 1873. He worked as a schoolmaster in England (1876), before training for the ministry at Amsterdam University (1877). After he failed to get a post in the Church, he went to live as an independent missionary among the Borinage miners.

"He was largely self-taught as an artist, although he received help from his cousin, Mauve. His first works were heavily painted, mud colored and clumsy attempts to represent the life of the poor (e.g., *Potato-Eaters,* 1885, Amsterdam), influenced by one of his artistic heroes, Millet. He moved to Paris in 1886, living with his devoted brother, Theo, who as a dealer introduced him to artists like Gauguin, Pissarro, Seurat and Toulouse-Lautrec. In Paris, he discovered color as well as the divisionist ideas which helped to create the distinctive dashed brushstrokes of his later work (e.g., *Père Tanguy,* 1887, Paris). He moved to Arles, in the south of France, in 1888, hoping to establish an artists' colony there, and was immediately struck by the hot reds and yellows of the Mediterranean, which he increasingly used symbolically to represent his own moods (e.g., *Sunflowers,* 1888, London, National Gallery). He was joined briefly by Gauguin in October 1888, and managed in some works to combine his own ideas with the latter's Synthetism (e.g., *The Sower,* 1888, Amsterdam), but the visit was not a success. A final argument led to the infamous episode in which Van Gogh mutilated his ear.

"In 1889, he became a voluntary patient at the St. Remy asylum, where he continued to paint, often making copies of artists he admired. His palette softened to mauves and pinks, but his brushwork was increasingly agitated, the dashes constructed into swirling, twisted shapes, often seen as symbolic of his mental state (e.g., *Ravine,* 1889, Otterlo). He moved to Auvers, to be closer to Theo in 1890–his last 70 days spent in a hectic program of painting. He died, having sold only one work, following a botched suicide attempt. His life is detailed in a series of letters to his brother (published 1959)."

– From "The Bulfinch Guide to Art History"

Materials for Further Research

Text on Vincent van Gogh displayed on the ArtLive site is supplied courtesy of Mark Harden.

Vincent van Gogh

BOOKS

Vincent Van Gogh
Myra Schapiro, Meyer Schapiro

This Harry Abrams-published book is an excellent and economical introduction. Meyer Schapiro was one of the greatest, most readable, art critics. The reproductions are not the greatest (this was published originally in 1983), but the writing more than makes up for any graphical deficiencies.

The Letters of Vincent Van Gogh
Vincent Van Gogh, Ronald De Leeuw (Editor), Arnold Pomerans (Translator)

The letters from Vincent to his beloved brother Theo are required reading for anyone who wants to understand the tortured artist. In them, van Gogh provides deep insights into his working process, providing details on his motifs and compositional decisions. These letters, with the sensitive commentary of De Leeuw, are almost an essential accompaniment to his paintings.

Vincent: A Complete Portrait : All of Vincent Van Gogh's Self Portraits, With Excerpts from His Writings
Bernard Denvir

Excellent graphics and an even more attractive price make this compilation hard to resist. Van Gogh's most searching artistic analysis was of himself, as his famous self-portraits show ... and this book includes them all.

Van Gogh in Saint Remy and Auvers/D2212P
R. Pickvance

This is the catalog to a 1986 show at the Metropolitan Museum of Art. The reproductions are good quality, and the essays well chosen, written by the world's foremost experts on van Gogh. This exhibition covered the final phase of Vincent's tragically short career.

The New Complete Van Gogh: Paintings, Drawings, Sketches
Jan Hulsker

When he says COMPLETE, he means it ... this is the real thing, with a price to match.

ARTICLES

Text about "Irises" from Meyer Schapiro, "Vincent Van Gogh"

Text about "The Poet's Garden" from Meyer Schapiro, "Vincent Van Gogh"

Text about "Self-portrait" from Meyer Schapiro, "Vincent Van Gogh"

Text about "The Sower" from J. van der Wolk, "Vincent Van Gogh: Paintings and Drawings"

Text about "The Starry Night" from J. van der Wolk, "Vincent Van Gogh: Paintings and Drawings"

ONLINE RESOURCES

David Brooks' passion for van Gogh pours out of every pixel in his "Vincent van Gogh Information Gallery", making it a must-see for van Gogh on the Web.

Nicolas Pioch's WebMuseum includes many images as well as a biography from the Encyclopaedia Brittanica.

Voyager has an online preview of their new "Van Gogh: Starry Night" CD-ROM, in which art historian Albert Boime debunks much of the "mad artist" mythology that has grown up around van Gogh.

Top of Page

van Gogh Biography

Text on Vincent van Gogh displayed on the ArtLive site is supplied courtesy of Mark Harden.

You decide to check out another Web site that showed up in your search. Answer the following questions using the Starry Night Gallery site on page 94. For statements preceded by T / F / N, circle T if the statement is true according to this Web site, F if the statement is false, and N if there is not enough information to know if the statement is true or false.

1. T / F / N   The author is a noted art critic and authority on van Gogh.

2. T / F / N   Because the author refers to van Gogh as "Vincent," we can assume they were personal friends.

3. T / F / N   Van Gogh's early works were sad and portrayed his sense of hopelessness.

4. T / F / N   Vincent van Gogh benefited from meeting other painters during his time in Paris.

5. T / F / N   The Japanese prints that van Gogh collected gave him pleasure.

6. What is your opinion of this site? Would you bookmark it?

7. If you were writing a paper for a class, which Web site—**ArtLive** or **Starry Night Gallery**—would you cite? Why?

St★rry Night Gallery

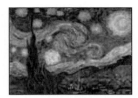

A discussion of Vincent van Gogh's paintings probably places me on the shakiest ground of my entire van Gogh website. As I mention on the introductory page, I have no formal training whatsoever in art criticism. All I can do, for what it's worth, is give a very subjective overview of the various periods of Vincent's works, and share a few personal impressions.

If you wish to see more of van Gogh's works, be sure to look through either my alphabetical listings of paintings or my world map. There are dozens of links to paintings within each and I hope to have hundreds more in the weeks and months to come.

I would divide van Gogh's works into the following nine categories (again, I must stress that these are my own categories and have no grounding in a proper, academic study of van Gogh's works—in addition, there is, of course, no clean transition from one category to the next. The categories can overlap and don't necessarily follow a precise chronological sequence):

- **Early Works:** Van Gogh's early drawings and paintings tend to centre on the lives of peasants and poor labourers, as well as on the bleak landscapes in which they find themselves. This is not to say that these works are bleak themselves or offer no signs of hope. Not at all. While van Gogh's early use of darker colours may suggest a melancholy atmosphere (as can be interpreted in *The Potato Eaters* at right), Vincent himself had a great admiration for the field workers and weavers he captured on canvas. In a letter to Theo he comments on the peasants of Nuenen:

  "The people here instinctively wear the most beautiful blue . . . when this fades and becomes somewhat discolored by the wind and weather, it is an infinite delicate tone that particularly brings out the flesh colors."

- **Paris Works and Pointillism:** As mentioned on the Biography page, Vincent's move to Paris in 1886 brought about a profound change in his approach to art. There are a number of explanations as to the reasons, not the least of which is van Gogh's introduction to other fellow painters at the time: Monet, Renoir, Sisley, Pissarro, Degas, Signac and Seurat. A number of van Gogh's works at the time are not only noticeably more adventurous in their use of colour, but also adopt a pointillist approach. In just a short period, we see van Gogh's style move from the dark to the vibrant; from the worker bent over a loom to a pair of lovers strolling through the park.

- **Japonaiseries:** The period in which Vincent painted in the traditional Japanese fashion is brief, but nonetheless extremely interesting. "Japonisme" was an influence that was particularly popular in the mid to late 19th century. Vincent was intrigued by the Japanese prints available to him at the time and wrote to Theo:

  "My studio is not so bad, especially as I have pinned a lot of little Japanese prints on the wall, which amuse me very much."

  In fact, there are only three surviving examples of Vincent's Japonaiseries, however, their inclusion at such a pivotal point in Vincent's artistic evolution suggest that they commanded an important influence on his changing style.

[next page]

Text on the paintings of Vincent van gogh displayed on the Starry Night site is supplied courtesy of David Brooks.

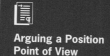

Reading Selections 1A–1C
News and Information

In our modern world an education is rapidly becoming a necessity if one hopes to earn a good living. The readings in this section provide you with the opportunity to examine your ideas about education. Your teacher may want you to talk over some of the issues in small groups before discussing answers with the class as a whole.

Before You Begin   The following questions are intended to focus your thoughts on education. The questions have no absolute right or wrong answer; each society has different opinions on the importance and structure of education. Indicate if you believe each statement is true (T) or false (F). Be prepared to give reasons and examples to support your answers.

1. _____ An education is a basic human right—every child is entitled to an education.

2. _____ Society must take responsibility for the education of all individuals.

3. _____ It is the responsibility of the family to provide an education for children.

4. _____ All children must attend school.

5. _____ School is not necessary for all children.

6. _____ A good education includes music, art, sports, social activities, etc.

7. _____ Schools should focus only on the "basics": reading, writing, and arithmetic.

8. _____ Education policy should be made at the national level, and all schools should follow a uniform plan.

9. _____ Schools should be controlled by the community in which they are located.

10. _____ Children are natural learners; education should nurture their interests and skills.

11. _____ Learning occurs primarily and most effectively in a carefully organized environment.

12. _____ The role of school is to help children learn how to function in the business world.

13. _____ Children must learn to follow the rules of society.

14. _____ Competition is essential for effective learning.

15. _____ If children are left on their own they will waste time.

16. _____ If children are encouraged to explore their interests, they will eventually learn everything that is important.

Selection 1A   Reference Book

Before You Begin   Take a few minutes to think about the following questions before you read
the selection below.

1. Can you describe the conditions under which you do your best work?

2. What are your favorite memories of school? Your least favorite memories?

3. How would you organize schools to encourage creativity and learning?

Beginning on page 98 is an excerpt from a book written for the layperson (the nonprofessional, such
as a parent, a grandparent, or an everyday citizen) who is interested in teaching and learning. Read it
and answer the questions that follow. Your teacher may want you to do the Vocabulary from Context
exercise on pages 102–3 before you begin reading.

Comprehension

Answer the following questions according to your understanding of the authors' point of view.
True/False items are indicated by a T / F preceding the statement.

1. What are the "creativity killers" the authors discuss? _____

_____

2. T / F   It is difficult to be creative when you are being observed.

3. T / F   Telling learners that they are doing a good job may hinder their creativity.

4. T / F   You should never reward a student for his or her accomplishments.

5. Do you think competition helps or hinders creativity? Give examples from your own experience.

_____

_____

6. T / F   Creativity requires freedom.

7. T / F   Teachers who want to encourage creativity should limit student choice.

8. T / F   Unreasonably high expectations can reduce creativity.

9. T / F   It is difficult to be creative on someone else's schedule.

The Creative Spirit

by Dan Goleman, Paul Kaufman, and Michael Ray

IF CREATIVITY is a child's natural state, what happens on the way to adulthood? Many of us will recognize ourselves in the sad tale of little Teresa Amabile, now a specialist in creativity.

"I was in kindergarten and my beloved teacher, Mrs. Bollier, had come to our home for an end-of-the-year conference with my mother. And, of course, I was eavesdropping on this conference from the next room."

Teresa was thrilled to hear Mrs. Bollier tell her mother, "I think Teresa shows a lot of potential for artistic creativity, and I hope that's something she really develops over the years."

"I didn't know what 'creativity' was," she recalls, "but it sure sounded like a good thing to have.

"When I was in kindergarten," she went on, "I remember rushing in every day, very excited about getting to the easel and playing with all these bright colors and these big paintbrushes we had. And there was a clay table set up where we had free access to all these art materials. I remember going home every day after kindergarten and telling my mother I wanted to play with crayons, I wanted to draw, I wanted to paint."

But kindergarten was to be the high point of Teresa's artistic career. The next year she entered a strict, traditional school, and things began to change. As she tells it, "Instead of having free access to art materials every day, art became just another subject, something that you had for an hour and a half every Friday afternoon."

Week after week, all through elementary school, it was the same art class. And a very restricted, even demoralizing one at that. "We would be given small reprints of one of the masterworks in painting, a different one every week. So, for example, I remember one week in second grade, we all got a small copy of da Vinci's *Adoration of the Magi*.

"This was meant for art appreciation, but that's not how our teacher used it. Instead we were told to take out our materials and copy it. Second-graders being asked to copy da Vinci—with their loose-leaf paper and their Crayola crayons. An exercise in frustration!

"You don't have the skill development at that age to even make all those horses and angels fit on the page, let alone make them look like anything. It was very demoralizing. You could see yourself that what you were doing was very bad.

From *The Creative Spirit* by Dan Goleman, Paul Kaufman, and Michael Ray (New York: Penguin, 1992).

"We weren't given any help developing skills. Worse, we were graded on these monstrosities that we produced, so we felt a heavy evaluation pressure. I was really aware at the time that my motivation for doing artwork was being completely wiped out. I no longer wanted to go home at the end of the day and take out my art materials and draw or paint."

THE CREATIVITY KILLERS

THE PSYCHOLOGICAL PRESSURES that inhibit a child's creativity occur early in life. Most children in preschool, kindergarten—even in first grade—love being in school. They are excited about exploring and learning. But by the time they are in the third or fourth grade, many don't like school, let alone have any sense of pleasure in their own creativity.

Dr. Amabile's research has identified the main creativity killers:

- **Surveillance:** hovering over kids, making them feel that they're constantly being watched while they're working. When a child is under constant observation, the risk-taking, creative urge goes underground and hides.

- **Evaluation:** making kids worry about how others judge what they're doing. Kids should be concerned primarily with how satisfied they are with their accomplishments, rather than focusing on how they are being evaluated or graded, or what their peers will think.

- **Rewards:** excessive use of prizes, such as gold stars, money, or toys. If overused, rewards deprive a child of the intrinsic pleasure of creative activity.

- **Competition:** putting kids in a desperate win-lose situation, where only one person can come out on top. Children should be allowed to progress at their own rate. (There can, however, be healthy competition that fosters team or group spirit.)

- **Over-control:** telling kids exactly how to do things—their schoolwork, their chores, even their play. Parents and teachers often confuse this kind of micromanagement with their duty to instruct. This leaves children feeling that any originality is a mistake and any exploration a waste of time.

- **Restricting Choice:** telling children which activities they should engage in instead of letting them follow where their curiosity and passion lead. Better to let a child choose what is of interest, and support that inclination.

- **Pressure:** establishing grandiose expectations for a child's performance. For example, those "hothouse" training regimes that force toddlers to learn the alphabet or math before they have any real interest can easily backfire and end up instilling an aversion for the subject being taught.

One of the greatest creativity killers, however, is more subtle and so deeply rooted in our culture that it is hardly noticed. It has to do with time.

If intrinsic motivation is one key to a child's creativity, the crucial element in cultivating it is time: open-ended time for the child to savor and explore a particular activity or material to make it his or her own. Perhaps one of the greatest crimes adults commit against a child's creativity is robbing the child of such time.

Children more naturally than adults enter that ultimate state of creativity called *flow*, in which total absorption can engender peak pleasure and creativity. In flow, time does not matter; there is only the timeless moment at hand. It is a state that is more comfortable for children than adults, who are more conscious of the passage of time.

"One ingredient of creativity is open-ended time," says Ann Lewin, Director of the Capital Children's Museum in Washington, D.C. The children's museum is an arena designed to draw children into the flow state. But, as Lewin sees there every day, there is a marked difference between the rhythms of the children who come there and the adults who bring them.

"Children have the capacity to get lost in whatever they're doing in a way that is much harder for an adult," she says. "Children need the opportunity to follow their natural inclinations, their own particular talents, to go wherever their proclivities lead them."

Unfortunately, children are interrupted, torn out of deep concentration; their desire to work something through is frustrated. Lewin explains: "Adults have the compulsion to march through and see everything. But there are hundreds of things that can deeply engross a child here, things they can spend hours with. And you see the adults pulling them away, tugging at them and telling them, 'Enough, stop it, let's go.'

"It's a terribly frustrating thing to be stopped when you're in the middle of the process. But we live in such a hurry-up way. So again and again children are stopped in the middle of things they love to do. They are scheduled. There isn't the time for children to relax into their own rhythm.

Critical Reading

The following questions are designed to give you an opportunity to explore ideas presented in "The Creative Spirit." Answer each question according to your understanding of the passage and your own experience. Some questions may have more than one correct answer. True/False items are indicated by a T / F preceding the statement.

1. T / F If we do not evaluate students, they will not learn how to do things correctly.

2. T / F Goals are necessary for learning.

3. At what point does a goal become unreasonable for a learner? Who sets goals for learning?

4. The authors assert that children arrive at school full of energy and curiosity but that by the third or fourth year, they have lost the sense of pleasure in their own learning. Do you agree or disagree? Why?

5. T / F Children must learn to complete tasks on time.

Discussion/Composition

1. Each of the "creativity killers" is listed below, paired with a word that expresses a similar or related idea. For each pair,

   a. define the difference between the two terms;

   b. discuss an experience in school when your creativity was encouraged or "killed." (You are not allowed to give this exercise as an example.) ;-)

surveillance	observation
evaluation	self-assessment
rewards	recognition
competition	personal achievement
control	support
restricting choice	guidance
pressure	goal setting

2. What is the relationship between structured, organized activity and individual creativity? Is it the responsibility of schools to encourage creativity in individual children or to promote cooperation and conformity to society's values? Can both be accomplished in the same school?

3. What is the relationship between learning and creativity? Is all learning creative? Can you think of situations where important learning occurs in spite of controls by school?

4. What is "flow" (described near the end of the article)? When was the last time you experienced flow? What were the circumstances? What can an individual learner do to create this experience for him- or herself? How should schools be organized to promote flow?

Vocabulary from Context

Both the ideas and the vocabulary in the following exercise are taken from "The Creativity Killers." Use the context provided to determine the meanings of the italicized words. Write a definition, synonym, or description of each of the italicized vocabulary items in the space provided.

A continuing debate in education concerns the tension between the need for children to be given freedom to explore and learn and the responsibility of school to organize their experience and structure their environment so that they learn attitudes and skills that are important for society. It is clear that children are naturally creative, curious, and original in their approach to learning. This *creativity* needs to be encouraged. As children begin to walk, usually between the ages of 12 months and 2 years, they begin to explore their surroundings. *Toddlers* are naturally curious; they want to explore, and they are not afraid to take risks, to try out new things. This is good; *risk taking* is a natural part of learning.

1. _____

2. _____

3. _____

But parents and teachers have a responsibility to make sure children are safe, and we also want children to learn the skills and attitudes considered appropriate by society. Schools need to create environments in which children learn what is expected of them when they grow up. The difficulty is structuring activities that help children learn without limiting them. When we *inhibit* them, we reduce the chances that they will develop their creativity. We want activities that provide guidance without overly *restricting* their choices. We want children to *savor* new experiences. Intense enjoyment of experiences is a natural state for youngsters, an *intrinsic* part of their natures.

4. _____

5. _____

6. _____

7. _____

An important aspect of this issue is related to the nature of learning and the institutional structures that encourage learning. For learning to occur, children have to find school motivating—it has to provide interesting and energizing activities that appeal to their interests, their loves, their passions. Whether they are playing

8. _____

9. _____

10. _____

11. _____

12. _____

alone or with *peers,* they have the ability to become so totally involved in their activity that they appear to become lost in time. This state of being totally *engrossed* in an activity is often referred to as *flow*—when learning is so involving that time doesn't matter. The *rhythm* of the activity is similar to the rhythm of the learner; like dancers who move together on the dance floor, the learner and the activity are working together. When the child's inner rhythm and the school's schedule are not the same, children's creativity suffers. And this is often a problem, because schools are organized by adults, who often follow the clock rather than their creativity. It is almost as if they are governed by clock *compulsions;* they seem to be driven or forced, unable to do anything without time limits.

The difficulty is in developing programs that support learning without inhibiting creativity. How do we provide structure without holding back creativity? How do you observe children, for example, without making them feel as if they are under *surveillance?* How do you stay close to them as they play without appearing to *hover?* At what point does some amount of concern for their well-being become too much, with this *excessive* attention limiting learning and creativity? We want children to have a healthy self-confidence in their abilities, and there are times when it is appropriate for them to attempt to do better than others. However, we do not want *competition* to become so important that they lose sight of the joy of learning. We don't want children to have too great a desire for success; a *desperate* desire to win actually makes learning more difficult. It is also true that when overly complex programs are imposed on children, the result is often *aversion* rather than attraction to learning activities. Programs such as preschool reading programs, or programs intended to boost children's intelligence through intense competition, are likely to have the opposite effect. School programs need to support children's *proclivities.* When activities support their natural inclinations, they will learn, naturally and easily.

13. _____

14. _____

15. _____

16. _____

17. _____

18. _____

19. _____

Figurative Language and Idioms

1. In the section "Surveillance," the authors say that constant observation causes the creative urge to "go underground and hide." What is meant by this?

2. In the final section, the authors comment that children have the ability to "get lost in" an activity. Do they see this as a good thing? Why or why not?

Below is an exerpt from an American textbook for schoolchildren. Read the selection, and answer the questions that follow.

American Values in Education

Our school system has developed as it has because the American people value education highly. Some of the traditional values which have developed over the years are:

1. Public education should be *free*. There should be no hidden charges to prevent any citizen from receiving a good education at public expense.

2. Schooling should be *equal* and open to all. No one should be discriminated against because of race, religion, or financial status.

3. The public schools should be *free of any creed or religion.* The schools of the United States are open to all Americans regardless of their religious beliefs. The Supreme Court has held that no special prayer or Bible reading shall be required. However, religious schools (sometimes called parochial schools) are permitted outside of the public school system.

4. Public schools are *controlled by the state and local governments* within which

they are located. Local school boards run the public schools under laws passed by the state legislature. The State Board of Education assists the local schools, but does not give orders to the district board. The United States Department of Education also assists with advice and information, but the actual control is located in the local school district, where the people know the local situation.

5. Attendance at school is *compulsory.* Parents cannot decide to keep their children out of school. Each state compels the attendance of young people, usually between the ages of 7 and 16.

6. Schooling should be *enriched* and not just confined to the fundamentals. Most Americans believe that schools should be places where young people can grow in body, mind, and spirit. Athletics, clubs, social events, and creative arts are a part of each person's education. Schools should be lively places where individuals are encouraged to develop to their greatest potential.

From *American Civics*, 2d ed. (New York: Harcourt Brace Jovanovich).

Critical Reading

Using the six "traditional values" of American education described above, summarize the educational philosophy of another country with which you are familiar. Where do you find similarities? What are the differences?

Discussion

1. Who should make decisions about the schools—parents? professional educators? elected officials? religious leaders? specially appointed experts? the children themselves? Read the statements below and discuss the pros and cons of each. With whom do you agree?

   a. Parents: "They are our kids. We know what is best for them. We should decide what they learn and how they are taught."

   b. Teachers: "What do parents know? We are the ones with the special training. We should make the decisions."

   c. Government officials: "We have the best view of the issues. We know the budget, and we understand the laws and how they apply. Only we can make the best decisions."

   d. Religious authorities: "Schools that teach facts but no values weaken the moral strength of the country. We can provide the wisdom and insight on which all teaching should be based."

   e. University experts: "We have studied the problems and done the research. We should be consulted before any decisions are made."

   f. Children: "It is our lives and education that are at stake. No decisions should be made without our advice and agreement."

2. Does the United States live up to the philosophical ideals listed above? Do you think other countries fulfill their educational goals? To what extent can a country live up to its educational ideals? Give examples to support your opinions.

An automobile accident has caused heartache and trouble for the Espino family of Brownsville, Texas. It has also caused difficulties for the Brownsville school system. In many ways, the following article challenges the ideas discussed in the previous article. Read the article, imagining that you know the little boy, Raul. Decide what you would do to solve his problems. Answer the comprehension and discussion questions that follow. Your teacher may want you to do the Vocabulary from Context exercise 1 on page 109 before reading.

Parents Seeking Cool Classroom for Son

1 BROWNSVILLE, Texas (AP) — School bells and the swelter of a waning Texas summer will greet children in Brownsville when they resume classes in a few weeks, but Raul Espino Jr. hopes that will not mean another semester of peering at his classmates from inside a plexiglass box that protects him from the heat.

2 The 7-year-old's parents asked a federal judge this week to order their son's entire classroom air-conditioned to free him from the transparent cubicle. An auto accident when he was an infant left the boy a paraplegic and his body unable to control its temperature.

3 **NONE OF THE** Brownsville Intermediate District's 28 primary or junior high schools, which open Aug. 25, have air-conditioning. The district's solution to Raul's problem was to put him in the box.

4 U.S. District Judge Filemon Vela said he would decide by Aug. 15 whether to grant the request from Ana and Raul Espino.

5 "Other alternatives have not been considered," Vela said. "We may be able to find a solution with the present setting."

6 The accident damaged the hypothalamus gland in Raul's brain that controls the body's temperature and some movement. He is confined to a wheelchair and must stay in an environment between 72 and 78 degrees.

7 Doctors say the injury did not affect his intelligence, and teachers call him an above-average student.

8 **WHEN HE** transferred last year from a school for the handicapped to Egly Elementary School, the box with a portable air-conditioning unit was built for him to use when temperatures climbed above 78 degrees. A two-way sound system was installed so he could converse with his teacher and classmates.

9 Mrs. Espino testified Monday that she was overjoyed to hear her son would be with normal children last school year, but then she became dismayed to learn that he would be confined to the cubicle.

10 After failing to persuade the Texas Education Agency and the state Board of Education to order classroom air-conditioning, the Espinos took their case to federal court, arguing that the district is violating a law that requires handicapped children be educated in the "least restrictive environment."

11 Local Superintendent Raul Besteio testified that he decided to build the box instead of air-conditioning the room for fear of jealousy among other parents and teachers. Besteio said he turned down a woman from Pennsylvania who offered to pay for air-conditioning because that would have been "discrimination."

12 **THE DISTRICT,** with a relatively low tax base in the Rio Grande Valley, cannot afford to air condition the classroom, he said.

13 No estimates of the cost of air conditioning were available, but based on costs at the three high schools in the 28,000-student district, it could come to $5,700 a room.

Reprinted by permission of The Associated Press.

Comprehension

Answer the following questions. Your teacher may want you to answer orally, in writing, or by underlining appropriate portions of the text. True/False items are indicated by a T / F preceding the statement. Some items may have more than one correct answer.

1. Why is Raul in a wheelchair? _____
_____

2. Why does Raul need an air-conditioned environment? _____
_____

3. Brownsville, Texas must be a warm place. From reading the article, what do you think are

typical temperatures during the school year? _____

4. How did the Brownsville school district solve Raul's need for an air-conditioned environment?
_____

5. T / F   Raul must stay in the plexiglass box all of the time.

6. T / F   Raul cannot see or hear his classmates from inside the plexiglass box.

7. Why do Raul's parents object to the box? _____
_____

8. T / F   The school district has worked cooperatively with the parents to solve Raul's problems.

9. T / F   The Brownsville school system cannot afford to air-condition any of its classrooms.

10. T / F   The Brownsville school district cannot afford to air-condition Raul's classroom.

11. How much would it cost to air-condition Raul's room? _____
_____

12. T / F   Apparently the Brownsville school district believes that primary and junior high school students can endure the heat better than high school students.

13. Judge Vela reports that he is exploring other options. What might they be? What alternatives can you think of that have not been mentioned? How do you think the problem would be solved where you are from?

_____

_____

_____

_____

_____

14. The superintendent of schools cited considerations of discrimination as one of the reasons that the situation had not been resolved (paragraph 11). In your opinion, which of the following situations constitute discrimination?

   a. A classroom whose environment makes it impossible for a handicapped student to work

   b. Providing air-conditioning for handicapped students but not for nonhandicapped students

   c. Providing air-conditioning for high school students but not for primary or junior high students

   d. Air-conditioning paid for by private sources rather than by public funds

   e. Air-conditioning only one classroom in a school

15. Do you think the superintendent's office is air-conditioned? _____

16. Do you think the writer of the newspaper article agrees with the Espinos or with the

   superintendent? _____

17. Use the six points from the textbook article to evaluate the Brownsville school district.

   What grade would you give it? _____

Discussion/Composition

1. Pretend you are one of the following people involved in the legal battle you have been reading about:

   a. the attorney representing the Espinos

   b. the attorney representing the Brownsville Intermediate District

   State your position on the issue of how Raul's special needs should be met and explain the reasoning behind your position.

2. Pretend you are the federal court judge responsible for deciding how to resolve the dispute between the Espinos and the Brownsville Intermediate District. What would your decision be? Explain your reasoning.

Vocabulary from Context

Exercise 1

Use the context provided to determine the meanings of the italicized words. Write a definition, synonym, or description of each of the italicized vocabulary items in the space provided.

1. _____ For many children in North America, school vacation begins in June. Classes usually *resume* in late August or early September.

2. _____ Because the walls of the room were *transparent* we could see everything that was going on in the next room.

3. _____ The problem was complex, and several different solutions were offered by teachers, parents, and administrators. It was the director's job to choose the best solution from among these *alternatives*.

4. _____ We did not like the solution that was proposed, and we argued for several days with the director, but we could not *persuade* her to change her mind.

5. _____ The boy was in a box where he could not move around or participate in all of the class activities. His parents felt that the box was far too *restrictive* and demanded a change.

Exercise 2

This exercise is designed to give you additional clues to determine the meanings of unfamiliar vocabulary items in context. In the paragraph of "Parents Seeking Cool Classroom for Son" indicated by the number in parentheses, find the word that best fits the meaning given. Your teacher may want to read these aloud as you quickly scan* the paragraph to find the answer.

1. (1) Which word means *extreme heat*?

2. (1) Which word means *looking at*?

3. (2) Which word means *a small enclosed space; a box*?

4. (2) Which word means *a person who cannot move his or her legs due to disease or injury*?

5. (6,10) Which word means *all that surrounds a person, including air, objects, etc.*?

6. (9) Which word means *surprised; alarmed; discouraged*?

7. (11) Which word means *envy; unhappiness caused by wanting what someone else has*?

8. (11) Which word means *unfair or unequal treatment*?

* For an introduction to scanning, see Unit 1.

Reading Selection 2
Newspaper Questionnaire

Before You Begin   Look at the following cartoon.

1. Why is the woman having trouble sleeping?

2. If you have a problem, what do you do? Do you try to avoid the problem? Do you simply worry about it? Or do you do something about it?

3. Do you think all people handle problems in the same way? Do you think people from different backgrounds and cultures respond differently to crises?

Efficient reading requires an understanding of the attitudes and experiences of the writer. Unless one has knowledge about or is able to infer an author's beliefs, it is possible to understand all of the sentences in a passage and yet not comprehend a writer's ideas.

Reading a newspaper in another language is an excellent way of drawing inferences about another culture. The following selection is a quiz that appeared in a newspaper in the United States. It was designed to provide people with the opportunity to measure their ability to handle problems. By taking the quiz, you should be able to gain an understanding of the kinds of problems experienced in the United States and the ways in which people attempt to deal with them.

Answer each of the questions. If you have trouble deciding what you would do in a given situation, choose the response that is closest to what you would do.

Between Friends reprinted with special permission of King Features Syndicate.

How Do You Handle Everyday Stress?

Psychologists are now convinced that day-to-day problems, which frequently seem unimportant, are what "take a lot out of you." Moreover, they can even affect the length of your life. Everybody faces day-to-day problems, but some can handle them better than others.

Would you like to know how well you can cope? In this quiz, circle the answer closest to the way you actually react in the situation described. If the situation is unfamiliar, circle the answer closest to the way you think you would handle it.

Answers at the end will tell you how well you are coping with everyday stress and may help you to improve your methods of dealing with problems.

1. You have become increasingly irritated with drivers who are "multitasking"—for example, talking on their cell phones as they drive. You have had several near accidents with such drivers.
   a. You honk and shake your fist at the offenders. Perhaps if they see the problems they are causing they will reform.
   b. You resolve to take a defensive driving course to learn how to deal with these drivers.
   c. You shake your head and keep on going. There's nothing to be done about crazy drivers.

2. You can't seem to stay on top of all the messages and demands on your time. It seems that faxes, email, and voice-mail messages pile up faster than you can respond to them.
   a. You start an anti-information campaign among your friends and co-workers to throw away faxes and delete every third email message without reading it, and you stop checking your voice mail.
   b. You buy a book that has sug- gestions for how to deal with the information age.
   c. You decide to devote more of your time to your messages, hoping to get on top of the situation.

3. You have just taken a new job. Although you like it a lot, you are amazed at the technological ignorance of your boss. He cannot complete the simplest computer application without your help, and you find that you are spending more and more time doing his work, rather than doing your own.
   a. You become extremely frustrated and complain to your co-workers.
   b. You volunteer to take the lead in developing technical training courses for your company.
   c. You take on the extra work rather than teach your boss how to do it.

4. Birthdays, weddings, anniversaries . . . it seems impossible to avoid spending money.
   a. You tell everyone to take you off their gift list so that you don't have to buy a gift.
   b. In spite of the expense you continue to enjoy selecting small, special gifts for any occasion.
   c. You give only to those who are most important to you.

5. You have an automobile accident with another car and you have to appear in court.
   a. The anxiety and inconvenience of appearing in court causes you to lose sleep.
   b. It's an unimportant event, one of those things that happen in life. You will reward yourself with a little gift after court.
   c. You forget about it. You will cope with it when the day comes.

6. You've had a fight with your neighbor and nothing was resolved.
   a. You go home, fix a strong drink, try to relax and forget about it.
   b. You call your lawyer to discuss a possible lawsuit.
   c. You work off your anger by taking a walk.

7. The pressures of modern-day

Adapted from "How Do You Handle Everyday Stress?" by Dr. Syvil Marquit and Marilyn Lane. Features and News Service.

living have made you and your spouse irritable.

a. You decide to take it easy and not be forced into any arguments.

b. You try to discuss irritating matters with a third person so that you can make your feelings known without an argument.

c. You discuss the problems with your spouse to see how you can take off some of the pressure.

8. A close friend is about to get married. In your opinion, it will be a disaster.

a. You convince yourself that your early fears are incorrect and hope for the best.

b. You decide not to worry because there's still time for a change of plans.

c. You decide to present your point of view; you explain your reasoning seriously to your friend.

9. You are worried about rising energy prices.

a. In spite of the cost, you do not change your lifestyle.

b. You turn down your thermostat, and you wear sweaters around the house.

c. Your anger toward the power company grows and you contemplate ways of getting revenge, but you send in your payments on time.

10. Finally your abilities have been recognized; you've been offered an important job.

a. You think of turning down the chance because the job is too demanding.

b. You analyze what the job requires and prepare yourself to do the job.

c. You begin to doubt if you can handle the added responsibility successfully.

11. You suspect that your rent or some other monthly expense will increase.

a. You pick up the mail anxiously each day and give a sigh of relief when the letter isn't there.

b. You decide not to be caught by surprise, and you plan how to handle the situation.

c. You feel that everyone is in the same situation and that somehow you'll cope with the increase.

12. Someone close to you has been seriously injured in an accident, and you hear the news by phone.

a. You hold back your feelings for the moment because other friends and relatives have to be told the news.

b. You hang up and burst into tears.

c. You call your doctor and ask for tranquilizers to help you through the next few hours.

13. You've won a big luxury car in a competition. You could use a car, but it seems this is going to change your life considerably.

a. You worry about the added problems your good luck will bring.

b. You sell it and buy a smaller car, banking the money left over.

c. You decide to enjoy the car and to worry about the added expense later.

14. Every holiday there is a serious argument in the family about whether to visit your parents or those of your spouse.

a. You make a rigid 5-year plan, which will require you to spend each holiday with different members of the family.

b. You decide that you'll spend important holidays with the members of the family you like best and ask others to join you for the lesser holidays.

c. You decide the fairest thing is not to celebrate with the family at all—and it's less trouble.

15. You're not feeling well.

a. You diagnose your own illness, then read about it.

b. You gather up your courage, talk about it at home, and go to see your doctor.

c. You delay going to the doctor thinking that you will eventually feel better.

Critical Reading

Now that you have indicated how you would react to these situations, return to the questions to predict the behaviors of others.

1. For each item, place a *C* (for native culture) next to the response that you believe would describe the behavior of people from your culture.

2. Place a *U* (for U.S. natives) next to the response that you believe would best describe the behavior of most people in the United States.

When you have finished, continue reading the article. You will learn how to score your responses and discover what the authors of this questionnaire consider healthy behavior. Be sure to score responses for yourself, others from your culture, and natives of the United States.

To find out how you cope with stress, score your answers according to the following chart:

Questions 1–3:   a = 3, b = 1, c = 2
Questions 4–8:   a = 3, b = 2, c = 1
Questions 9–15:   a = 2, b = 1, c = 3

The lower your total score, the better able you are to cope with your problems. If you scored 23 or less, the advice that follows may be normal behavior for you. (Perhaps you can teach others how to be calm.)

If you scored over 23, here are some ways to handle stress conditions effectively. Don't put difficult situations to one side thinking they will go away. Eventually you will have to deal with them anyway. Don't make decisions that will cause you stress later. It's better to face reality at the beginning. For example, don't accept an invitation if you know you won't be able to attend when the time comes.

In order to avoid problems later, think things through in advance. In facing a problem, don't guess about the future or let your imagination run away with you; find out what the true situation is, then handle it.

Most of the time what you may be fearing will never happen. When you get upset about an unavoidable stress-filled event, do something physical to work it off. When tragedy strikes, as it does to all of us, don't be afraid to show your emotions.

Discussion/Composition

1. What can you infer from this quiz about the kinds of problems faced by people in the United States? How are these similar to and different from problems faced by people everywhere?

2. The choices below each question in the quiz describe some of the ways people in the United States cope with problems. Compare and contrast the ways in which you, people from your culture, and a "typical American" might respond to these situations. Which responses are similar? Which do you find strange? Be sure to give examples.

3. This questionnaire reveals a lot about modern life. Are there items that you think would be answered differently by men and women? By individuals from different cultures? By people of different ages? Social scholars would say that your answers reveal as much about you as about society. How would you support your answers? Did you reach your conclusions through observation and research, or did you merely report your stereotypes? How do you know? How would you conduct research on this issue?

   To learn more about stereotypes, see "The Stereotype of Stereotypes," pages 115–16.

4. The cartoon that follows is taken from the comic strip "Sally Forth." Sally and her husband Ted are a "modern couple" who both have careers outside the home. When they have problems, they try to face these with humor. In this cartoon, Sally is considering how she deals with stress. What is Sally's source of stress? Is Sally the kind of person who tries to avoid the problem, simply worries about it, or tries to do something about it?

Vocabulary Review

Circle the word or phrase that is not similar in meaning.

deal with   demand   handle   cope with   respond to   stay on top of

Reading Selection 3
Science Reporting

Before You Begin

1. What are stereotypes? Can you give an example of stereotypes you have about other nations? Can you give an example of a mistaken stereotype that others have about your country/culture?

2. Are stereotypes good or bad?

Do stereotypes represent incorrect prejudices, or do they function as useful first steps in cross-cultural contact? Read "The Stereotype of Stereotypes" to see what you think. First, read the article quickly to get an overall sense of the arguments presented. Then do Comprehension exercise 1. Your teacher may want you to do Vocabulary from Context exercise 1 on page 119 before you begin reading.

The Stereotype of Stereotypes

Bruce Bower

1 Psychologist Yueh-Ting Lee received an electronic mail message several years ago that included some barbed observations about the quality of life in several countries. "Heaven is a place with an American house, Chinese food, British police, a German car, and French art." Lee's correspondent wrote, "Hell is a place with a Japanese house, Chinese police, British food, German art, and a French car."

2 While these national stereotypes fall short of absolute truths, asserts Lee of Westfield (Mass.) State College, they are accurate enough to give the aphorism its humorous punch. Houses in the United States indeed boast more space, on average, than Japanese dwellings. A Chinese inn probably holds greater culinary potential than a British pub.

3 In this respect, stereotypes, rather than representing unjustified prejudices, typically function as thought-efficient starting points for understanding other cultures and social groups, as well as the individuals who belong to them, Lee holds.

4 "Stereotypes are probabilistic beliefs we use to categorize people, objects, and events," Lee proposes. "We have to have stereotypes to deal with so much information in a world with which we are often uncertain and unfamiliar."

5 Many psychologists find this opinion about as welcome as a cut in their research grants. They view stereotyping as a breeding ground for errant generalizations about others that easily lead to racism, sexism, and other forms of bigotry.

6 In the realm of stereotypes, intelligence gives way to misjudgment, maintains Charles Stangor of the University of Maryland at College Park. People employ stereotypes mainly to simplify how they think about others and to enhance their views of themselves and the groups to which they belong, Stangor holds. In the hands of politically powerful folks, stereotypes abet efforts to stigmatize and exploit selected groups, he adds.

7 Stangor's argument fails to give stereotypes their due as often helpful, if not absolutely precise, probes of the social world, Lee responds. He contends that a growing body of research suggests that in many real-life situations, stereotypes accurately capture cultural or group differences.

8 For more than 60 years, scientists have treated stereotypes as by definition erroneous, illogical, and inflexible. This view was voiced in journalist Walter Lippman's 1922 book *Public Opinion,* in which he argued that stereotypes of social groups invariably prove incomplete and biased.

9 In the 1950s, psychologist Gordon W. Allport characterized stereotypes as invalid beliefs about all members of a group. Allport treated the opinion "all Germans are efficient" as a stereotype, but not "Germans, on average, are more efficient than people in other countries." Debate arose at that time over whether some stereotypes encase a "kernel of truth."

From *Science News,* June 29, 1996.

10 Lippman's fear that stereotypes cause social harm gained particular favor after 1970, as psychologists rushed to expose errors and biases in social judgments. Recently, however, psychologists have shown more interest in delineating the extent to which decision making proves accurate in specific contexts.

11 Lee's approach to stereotypes falls squarely within the focus on accuracy of judgment. His interest in how people comprehend ethnic and cultural differences intensified after he emigrated from China to the United States in 1986 to attend graduate school. At that point, he began to suspect that a keener scientific understanding of stereotypes might have valuable applications. For instance, Lee asserts, efforts at conflict resolution between ethnic groups or nations may work best if both sides receive help in confronting real cultural differences that trigger mutual animosities.

12 "Group differences, not prejudice, are the root cause of tension and conflict between various cultural and racial groups," he contends. "The most effective way to improve intergroup relations is to admit and to discuss frankly the existing differences at the same time explaining that there is nothing wrong with being different."

13 Bridge-building efforts of this kind counteract the natural tendency to emphasize negative features in stereotypes, argues Reuben M. Baron of the University of Connecticut in Storrs. Humans evolved in groups that negotiated a dangerous world, he states. Our ancestors must have relied on stereotypes to marshal quick responses to potential threats, such as distinguishing predators from prey, friends from enemies, and fellow group members from outsiders, Baron asserts.

14 The ability to categorize individuals into "types" may also have been crucial for communicating with others as groups grew in size and complexity, Baron proposes. In large communities, stereotypes capitalized on people's propensity to fill social roles that match their own personal qualities. Warriors in an ancient society, for instance, might reasonably have been stereotyped as aggressive and unemotional, while storytellers and musicians were accurately tagged as expressive and friendly.

15 Despite their handiness, even accurate stereotypes can result in mistaken beliefs about others, according to Baron.

16 Consider the misunderstandings over punctuality that develop between Mexican and U.S. businesspeople. Lee says that north of the border, Mexicans get stereotyped as "the mañana people" because of their tendency to show up for meetings considerably after prearranged times and to miss deadlines for completing assigned tasks. U.S. officials may see this trait as unforgivable deal breaking, whereas their Mexican counterparts—who do not dispute their own tardiness—deride Americans as "robots" who rigidly reach conclusions by specified dates before gathering all relevant data and fully grasping the issues.

17 Businesspeople from each culture perceptively categorize the behavior of those in the other group but misunderstand the cultural roots of their different time perspectives, Lee says.

18 Such subtleties of stereotyping have gone largely unexplored, remarks David C. Funder, a psychologist at the University of California, Riverside. Most research of the past 25 years has tried to catalog the ways in which expectations about social categories distort a person's judgment, usually by placing the individual in laboratory situations intended to elicit racial or sexual stereotypes.

19 This approach neglects to ask whether people in a wide array of real-life situations incorporate accurate information into their stereotypes, Funder holds.

20 "We desperately need to know which of the judgments we make of each other and of ourselves are right, which are wrong, and when," Funder contends. ■

Comprehension

Exercise 1

The following questions check your understanding of the main ideas in "The Stereotype of Stereotypes." Indicate if each of the statements below is true (T) or false (F) according to the article.

1. T / F   According to Yueh-Ting Lee, national stereotypes represent unjustified prejudices.

2. T / F   Some researchers believe that we need stereotypes to deal with a large and dangerous world.

3. T / F   Charles Stangor believes that stereotypes accurately reflect cultural or group differences.

4. T / F   Charles Stangor believes that stereotypes can be used by the powerful to harm the less powerful.

5. T / F   For much of the last century, psychologists and writers believed that stereotypes were invalid.

6. T / F   Our ancestors may have used stereotypes to survive in a complex and dangerous world.

7. T / F   Lee believes that understanding stereotypes can be helpful in understanding others.

8. T / F   Lee and Baron see no dangers in stereotypes.

9. T / F   The article demonstrates why further research is not necessary.

Exercise 2

Look back at the article to complete the following task. "The Stereotype of Stereotypes" presents a variety of points of view and research on stereotypes. Below is a list of researchers and writers cited in the article. Put a P next to the names of those who see positive effects of stereotypes. Put an N next to those who are reported to have negative opinions of stereotypes.

1. _____ Yueh-Ting Lee

2. _____ Charles Stangor

3. _____ Walter Lippman

4. _____ Gordon W. Allport

5. _____ Reuben M. Baron

6. _____ David C. Funder

Critical Reading

1. What does the title "The Stereotype of Stereotypes" mean? Do you think that we have stereotypes about stereotypes?

2. In paragraphs 6 and 7, the author contrasts the views of Stangor and Lee concerning the effects of stereotypes. With whom do you agree? When does a useful generalization about other people become a harmful stereotype?

3. Yueh-Ting Lee (paragraph 11) believes that people can use stereotypes to help with conflict resolution. Can you give an example from your own experience? Do you agree or disagree with Lee?

4. a. Did you enjoy the joke that began this article? Why or why not? When they work, what makes such jokes funny? When are they not funny?

   b. The following question is meant in fun. Every culture has stereotypes and generalizations about other groups. If you or those in your home culture were writing the email message, what would be good and bad characteristics of different countries? Fill in the chart below in the spirit of fun; be careful to respect the feelings of your classmates.

	Good	Bad
Food		
Car		
Art		
House		
Toilet paper		

   c. Give examples of ways by which you might discover that your stereotypes are inaccurate.

Discussion/Composition

1. By and large, do you believe stereotypes are positive or negative? You will be debating this issue. In preparation, go through "The Stereotype of Stereotypes" and put a *P* next to any arguments that would support a positive view of stereotypes. Put an *N* next to negative arguments. Work with your classmates to develop a debate. (Do you believe that using a debate format to clarify your thoughts is a stereotypically North American way to proceed?)

2. If you were going to develop a high school curriculum on stereotypes, what would you teach? Work with your classmates to develop a list of ideas and a list of possible activities.

3. In paragraph 5 the author says that many psychologists find Lee's opinions "about as welcome as a cut in their research grants." What does this mean? What does it tell us about scientists and their research grants? Can you make up other expressions using this phrasing, for example, "about as welcome as running out of gas in the desert"?

4. Below is a statement by Yueh-Ting Lee, quoted in the article (paragraph 12).

   Group differences, not prejudice, are the root cause of tension and conflict between various cultural and racial groups.

   What does this mean? Do you agree or disagree? Which do you think is the major cause of cultural conflict: real differences between groups or prejudice? Support your position orally or in writing by presenting reasons and examples.

Vocabulary from Context

Note: because "The Stereotype of Stereotypes" is especially rich in unfamiliar vocabulary, the following sections include quite a few vocabulary activities. After you do exercise 1, your teacher may ask you to complete only some of the activities that follow.

Exercise 1

Both the ideas and the vocabulary in the following exercise are taken from "The Stereotype of Stereotypes." Use the context provided to determine the meanings of the italicized words. Write a definition, synonym, or description of each of the italicized vocabulary items in the space provided.

1. _____

2. _____

3. _____

4. _____

5. _____

6. _____

7. _____

8. _____

9. _____

Are stereotypes always bad? Many people believe that stereotypes are the equivalent of *prejudices:* negative opinions without any basis in fact. If people decide that they don't like anyone with brown hair, for example, they are simply *biased* against brown-haired folks. Racism and sexism are other forms of *bigotry.* Many worry that stereotypes are always dangerous. They can be used to *stigmatize* groups, to mark them as shameful and dishonored. Stereotypes can be used by people in power to *exploit* other people, as an excuse to treat them unfairly and take advantage of them. The problem with stereotypes is that they are most often without any basis in fact—they tend to be *unjustified* and *erroneous.* Although not all stereotypes are completely false, this *tendency* of stereotypes to be negative and erroneous is what worries many. This *propensity* of humans to believe good things about themselves and bad things about others is what makes many people mistrust all stereotypes.

10. _____

11. _____

12. _____

13. _____

14. _____

Others feel that stereotypes reflect a bit of truth, that they reflect real differences between people. In this sense, stereotypes help people make sense of the world, keep them safe, and therefore cannot be overlooked. Stereotypes might even *abet* efforts to make peace. It may be that the only way to make true peace in the world is to face the differences that cause strong dislikes between different cultures. The theory is that if people *confront* the causes of their *animosities,* they can begin to solve intercultural misunderstandings. It may be that people can come to understand the source of cultural characteristics and not find these *traits* so frustrating.

Clearly stereotyping requires more study. It's a complex issue that requires delicate reasoning, making fine distinctions, and looking for the less obvious. The new researchers on stereotypes hope to bring this *subtlety* to their investigations.

Exercise 2

This exercise is designed to give you additional clues to determine the meanings of unfamiliar vocabulary items in context. In the paragraph of "The Stereotype of Stereotypes" indicated by the number in parentheses, find the word or phrase that best fits the meaning given. Your teacher may want to read these aloud as you quickly scan* the paragraph to find the answer.

1. (6) What word means *to improve; to make more attractive*?

2. (7) What word means *analyses; studies; assessments; examinations*?

3. (10) What word means *outlining; defining; describing*?

4. (11) What word means *sharper; more precise or accurate*?

5. (13) What word means *to organize; to manage; to come up with*?

6. (16) What word means *being on time*?

7. (16) What word means *time limits; cut-off dates; target dates*?

8. (19) What phrase means *doesn't ask; fails to deal with*?

9. (19) What phrase means *a large number; a broad range*?

Exercise 3

This exercise should be done after you have finished reading "The Stereotype of Stereotypes." The exercise is designed to give you practice using context clues to guess the meaning of unfamiliar vocabulary. Give a definition, synonym, or description of each of the words below. The number in parentheses indicates the paragraph in which the word can be found. Your teacher may want you to do these orally or in writing.

1. (2) dwellings _____

2. (6) realm _____

3. (6) employ _____

4. (9) invalid _____

5. (9) encase _____

6. (13) counteract _____

7. (14) crucial _____

8. (14) tagged _____

9. (16) tardiness _____

10. (18) distort _____

_____

*For an introduction to scanning, see Unit 1.

Figurative Language and Idioms

In the paragraph indicated by the number in parentheses, find the phrase that best fits the meaning given. Your teacher may want to read these aloud as you quickly scan* the paragraph to find the answer.

1. (2)   What phrase means *are not; are less than*?

2. (7)   What phrase means *to give credit; to give what is deserved; to be fair*?

3. (10) What phrase means *became popular; developed support*?

4. (11) What phrase means *peacemaking; solving disagreements*?

5. (13) What phrase means *peacemaking; creating relationships across groups*?

Dictionary Study

Many words have more than one meaning. When you use a dictionary to discover the meaning of an unfamiliar word or phrase, you need to use the context to determine which definition is appropriate. The sentences below are based on "The Stereotype of Stereotypes." Use the portions of the dictionary provided to select the best definition for each of the italicized words. Write the number of the definition in the space provided.

_____ 1. While these national stereotypes don't represent absolute truths, they are accurate enough to give the joke its humorous *punch*.

_____ 2. Houses in the United States may indeed *boast* more space, on average, than Japanese dwellings.

_____ 3. A growing body of research suggests that in many real-life situations, stereotypes accurately *capture* cultural or group differences.

_____ 4. Humans evolved in groups that *negotiated* a dangerous world.

_____ 5. In large communities, stereotypes *capitalized* on people's tendency to fill social roles that matched their own personal qualities.

---

*For an introduction to scanning, see Unit 1.

punch¹ (pŭnch) *n.* **1.** A tool for circular or other piercing. **2.** A tool for forcing a pin, bolt, or rivet in or out of a hole. **3.** A tool for stamping a design on a surface. **4.** A tool for making a countersink. — *intr. & tr.v.* **punched, punch·ing, punch·es.** To use a punch or use a punch on. [ME *pounce, punche* < OFr. *poinçon, ponchon.* See PUNCHEON¹. V. < ME *pouncen, punchen,* to prick < OFr. *poinçoner, ponchoner,* to emboss with a punch. See PUNCH².]

punch² (pŭnch) *tr.v.* **punched, punch·ing, punch·es. 1.** To hit with a sharp blow of the fist. **2.a.** To poke or prod with a stick. **b.** *Western U.S.* To herd (cattle). **3.** To depress (a key or button, for example) in order to activate a device or perform an operation. — *n.* **1.** A blow with the fist. **2.** Vigor or drive. — *phrasal verbs.* **punch in.** To check in formally at a job upon arrival. **punch out. 1.** To check out formally at a job upon departure. **2.** *Slang.* To eject from a military aircraft. — *idiom.* **beat to the punch.** To make the first decisive move. [ME *punchen,* to thrust, prod, prick < OFr. *poinçonner, ponchonner,* to emboss with a punch < *poinçon, ponchon,* pointed tool. See PUNCHEON¹.] — **punch′less** *adj.*

punch³ (pŭnch) *n.* A beverage of fruit juices and sometimes carbonated water, often spiced and mixed with wine or liquor. [Perh. < Hindi *pañc-,* five- < Skt. *pañca,* (< the hypothesis that it was originally prepared from five ingredients). See **penkʷe*.]

boast¹ (bōst) *v.* **boast·ed, boast·ing, boasts.** — *intr.* To glorify oneself in speech; talk in a self-admiring way. — *tr.* **1.** To speak of with excessive pride. **2.** To possess or own (a desirable feature). **3.** To contain; have. — *n.* **1.** The act or an instance of bragging. **2.** A source of pride. [ME *bosten* < *bost,* a brag.] — **boast′er** *n.* — **boast′ful** *adj.* — **boast′ful·ly** *adv.* — **boast′ful·ness** *n.*

boast² (bōst) *tr.v.* **boast·ed, boast·ing, boasts.** To shape or form (stone) roughly with a broad chisel. [?]

cap·ture (kăp′chər) *tr.v.* **-tured, -tur·ing, -tures. 1.** To take captive, as by force or craft; seize. **2.** To gain possession or control of, as in a game or contest. **3.** To attract and hold: *capture the imagination.* **4.** To succeed in preserving in lasting form: *capture a likeness.* — *n.* **1.** The act of catching, taking, or winning, as by force or skill. **2.** One that has been seized, caught, or won. **3.** *Phys.* The phenomenon in which an atom or a nucleus absorbs a subatomic particle. [< Fr., capture < OFr. < Lat. *captūra* < *captus,* p.part. of *capere,* to seize. See **kap-*.]

ne·go·ti·ate (nĭ-gō′shē-āt′) *v.* **-at·ed, -at·ing, -ates.** — *intr.* To confer with another or others in order to come to terms or reach an agreement. — *tr.* **1.** To arrange or settle by discussion and mutual agreement. **2.a.** To transfer title to or ownership of (a promissory note, for example) to another party by delivery or by delivery and endorsement in return for value received. **b.** To sell or discount (securities, for example). **3.a.** To succeed in going over or coping with. **b.** To succeed in accomplishing or managing. [Lat. *negōtiārī, negōtiāt-,* to transact business < *negōtium,* business : *neg-,* not; see **ne*** + *ōtium,* leisure.] — **ne·go·ti·a′tor** *n.* — **ne·go′tia·to·ry** (-shə-tôr′ē, -tōr′ē, -shē-ə-) *adj.*

cap·i·tal·ize (kăp′ĭ-tl-īz′) *v.* **-ized, -iz·ing, -iz·es.** — *tr.* **1.** To use as or convert into capital. **2.** To supply with capital or investment funds. **3.** To authorize the issue of a certain amount of capital stock of. **4.** To convert (debt) into capital stock or shares. **5.** To calculate the current value of (a future stream of earnings or cash flows). **6.** To include (expenditures) in business accounts as assets instead of expenses. **7.a.** To write or print in capital letters. **b.** To begin a word with a capital letter. — *intr.* To turn something to one's advantage; benefit. — **cap′i·tal·iz′a·ble** *adj.*

Vocabulary Review

Three of the words in each line below are similar or related in meaning. Circle the word that does not belong.

1. prejudice	bias	accuracy	bigotry
2. justified	erroneous	illogical	invalid
3. tendency	animosity	propensity	inclination
4. stereotype	generalization	oversimplification	trait
5. qualities	characteristics	deadlines	traits

From *The American Heritage College Dictionary,* 3d ed. (Boston: Houghton Mifflin, 2000).

Nonprose Reading
Questionnaire

Before You Begin   Before completing the questionnaire below, take a few minutes to think about the following.

1. What activities are you good at? What do you enjoy doing?

2. What do you struggle with? What are the things that you do not enjoy doing?

3. How intelligent are you?

4. Have you ever considered that the answer to question 3 is related to the answers to questions 1 and 2? How could this be?

Scholars agree that intelligence is far more complex than commonly thought. Howard Gardner, of Harvard University, has determined that there are multiple intelligences and that people vary in the ways they think and problem solve.*

> For more information about multiple intelligences, check out Gardner's Web site: **http://edweb.gsn.org/edref.mi.th.html**.

This questionnaire is designed to help you understand how Gardner's theory of multiple intelligences might relate to the ways that you study languages. Respond to each statement, indicating the extent to which you think it represents your way of thinking and problem solving, and then continue with the activities on pages 125 and 126.

---

*For an explanation of nonprose reading, see Unit 1.

Strongly Disagree				Strongly Agree	
1 2 3 4 5	1. I see words in my mind before I write them down.
1 2 3 4 5	2. I am interested in new developments in science.
1 2 3 4 5	3. I can generally find my way around unfamiliar territory.
1 2 3 4 5	4. I find it difficult to sit still for long periods of time.
1 2 3 4 5	5. I know the tunes of many songs.
1 2 3 4 5	6. I prefer to use a dictionary when I encounter a word I do not know.
1 2 3 4 5	7. I listen to music all the time, even when studying.
1 2 3 4 5	8. I am considered a leader by others.
1 2 3 4 5	9. I remember the lyrics to songs after hearing them once or twice.
1 2 3 4 5	10. I use symbols and charts to solve problems.
1 2 3 4 5	11. I like books. Reading is a favorite pastime.
1 2 3 4 5	12. I like to physically practice a new skill rather than just study it.
1 2 3 4 5	13. I have ideas and opinions that set me apart from the majority of my peers.
1 2 3 4 5	14. I like to play word games.
1 2 3 4 5	15. I have set goals for my life, and I work to achieve those goals.
1 2 3 4 5	16. I engage in sports and physical activity regularly.
1 2 3 4 5	17. I can easily compute mathematical problems in my head.
1 2 3 4 5	18. I have vivid dreams at night.
1 2 3 4 5	19. I search for patterns, regularities, or logical sequences in everyday events.
1 2 3 4 5	20. I prefer group activities rather than doing things alone.
1 2 3 4 5	21. I like to sing.
1 2 3 4 5	22. I am able to learn and remember things better when I see them written down.
1 2 3 4 5	23. My best ideas come to me when I am jogging or exercising.
1 2 3 4 5	24. I prefer illustrated textbooks.
1 2 3 4 5	25. I prefer to measure, categorize, and analyze when problem solving.
1 2 3 4 5	26. I feel comfortable in a crowd.
1 2 3 4 5	27. I have at least three close friends.
1 2 3 4 5	28. I am well coordinated.
1 2 3 4 5	29. I consider myself to be strong willed and independent.
1 2 3 4 5	30. I enjoy working with others on problem-solving tasks.
1 2 3 4 5	31. I regularly spend time alone meditating or reflecting on important matters.
1 2 3 4 5	32. I am sensitive to color.
1 2 3 4 5	33. I often draw or doodle while thinking, talking, or problem solving.
1 2 3 4 5	34. I often choose to spend time alone rather than seek out friends for company.
1 2 3 4 5	35. I sometimes catch myself singing a song from a TV program or a movie I recently saw.

Scoring your questionnaire

Total your scores for each of the following types of intelligence, and enter your scores in the blanks.

____ Linguistic Intelligence: Items 1, 6, 11, 14, 22

____ Logical-Mathematical Intelligence: Items 2, 10, 17, 19, 25

____ Spatial Intelligence: Items 3, 18, 24, 32, 33

____ Bodily-Kinesthetic Intelligence: Items 4, 12, 16, 23, 28

____ Musical Intelligence: Items 5, 7, 9, 21, 35

____ Interpersonal Intelligence: Items 8, 20, 26, 27, 30

____ Intrapersonal Intelligence: Numbers 13, 15, 29, 31, 34

1. This is not a scientifically constructed questionnaire. Nevertheless, the scores indicate your strengths in problem solving and your preferred ways of learning. High scores (between 19 and 25 points) indicate that you have a preference for, or a special skill in, a particular way of solving problems, that you are "intelligent" in that particular way. Low scores suggest that these may not be your preferred ways of learning. Enter your scores in the appropriate cells of the table below.

	Low (5–11)	Moderate (12–18)	High (19–25)
1. Linguistic Intelligence			
2. Logical-Mathematical Intelligence			
3. Spatial Intelligence			
4. Bodily-Kinesthetic Intelligence			
5. Musical Intelligence			
6. Interpersonal Intelligence			
7. Intrapersonal Intelligence			

2. In pairs or small groups, talk with classmates who have similar strengths to yours, who have scored themselves high in the same areas. Using the following list as a guide, develop a profile of the language class that would best meet your needs. Each item describes an activity that might help you learn a second language. Check (✔) those activities that you and your classmates would find helpful, given your particular intelligence profile.

_____ a. Making charts to learn verb tenses or other vocabulary

_____ b. Using charts or visual aids made by other people

_____ c. Learning songs in the second language

_____ d. Presenting skits or short dialogues that illustrate an idea in the native language

_____ e. Writing short skits or dialogues

_____ f. Doing workbook exercises or end-of-chapter assignments

_____ g. Learning new vocabulary through art projects—painting or building things

_____ h. Interacting with native speakers in the community

_____ i. Performing services for children or the elderly

_____ j. Teaching someone else a skill that you have to learn

_____ k. Playing on a sports team with native speakers of the target language

_____ l. Joining a choir or theater group

_____ m. Signing up for a class that will require you to use the target language

_____ n. Getting a job

_____ o. Drawing a concept to represent an idea in the target language

_____ p. Keeping a journal in the target language that helps you reflect on your language learning experiences

_____ q. Producing videos with native speakers

_____ r. Exchanging email with native speakers

_____ s. Marrying a native speaker

_____ t. Joining chat rooms on the Internet

Can you think of other activities that would be helpful?

_____ u. _____

_____ v. _____

_____ w. _____

Word Study
Context Clues

In the following exercise, do NOT try to learn the italicized words. Concentrate on developing your ability to guess the meanings of unfamiliar words using context clues. Read each sentence carefully and write a definition, synonym, or description of the italicized word on the line provided.*

1. _____ The major points of your plan are clear to me, but the details are still *hazy*.

2. _____ By *anticipating* the thief's next move, the police were able to arrive at the bank before the robbery occurred.

3. _____ All of the palace's laundry, when gathered for washing, formed a *massive* bundle that required the combined efforts of all the servants to carry.

4. _____ "Give me specific suggestions when you criticize my work," said the employee. "*Vague* comments do not help me improve."

5. _____ The apple *appeased* my hunger temporarily, but I could still eat a big dinner.

6. _____ After the workers walked off the job, a committee met to try to discover what could have *provoked* such action.

7. _____ The audience *manifested* its pleasure with hearty laughter.

8. _____ The nation's highway death *toll* has increased every year since the invention of the automobile.

_____

*For an introduction to using context clues, see Unit 1.

9. _____ The worker's lives were *wretched;* they worked from morning to night in all kinds of weather, earning only enough money to buy their simple food and cheap clothes.

10. _____ In a series of bold moves, government attorneys attacked the *mammoth* computer company, saying that the size of the business endangered the financial freedom of the individual buyer.

Exercise 2

This exercise is designed to give you practice using context clues from a passage. Use your general knowledge along with information from the entire text below to write a definition, synonym, or description of the italicized word on the line provided. Read through the entire passage before making a decision. Note that some of the words appear more than once; by the end of the passage you should have a good idea of their meaning. Do not worry if your definition is not exact; a general idea of the meaning will often allow you to understand the meaning of a written text.

Hummingbirds: A Portrait of the Animal World

The hummingbird is truly extraordinary. It is, of course, most famous for its *diminutive* size; even the largest of these little birds weighs barely half an ounce; the tiniest, at barely two inches long, is the smallest of all warm-blooded creatures. But the hummingbird is *notable* for many other reasons. Its ability to *hover,* seemingly motionless, in midair and even to fly upside down is amazing. Its vividly hued iridescent plumage gives it a remarkable appearance. And its specialized feeding habits, its extraordinary migration patterns, and its unusual courtship and mating rituals make it *unique* in the realm of *ornithology.*

diminutive: _____

notable: _____

hover: _____

unique: _____

ornithology: _____

Adapted from the dust jacket of *Hummingbirds: A Portrait of the Animal World* by Hal H. Wyss (New York: TODTRI Book Publishers, 1999).

Word Study
Stems and Affixes

Below is a list of some commonly occurring stems and affixes.* Study their meanings, and then do the exercises that follow. Your teacher may ask you to give examples of other words you know that are derived from these stems and affixes.

Prefixes

a-, an-	without, lacking, not	atypical, apolitical
bene-	good	benefit, benefactor
bi-	two	bicycle, binary
mis-	wrong	misspell, mistake
mono-	one, alone	monarch, monopoly
poly-	many	polynomial, polytechnic
syn-, sym-, syl-	with, together	symphony, sympathy

Stems

-anthro-, -anthropo-	human	anthropology
-arch-	first, chief, leader	patriarch, monarch, archbishop
-fact-, -fect-	make, do	affect, benefactor, factory
-gam-	marriage	monogamy, polygamous
-hetero-	different, other	heterosexual, heterogeneous
-homo-	same	homogenized milk
-man-, -manu-	hand	manually, manage
-morph-	form, structure	polymorphous
-onym-, -nomen-	name	synonym, nomenclature
-pathy-	feeling, disease	sympathy, telepathy, pathological
-theo-, -the-	god	theology, polytheism

Suffixes

-ic, -al	relating to, having the nature of	comic, musical
-ism	action or practice, theory or doctrine	Buddhism, communism
-oid	like, resembling	humanoid

*For a list of all stems and affixes taught in *Reader's Choice*, see the Appendix.

Exercise 1

For each item, select the best definition of the italicized word, or answer the question.

1. The small country was ruled by a *monarch* for 500 years.

   _____ a. king or queen

   _____ b. single family

   _____ c. group of the oldest citizens

   _____ d. group of the richest citizens

2. He was interested in *anthropology*.

   _____ a. the study of apes

   _____ b. the study of insects

   _____ c. the study of royalty

   _____ d. the study of humans

3. Some citizens say the election of William Blazer will lead to *anarchy*.

   _____ a. a strong central government

   _____ b. a government controlled by one person

   _____ c. the absence of a controlling government

   _____ d. an old-fashioned, outdated government

4. If a man is a *bigamist,* he

   _____ a. is married to two women.

   _____ b. is divorced.

   _____ c. has two children.

   _____ d. will never marry.

5. Which of the following pairs of words are *homonyms*?

   _____ a. good   bad

   _____ b. Paul   Peter

   _____ c. lie   die

   _____ d. two   too

6. Which of the following pairs of words are *antonyms*?

   _____ a. sea   see

   _____ b. wet   dry

   _____ c. read   read

   _____ d. Jim   Susan

7. The reviewer criticized the poet's *amorphous* style.

   _____ a. unimaginative

   _____ b. unusual

   _____ c. stiff, too ordered

   _____ d. lacking in organization and form

8. Dan says he is an *atheist*.

_____ a. one who believes in one god

_____ b. one who believes there is no god

_____ c. one who believes in many gods

_____ d. one who is not sure if there is a god

9. There was a great *antipathy* between the brothers.

_____ a. love

_____ b. difference

_____ c. dislike

_____ d. resemblance

10. Which circle is *bisected*?

a.   b.   c.   d.

11. This design is symmetric: ○ □ ▯ □ ○

Which of the following designs is *asymmetric*?

a. □ ▯ □   b. □ □ ▯ □ □   c. ○ ∘ ○   d. □ ▯ ▯

12. Consider the following sentences:

Many automobiles are *manufactured* in Detroit.
The authors must give the publisher a *manuscript* of their new book.

How are the meanings of *manufacture* and *manuscript* different from the meanings of the stems from which they are derived? _____

_____

Exercise 2

Word analysis can help you to guess the meanings of unfamiliar words. Using context clues and what you know about word parts, write a synonym, description, or definition of the italicized word.

1. _____ Doctors say that getting regular exercise is *beneficial* to your health.

2. _____ He's always *mislaying* his car keys, so he keeps an extra set in the garage.

3. _____ Because some of our patients speak Spanish and some speak English, we need a nurse who is *bilingual*.

4. _____ My parents always told me not to *misbehave* at my grandparents' house.

5. _____ Some people prefer to remain *anonymous* when they call the police to report a crime.

Exercise 3

Following is a list of words containing some of the stems and affixes introduced in this unit and the previous one. Definitions of these words appear on the right. Put the letter of the appropriate definition next to each word.

1. _____ archenemy
2. _____ archetype
3. _____ anthropoid
4. _____ benediction
5. _____ benefactor
6. _____ manicure

a. care of the hands and fingernails
b. the saying of a blessing
c. resembling humans
d. one who performs good deeds
e. a chief opponent
f. the original model or form after which a thing is made

7. _____ monotheism
8. _____ polytheism
9. _____ polygamy
10. _____ monogamy
11. _____ heterogeneous
12. _____ homogeneous

a. made up of similar parts
b. belief in one god
c. the practice of having one marriage partner
d. the practice of having several marriage partners
e. consisting of different types; made up of different types
f. belief in more than one god

Sentence Study
Comprehension

Read the following sentences carefully.* The questions that follow are designed to test your comprehension of complex grammatical structures. Select the *best* answer.

1. My discovery of Tillie Olsen was a gift from a friend; years ago she gave me her copy of *Tell Me a Riddle* because she liked the stories and wanted to share the experience.

   What do we know about Tillie Olsen?

   _____ a. She is a friend.

   _____ b. She likes stories.

   _____ c. She gives gifts.

   _____ d. She is an author.

2. A few government officials even estimate that the flood has created more than half a million refugees who need immediate food, clothing, and shelter.

   Exactly how many refugees are there?

   _____ a. half a million

   _____ b. over half a million

   _____ c. We don't know exactly.

   _____ d. Only a few government officials know the exact figure.

3. The Green Tiger Press believes that the relatively unknown work of great children's illustrators are sources of vast beauty and power and is attempting to make these treasures more easily available.

   What is the goal of this printing company?

   _____ a. to publish more children's books

   _____ b. to develop powerful stories

   _____ c. to make children's illustrations more easily available

   _____ d. to encourage artists to become children's illustrators

---

*For an introduction to sentence study, see Unit 3.

4. Although he calls the $1,000 donation "a very generous amount, especially in these times," the president expresses hope that the project will attract additional funds from companies and other sources so that it can continue beyond this first year.

What does the president know about the project?

_____ a. It will cost only $1,000.

_____ b. It is very special.

_____ c. Special sources will support it.

_____ d. It cannot continue without additional funding.

5. Any thought that this new custom will remain unchanged—or in Europe will remain uniquely English—is ridiculous.

What does the author believe about the new custom?

_____ a. It will remain limited.

_____ b. The custom will change.

_____ c. Acceptance of the custom is ridiculous.

_____ d. The custom will remain in Europe.

6. Robust and persistent sailors gathered from all the sea-faring nations set out on voyages that laid foundations for great empires with no other power than sail and oar.

Why were these voyages important?

_____ a. Sailors came from many countries.

_____ b. The voyages laid the foundations for sea-faring nations.

_____ c. The foundations for empires were established.

_____ d. Sea-faring nations lost their power.

7. Young people need to develop the values, attitudes, and problem-solving skills essential to their participation in a political system that was designed, and is still based, on the assumption that all citizens would be so prepared.

What is the basic assumption of this political system?

_____ a. All people will be capable of participation.

_____ b. All people participate in the system.

_____ c. All people should have the same values and attitudes.

_____ d. Most people cannot develop the skills to participate in the system.

8. While we may be interested in the possibilities of social harmony and individual fulfillment to be achieved through nontraditional education, one cannot help being cautious about accepting any sort of one-sided educational program as a cure for the world's ills.

How does the author feel about nontraditional education?

_____ a. He believes that it has no possibility of success.

_____ b. He doubts that it can cure the world's ills.

_____ c. He feels that it is a cure for the world's ills.

_____ d. He believes that it will bring social harmony.

9. The complexity of the human situation and the injustice of the social order demand far more fundamental changes in the basic structure of society itself than some politicians are willing to admit in their speeches.

What is necessary to correct the problems of society?

_____ a. basic changes in its structure

_____ b. fewer political speeches

_____ c. honest politicians

_____ d. basic changes in political methods

Paragraph Reading
Restatement and Inference

Each paragraph below is followed by five statements. The statements are of four types.

1. Some of the statements are restatements of ideas in the original paragraph. They give the same information in a different way.

2. Some of the statements are inferences (conclusions) that can be drawn from the information given in the paragraph.

3. Some of the statements are false based on the information given.

4. Some of the statements cannot be judged true or false based on the information given in the original paragraph.

Put a check (✔) next to all restatements and inferences (types 1 and 2). *Note:* do not check a statement that is true of itself but cannot be inferred from the paragraph.

Example | Often people who hold higher positions in a given group overestimate their performance, while people in the lowest levels of the group underestimate theirs. While this may not always be true, it does indicate that often the actual position in the group has much to do with the feeling of personal confidence a person may have. Thus, members who hold higher positions in a group or feel that they have an important part to play in the group will probably have more confidence in their own performance.

_____ a. If people have confidence in their own performance, they will achieve high positions in a group.

_____ b. If we let people know they are an important part of a group, they will probably become more self-confident.

_____ c. People who hold low positions in a group often overestimate their performance.

_____ d. People in positions of power in a group may feel they do better work than they really do.

_____ e. People with higher positions in a group do better work than other group members.

Explanation

_____ a. This cannot be inferred from the paragraph. We know that people who hold high positions have more self-confidence than those who don't. However, we don't know that people with more confidence will achieve higher status. Confidence may come only *after* one achieves a higher position.

__✔__ b. This is an inference that can be drawn from the last sentence in the paragraph. We know that if people feel they have an important part to play in a group, they will probably have more self-confidence. We can infer that if we let people know (and therefore make them feel) that they have an important part to play, they will probably become more self-confident.

_____ c. This is false. The first sentence states that the people in the lowest levels of a group underestimate, not overestimate, their performance.

✓ d. This is a restatement of the first sentence. People who hold higher positions tend to overestimate their performance: they may feel they do better work than they really do.

_____ e. We do not know this from the paragraph. We know that people who hold higher positions often _think_ they do better work than others in a group. (They "overestimate their performance.") We do not know that they actually do better work.

Paragraph 1 | Like any theory of importance, that of social or cultural anthropology was the work of many minds and took on many forms. Some, the best known of its proponents, worked on broad areas and attempted to describe and account for the development of human civilization in its totality. Others restricted their efforts to specific aspects of the culture, taking up the evolution of art, or the state, or religion.

_____ a. Social anthropology concerns itself with broad areas while cultural anthropology concerns itself with specific aspects of culture.

_____ b. Cultural anthropologists, also known as social anthropologists, may work in either broad or restricted areas.

_____ c. Cultural anthropology is a new field of study.

_____ d. Any important area of study requires the work of many minds and is therefore likely to have different approaches.

_____ e. The best-known people in cultural anthropology attempted to describe the development of human civilization.

Paragraph 2 | I saw by the clock of the city jail that it was past eleven, so I decided to go to the newspaper immediately. Outside the editor's door I stopped to make sure my pages were in the right order; I smoothed them out carefully, stuck them back in my pocket, and knocked. I could hear my heart thumping as I walked in.

_____ a. The teller of this story has just left the city jail.

_____ b. He has been carrying his papers in his pocket.

_____ c. We know that the storyteller is a newspaper writer by profession.

_____ d. We might infer that the storyteller is going to show his papers to the editor.

_____ e. The meeting is important for the storyteller.

Paragraph 3 | *First Light* tells the story of astronomers at the Palomar Observatory in the San Gabriel Mountains of California who peer through the amazing Hale Telescope at the farthest edges of space, attempting to solve the riddle of the beginning of time. "Science is a lot weirder and more human than most people realize," Preston writes in his foreword to this revised and updated edition of his first book, and he skillfully weaves together stories of the eccentricities of his characters and the technical wonders of their work to create a riveting narrative about what scientists do and why they do it. The telescope itself is the main character. It is huge, seven stories tall, the heaviest working telescope on earth, with a mirror that is two hundred inches wide and took fourteen years to cast and polish. Although there are now larger telescopes and telescopes in space, the Hale telescope is still used by astronomers on almost every clear night. Preston's rendering of their obsessions and adventures is a witty and illuminating portrait of scientists in action and a luminous story of what modern astronomy is all about.

_____ a. *First Light* is the title of a book.

_____ b. This paragraph was written by the author of *First Light*.

_____ c. The purpose of *First Light* is to detail the eccentricities of scientists.

_____ d. *First Light* tells the story of the astronomers who use the Hale Telescope.

_____ e. The author of the paragraph likes *First Light*.

Paragraph 4 | The Incas had never acquired the art of writing, but they had developed a complicated system of knotted cords called *quipus*. These were made of the wool of the alpaca or llama, dyed in various colors, the significance of which was known to the officials. The cords were knotted in such a way as to represent the decimal system. Thus an important message relating to the progress of crops, the amount of taxes collected, or the advance of an enemy could be speedily sent by trained runners along the post roads.

_____ a. Because they could not write, the Incas are considered a simplistic, poorly developed society.

_____ b. Through a system of knotted cords, the Incas sent important messages from one community to another.

_____ c. Because runners were sent with cords, we can safely assume that the Incas did not have domesticated animals.

_____ d. Both the color of the cords and the way they were knotted formed part of the message of the *quipus*.

_____ e. The *quipus* were used for important messages.

Paragraph 3 adapted from the dust jacket of *First Light: The Search for the Edge of the Universe* by Richard Preston, rev. ed. (New York: Random House, 1996).

Paragraph 5 There was a time when scholars held that early humans lived in a kind of beneficent anarchy, in which people were granted their rights by their fellows and there was no governing or being governed. Various early writers looked back to this Golden Age but the point of view that humans were originally *children of nature* is best known to us in the writings of Rousseau, Locke, and Hobbes. These men described the concept of *social contract*, which they said had put an end to the *state of nature* in which the earliest humans were supposed to have lived.

_____ a. For Rousseau, Locke, and Hobbes, the concept of *social contract* put an end to the time of beneficent anarchy in which early humans lived.

_____ b. According to the author, scholars today do not hold that early humans lived in a state of anarchy.

_____ c. Only Rousseau, Locke, and Hobbes wrote about early humans as *children of nature*.

_____ d. The early writers referred to in this passage lived through the Golden Age of early humans.

_____ e. We can infer that the author of this passage feels that concepts of government have always been present in human history.

Discourse Focus
Careful Reading / Drawing Inferences

Mystery stories, like most other texts, require readers to note important facts and draw inferences based on these. To solve the following mysteries, you must become a detective, drawing inferences from the clues provided. Each mystery below has been solved by the fictional Professor Fordney, a master detective—the expert the police call for their most puzzling cases. Your job is to match wits with the great professor. Your teacher may want you to work with your classmates to answer the question following each mystery. Be prepared to defend your solution with details from the passage.

Mystery 1:
Class Day

"I shall tell you," Fordney said to his class some years ago, of an exploit of the famed scientist, Sir Joshua Beckwith, Professor of Egyptology in London.

"He had uncovered an ancient tomb in Egypt and, through his undisputed knowledge and ability to read hieroglyphics, had definitely established the date of the birth and the reign of a great Pharaoh whose mummy he had discovered. A man of volatile temper, and emphatic scientific views which he did not hesitate to express in exposing charlatanism, he had many enemies.

"The British Museum soon received a message, signed by Sir Joshua Beckwith, which in part read as follows: 'Have discovered the tomb of an important Pharaoh who reigned from 1410 to 1428 B.C. and who died at the age of 42 years, leaving two sons and two daughters. Great wealth found in sarcophagus. One of his sons died shortly after his reign began, etc. . . . '

"The museum officials at first were astonished," continued Fordney, "but examination of the communication quickly told them it was either a very stupid fake or an attempt at a 'practical joke'!

"They were right in their belief that the message did not come from Sir Joshua Beckwith. He did make a most important discovery—but how did the Museum authorities know the communication was not authentic?"

How did they know? _____

_____

From *Minute Mysteries* by Austin Ripley (New York: Pocket Books).

**Mystery 2:
Ruth's
Birthday**

A multitude of small accidents had delayed Ruth Mundy. The battery in her car had gone dead and she had to call a cab; she had mislaid the key to the strong box! Just as the taxi pulled up she located it. Hastily snatching from the dresser drawer two twenty-dollar bills, one old and crumpled, one crisp and new, she thrust them loosely into her bag. In her hurry, the perfume bottle on the dresser upset, spilling perfume on her lovely moire purse! If this kept up she'd be late for her birthday party! Now, where was that book she was to return? She was sure she had just put it on the dresser! Finally locating it under her coat on the bed, she grabbed it and ran.

Once in the taxi she opened her bag and fumbled for her vanity case. Its clasp opened and she stuck her finger in the paste rouge. Another casualty! Well, it didn't get on anything else, that was one break. Removing all traces of the rouge with her handkerchief, she threw it away.

Arriving at the Mayflower Hotel she handed the driver a bill. While she waited for her change Professor Fordney alighted from his car and greeted her with a "Hello Ruth."

Acknowledging the greeting she turned to the driver. "You've made a mistake. This is change for five. I gave you a twenty."

"Oh no, lady! You gave me five dollars!"

Fordney listened amused while Ruth excitedly proved she'd given the driver a twenty-dollar bill.

"How's that, Professor?" she laughed.

How did Ruth prove her story? _____

_____

**Mystery 3:
The
Ex-Wife
Murder**

"Who shot her?" cried Rogers as he rushed into the hospital three minutes after his ex-wife died from a bullet through her head.

"Just a minute," Professor Fordney said. "I'd like to ask you a few questions . . . routine, you know. Although divorced for the past six months, you have been living in the same house with your ex-wife, have you not?"

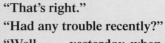

"That's right."

"Had any trouble recently?"

"Well . . . yesterday when I told her I was going on a business trip, she threatened suicide. In fact, I grabbed a bottle of iodine from her as she was about to drink it. When I left last evening at seven, however, telling her I was spending the night with friends in Sewickley, she made no objections. Returning to town this afternoon," he continued, "I called my home and the maid answered."

"Just what did she say?"

"'Oh, Mr. Rogers, they took poor mistress to St. Anne's hospital 'bout half an hour ago. Please hurry to her!' She was crying so I couldn't get anything else out of her; then I hurried here. Where is she?"

"The nurse here will direct you," responded the Professor. "A queer case this, Joe," said Inspector Kelley, who had been listening to the conversation. "These moderns are a little too much for me! A man and woman living together after being divorced six months!"

"A queer case, indeed, Jim," sighed Fordney. "You'd better detain Rogers. If he didn't shoot her himself, I'm confident he knows who did."

Why did the Professor advise the Inspector to detain Rogers? _____

_____

Mystery 4:
Case #463

At 8:10 P.M., July 4, 1945, Miss Ruby Marshall left her apartment on the fifth floor of the Hotel Oakwood. As she walked toward the elevator she passed Jane McGuire. The fourteen-year-old child had her Scottish terrier on a long leash and as they came opposite each other the dog growled and leaped at Miss Marshall. The woman screamed and ran back to her apartment.

Thirty minutes later Mrs. McGuire had a call from police headquarters informing her that Miss Marshall had received first aid at Mercy Hospital for a wound on the knee where the McGuire dog had bitten her. Invalided for the past two years, Mrs. McGuire was unable to look into the situation herself. She immediately called her friend, Professor Fordney, informing him of the above and asking him to look into the matter.

He found Miss Marshall sitting on a chair in the emergency ward, about to leave the hospital. Receiving permission to examine the wound from the doctor who had just taken care of her, Fordney raised Miss Marshall's immaculate evening dress, noticed her hose were rolled below her knees, removed the bandage and found cauterized marks on the right knee cap. Turning to the physician he inquired, "Are you sure those are teeth marks?"

"Why . . . they look like it to me!"

Lowering the woman's dress, the Professor told her, "You certainly didn't show much intelligence in trying to frame this charge against Mrs. McGuire, toward whom you hold a personal grudge. Her dog did not bite you!"

How did he know? _____

_____

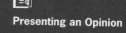

Reading Selections 1A–1B
News and Advertisement

The following reading selections document the continuing controversy over smoking.

Selection 1A   Newspaper Advertisement

Before You Begin

1. Are there disagreements between smokers and nonsmokers in your country about smoking in public?

2. One purpose of advertising is to persuade people that something they disagree with might be reasonable. If you were trying to develop a prosmoking advertisement at a time when cigarette smoking is under attack, what kind of advertisement would you create?

Below is an advertisement in favor of smokers' rights. Read it through once to see how persuasive you think it is. Then complete the exercises that follow. Your teacher may want you to work in groups or pairs.

Recognizing a Point of View

This exercise should be completed after you have finished reading "Smoking in Public: Live and Let Live." Below you will find portions of the advertisement followed by four statements. Put a check (✔) next to those statements that reflect the underlying beliefs or point of view of the original text.

1. Ours is a big world, complex and full of many diverse people. People with many varying points of view are constantly running up against others who have differing opinions. Those of us who smoke are just one group of many.

_____ a. Smokers are simply another group in the U.S., such as Greek Americans.

_____ b. Smokers can be thought of as people with a different point of view rather than as a group who engage in a particular behavior.

_____ c. People should like smokers.

_____ d. Smokers are people too.

Smoking in Public: Live and Let Live

Ours is a big world, complex and full of many diverse people. People with many varying points of view are constantly running up against others who have differing opinions. Those of us who smoke are just one group of many. Recently, the activism of nonsmokers has reminded us of the need to be considerate of others when we smoke in public.

But, please! Enough is enough! We would like to remind nonsmokers that courtesy is a two-way street. If you politely request that someone not smoke you are more likely to receive a cooperative response than if you scowl fiercely and hurl insults. If you speak directly to someone, you are more likely to get what you want than if you complain to the management.

Many of us have been smoking for so long that we sometimes forget that others are not used to the aroma of burning tobacco. We're human, and like everyone else we occasionally offend unknowingly. But most of us are open to friendly suggestions and comments and quite willing to modify our behavior to accommodate others.

Smokers are people, too. We laugh and cry. We have hopes, dreams, aspirations. We have children, and mothers, and pets. We eat hamburgers with everything on them and salute the flag at Fourth of July picnics. We hope you'll remember that the next time a smoker lights up in public.

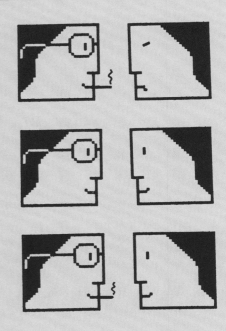

Just a friendly reminder from your local Smokers' Rights Association.

2. We would like to remind nonsmokers that courtesy is a two-way street. If you politely request that someone not smoke you are more likely to receive a cooperative response than if you scowl fiercely and hurl insults. If you speak directly to someone, you are more likely to get what you want than if you complain to the management.

_____ a. Nonsmokers have not been polite to smokers.

_____ b. Nonsmokers should never complain to the management.

_____ c. Smokers have always been cooperative.

_____ d. If nonsmokers were more polite, smokers would be more cooperative.

3. Smokers are people, too. We laugh and cry. We have hopes, dreams, aspirations. We have children, and mothers, and pets. . . . We hope you'll remember that the next time a smoker lights up in public.

_____ a. Smokers are not always treated like people.

_____ b. Nonsmokers should be nicer to smokers because they have mothers.

_____ c. When smokers light up in public, we should remember that we all have many things in common.

_____ d. Having a pet makes you a nice person.

Evaluating a Point of View

1. Check (✔) all of the following that are assumptions of this passage.

_____ a. Secondary smoking (being near people who smoke) can kill you.

_____ b. Smokers might be uncooperative if nonsmokers are not polite.

_____ c. Smokers are people too.

2. Now look at the statements listed under question 1. Check (✔) all those with which you agree.

Discussion

1. Who do you think wrote this advertisement? What purpose does it serve?

2. What is your reaction to this advertisement? Is your opinion of smokers different now than before you read it?

3. What do you think makes the ad persuasive? Unpersuasive?

Composition

Develop an anti- or prosmoking advertisement.

Before You Begin   1. Why do children begin to smoke?

2. Do you believe that children should be discouraged from beginning to smoke?

3. Should governments take actions to control advertising aimed at children?

Some magazines and newspapers present "special reports," often the result of long-term research, on topics of particular interest to their readers. When this kind of report suggests that it has uncovered hidden information, it is called an exposé (pronounced *expozAY*). The exposé that follows is from *Reader's Digest,* which claims to be the "world's most widely read magazine." Originating in the United States, it is published throughout the world, in 14 languages and in editions for the blind. The article that follows, however, is directed especially at U.S. citizens.

Below are the title, the epigram, and some emphasized quotes that appeared with this article. On the basis of these, what do you expect the article to be about?

AMERICA'S NEW MERCHANTS OF DEATH

Pushed by decreasing sales at home, U.S. tobacco companies are marketing cigarettes abroad. Among those lured by their clever advertising: the world's children. And Washington is lending a hand.

"From television ads we know that everyone in America smokes."
—Georgina Becci, age 13,
Buenos Aires, Argentina

"I feel a lot more important smoking Lucky Strike—it costs more and has a lot of class. It's an American original!"
—Francisco Queman, 16,
Santiago, Chile

"I like Parliaments the best, but if I were a boy I'd probably be smoking Marlboros. They make the boys feel like men."
—Huang Mei-Chun, 13,
Taipei, Taiwan

Skimming

The theme or main idea of this article is found in paragraphs 5 and 6. Read these first and then skim* the article to discover how children worldwide are made smokers. Your teacher may want you to do Vocabulary from Context exercise 1 on pages 152–54 before you begin reading.

---

* For an introduction to skimming, see Unit 1.

AMERICA'S NEW MERCHANTS OF DEATH

1 IN GERMANY, three women in black miniskirts set up a table beside a Cadillac in the center of Dresden. In exchange for an empty pack of local cigarettes, they offer passersby a pack of Lucky Strikes and a leaflet that reads: "You just got hold of a nice piece of America. Lucky Strike is the original...a real classic." Says German physician Bernhard Humburger, who studies youth smoking, "Adolescents time and again receive cigarettes at such promotions."

2 • A Jeep decorated with the yellow Camel logo pulls up in front of a high school in Buenos Aires. The driver, a blond woman, begins handing out cigarettes to 15- and 16-year-olds during their lunch break.

3 • In Malaysia, a man responds to a television commercial for "Salem High Country Holidays." When he tries to book a trip, he is refused; the $2.5-million-a-year operation exists only to advertise Salem on TV. This promotes Salem cigarettes without breaking the law.

4 • At a video arcade in Taipei, free U.S. cigarettes lie atop each game. "As long as they're here, I may as well try one," says a high-school girl in a Chicago Bears T-shirt. Before the United States entered the Taiwanese cigarette market, such giveaways were uncommon at places frequented by adolescents.

5 A *Reader's Digest* investigation covering 20 countries on five continents has revealed that millions of children are being lured into nicotine addiction by U.S. cigarette makers. In several nations, U.S. tobacco companies have being fighting laws that curtail cigarette use by young people and are cleverly violating the spirit of the curbs on advertising. Their activities clearly show a disregard for public health.

6 But the most shocking finding is that children are being lured into smoking in the name of the United States itself. In some countries, tobacco companies never would have gotten a start without the help of a powerful ally: the U.S. government.

7 Although domestic sales have dropped for eight straight years, and by the year 2000 only one in seven people in the U.S. will likely smoke, sales outside the U.S. have more than tripled since 1985. Smoking rates in developing countries are climbing more than two percent a year. Most troubling is the rise in youth smoking. In the Philippines, 22.7 percent of people under 18 smoke. In some Latin American cities, the teenage rate is a shocking 50 percent. In Hong Kong, children as young as seven are smoking.

8 Why are the young so important? Because millions of adult smokers either kick their habit or die each year, the cigarette industry depends on attracting new customers. Most smokers begin between ages 12 and 16; if a young person hasn't begun by 18, he or she is unlikely ever to smoke.

9 "Tobacco is a growth industry, and we are gaining in volume and share in markets around the world," Philip Morris assured stockholders in its 1991 annual report.

10 "Growth prospects internationally have never been better," reported Dale Sisel, chief executive officer of R.J. Reynolds (RJR) Tobacco International at last summer's international tobacco conference in Raleigh, N.C. "We all produce and sell a legal product that more than one billion consumers around the world use every single day."

11 Unmentioned at the conference was the fact that smoking is one of the leading causes of premature death, linked to cancers of the mouth, lung, esophagus, kidney, pancreas, bladder, and cervix, as well as to heart disease. Or that, according to the World Health Organization, tobacco will prematurely kill 200 million who are now children and eventually wipe out ten percent of the world's population. This grim prospect is due in no small part to the spectacular U.S. invasion of international markets.

12 "The American people need to know precisely how their companies and government are promoting smoking among the world's children," says Dr. Carlos Ferreyra Nunez, president of the Argentine Association of Public Health. "If they knew the full story, I believe they would stop this outrage."

13 Here is that story.

Pervasive Influence

14 TOBACCO ADVERTISING is more pervasive in other parts of the world than in the U.S. African merchants can get their shops painted to look like a pack of Marlboros. The Camel logo appears on store awnings and taxis in Warsaw. Christmas trees in Malaysian discos are decorated free by Kent—with balls and stars bearing the Kent logo. In Mexico, one in five TV commercials is for cigarettes. On an average day, 60 spots for U.S. brands appear on Japanese TV, many of them during programs watched by teens.

15 Although their marketing budgets are secret, tobacco companies have increased their spending for international advertising, adding substantially to the $4 billion spent yearly in the United States. "It's crucial for them," says Richard Pollay, professor of marketing at the University of British Columbia. "Familiarity in advertising leads to trust."

16 Tobacco spokespeople insist that cigarette advertising draws only people who already smoke. But an ad executive who worked until recently on the Philip Morris account disagrees. "You don't have to be a genius to figure out what's going on. Just look at the ads. It's ridiculous for them to deny that a cartoon character like Joe Camel isn't attractive to kids."

17 Dr. John L. Clowe, president of the American Medical Association, says, "It is clear that advertising encourages tobacco use among children. And, despite tobacco-industry denials, ads like Joe Camel are especially appealing to adolescents, equating smoking with sex, athleticism, even success."

18 Numerous independent studies support this view. Time and again they have shown that cigarette advertising creates an environment in which young people are more likely to smoke. That may explain why the U.S. Centers for Disease Control found that smokers between ages 12 and 18 prefer Marlboro, Newport and Camel—three of the most advertised brands.

Brand-Stretching

19 LIKE THE UNITED STATES, some developing countries have banned cigarette commercials on TV and radio. This doesn't stop the tobacco companies, however. To keep their logos before the public, they use "brand-stretching"—advertising nontobacco products and services named after their brands. Most of these items have special appeal to young people: Marlboro jeans and jackets, for example.

20 In Malaysia, a music store called Salem Power Station wraps customers' tapes and CDs in plastic bags bearing the Salem logo, and television carries an MTV-like show called "Salem Power-hits." A Budapest radio station broadcasts a rock program called the Marlboro Hit Parade, and in China, Philip Morris sponsors the Marlboro American Music Hour. Rock concerts are especially effective.

21 Sports sponsorship is even more insidious, for it implies

From *Reader's Digest*, April 1993. Reprinted without adaptations.

that smoking and fitness mix. Tobacco logos appear at events of every description, from cycling in Morocco to badminton in Indonesia. There's the Salem Open Tennis Tournament in Hong Kong and the Kent International Sailing Regatta, to name just two. U.S. tobacco companies spent $100 million sponsoring sports last year.

22 Tobacco companies regularly skirt laws against TV commercials. In Shanghai, Philip Morris sponsors spots for "The World of Marlboro." Except that cigarettes aren't mentioned, they are identical to a Marlboro commercial: the Marlboro man and his horse splash across a stream, the man dismounts and gazes toward mountains that look like the Rockies.

23 Unfortunately, many of the children who succumb to brand-stretching find habits that begin as cobwebs end up as steel cables. At a McDonald's in Malaysia, Sunil Ramanathan, 16, finishes off a Big Mac, lights a Marlboro and inhales deeply. He says he's smoked since he was ten. "I know smoking is bad for me, but I can't stop. I try to quit, but after one day I start again."

Easy Access

24 JUST OFF Taipei's busy Keelung Road, high-school students begin arriving at the Whiskey A Go-Go disco about 9 P.M., and soon the room is a sea of denim. On each table are free packs of Salems. Before long, the place is full of smoke.

25 "American tobacco companies spend more than a quarter of a billion dollars every year giving away cigarettes, many of which are smoked by children and teenagers," says Joe Tye, editor of the newsletter *Tobacco Free Youth Reporter*, "If they can get a youngster to smoke a few packs, chances are he'll be a customer for life."

26 Of the seven under-18 students assembled at the Beltram High School in Buenos Aires, five say they have been offered free Camels. None was asked his age. One, Ruben Paz, 16, said he

got his from a "blond, American-looking girl" handing out cigarettes from "the Camel Jeep" at the school door.

Sell America

27 "MANY AFRICAN children have two hopes," says Paul Wangai, a physician in Nairobi, Kenya. "One is to go to heaven, the other to America. U.S. tobacco companies profit from this by associating smoking with wealth. It's not uncommon to hear children say they start because of the glamorous lifestyle associated with smoking."

28 Cigarette advertising outside the United States focuses heavily on U.S. lifestyles; indeed, the ads are seen as a way of learning about the United States itself. A letter from secretarial students in China appeared in the Petaluma, California, *Argus-Courier:* "Every day we listen to the Marlboro Music Hour. We enjoy Elvis Presley and Michael Jackson. We smoke American cigarettes and wear American clothes. We are eager to gain more information about American life."

29 To hear the children of the rest of the world tell it, everyone in the U.S. smokes. The truth is, the United States has one of the *lowest* smoking rates—25.5 percent of the population.

30 Yet because of advertising, U.S. cigarettes are considered a sign of style and sophistication. In Bangkok, young Thais sew Marlboro logos on their jackets and jeans. At the city's Wat Nai Rong High School, 17-year-old Wasana Warathongchai says smoking makes her feel "sophisticated and cosmopolitan, like America." She associates Marlboros with "jeans and denim jackets, Pizza Hut, everything we like about America."

Friends in High Places

31 THE THEME of last summer's Raleigh conference was "The Tobacco Industry to the Year 2000," and on hand were two experts from

the U.S. Department of Agriculture to help the industry sell tobacco overseas.

32 …Wait a minute. Didn't the U.S. government decide in 1964 that cigarettes are a major cause of death and disease, and doesn't the U.S. government discourage its own citizens from smoking? Then how can we encourage people of other nations to smoke?

33 For many years, Japan, Korea, Taiwan and Thailand imposed strong trade restrictions on imported cigarettes. But U.S. tobacco companies joined forces with the Office of the U.S. Trade Representative (USTR) to enter these Asian markets.

34 The weapon Washington has used was Section 301 of the old Trade Act of 1974. It empowers the USTR to retaliate—with punitive tariffs—against any nation thought to have imposed unfair barriers on U.S. products.

35 Here is a recent example. When the USTR began an investigation of Japanese trading practices, a U.S. senator stepped in on behalf of the tobacco industry. He sent a letter to the Japanese prime minister suggesting he could not support a substantial U.S. military presence in the Pacific or help change anti-Japanese trade attitudes in Congress unless Japan opened its cigarette market.

36 "I urge that you establish a timetable for allowing U.S. cigarettes a specific share of your market," the senator wrote. "I suggest a total of 20 percent within 18 months." Three months later, the Japanese government agreed to open its markets more.

37 The results have been devastating. Before the U.S. tobacco companies arrived, smoking rates were declining slightly in Japan, but in the past five years, cigarette consumption by minors has increased 16 percent. Among Taiwanese high-school students, the smoking rate climbed 14 percent. The number of Thai smokers ages 15 to 19 increased 24 percent, with similar increases for Korean school boys.

38 "We were making progress in discouraging smoking, but all has been washed away by the flood of American advertising," says David D. Yen, chair of an antismoking group in Taiwan. "We want your friendship, but not your tobacco."

39 The U.S. cigarette business is booming. Exports are soaring, factories being built. And at the end of the rainbow lies China, with 300 million smokers—30 percent of the world market.

40 "This vastly larger marketplace means a whole new world of opportunities," RJR's Dale Sisel told the Raleigh conference. Expansion abroad, he continued, would "pave the way for a bigger and brighter future."

41 That kind of talk makes Argentina's Dr. Ferreyra Nunez shake with anger. "U.S. tobacco companies know their product causes death. Yet they promote smoking among children. What must these people think? Don't they have children of their own?"

You Can Stop This Outrage

42 PUBLIC OPINION is more powerful than the tobacco lobby. If you agree that it's wrong for the United States to promote the sale abroad of a health hazard that we discourage at home, write a letter to the President. Ask him to order the United States Trade Representative to stop helping the tobacco companies open cigarette markets overseas. Urge him to support curbs on tobacco advertising in other countries like those already in place here. And send copies of your letter to your Representatives in Congress.

43 The President's address is The White House, Washington, D.C. 20500. (Fax number: 202:555-2461)

AUTHOR'S NOTE: William Ecenbarger is a *Reader's Digest* staff writer. He is a previous winner of the George Polk Award for Investigative Journalism.

Comprehension

Answer the following questions. True/False items are indicated by a T / F preceding the statement.

1. T / F   U.S. tobacco companies encourage young people to smoke.

2. T / F   The tobacco companies deny that their advertising causes people to begin to smoke.

3. Why are young people an important market for cigarette makers?

   _____

4. T / F   Tobacco advertising is more pervasive in other parts of the world than in the U.S.

5. The article states that the investigation has covered five continents. What are the five continents from which examples are given in this article?

   _____

6. T / F   U.S. tobacco companies often break the law in other countries by their advertising.

7. What is "brand-stretching"? _____

8. T / F   Research shows that cigarette advertising creates an environment in which young people are more likely to smoke.

9. According to the article, why is sports sponsorship "insidious"?

10. T / F   The younger you are when you begin to smoke, the easier it is to quit.

11. Why does cigarette smoking outside the U.S. focus heavily on U.S. lifestyles?

   _____

12. T / F   In Asia, unlike other parts of the world, cigarette advertising has had little effect on smoking rates among minors.

13. The article states (paragraph 39) that "at the end of the rainbow lies China." What does this mean?

   _____

14. T / F   Doctors and public health officials in developing countries are not aware of the health risks of smoking.

15. The article refers to the U.S. government as a "powerful ally" of the tobacco industry. What has been the role of the U.S. government in helping sell cigarettes?

   _____

16. What does the author of this article want readers in the U.S. to do?

   _____

Critical Reading

1. This article was written in the 1990s. Why do you think the advertising practices described in this article continue? Who benefits from them in the U.S.? Who might benefit from them in your country/community? Are there ways that you benefit from them?

2. Did this article affect your attitudes toward

   - cigarette companies?
   - government officials?

   In your opinion, what made the article effective? Not effective?

Discussion/Composition

1. The following is from a report prepared for a tobacco company by a company specializing in marketing and research. The report recommends that the following types of advertising should be targeted at young people.

   - Present the cigarette as one of a few initiations into the adult world.
   - Present the cigarette as part of the illicit pleasure category of products and activities.
   - To the best of your ability (considering some legal constraints), relate the cigarette to "pot [marijuana]," wine, beer, sex, etc.
   - Don't communicate health or health-related points.

   Do you believe that there should be any control on the advertising of cigarettes targeted at young people? Support your position.

2. Write a letter to the President of the United States giving your opinion about the practices of U.S. cigarette companies internationally.

Vocabulary from Context

Exercise 1

Both the ideas and the vocabulary in the following exercise are taken from "America's New Merchants of Death." Use the context provided to determine the meanings of the italicized words. Write a definition, synonym, or description of each of the italicized vocabulary items in the space provided.

1. _____

2. _____

3. _____

4. _____

Usually *merchants* sell objects that people need, that make their lives better. However, the salespeople who *promote* cigarette smoking among young people may be making America a "merchant of death." Increasingly, American cigarette companies advertise, not in the U.S., but *overseas*. Outside the U.S., advertising shows cigarettes as part of the American lifestyle. In these ads, cigarettes ARE America, and smokers are presented as rich, attractive, and romantic. These ads are meant to *appeal to* young people, and as a result of these romantic pictures, children

5. _____

6. _____

7. _____

8. _____

9. _____

10. _____

11. _____

12. _____

13. _____

14. _____

15. _____

16. _____

17. _____

18. _____

19. _____

20. _____

21. _____

22. _____

23. _____

around the world are being *lured* into cigarette smoking at a very young age. Once they begin to smoke, they are unlikely to be able to stop; cigarette smoking becomes a *habit.* This nicotine *addiction* is very hard to break. If children *succumb to* this advertising and begin to smoke before they are 18 years old, they may become smokers for life.

Tobacco companies *deny* that they create new smokers; instead, they say that they only appeal to those who already smoke. However, experts say that it is clear that advertising encourages children to smoke.

The health effects on nations can be *devastating:* every year, millions of people die from the effects of smoking, and nations spend millions of dollars on related health costs.

The problem for U.S. cigarette companies is that smoking in the United States is decreasing. *Stockholders* want to see the companies they own make money. Because their sales in the U.S. have decreased, they are expanding their markets *abroad.* If companies can create more smokers, they will be rich.

Many nations realize the dangers of smoking and have tried to *ban* ads completely so that children never see them, or at least *curtail* smoking advertisements so that they are not widespread. But these controls are often not successful; by and large, they have not *curbed* cigarette advertising. Through their activities, U.S. companies *violate* the meaning of these laws even if they obey the wording of the laws. There are a number of ways in which these companies violate the *spirit* of laws intended to protect young people from cigarettes.

As one example, some companies don't advertise their cigarettes, but they give them away free. Even more *insidious* is the involvement of cigarette companies in sports events. They appear to be promoting a sports event when, in fact, they are selling cigarettes. It is harmful in the long run when cigarette companies *sponsor* sports events and music concerts which otherwise might not be performed for lack of money. At these events, young people see the names and familiar pictures of cigarette *brands* such as Camel all around them. If they see the familiar camel *logo,* for example, even if cigarettes are not mentioned, the young people will be more likely to choose that brand when they begin to smoke. As a result of advertising at sponsored events, youth live in an environment in which cigarette smoking is all around them and, when these ads are *pervasive,* smoking seems normal.

For those who worry about youth smoking, these actions are an *outrage,* but there is little they can do about their anger. Some governments have tried to pass laws to keep U.S. cigarettes out of

24. _____

25. _____

26. _____

27. _____

28. _____

29. _____

their countries; however, these *barriers* have been met with counteractions on the part of the U.S. It has *retaliated* by making it more difficult for these governments to sell their products in the U.S. The U.S. government creates trade *tariffs* that add costs to any products bought from these countries. These *punitive* actions punish nations for trying to protect their children.

The result has been an increase in young smokers worldwide. Cigarette sales are *soaring,* with great increases around the world. For U.S. companies in particular, the sale of cigarettes internationally is *booming*—new factories are being built and they have an increasing share of the world market.

Exercise 2

This exercise is designed to give you additional clues to determine the meanings of unfamiliar vocabulary items in context. In the paragraph of "America's New Merchants of Death" indicated by the number in parentheses, find the word that best fits the meaning given. Your teacher may want to read these aloud as you quickly scan* the paragraph to find the answer.

1. (1) Which word means *a printed sheet of paper?*

2. (1) Which word means *not a copy; the first?*

3. (1) Which word means *a perfect example; first class?*

4. (5) Which word means *lack of concern?*

5. (6) Which word means *friend; helper?*

6. (10) Which word means *expectations; chances?*

7. (21) Which word means *health?*

8. (31) Which word means *topic; subject; focus?*

Exercise 3

This exercise should be done after you have finished reading "America's New Merchants of Death." The exercise is designed to give you practice using context clues to guess the meaning of unfamiliar vocabulary in the article. Give a definition, synonym, or description of each of the words below. The number in parentheses indicates the paragraph in which the word can be found. Your teacher may want you to do these orally or in writing.

1. (1) passersby _____

2. (4) giveaways _____

*For an introduction to scanning, see Unit 1.

3. (4) frequented _____

4. (7) domestic _____

5. (9) growth industry _____

6. (36) timetable _____

Figurative Language and Idioms

In the paragraph indicated by the number in parentheses, find the phrase that best fits the meaning given. Your teacher may want to read these aloud as you quickly scan* the paragraph to find the answer.

1. (8) What phrase means *quit; become free of their addiction?*

2. (23) What phrase means *are harmless and easy to free oneself from in the beginning but become traps and are impossible to give up?*

3. (24) What phrase means *full of young people in blue jeans?*

4. (33) What phrase means *worked together?*

5. (39) What phrase means *the biggest prize; the greatest dream?*

6. (40) What phrase means *make possible; prepare the way?*

Stems and Affixes

The words in the left column are taken from "America's New Merchants of Death." Use your knowledge of stems and affixes** and the context to match each word on the left with its synonym or definition on the right. The number in parentheses indicates the paragraph in which the word can be found.

1. _____ miniskirt (1)   a. put in place; established; brought about

2. _____ invasion (11)   b. items sent or carried out of one country or another

3. _____ sophistication (30)   c. a short skirt worn several inches above the knee

4. _____ imposed (33)   d. arrival or incoming of something harmful

5. _____ imported (33)   e. knowledgeable in the ways of the world

6. _____ exports (39)   f. brought in from another country

_____

*For an introduction to scanning, see Unit 1.
**For a list of all stems and affixes taught in *Reader's Choice,* see the Appendix.

Dictionary Study

Many words have more than one meaning. When you use the dictionary to discover the meaning of an unfamiliar word or phrase, you need to use the context to determine which definition is appropriate. The sentences below are based on "America's New Merchants of Death." Use the portions of the dictionary provided to select the best definition for each of the italicized words below. Write the number of the definition in the space provided.

_____ 1. In Malaysia, a man responds to a television commercial for "Salem High Country Holidays"; when he tries to *book* a trip, he is refused by the office manager.

_____ 2. Tobacco spokespeople insist that cigarette advertising *draws* only people who already smoke.

_____ 3. Tobacco companies regularly *skirt* laws against TV commercials.

_____ 4. On TV in Shanghai, Philip Morris sponsors *spots* for "The World of Marlboro."

Vocabulary Review

Two of the words in each line below are similar or related in meaning. Circle the word that does not belong.

1. exported   curbed   curtailed

2. overseas   abroad   sophisticated

3. addiction   invasion   habit

4. tariff   barrier   addiction

5. devastating   booming   soaring

6. spots   machines   ads

7. glamorous   sophisticated   insidious

book \'bůk\ *n* [ME, fr. OE *bōc;* akin to OHG *buoh* book, Goth *boka* letter] (bef. 12c) **1 a :** a set of written sheets of skin or paper or tablets of wood or ivory **b :** a set of written, printed, or blank sheets bound together into a volume **c :** a long written or printed literary composition **d :** a major division of a treatise or literary work **e :** a record of a business's financial transactions or financial condition — often used in pl. ⟨the ∼s show a profit⟩ **2** *cap* **:** BIBLE 1 **3 :** something that yields knowledge or understanding ⟨the great ∼ of nature⟩ ⟨her face was an open ∼⟩ **4 a :** the total available knowledge and experience that can be brought to bear on a task or problem ⟨tried every trick in the ∼⟩ ⟨the ∼ on him is that he can't hit a curveball⟩ **b :** the standards or authority relevant in a situation ⟨run by the ∼⟩ **5 a :** all the charges that can be made against an accused person ⟨threw the ∼ at him⟩ **b :** a position from which one must answer for certain acts : ACCOUNT ⟨bring criminals to ∼⟩ **6 a :** LIBRETTO **b :** the script of a play **c :** a book of arrangements for a musician or dance orchestra : musical repertory **7 a :** a packet of items bound together like a book ⟨a ∼ of stamps⟩ ⟨a ∼ of matches⟩ **8 a :** BOOKMAKER **b :** the bets registered by a bookmaker; *also* **:** the business or activity of giving odds and taking bets **9 :** the number of tricks a cardplayer or side must win before any trick can have scoring value — **book·able** \'bů-kə-bəl\ *adj* — **book·ful** \'bůk-,fůl\ *n* — **in one's book :** in one's own opinion — **in one's good books :** in favor with one — **one for the book :** an act or occurrence worth noting — **on the books :** on the records
²book *adj* (13c) **1 :** derived from books and not from practical experience ⟨∼ learning⟩ **2 :** shown by books of account ⟨∼ assets⟩
³book *vt* (1807) **1 a :** to register (as a name) for some future activity or condition (as to engage transportation or reserve lodgings) ⟨∼ed to sail on Monday⟩ **b :** to schedule engagements for ⟨∼ the band for a week⟩ **c :** to set aside time for **d :** to reserve in advance ⟨∼ two seats at the theater⟩ ⟨were all ∼ed up⟩ **2 a :** to enter charges against in a police register **b** *chiefly Brit* **:** to charge (as a soccer player) with an infraction of the rules ∼ *vi* **1 :** to make a reservation ⟨∼ through your travel agent⟩ **2** *chiefly Brit* **:** to register in a hotel — usu. used with *in* — **book·er** *n*

draw \'dró\ *vb* **drew** \'drü\; **drawn** \'drón, 'drän\; **draw·ing** [ME *drawen, dragen,* fr. OE *dragan;* akin to ON *draga* to draw, drag] *vt* (bef. 12c) **1 :** to cause to move continuously toward or after a force applied in advance : PULL ⟨∼ your chair up by the fire⟩: as **a :** to move (as a covering) over or to one side ⟨∼ the drapes⟩ **b :** to pull up or out of a receptacle or place where seated or carried ⟨∼ water from the well⟩ ⟨drew a gun⟩; *also* **:** to cause to come out of a container ⟨∼ water for a bath⟩ **2 :** to cause to go in a certain direction (as by leading) ⟨drew him aside⟩ **3 a :** to bring by inducement or allure : ATTRACT ⟨honey ∼s flies⟩ **b :** to bring in or gather from a specified group or area ⟨a college that ∼s its students from many states⟩ **c :** BRING ON, PROVOKE ⟨drew enemy fire⟩ **d :** to bring out by way of response : ELICIT ⟨drew cheers from the audience⟩ **e :** to receive in the course of play ⟨the batter *drew* a walk⟩ ⟨∼ a foul⟩ **4 :** INHALE ⟨drew a deep breath⟩ **5 a :** to extract the essence from ⟨∼ tea⟩ **b :** EVISCERATE ⟨plucking and ∼ing a goose before cooking⟩ **c :** to derive to one's benefit ⟨drew inspiration from the old masters⟩ **6 :** to require (a specified depth) to float in ⟨a ship ∼s 12 feet of water⟩ **7 a :** ACCUMULATE, GAIN ⟨∼ing interest⟩ **b :** to take (money) from a place of deposit **c :** to use in making a cash demand ⟨∼ing a check against his account⟩ **d :** to receive regularly or in due course ⟨∼ a salary⟩ **8 a :** to take (cards) from a stack or from the dealer **b :** to receive or take at random

skirt \'skərt\ *n* [ME, fr. ON *skyrta* shirt, kirtle — more at SHIRT] (14c) **1 a** (1) **:** a free-hanging part of an outer garment or undergarment extending from the waist down (2) **:** a separate free-hanging outer garment or undergarment usu. worn by women and girls covering some or all of the body from the waist down **b :** either of two usu. leather flaps on a saddle covering the bars on which the stirrups are hung **c :** a cloth facing that hangs loosely and usu. in folds or pleats from the bottom edge or across the front of a piece of furniture **d :** the lower branches of a tree when near the ground **2 a :** the rim, periphery, or environs of an area **b** *pl* **:** outlying parts (as of a town or city) **3 :** a part or attachment serving as a rim, border, or edging **4 :** a girl or woman — **skirt·ed** *adj*
²skirt *vt* (1602) **1 :** to form or run along the border or edge of : BORDER **2 a :** to provide a skirt for **b :** to furnish a border or shield for **3 a :** to go or pass around or about; *specif* **:** to go around or keep away from in order to avoid danger or discovery **b :** to avoid esp. because of difficulty or fear of controversy ⟨∼ed the issue⟩ **c :** to evade or miss by a narrow margin ⟨having ∼ed disaster —Edith Wharton⟩ ∼ *vi* **:** to be, lie, or move along an edge or border — **skirt·er** *n*

spot \'spät\ *n* [ME; akin to MD *spotte* stain, speck, ON *spotti* small piece] (13c) **1 :** a taint on character or reputation : FAULT ⟨the only ∼ on the family name⟩ **2 a :** a small area visibly different (as in color, finish, or material) from the surrounding area **b** (1) **:** an area marred or marked (as by dirt) (2) **:** a circumscribed surface lesion of disease (as measles) or decay ⟨∼s of rot⟩ ⟨rust ∼s on a leaf⟩ **c :** a conventionalized design used on playing cards to distinguish the suits and indicate values **3 :** an object having a specified number of spots or a specified numeral on its surface **4 :** a small quantity or amount : BIT **5 a :** a particular place, area, or part **b :** a small extent of space **6** *pl usu* **spot :** a small croaker (*Leiostomus xanthurus*) of the Atlantic coast with a black spot behind the opercula **7 a :** a particular position (as in an organization or a hierarchy) **b :** a place or appearance on an entertainment program **8 :** SPOTLIGHT **9 :** a position usu. of difficulty or embarrassment **10 :** a brief announcement or advertisement broadcast between scheduled radio or television programs **11 :** a brief segment or report on a broadcast esp. of news — **on the spot 1 :** at once : IMMEDIATELY **2 :** at the place of action **3 a :** in a responsible or accountable position **b :** in a difficult or trying situation
²spot *vb* **spot·ted; spot·ting** *vt* (14c) **1 :** to stain the character or reputation of : DISGRACE **2 :** to mark in or with a spot : STAIN **3 :** to locate or identify by a spot **4 a :** to single out : IDENTIFY; *esp* **:** to note as a known criminal or a suspicious person **b :** DETECT, NOTICE ⟨∼ a mistake⟩ **c** (1) **:** to locate accurately ⟨∼ an enemy position⟩ (2) **:** to cause to strike accurately ⟨∼ the battery's fire⟩ **5 a :** to lie at intervals in or over : STUD **b :** to place at intervals or in a desired spot ⟨∼ field telephones⟩ **c :** to fix in or as if in the beam of a spotlight **d :** to schedule in a particular spot or at a particular time **6 :** to remove a spot from **7 :** to allow as a handicap ∼ *vi* **1 :** to become stained or discolored in spots **2 :** to cause a spot **3 :** to act as a spotter; *esp* **:** to locate targets **4 :** to experience abnormal and sporadic bleeding in small amounts from the uterus — **spot·ta·ble** \'spä-tə-bəl\ *adj*

From *Merriam-Webster's Collegiate Dictionary* (Springfield, Mass.: Merriam-Webster).

Reading Selection 2
Magazine Article

Before You Begin   1. Why do people get married? Why do some people choose never to marry?

2. How do you think young people who are considering marriage should be prepared? Is it the responsibility of the family, the school, or religious institutions?

3. If you were to design a high school course to prepare young people for married life, what topics would you include?

A high school teacher in Oregon has developed an unusual course for helping young people make intelligent decisions about marriage. Read the following article to see how you feel about Mr. Allen's "Conjugal Prep." Then answer the Comprehension questions. You may want to do the Vocabulary from Context exercise on pages 160–61 before you begin reading.

Comprehension

Answer the following questions. Your teacher may want you to answer orally, in writing, or by underlining appropriate portions of the text. True/False items are indicated by a T / F preceding the statement.

1. T / F   The course taught by Cliff Allen requires students to marry, buy a house, and get a divorce.

2. T / F   Allen believes that traditional courses do not adequately prepare young people for married life.

3. What are the nitty-gritty problems that Allen's students must face during the course?

   _____

   _____

4. T / F   One member of a "newlywed couple" must get a job.

5. How long does the course last? _____ How long are the couples "married"?

   _____

6. What are some of the events of married life that the students "experience"? _____

   _____

7. What are examples of the disasters that strike couples in the eighth week of the course?

   _____

   _____

Conjugal Prep

1   The bridegroom, dressed in a blue blazer and brown suede Adidas sneakers, nervously cleared his throat when his bride, in traditional white, walked down the classroom aisle. As the mock minister led the students—and ten other couples in the room—through the familiar marriage ceremony, the giggles almost drowned him out. But it was no laughing matter. In the next semester, each "couple" would buy a house, have a baby—and get a divorce.

2   In a most unusual course at Parkrose (Ore.) Senior High School, social-science teacher Cliff Allen leads his students through the trials and tribulations of married life. Instead of the traditional course, which dwells on the psychological and sexual adjustments young marrieds must face, Allen exposes his students to the nitty-gritty problems of housing, insurance and child care. "No one tells kids about financial problems," says Allen, 36. "It's like sex—you don't talk about it in front of them."

3   Students act out in nine weeks what normally takes couples ten years to accomplish. In the first week, one member of each couple is required to get an after-school job—

a real one. During the semester, the salary, computed on a full-time basis with yearly increases factored in, serves as the guideline for their lifestyle. The third week, the couples must locate an apartment they can afford and study the terms of the lease.

4   **Disaster:** In the fifth week, the couples "have a baby" and then compute the cost by totaling hospital and doctor bills, prenatal and postnatal care, baby clothes and furniture. In week eight, disaster strikes: the marriages are strained to the breaking point by such calamities as

a mother-in-law's moving in, death, or imprisonment. It's all over by week nine (the tenth year of marriage). After lectures by marriage counselors and divorce lawyers and computations of alimony and child support, the students get divorced.

5   Allen's course, which has "married" 1,200 students since its inception five years ago, is widely endorsed by parents and students. Some of the participants have found the experience chastening to their real-life marital plans. "Bride" Valerie Payne, 16, and her "groom," David Cooper, 19, still plan to marry in July, but, said Cooper, the course pointed out "the troubles you can have." The course was more unsettling to Marianne Baldrica, 17, who tried "marriage" last term with her boyfriend Eric Zook, 18. "Eric and I used to get along pretty well before we took the course together," Marianne said. "But I wanted to live in the city, he wanted the country. He wanted lots of kids, I wanted no kids. It's been four weeks since the course ended and Eric and I are just starting to talk to each other again."

—Linda Bird Francke with Mary Alice Kellogg in Parkrose, Ore.

8.   How has the course affected the marriage plans of some of the students? _____

_____

9.   Do you think young people in your country/community should be required to take such a course?

_____

10.   Would this course be of interest to gay and lesbian students? _____

_____

"Congual Prep," *Newsweek.*

Discussion/Composition

1. Compare and contrast the customs and values of the United States (as revealed in this article) with those of your country or community with respect to the following areas:

   a. age at which people marry

   b. role of the school in preparing young people for marriage

   c. amount of individual freedom in choosing marriage partners

   d. "crises" likely to be faced by married couples

2. Marriage rates in the United States are dropping. Here are some predictions for the twenty-first century.

   • Nearly one-quarter of adults will never marry.
   • The divorce rate will level off, but it will still be more than twice as high as it was in the 1970s.
   • Before they marry for the first time, more and more couples will live together. (That rate more than quadrupled in the last three decades of the twentieth century.)

   a. Are the predictions above likely to prove true also for your country/community? Why do you think this is or isn't the case?

   b. What do you think are reasons why people in the U.S. might be marrying later? Why do you think more people never marry?

   c. Why do you think courses such as the one described in "Conjugal Prep" are being developed?

Vocabulary from Context

Both the ideas and the vocabulary in the following passage are taken from "Conjugal Prep." Use the context provided to determine the meanings of the italicized words. Write a definition, synonym, or description of each of the italicized vocabulary items in the space provided.

1. _____

2. _____

3. _____

    In Mr. Allen's high school class, all the students have to "get married." However, the wedding ceremonies are not real ones but imitations. These *mock* ceremonies sometimes become so noisy that the loud laughter *drowns out* the voice of the "minister." Even the two students getting married often begin to *giggle*.

4. _____

    The teacher, Mr. Allen, believes that marriage is a difficult and serious business. He wants young people to understand that there are many changes that must take place after marriage. He believes that the need for these psychological and financial *adjustments* should be understood before people marry.

5. _____

6. _____

7. _____

8. _____

9. _____

10. _____

11. _____

Mr. Allen doesn't only introduce his students to major problems faced in marriage such as illness or unemployment. He also *exposes* them to the *nitty-gritty* problems they will face every day. He wants to introduce young people to all the *trials and tribulations* that can *strain* a marriage to the breaking point. He even familiarizes his students with the problems of divorce and the fact that divorced men must pay child support money for their children and sometimes pay monthly *alimony* to their wives.

It has been *unsettling* for some of the students to see the problems that a married couple often faces. Until they took the course, they had not worried much about the problems of marriage. However, both students and parents feel that Mr. Allen's course is valuable and have *endorsed* the course publicly. Their statements and letters supporting the class have convinced the school to offer the course again.

Cartoonists Look at Marriage

On page 162 are some cartoonists' views of marriage that have appeared in newspapers in the United States.

1. Which cartoons do you find amusing? Which ones would not be found amusing in your country/community?

2. Do any of these cartoons illustrate problems for which Allen's course attempts to prepare young people?

3. Are there situations presented here that reveal universal problems presented by marriage?

LOVE HANDLES By H. Brown

SALLY FORTH by Greg Howard

SALLY FORTH

Doonesbury By Garry Trudeau

Reading Selection 3
Science Reporting

Before You Begin

1. Here are some common English sayings. What do they mean? Do they contain some elements of truth? Are there similar sayings in the languages you speak?

   a. Like father, like son.
   b. He's a chip off the old block.
   c. The apple never falls far from the tree.

2. How might recent discoveries in genetics contribute to an understanding of the assumptions that underlie these sayings?

3. In discussions of personality, most explanations can be described as emphasizing "nature" or "nurture." Where do you stand with regard to these explanations?

4. Would you care if others had a copy of your medical records and learned about your genetic makeup?

Recent discoveries by scientists working on the Human Genome Project have been reported in scholarly publications and the popular press. They report success in mapping the human genome. Gene mapping is the process of identifying which genes lie where on the DNA strands that make up biological inheritance. The following article, which appeared in newspapers across the United States, examines potential dangers of the research.

Skimming and Scanning

Skim the article quickly to discover the author's main ideas, and study the accompanying illustration. Then scan to answer the following questions.*

1. Look at the illustration on page 165. What is the human genome?

2. What sort of discrimination could gene mapping encourage?

Now read the article more carefully. Your teacher may want you to do the Vocabulary from Context exercise on pages 168–69 before you begin reading.

For further discussion of issues surrounding genetic research, see "Grains of Hope," pages 258–60.

---

*For an introduction to skimming and scanning, see Unit 1.

Gene mapping may foster discrimination

■ Employers could reject new hires predisposed to disease.

by PAUL RECER

'Without adequate safeguards, the genetic revolution could mean one step forward for science and two steps backward for civil rights.'

—Sens. James Jeffords, R-Vt., and Tom Daschle, D-S.D.

WASHINGTON — Mapping the human genome opens a new era for medical science— and a new frontier for potential discrimination.

New genetic research may make it possible to identify an individual's lifetime risk of cancer, heart attack and other diseases. Experts worry that this information could be used to discriminate in hiring, promotions, or insurance.

Employers and insurers could save millions of dollars if they could use predictive genetics to identify in advance, and then reject, workers or policy applicants who are predisposed to develop chronic disease.

Thus, genetic discrimination could join the list of other forms of discrimination: racial, ethnic, age and sexual.

Genetic discrimination is drawing attention this week because of the first publication of the complete human genome map and sequence. Two versions, virtually identical, were compiled separately by an international public consortium and by a private company.

The journal *Nature* is publishing the work of the public consortium and the journal *Science* is publishing the sequence by Celera Genomics, a Rockville, Md., company.

Fear of such discrimination already is affecting how people view the medical revolution promised by mapping the human genome. A Time/CNN poll last summer found that 75 percent of 1,218 Americans surveyed did not want insurance companies to know their genetic code, and 84 percent wanted that information withheld from the government.

"There has been widespread fear that an individual's genetic information will be used against them," said Sen. Bill Frist, R-Tenn. "If we truly wish to improve quality of health care, we must begin taking steps to eliminate patients' fears."

The Equal Employment Opportunity Commission filed its first lawsuit challenging genetic testing last week in U.S. District Court in the Northern District of Iowa.

Burlington Northern Santa Fe Railroad was charged in the suit with conducting genetic testing on employees without their permission. At least one worker was threatened with dismissal unless he agreed to the test, the agency charges.

The EEOC said the genetic tests were being run on employees who filed for worker's compensation as the result of carpal tunnel syndrome, a type of repetitive motion injury common to keyboard operators. Some studies have suggested that a mutation on chromosome 17 predisposes to the injury.

A survey of 2,133 employers this year by the American Management Association found that seven are using genetic testing for either job applicants or employees, according to the journal *Science*.

Many experts believe the only solution to potential genetic discrimination is a new federal law that specifically prohibits it.

"Genetic testing has enormous potential for improving health care in America, but to fully utilize this new science, we must eliminate patients' fears and the potential for insurance discrimination," said Frist, the only physician in the Senate.

Frist and Sen. Olympia Snowe, R-Maine, are introducing legislation that would prevent insurance companies from requiring genetic testing and ban the use of genetic information to deny coverage or to set rates.

Writing this week in the journal *Science*, Senators James M. Jeffords, R-Vt., and Tom Daschle, D-S.D., say they both favor legislation prohibiting genetic discrimination. "Without adequate safeguards, the genetic revolution could mean one step forward for science and two steps backward for civil rights," they write. "Misuse of genetic information could create a new underclass: the genetically less fortunate."

From the *Ann Arbor News,* February 12, 2001.

The human genome

The human genome is the genetic code contained in the tightly coiled strands of 23 pairs of chromosomes in each cell's nucleus.

The Human Genome Project and Celera Genomics have been racing to be the first to decode the three billion base pairs that make up the human genome and to identify genes revealed in the process.

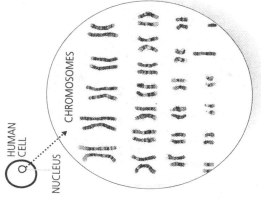

HUMAN CELL

NUCLEUS

CHROMOSOMES

Chromosomes

Mostly made of long chains of a chemical called DNA, chromosomes carry thousands of genes, the specific portions of DNA that contain hereditary instructions.

DNA

The hereditary instructions of genes are written in a four-letter code. Each letter corresponds to one of the chemical components of DNA: A, G, C, T.

A ADENINE
T THYMINE
G GUANINE
C CYTOSINE

DNA

The bases are linked so that A always links to T, and C always links to G.

Gene discovery

To find genes, computer programs have been developed that search the raw sequence for characteristic patterns of As, Ts, Cs and Gs.

GENE

ISOLATED GENE

The genes are scattered in portions along the DNA, but are read as whole sets of hereditary instructions.

DNA SEQUENCE

A T A T A T A T A T A
A T A T A T A T A T A
A T A T A T A T A T A
A T A T A T A T A T A

ISOLATED GENE

A T A T A T A T A T A
A T A T A T A T A T A
A T A T A T A T A

Scientists hope identifying disease-causing genes will improve detection and treatment of the disease and offer new approaches for prevention. There are up to 40,000 genes in the human genome.

Complete reports online

The world's two leading scientific journals are publishing reports by the competing teams online today. Science magazine is publishing the work by the private company Celera. Nature is publishing the work of an international public consortium.

Science magazine
▶ Web site:
www.sciencemag.org

Nature Science
▶ Web site:
www.nature.com

From the *Seattle Post-Intelligencer/New York Times*, February 12, 2001.

Comprehension

Exercise 1

Indicate if each of the statements below is true (T) or false (F) based on "Gene Mapping May Foster Discrimination" or inferences that can be drawn from the article.

1. T / F   As a result of research on the human genome, doctors will be able to make better decisions about their patients.

2. T / F   Genome mapping could help you make lifestyle decisions.

3. T / F   Businesses could use genetic information to make decisions about employees.

4. T / F   According to a Time/CNN poll conducted around the time of the publication of the article, the majority of Americans do not want insurance companies or the government to know their genetic code.

5. T / F   The Equal Employment Opportunity Commission supports widespread genetic testing as a way to improve the nation's economy.

6. T / F   A mutation on a chromosome may be a cause of injured or sore wrists.

Exercise 2

Examine the illustration describing the human genome. Answer the following questions. True/False questions are indicated by a T / F preceding the item.

1. T / F   The human genome contains the information that determines your physical appearance and other characteristics.

2. T / F   Each human cell contains a nucleus with 23 pairs of chromosomes.

3. T / F   Each chromosome contains thousands of genes.

4. T / F   Genes are sections of DNA that contain instructions for how you look and act.

5. T / F   There are four chemical components of DNA.

6. How many genes are contained in the human genome?

7. Where might you go for more information about the Human Genome Project?

Critical Reading

1. Following is a list of potential consequences of the genome project. Put a plus sign (+) next to those that you believe are positive and a minus sign (−) next to those that you believe are negative.

   a. _____ You will know your genetic history.

   b. _____ Genetic counselors will be able to give advice to couples who are considering having children.

   c. _____ Employers will be able to hire people with healthy family histories.

   d. _____ Doctors will be able to make more precise prescriptions.

   e. _____ Researchers will be able to suggest ways of improving babies.

   f. _____ Surgeons will be able to modify your genetic structure so that you can live longer.

   g. _____ Insurance companies will be able to save money by insuring only healthy individuals.

   h. _____ It will be possible for the government to issue ID cards with individuals' genetic profiles on them.

   i. _____ The armed forces will be able to recruit individuals whose genetic history indicates that they will be good soldiers.

   j. _____ Universities will be able to recruit students with strong academic potential.

   k. _____ Selective decisions before marriage could result in children whose genetic profiles promise genius in the arts, sports, or other areas.

   l. _____ Countries could improve their chances of healthy citizens by issuing guidelines for marriage and childbearing.

   m. _____ Parents could make medical decisions about their children long before a potential disease appeared.

   n. _____ Young people could learn about their health risks in time to alter their lifestyle choices and improve their chances for a healthy future.

2. Who are the following individuals, and what are their scientific qualifications? What role do they play in the debate over genetics and discrimination?

   a. Paul Recer
   b. Bill Frist
   c. Olympia Snowe
   d. Tom Daschle

Discussion/Composition

1. Which potential consequence of genetic mapping most excites or most worries you? Why?

2. Should an employer be required to hire a worker who is otherwise qualified for a job but whose family history indicates a risk of a serious illness? Consider the issue from the perspective of both employer and employee. Present your perspective either orally or in writing. Include reasons and examples.

Vocabulary from Context

Both the ideas and the vocabulary in the following passage are taken from "Gene Mapping May Foster Discrimination." Use the context provided to determine the meanings of the italicized words. Write a definition, synonym, or description of each of the italicized vocabulary items in the space provided.

1. _____

2. _____

3. _____

4. _____

5. _____

6. _____

7. _____

8. _____

9. _____

The gene is often called the building block of life because it is the smallest unit to carry information from one generation to another. Scientists working in the field of *genetics* are able to understand how one generation inherits important characteristics from the previous generation. But we are able to understand much more than merely why a particular family has a large number of red-haired children. We are also able to discover whether an individual is likely to live a long life or suffer from particular diseases. This is called *predictive genetics,* and the benefits of such research are many.

This description of the genetic code of the human being has long been the goal of scientists. Doctors are interested in this research because of the possibilities it would provide for treating long-term illnesses. The treatment of *chronic* diseases such as asthma and diabetes, for example, could be greatly improved by early diagnosis. There is also the possibility that an understanding of *mutations* in genetic sequences could be used to cure disease. Some researchers believe, for example, that genetic changes are responsible for many common diseases. Predictive genetics can also help in situations where there is a *predisposition* for illness. In some cases, a family history indicates a high probability of developing a disease. Genetic mapping could indicate if that will happen, thereby increasing the chances of early diagnosis and treatment.

While no one doubts the benefits of gene mapping, it is also true that there is a dark side to all this knowledge. As with all scientific advances, the possibility exists that knowledge would be used to violate basic human rights. For example, you might be denied a job or a chance to move up in the company because your genetic map indicates that you have a high probability of contracting a certain disease. The possibility that this would be used as a reason not to hire an employee or *promote* within the company is what worries people.

The *insurance* industry is another area where these concerns arise. Insurance companies provide financial security for people by promising that they will continue to be paid in the event that they are unable to work. There is widespread fear that employees needing *workers' compensation* would be denied because of their genetic history. This type of *discrimination* is illegal, just as it is illegal to reject you because of your gender or race. However, the dangers increased recently because of research reports published in

10. _____

11. _____

12. _____

13. _____

two respected journals, *Nature* and *Science,* which describe the work of scientists to map the human *genome*.

Many experts believe that the only way to address this risk is to pass national laws that *prohibit* discrimination. Such laws would forbid employers from failing to promote an employee or from *dismissing* an employee from the company merely because of genetic makeup. It is clear that such laws would not *eliminate* genetic discrimination entirely, but they would greatly reduce such practices.

Nonprose Reading
Poetry

Because the goal of reading is to (re)create meaning, we can say that reading involves solving a puzzle for which the clues are the words we read. Reading poetry* can be the most exciting kind of reading because more of the meaning seems hidden. The author provides the fewest but the richest clues. All of your reading skills will be needed if you are to "solve" the poems in this section.

Each of the following poems describes something. Read each poem carefully to discover what is being described; do not be concerned if you do not know the meaning of some vocabulary items. If you are having trouble arriving at an answer, read the poem again. If the poem is still not clear, answering the questions on page 174 will give you more clues.

Living Tenderly

My body a rounded stone
with a pattern of smooth seams.
My head a short snake,
retractive, projective,
My legs come out of their sleeves
or shrink within,
and so does my chin.
My eyelids are quick clamps.
My back is my roof.
I am always at home.
I travel where my house walks.
It is a smooth stone.
It floats within the lake,
or rests in the dust.
My flesh lives tenderly
inside its bone.

May Swenson

What is it? _____

Poems from *Poems to Solve,* by May Swenson (New York: Charles Scribner's Sons).
*For an explanation of nonprose reading, see Unit 1.

Southbound on the Freeway

A tourist came in from Orbitville,
parked in the air, and said:

The creatures of this star
are made of metal and glass.

Through the transparent parts
you can see their guts.

Their feet are round and roll
on diagrams—or long

measuring tapes—dark
with white lines.

They have four eyes.
The two in back are red.

Sometimes you can see a 5-eyed
one, with a red eye turning

on the top of his head.
He must be special—

The others respect him,
and go slow,

when he passes, winding
among them from behind.

They all hiss as they glide,
like inches, down the marked

tapes. Those soft shapes,
shadowy inside

the hard bodies—are they
their guts or their brains?

May Swenson

What is it? _____

By Morning

Some for everyone
    plenty

    and more coming

Fresh   dainty   airily arriving
    everywhere at once

Transparent at first
    each faint slice
    slow   soundlessly tumbling
    then quickly thickly a gracious fleece
    will spread like youth   like wheat
    over the city

Each building will be   a hill
    all sharps made round

    dark worn noisy arrows made still
    wide   flat   clean   spaces

Streets will be fields
    cars be   fumbling sheep

A deep bright harvest will be seeded
    in a night

By morning we'll be   children
    feeding on manna

    a new loaf on every doorsill

                    May Swenson

What is it? _____

Comprehension

"Living Tenderly": What is it?

1. What is the shape of its body?

2. What does its head look like?

3. T / F   Its legs don't move.

4. T / F   It carries its home wherever it goes.

5. T / F   It lives only in dry places.

"Southbound on the Freeway": What does the tourist see?

1. From where is the tourist observing the creatures?

2. What are the creatures made of?

   a. Describe their feet.

   b. Describe their eyes.

3. What is it that is described as "dark with white lines"?

4. What is different about the special ones:

   a. in appearance?

   b. in the way they affect the behavior of the other creatures?

5. What is a freeway?

"By Morning": What is it?

1. Which adjectives describe how it arrives?

2. How does it look at first?

3. What could make buildings suddenly look like hills?

4. What happens to the cars?

5. What could happen in the night to change a city like this?

Word Study
Context Clues

Exercise 1

In the following exercise do NOT try to learn the italicized words. Concentrate on developing your ability to guess the meanings of unfamiliar words using context clues. Read each sentence carefully and write a definition, synonym, or description of the italicized word on the line provided.

1. _____ It is difficult to list all of my father's *attributes* because he has so many different talents and abilities.

2. _____ Mary, the president of the family council, *conferred* upon Robert the title of vice president, because she thought he would do a good job.

3. _____ The main character in the movie was tall, fat, and middle-aged. The supporting actor was older, almost as *plump,* and much shorter.

4. _____ When Mark was in one of his *pedantic* moods, he assumed the manner of a distinguished professor and lectured for hours, on minute, boring topics.

5. _____ Many members of the old wealthy families in society held themselves *aloof* from Gatsby, refusing even to acknowledge his existence.

6. _____ I became angrier and angrier as Don talked, but I *refrained* from saying anything.

7. _____ Mr. Doodle is always busy in an *ineffectual* way; he spends hours running around accomplishing nothing.

8. _____ Laura was proud of the neat rows of *marigolds* in her flower beds, which she tended with great care.

9. _____ Most dentists' offices are *drab* places, but Emilio's new office is a bright, cheerful place.

10. _____ The inner and outer events of a plant are interdependent; but this isn't saying that the *skin, cortex, membrane,* or whatever you want to call the boundary of the individual, is meaningless.

Exercise 2

This exercise is designed to give you practice using context clues from a passage. Use your general knowledge along with information from the entire text below to write a definition, synonym, or description of the italicized word on the line provided. Read through the entire passage before making a decision. Note that some of the words appear more than once; by the end of the passage you should have a good idea of their meaning. Do not worry if your definition is not exact; a general idea of the meaning will often allow you to understand the meaning of a written text.

Babies Sound Off: The Power of Babble

There is more to the *babbling* of a baby than meets the ear. A handful of scientists are picking apart infants' utterances and finding that not only is there an ordered *sequence* of vocal stages between birth and the first words, but in *hearing-impaired* babies a type of *babbling* thought to signal an emerging capacity for speech is delayed and distorted.

"The traditional wisdom [among developmental researchers] is that deaf babies *babble* like hearing babies," says linguist D. Kimbrough Oller of the University of Miami (Fla.) "This idea is a *myth*." Oller reported his latest findings on hearing and deaf infants last week at a National Institutes of Health seminar in Bethesda, Md. He and his colleagues demonstrated some years ago that hearing babies from a variety of language communities start out by cooing and gurgling; at about 7 months of age, they start to produce *sequences* of the same syllables (for instance, "da-da-da" or "dut-dut-dut") that are classified as *babbling* and can be recorded and acoustically measured in the laboratory, with words or wordlike sounds appearing soon after 1 year of age. *Babbling*—the emitting of identifiable consonant and vowel sounds—usually disappears by around 18 to 20 months of age.

In a just-completed study, Oller and his co-workers found that repeated *sequences* of syllables first appeared among 21 hearing infants between the ages of 6 and 10 months; in contrast, these vocalizations emerged among 9 severely to profoundly deaf babies between the ages of 11 and 25 months. In addition, deaf babies *babbled* less frequently than hearing babies, produced fewer syllables, and were more likely to use single syllables than repeated *sequences*.

From *Science News.*

babbling: _____

sequence: _____

hearing-impaired: _____

myth: _____

Word Study
Stems and Affixes

Below is a list of some commonly occurring stems and affixes.* Study their meanings, and then do the exercises that follow. Your teacher may ask you to give examples of other words you know that are derived from these stems and affixes.

Prefixes		
multi-	many	multiply, multiple
peri-	around	periscope, perimeter
semi-	half, partly	semisweet, semicircle
tri-	three	triangle
ultra-	beyond, excessive, extreme	ultramodern
uni-	one	unicycle, unify, universe

Stems		
-aster-, -astro-, -stellar-	star	astronomy, stellar
-auto-	self	automobile, automatic
-bio-	life	biology
-cycle-	circle	bicycle, cycle
-mega-	great, large	megaton, megalopolis
-mort-	death	mortal, immortality
-phil-	love	philosophy
-polis-	city	metropolis
-psych-	mind	psychology
-soph-	wise	philosophy, sophomore

Suffixes		
-ity	condition, quality, state of being	unity, ability
-ness	condition, quality, state of being	sadness, happiness

---

*For a list of all stems and affixes taught in *Reader's Choice,* see the Appendix.

For each item, select the best definition of the italicized word or phrase, or answer the question.

1. To apply to some universities, you must fill out the application form and include a short *autobiography*.

   _____ a. sample of your writing   _____ c. list of courses you have taken

   _____ b. account of your life written by you   _____ d. list of schools you have attended

2. The police officer used a *megaphone*.

   _____ a. a portable radio   _____ c. an instrument to make one's voice louder

   _____ b. a long stick   _____ d. a telephone in the car

3. Dr. Swanson has written articles about *interstellar* travel.

   _____ a. underwater   _____ c. high-speed

   _____ b. long-distance   _____ d. outer space

4. Janet is interested in *autographs* of famous people.

   _____ a. pictures   _____ c. families

   _____ b. personalities   _____ d. signatures

5. An *asterisk* is a written symbol that looks like _____

   _____ a. /.   _____ c. %.

   _____ b. *.   _____ d. @.

6. The government is financing a study of the effects on humans of living in a *megalopolis*.

   _____ a. an apartment in a large building   _____ c. a dangerous part of a city

   _____ b. an extremely large city   _____ d. a city with a large police force

7. Children learning to ride bicycles probably already know how to ride a _____

   _____ a. unicycle.   _____ c. tricycle.

   _____ b. megacycle.   _____ d. motorcycle.

8. What is the perimeter of this rectangle?

   _____ a. 14   _____ c. 2

   _____ b. 4   _____ d. 5

9. *Nautical* means *pertaining to sailors, ships, or navigation.* Explain how the word *astronaut* is formed.

_____

_____

10. Why are the clothes that nurses, police officers, and soldiers wear called *uniforms*?

_____

_____

11. People who study population often speak of the world mortality rate. What is the opposite of *mortality rate*?

_____

_____

Exercise 2

Word analysis can help you to guess the meanings of unfamiliar words. Using context clues and what you know about word parts, write a synonym, description, or definition of the italicized word or phrase.

1. _____   I enjoy reading *biographies* of jazz performers.

2. _____   The Morrises hired a full-time nurse to help them care for their newborn *triplets*.

3. _____   The new art museum will be named for the *multimillionaire* who donated the money to build it.

4. _____   About 5.4 million people live in the Detroit *metropolitan* area.

5. _____   All the hospital's private rooms were occupied, so Michelle had to stay in a *semiprivate* one.

6. _____   Winston Churchill wrote a *multivolume* history of World War II.

7. _____   Race car drivers need to have good *peripheral* vision so they can see another car driving alongside them without turning their heads.

8. _____   That jeweler doesn't cut diamonds; he works mainly with *semiprecious* stones such as opals.

9. _____   He was shot during the robbery, but it is not a *mortal wound*.

10. _____   My teeth are falling out; my dentist wants me to make an appointment with a *periodontist*.

11. _____   The president's *popularity* with the voters has never been greater than it is today.

Exercise 3

Following is a list of words containing some of the stems and affixes introduced in this unit and the previous ones. Definitions of these words appear on the right. Put the letter of the appropriate definition next to each word.

1. _____ psychologist
2. _____ philanthropist
3. _____ sophisticated
4. _____ biochemist
5. _____ biology
6. _____ antibiotic

a. worldly-wise; knowing; finely experienced

b. a substance capable of killing microorganisms

c. the science of life or living matter

d. one who studies the chemistry of living things

e. one who shows love for humanity by doing good works for society

f. one who studies mental processes and behavior

---

7. _____ multicolored
8. _____ asteroid
9. _____ periscope
10. _____ astronomer
11. _____ unilateral
12. _____ bilateral

a. starlike; shaped like a star

b. affecting two sides or parties

c. having many colors

d. pertaining to, involving, or affecting only one side

e. a scientific observer of the planets, stars, and outer space

f. an optical instrument that allows a submarine to observe the surface from below the water

---

13. _____ cycle

14. _____ semicircle

15. _____ trilogy

16. _____ astrology

17. _____ ultraviolet

18. _____ ultranationalism

a. a recurring period of time in which certain events repeat themselves in the same order and at the same intervals

b. the study of the influence of the stars on human affairs

c. excessive devotion to national interests as opposed to international considerations

d. a series or group of three related dramas, operas, novels, etc.

e. invisible rays of the spectrum lying beyond the violet end of the visible spectrum

f. a half circle

Sentence Study
Restatement and Inference

Each sentence below is followed by five statements.* The statements are of four types.

1. Some of the statements are restatements of the original sentence. They give the same information in a different way.

2. Some of the statements are inferences (conclusions) that can be drawn from the information given in the original sentence.

3. Some of the statements are false based on the information given.

4. Some of the statements cannot be judged true or false based on the information given in the original sentence.

Put a check (✔) next to all restatements and inferences (types 1 and 2). *Note:* do not check a statement that is true of itself but cannot be inferred from the sentence given.

Example	Heavy smokers and drinkers run a fifteen times greater risk of developing cancer of the mouth and throat than nonsmokers and nondrinkers.

_____ a. Cancer of the mouth and throat is more likely to occur in heavy smokers and drinkers than in nonsmokers and nondrinkers.

_____ b. People who never drink and smoke will not get mouth or throat cancer.

_____ c. Heavy drinkers who run have a greater risk of developing cancer than nondrinkers.

_____ d. People who don't smoke and drink have less chance of getting cancer of the mouth and throat than those who smoke and drink heavily.

_____ e. People would probably be healthier if they did not drink and smoke too much.

Explanation

__✔__ a. This is a restatement of the original sentence. If heavy smokers and drinkers run a greater risk of developing cancer than those who do not drink or smoke, then cancer is more likely to occur in heavy smokers and drinkers.

_____ b. It is not true that people who never smoke and drink will never get mouth or throat cancer. We only know that they are *less likely* to get this kind of cancer.

_____ c. The word *run* in the original sentence is part of the phrase *to run a risk,* which means *to be in danger.* The sentence does not tell us anything about heavy drinkers who enjoy the sport of running.

---

*For an introduction to sentence study, see Unit 3.

_✔_ d. This is a restatement of the original sentence. If people who drink and smoke heavily have a greater chance of getting mouth and throat cancer than those who don't, then it must be true that those who don't smoke and drink heavily have less chance of developing this kind of cancer.

_✔_ e. This is an inference that can be drawn from the information given. If people who smoke and drink heavily run a high risk of developing cancer, then we can infer that people probably would be healthier if they didn't smoke and drink too much (heavily).

1. Nine out of ten doctors responding to a survey said they recommend our product to their patients if they recommend anything.

    _____ a. Nine out of ten doctors recommend the product.

    _____ b. Of the doctors who responded to a survey, nine out of ten doctors recommend the product.

    _____ c. If they recommend anything, nine out of ten doctors responding to a survey recommend the product.

    _____ d. Most doctors recommend the product.

    _____ e. We don't know how many doctors recommend the product.

2. This organization may succeed marvelously at what it wants to do, but what it wants to do may not be all that important.

    _____ a. The organization is marvelous.

    _____ b. The organization may succeed.

    _____ c. Although the organization may reach its goals, the goals might not be important.

    _____ d. What the organization wants is marvelous.

    _____ e. The author questions the goals of the organization.

3. This book contains a totally new outlook that combines the wisdom of the past with scientific knowledge to solve the problems of the present.

    _____ a. Problems of the past and present are solved in this book.

    _____ b. In this book, current knowledge and past wisdom are combined to solve current problems.

    _____ c. Only by using knowledge of the past and present can we solve problems.

    _____ d. None of today's problems can be solved without scientific knowledge.

    _____ e. This book is different because it combines the wisdom of the past with scientific knowledge.

4. Like other timeless symbols, flags have accompanied humankind for thousands of years, gaining ever wider meaning, yet losing none of their inherent and original force.

_____ a. In spite of losing some of their original force, flags are a timeless symbol that has accompanied humankind for thousands of years.

_____ b. Flags have existed for thousands of years.

_____ c. Timeless symbols typically gain wider meaning while not losing their inherent force.

_____ d. Thousands of years ago flags accompanied humankind, but through time they have lost their force.

_____ e. Because flags are considered a timeless symbol, they have gained continually wider meaning without losing their inherent original force.

5. When there is an absence of reliable information about drugs, the risks involved in using them are greatly increased.

_____ a. There is no reliable information about drugs.

_____ b. Using drugs is more dangerous when we don't know what effects and dangers are involved.

_____ c. The risks involved in using drugs have increased.

_____ d. People should try to find out about drugs before using them.

_____ e. There are no risks involved in using drugs if we have reliable information about them.

6. The project of which this book is the result was first suggested in the summer of 2000, in the course of some leisurely conversations at the foot of and (occasionally) on top of the Alps of western Austria.

_____ a. This book was written in 2000.

_____ b. This book was written in Austria.

_____ c. This book is a collection of conversations held in 2000.

_____ d. This book is the end result of a project.

_____ e. This book is about western Austria.

7. Los Angeles's safety record with school buses is generally a good one, but of course this record is only as good as the school bus drivers themselves.

_____ a. In spite of a generally good safety record for their school buses, Los Angeles school bus drivers are not very good.

_____ b. If school bus drivers are not very good, the town's school bus safety record will not be very good either.

_____ c. If cities wish to maintain good safety records with school buses, they should hire good school bus drivers.

_____ d. With better school buses, drivers will be able to maintain better safety records.

_____ e. Los Angeles's safety record with school buses has improved because better bus drivers have been hired.

8. Taxes being so high, the descendants of the wealthy class of the nineteenth century are being forced to rent out their estates to paying guests.

_____ a. In the nineteenth century, the wealthy class rented out its estates.

_____ b. Because of high taxes, families that were rich one hundred years ago now rent out their estates.

_____ c. Guests pay high taxes when they rent old estates.

_____ d. Some families that were once wealthy are having trouble paying their taxes.

_____ e. High taxes have changed the lives of some of the old wealthy families.

9. According to the definition of Chinese traditional medicine, acupuncture is the treatment of disease—not just the alleviation of pain—by inserting very fine needles into the body at specific points called loci.

_____ a. The author believes some people do not know that acupuncture can be used to treat illness.

_____ b. Finely pointed needles called loci are used in acupuncture.

_____ c. In Chinese traditional medicine, acupuncture is known to treat disease and alleviate pain.

_____ d. Those using acupuncture treat disease by placing needles into the body at specific points.

_____ e. Only those who practice traditional Chinese medicine use acupuncture.

10. It would be difficult to overpraise this book.

_____ a. This is a difficult book.

_____ b. This book deserves much praise.

_____ c. It is difficult not to overpraise this book.

_____ d. It is difficult to praise this book.

_____ e. The author of this sentence thinks this is an excellent book.

Paragraph Analysis
Reading for Full Understanding

The paragraph exercises in Units 1 and 3 require you to determine the main idea of a passage. This exercise and the one in Unit 11 require much more careful reading. Each selection is followed by a number of questions. The questions are designed to give you practice in

1. determining the main idea

2. understanding supporting details

3. drawing inferences

4. guessing vocabulary items from context

5. using syntactic and stylistic clues to understand selected portions of the paragraphs

Read each paragraph carefully. Try to determine the author's main idea while attempting to remember important details. For each of the questions below, select the *best* answer. You may refer to the passage to answer the questions.

Example

1   It is not often realized that women held a high place in southern
2 European societies in the 10th and 11th centuries. As a wife, the woman
3 was protected by the setting up of a dowry or *decimum.* Admittedly, the
4 purpose of this was to protect her against the risk of desertion, but in
5 reality its function in the social and family life of the time was much more
6 important. The *decimum* was the wife's right to receive a tenth of all her
7 husband's property. The wife had the right to withhold consent, in *all*
8 transactions the husband would make. And more than just a right: the
9 documents show that she enjoyed a real power of decision, equal to that
10 of her husband. In no case do the documents indicate any degree of
11 difference in the legal status of husband and wife.
12   The wife shared in the management of her husband's personal property,
13 but the opposite was not always true. Women seemed perfectly prepared
14 to defend their own inheritance against husbands who tried to exceed
15 their rights, and on occasion they showed a fine fighting spirit. A case in
16 point is that of María Vivas, a Catalan woman of Barcelona. Having agreed
17 with her husband Miró to sell a field she had inherited, for the needs of
18 the household, she insisted on compensation. None being offered, she
19 succeeded in dragging her husband to the scribe to have a contract duly
20 drawn up assigning her a piece of land from Miró's personal inheritance.
21 The unfortunate husband was obliged to agree, as the contract says, "for
22 the sake of peace." Either through the dowry or through being hot-
23 tempered, the Catalan wife knew how to win herself, within the context
24 of the family, a powerful economic position.

From Sylvia L. Thrupp, ed., *Early Medieval Society* (New York: Appleton-Century Crofts).

1. A *decimum* was _____

   _____ a. the wife's inheritance from her father.

   _____ b. the gift of money to the new husband.

   _____ c. a written contract.

   _____ d. the wife's right to receive one-tenth of her husband's property.

2. In the society described in the passage, the legal standing of the wife in marriage was _____

   _____ a. higher than that of her husband.

   _____ b. lower than that of her husband.

   _____ c. the same as that of her husband.

   _____ d. higher than that of a single woman.

3. What compensation did María Vivas get for the field?

   _____ a. some of the land Miró had inherited

   _____ b. a tenth of Miró's land

   _____ c. money for household expenses

   _____ d. money for Miró's inheritance

4. Could a husband sell his wife's inheritance?

   _____ a. no, under no circumstances

   _____ b. yes, whenever he wished to

   _____ c. yes, if she agreed

   _____ d. yes, if his father-in-law agreed

5. Which of the following is NOT mentioned as an effect of the dowry system?

   _____ a. The husband had to share the power of decision in marriage.

   _____ b. The wife was protected from desertion.

   _____ c. The wife gained a powerful economic position.

   _____ d. The husband was given control over his wife's property.

Explanation

1. (d) This is a restatement of a part of the passage. If you did not remember the definition of the word *decimum,* you could have scanned* for it quickly and found the answer in lines 6 and 7.

---

*For an introduction to scanning, see Unit 1.

2. (c) This is the main idea of the paragraph. The high place of women in the society is introduced in the first sentence. In lines 9 and 10 the author states that a woman enjoyed a legal power of decision equal to that of her husband. The last sentence tells us that, within the context of the home, women held a powerful economic position.

3. (a) This tests your understanding of details. In lines 18, 19, and 20 the author states that María Vivas forced her husband to agree to a contract giving her a piece of land from his inheritance.

4. (c) This is an inference. In lines 7 and 8 the author states that the wife could refuse to agree to any business agreements the husband might want to make. Thus, we can infer that a husband could only sell his wife's inheritance if she agreed. Furthermore, in lines 16, 17, and 18, the fact that María Vivas allowed her husband to sell a field she had inherited indicates that her agreement was necessary.

5. (d) Items a, b, and c serve as a summary of the ideas of the passage.

   (a) Lines 9 and 10 tell us that wives enjoyed a real power of decision; lines 12 and 13 state that a wife shared in the management of her husband's estate.

   (b) Lines 3 and 4 state that the purpose of the dowry was to protect wives from desertion.

   (c) The final sentence states that, within the context of the family, the wife was able to win a powerful economic position.

   (d) Nowhere does it state that a husband was given control over a wife's property, and in several instances the opposite is stated (see questions 3 and 4).

Paragraph 1

1   Today is the anniversary of that afternoon in April a year ago that I first
2   saw the strange and appealing doll in the window of Abe Sheftel's
3   stationery and toy shop on Third Avenue near Fifteenth Street, just around
4   the corner from my office, where the plate on the
5   door reads: Dr. Samuel Amory. I remember just
6   how it was that day: the first hint of spring floated
7   across the East River, mixing with the soft-coal
8   smoke from factories and the street smells of the
9   poor neighborhood. As I turned the corner on my
10   way to work and came to Sheftel's, I was made
11   once more aware of the poor collection of toys in
12   the dusty window, and I remembered the
13   approaching birthday of a small niece of mine in
14   Cleveland, to whom I was in the habit of sending
15   modest gifts. Therefore, I stopped and examined
16   the window to see if there might be anything
17   appropriate, and looked at the confusing collec-
18   tion of unappealing objects—a red toy fire engine, some lead soldiers,
19   cheap baseballs, bottles of ink, pens, yellowed stationery, and garish

From Paul Gallico, "The Enchanted Doll," in *Story and Structure*, ed. Laurence Perrine (New York: Harcourt, Brace and World).

20　cardboard advertisements for soft-drinks. And thus it
21　was that my eyes eventually came to rest upon the
22　doll tucked away in one corner, a doll with the
23　strangest, most charming expression on her face. I
24　could not wholly make her out, due to the shadows
25　and the film through which I was looking, but I was
26　aware that a tremendous impression had been made
27　upon me, as though I had run into a person, as one
28　does sometimes with a stranger, with whose
29　personality one is deeply impressed.

1. What made an impression on the narrator?

_____ a. the doll's unusual face

_____ b. the collection of toys

_____ c. a stranger he met at the store

_____ d. the resemblance of the doll to his niece

2. Why does the narrator mention his niece?

_____ a. She likes dolls.

_____ b. The doll looks like her.

_____ c. She lives near Sheftel's.

_____ d. He was looking for a gift for her.

3. Why did the narrator go past Sheftel's?

_____ a. He was on his way to work.

_____ b. He was looking for a present for his niece.

_____ c. He wanted to buy some stationery.

_____ d. He liked to look in the window.

4. The story takes place in the _____

_____ a. early summer.

_____ b. midsummer.

_____ c. early spring.

_____ d. late spring.

5. When was the story written?

_____ a. one year after the incident   _____ c. in the narrator's old age

_____ b. right after the incident   _____ d. on the narrator's birthday

6. Most of the things in the store window were _____

_____ a. expensive.   _____ c. neatly arranged.

_____ b. appealing.   _____ d. unattractive.

Paragraph 2

1   Linguists believe that the languages of about one-third of the human
2 race all developed from one Indo-European language. But who were
3 the speakers of this ancient language? Linguistic detective work offers
4 some clues. It is sometimes said that you can deduce a people's history
5 from the words they use. Study of some fifty ancient vocabularies has
6 led to a reconstruction of the lifestyle of the first Indo-Europeans, a
7 vanished people. From the words they used, it seems likely that they
8 lived a half-settled, half-nomadic existence. They had horses, oxen,
9 and sheep. They plowed, planted, worked leather, and wove wool.
10 They worshipped gods who are clear ancestors of Indian, Mediter-
11 ranean, and Celtic deities. However, exactly who the original
12 Indo-Europeans were and when they lived remains a hotly debated
13 mystery. According to an early theory, they lived in Mesopotamia, but

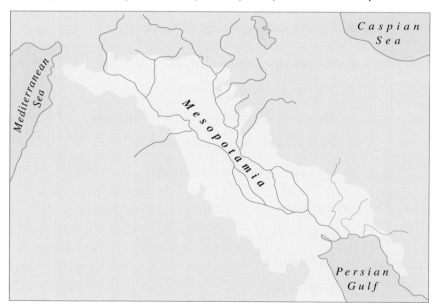

From *The Story of English* by Robert McCrum, William Cran, and Robert MacNeil (New York: Penguin, 1986).

14   this idea was exploded by nineteenth-century archaeology. Today, some
15   argue for the Krugan culture of the Russian steppes, others for the
16   farming culture of the Danube valley. The most widely accepted theory
17   locates the Indo-Europeans in a cold, northern climate where common
18   words for snow and wolf were important. None of these prehistoric
19   languages had a word for the sea. From this, and from our knowledge
20   of nature, it is clear that the Indo-Europeans must have lived some-
21   where in northern central Europe.

1. What would be a good title for this passage?

_____ a. In Search of Ancient Indo-Europeans   _____ c. Prehistoric Lifestyles in Europe

_____ b. The Mistakes of Early Archaeologists   _____ d. Prehistoric Vocabularies

2. According to the author, what has helped us understand the lifestyle of the original Indo-Europeans?

_____ a. studying their writings   _____ c. studying their gods

_____ b. studying prehistoric languages   _____ d. studying ancient climate data

3. None of the prehistoric languages studied had a word for *sea*. According to the passage, what kind of information about the Indo-Europeans does this provide?

_____ a. information about where they lived

_____ b. information about how they traveled

_____ c. information about when they lived

_____ d. information about what gods they worshipped

4. What does *exploded* mean in line 14?

_____ a. developed

_____ b. strengthened

_____ c. explained

_____ d. disproved

5. According to the passage, what was one thing that nineteenth-century archaeology showed?

_____ a. that the Krugan culture began in Mesopotamia

_____ b. that the first Indo-Europeans did not live in Mesopotamia

_____ c. that the earliest Indo-Europeans lived in Mesopotamia

_____ d. that there was a disastrous explosion in ancient Mesopotamia

6. What do some people think that the Krugan culture might be?

_____ a. a tribe that lived in Mesopotamia

_____ b. a farming culture in the Danube valley

_____ c. the original Indo-Europeans

_____ d. a tribe that lived near a sea

7. Where do you think this passage probably appeared?

_____ a. in an article meant for a general audience

_____ b. in an article meant for linguists

_____ c. in an article for specialists in archaeology

_____ d. in an article for specialists in history

Paragraph 3

1   It was not yet eleven o'clock when a boat crossed the river with a
2   single passenger who had obtained his transportation at that unusual
3   hour by promising an extra fare. While the youth stood on the landing-
4   place searching in his pockets for money, the ferryman lifted a lantern,
5   by the aid of which, together with the newly risen moon, he took a
6   very accurate survey of the stranger's figure. He was a young man of
7   barely eighteen years, evidently country bred, and now, as it seemed,
8   on his first visit to town. He was wearing a rough gray coat, which was
9   in good shape, but which had seen many winters before this one. The
10 garments under his coat were well constructed of leather, and fitted
11 tightly to a pair of muscular legs; his stockings of blue yarn must have
12 been the work of a mother or sister, and on his head was a three-
13 cornered hat, which in its better days had perhaps sheltered the grayer
14 head of the lad's father. In his left hand was a walking stick, and his
15 equipment was completed by a leather bag not so abundantly stocked
16 as to inconvenience the strong shoulders on which it hung. Brown,
17 curly hair, well-shaped features, bright, cheerful eyes were nature's
18 gifts, and worth all that art could have done for his adornment. The
19 youth, whose name was Robin, paid the boatman, and then walked
20 forward into the town with a light step, as if he had not already traveled
21 more than thirty miles that day. As he walked, he surveyed his
22 surroundings as eagerly as if he were entering London or Madrid,
23 instead of the little metropolis of a New England colony.

1. What time of year was it in this story?

_____ a. spring   _____ c. fall

_____ b. summer   _____ d. winter

From Nathaniel Hawthorne, *Selected Tales and Sketches,* ed. H. Waggooner Hyatt (Chicago: Holt, Rinehart and Winston).

2. At what time of day did Robin cross the river?

_____ a. morning

_____ b. midday

_____ c. late afternoon

_____ d. night

3. The boatman was willing to take Robin across the river because _____

_____ a. he wanted to make extra money.

_____ b. he saw that Robin was young and rich.

_____ c. he was going to row across the river anyway.

_____ d. he felt sorry for him because Robin looked poor.

4. The stockings that Robin wore were obviously ___

_____ a. well worn.

_____ b. very expensive.

_____ c. handmade.

_____ d. much too big.

5. From the way he looked, it was evident that Robin was _____

_____ a. a wealthy merchant's son.

_____ b. a country boy.

_____ c. a soldier.

_____ d. a foreigner.

6. Robin was apparently going to the town _____

_____ a. to buy new clothes.

_____ b. for the first time.

_____ c. for the first time in several years.

_____ d. on one of his regular trips there.

7. How did Robin appear as he walked into town?

_____ a. He was cheerful and excited.

_____ b. He was tired.

_____ c. He seemed very sad.

_____ d. He seemed frightened by his strange surroundings.

8. How far had Robin traveled?

_____ a. over thirty miles

_____ b. from Madrid

_____ c. from a nearby town

_____ d. from London

Paragraph 4 | 1   Fifty volunteers were alphabetically
          | 2   divided into two equal groups, Group A to
          | 3   participate in a seven-week exercise
          | 4   program, and Group B to avoid deliberate
          | 5   exercise of any sort during those 7 weeks.
          | 6   On the day before the exercise program
          | 7   began, all 50 men participated in a step-
          | 8   test. This consisted of stepping up and
          | 9   down on a 16-inch bench at 30 steps per
          | 10 minute for 5 minutes. One minute after
          | 11 completion of the step-test, the pulse rate
          | 12 of each subject was taken and recorded.
          | 13 This served as the pretest for the experiment.
          | 14 For the next 7 weeks, subjects in the experi-
          | 15 mental group (Group A) rode an Exercycle

16 (a motor-driven bicycle-type exercise machine) for 15 minutes each
17 day. The exercise schedule called for riders to ride relaxed during the
18 first day's ride, merely holding on to the handle bars and foot pedals as
19 the machine moved. Then, for the next 3 days, they rode relaxed for
20 50 seconds of each minute, and pushed, pulled, and pedaled actively
21 for 10 seconds of each minute. The ratio of active riding was increased
22 every few days, so that by the third week it was half of each minute,
23 and by the seventh week the riders were performing 15 solid minutes
24 of active riding.
25   At the end of the seven weeks, the step-test was again given to both
26 groups of subjects, and their pulses taken. The post-exercise pulse rates
27 of subjects in the experimental group were found to have decreased an
28 average of 30 heart beats per minute, with the lowest decrease 28 and
29 the highest decrease 46. The pulse rates of subjects in the control group
30 remained the same or changed no more than 4 beats, with an average
31 difference between the initial and final tests of zero.

1. How many people were in each group?

_____ a. 100   _____ c. 25

_____ b. 50   _____ d. 15

2. The step-test was given _____

_____ a. after each exercise period.

_____ b. at the beginning and at the end of the seven-week period.

_____ c. only once, at the beginning of the seven-week period.

_____ d. twice to the men in Group A and once to the men in Group B.

From James E. Haney, "Health and Motor Behavior: Measuring Energy Expenditures," *Research News.*

3. When were pulse rates taken?

_____ a. after each exercise period

_____ b. every day

_____ c. after the step-tests

_____ d. every time the ratio of active riding was increased

4. The exercise schedule was planned so that the amount of active riding _____

_____ a. increased every few days.

_____ b. varied from day to day.

_____ c. increased until the third week and then was kept constant.

_____ d. increased every exercise period.

5. What did Group A do in their program?

_____ a. They stepped up and down on a bench each day.

_____ b. They pushed and pulled on exercise handles every day.

_____ c. They rode on an Exercycle every day.

_____ d. They refrained from any exercise.

6. The post-exercise pulse rates of Group B were found on the average to have _____

_____ a. not changed.

_____ b. gone down 28 beats per minute.

_____ c. gone down 30 beats per minute.

_____ d. gone down 4 beats per minute.

7. This paragraph implies that _____

_____ a. most people do not get enough exercise.

_____ b. a high pulse rate is desirable.

_____ c. regular exercise can strengthen your heart.

_____ d. everyone should exercise 15 minutes a day.

Paragraph 5

1   In the second half of each year, many powerful storms are born in
2   the tropical Atlantic and Caribbean seas. Of these, only about half a
3   dozen generate the strong, circling winds of 75 miles per hour or more
4   that give them hurricane status, and several usually make their way to
5   the coast. There they cause millions of dollars of damage, and bring
6   death to large numbers of people.
7   The great storms that hit the coast start as innocent circling distur-
8   bances hundreds—even thousands—of miles out to sea. As they travel
9   aimlessly over water warmed by the summer sun, they are carried
10 westward by the trade winds. When conditions are just right, warm,
11 moist air flows in at the bottom of such a disturbance, moves upward
12 through it and comes out at the top. In the process, the moisture in this
13 warm air produces rain, and with it the heat that is converted to energy
14 in the form of strong winds. As the heat increases, the young hurricane
15 begins to swirl in a counterclockwise motion.
16   The average life of a hurricane is only about nine days, but it contains
17 almost more power than we can imagine. The energy in the heat
18 released by a hurricane's rainfall in a single day would satisfy the entire
19 electrical needs of the United States for more than six months. Water,
20 not wind, is the main source of death and destruction in a hurricane. A
21 typical hurricane brings 6- to 12-inch downpours resulting in sudden
22 floods. Worst of all is the powerful movement of the sea—the mountains
23 of water moving toward the low-pressure hurricane center. The water
24 level rises as much as 15 feet above normal as it moves toward shore.

1. When is an ordinary tropical storm called a hurricane?

_____ a. when it begins in the Atlantic and Caribbean seas

_____ b. when it hits the coastline

_____ c. when it is more than 75 miles wide

_____ d. when its winds reach 75 miles per hour

2. What is the worst thing about hurricanes?

_____ a. the destructive effects of water

_____ b. the heat they release

_____ c. that they last about nine days on the average

_____ d. their strong winds

From E. Hughes, "Hurricane Warning," *Reader's Digest.*

3. The counter-clockwise swirling of the hurricane is brought about by _____

_____ a. the low-pressure area in the center of the storm.

_____ b. the force of waves of water.

_____ c. the trade winds.

_____ d. the increasing heat.

4. Apparently the word *downpour* means _____

_____ a. heavy rainfall.

_____ b. dangerous waves.

_____ c. the progress of water to the hurricane center.

_____ d. the energy produced by the hurricane.

Discourse Focus
Prediction

Reading is an active process. Meaning does not exist only on the page or in the mind of the reader. It is created by an active *interaction* between reader and text. Based on their general knowledge and the information in a text, good readers develop predictions about what they will read next; then they read to see if their expectations will be confirmed. If they are not confirmed, readers reread, creating new predictions. Most often, however, readers are not greatly surprised; readers continue reading. This exercise is designed to give you practice in the process of consciously developing and confirming expectations. You will read an article, stopping at several points to consider what you expect to read about next. Readers cannot always predict precisely what an author will talk about next, but you can practice using clues from the text and your general knowledge to more efficiently predict content.

The Troubled State of Calculus
A Push to Revitalize College Calculus Teaching Has Begun

Calculus: a large lecture hall, 200 or so bored students, a lecturer talking to a blackboard filled with Greek symbols, a thick, heavy textbook with answers to even-numbered problems, a seemingly endless chain of formulas, theorems and proofs.

Example

1. Above are the title, the subtitle, and an inset from an article on calculus. On the basis of these, what aspect of calculus do you think the article might be about? List two possibilities.

   _____

   _____

2. Does the author seem to think that calculus instruction is successful or unsuccessful at the present time? _____ What words give you this impression? _____

   _____

Adapted from *Science News*.

Explanation

1. The main title indicates that calculus instruction is *troubled*. The subtitle tells us that there is a movement to improve calculus teaching. The inset describes a "typical," boring calculus class, suggesting what is troubled and what needs to be improved. Based on this information in the text you might have decided that the article would be about such things as current problems with calculus instruction and about proposals for improving instruction. If you have personal knowledge of calculus instruction, you may have some more specific ideas about the kinds of problems and solutions that might be mentioned.

2. Obviously the author has a negative opinion of calculus instruction. He refers to it as *troubled* in the main title and indicates a need to *revitalize* (to give new life to) it in the subtitle. The inset describes a *large* lecture hall, with *bored* students and *heavy* books: the opposite of a lively situation.

3. Before you continue reading the article, decide how you expect it to begin. Remember, you cannot always predict precisely what an author will do, but you can use knowledge of the text and your general knowledge to make good guesses. Which of the following seems the most likely beginning?

    a. The author will describe traditional ways of teaching calculus.

    b. The author will describe math instruction in general.

    c. The author will describe new ways to teach calculus.

    d. The author will describe the general state of calculus instruction.

Now read to see if your expectations are confirmed.

by Ivar Peterson

More than half a million students take an introductory calculus course in any given year, and the number is growing. A large proportion have no choice. Calculus is a barrier that must be overcome on the way to a professional career in medicine or engineering. Even disciplines like history now sometimes require some college mathematics. But for many people in the last few years who have passed through such a course, the word *calculus* brings back painful memories.

4. The article appears to be critical of current teaching practices. Is this what you expected?

5. Did you expect the article to begin with a general description of calculus instruction?

6. What do you expect to read about next? What words or phrases point in this direction? What do you know about calculus and schools in general that would lead you to predict this?

Now read to see if your expectations are confirmed.

In many universities about half of the students who take introductory calculus fail the course. A surprisingly large number must take the course several times to get through. At the same time, engineering and physical sciences professors complain that even the students who pass don't know very much about calculus and don't know how to use it.

"The teaching of calculus is a national disgrace," says Lynn A. Steen, president of the Mathematical Association of America, based in Washington, D.C., and a professor at St. Olaf College in Northfield, Minn. "Too often calculus is taught by inexperienced instructors to ill-prepared students in an environment with insufficient feedback," he says. "The result is a serious decline in the number of students pursuing advanced mathematics, and a majority of college graduates who have learned to hate mathematics."

7. Were your expectations confirmed? If not, why not? Did you misunderstand something in the previous section? Do you think your expectations were valid? Would they provide a better outline for the author than the one he used?

8. At this point, the author has summarized his criticisms of the teaching of calculus. What do you think he will say next?

_____

_____

Discuss your choices with your classmates. Then read to see if your expectations are confirmed.

Now a small group of educators has started a movement to change what is taught in an introductory calculus course, to improve the way it is taught, and to bring the teaching of calculus into the computer age. Earlier this year, 25 faculty members, administrators, scientists, and others representing diverse interests met at Tulane University in New Orleans to see what could be done.

One big surprise was a general agreement that there is room for change. When participants came to the meeting, says mathematician Peter L. Renz of Bard College in Annandale-on-Hudson, N.Y., although they recognized the problem, "we all believed that there was nothing we could do about calculus." Yet despite this pessimism, many of the participants brought worthwhile suggestions.

9. Were your expectations confirmed in these two paragraphs?

10. What do you think the author will do next? What aspects of the text and your general knowledge help you to create this prediction?

_____

_____

_____

Read to see if your expectations are confirmed.

A key question is the role of hand-held calculators and computers. For the price of a calculus textbook, students can buy a scientific calculator. "The first thing that one can do on that basis is to eliminate an awful lot of the routine problems," says mathematician Ronald G. Douglas, dean of the physical sciences school at the State University of New York at Stony Brook. The ideas are still important, and instructors may need some of these techniques to illustrate what is going on, he says, but drilling stu-dents in something that any calcula-tor or computer can now do becomes much less important.

The conference participants agreed that the routine use of calculators would help shift the focus of calculus back to its fundamental ideas and away from students mechanically plugging numbers into formulas to get "nice" answers. Until now, says Douglas, "all we've been teaching people in some sense has been a kind of pattern recognition."

11. Were your predictions confirmed?

12. What other kinds of problems and solutions do you predict are discussed in the final sections of this article? Be prepared to defend your predictions.*

_____

_____

_____

*The rest of this article is not reprinted here; however, a summary of the ideas can be found in the Answer Key.

Science Reporting

Supporting Data Proposals

Magazine Article

Comparison and Contrast

Short Story

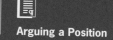
Arguing a Position

Reading Selections 1A–1B
Technical Prose and Science Reporting

Following are two magazine articles that present information about patterns of population growth. When writing about technical subjects, authors sometimes include graphics (such as graphs, tables, charts, and maps) because such visual aids present information clearly and concisely. You will need to use information from both the graphics and the text in these articles in order to complete the comprehension exercises.

Selection 1A   Magazine Graphic

Before You Begin

1. Imagine that twice as many people live in your community as live there now. What effects would the increased population have on the way you live, eat, and work?

2. Now imagine that the population has not increased where you live but that it has doubled in other countries. Would you care? Why or why not?

Check Your Assumptions

Readers begin reading with their own knowledge and assumptions. What we read may either confirm or contradict these beliefs and knowledge. Before you read "Six Billion . . . and Counting," answer these questions based on what you already believe about world population. Be sure to write down your guesses.

1. Is the population increasing in your country?

2. Is the world's population increasing?

3. Is the world's rate of population growth rising?

4. Do population predictions made today confirm predictions made in the past?

5. On which continent is population rising the fastest?

Getting Oriented

Look at the graphics that accompany "Six Billion . . . and Counting" to understand how the information is organized, and then answer the question that follows.

1. Which graphic(s) in the article would you look at to get information about each of the following?

   a. the population of individual countries

   b. total world population

   c. predictions about population

   d. growth of cities

   e. which parts of the world are most densely populated

Comprehension

Exercise 1

Skim* "Six Billion . . . and Counting" to get a general understanding of the information contained in the text and the graphics. Pay attention to the bold print. Your teacher may want to set a time limit to encourage you to read quickly.

1. Now that you have skimmed the article, quickly scan** to (re)check the text and graphics to see how accurate you were on the Check Your Assumptions questions (p. 203). Write the correct answers next to your guesses.

Exercise 2

Now scan the article and the accompanying graphics to answer the following questions. True/False items are indicated by a T / F preceding a statement. Your teacher may want to read these questions aloud as you scan for the answers.

Graphic 1: Map

1. T / F   The current population growth rate for the world is 1.7 percent.

2. T / F   The world's population is now growing more slowly than it was in 1987.

3. T / F   Some experts say that world population will stop increasing when it reaches 10 billion.

---

*For an introduction to skimming, see Unit 1.
**For an introduction to scanning, see Unit 1.
"Six Billion . . . and Counting" from *Time,* October 18, 1999. © 1999 Time, Inc. Reprinted by permission.

Six Billion ... and Counting

On Oct.12, 1999, give or take a few days, the world's population reached an alarming milestone. But the growth rate has begun to ease, and next century's rise will not be as steep as modern-day Malthusians once predicted

1 ▶ The worst crunch is coming to the poorest regions

Population density
Darker colors represent more densely populated areas of the globe, as measured in 1 km squares

Population per sq km
0   100   40,000

Growth is slowing ...
As recently as 1987, the head count rose by 1.7%, or 86 million. In 1999 the increase was down to 1.3%, or 78 million. Experts think the population may stabilize at 10 billion after 2200 if the deceleration continues

... for diverse reasons ...
Increased education and use of family planning have pushed down fertility rates all over the globe. On the negative side, mortality has been driven up by the spread of AIDS, especially in Africa

... but threats remain
If poor countries develop their economies in the same wasteful way industrial nations have, population growth will put an increasing burden on food and water supplies and the habitat of endangered species

2 ▶ In the future, a new world order looms

Most populous countries, 1999

1. China	1,267 million
2. India	998 million
3. U.S.	276 million
4. Indonesia	209 million
5. Brazil	168 million
6. Pakistan	152 million
7. Russia	147 million
8. Bangladesh	127 million
9. Japan	127 million
10. Nigeria	109 million

Population will keep soaring in less developed countries, North America's will plateau, and Europe's will start to fall

1999		**2050** (proj.)	
■ Asia	61%	■ Asia	60%
■ Africa	13%	■ Africa	20%
■ Europe	12%	■ S. America	9%
■ S. America	9%	■ Europe	7%
■ N. America	5%	■ N. America	4%

Most populous countries, 2050

1. India	1,529 million
2. China	1,478 million
3. U.S.	349 million
4. Pakistan	345 million
5. Indonesia	312 million
6. Nigeria	244 million
7. Brazil	244 million
8. Bangladesh	212 million
9. Ethiopia	169 million
10. Congo	160 million

4 ▶ Megacities will multiply

The number of cities with 10 million or more people is expected to keep surging

1960	■ ■ 2
1999	■ ■ ■ ■ ■ ■
	■ ■ ■ ■ ■ ■
	■ ■ ■ ■ ■ 17
2015	■ ■ ■ ■ ■ ■
(proj.)	■ ■ ■ ■ ■ ■
	■ ■ ■ ■ ■ ■
	■ ■ ■ ■ ■ ■
	■ ■ 26

Sources: Keith Clarke and Ann Ricchiazzi (NCGIA), Jason Simpson (ADL)/UC at Santa Barbara; United Nations Population Fund
TIME Graphic by Joe Zeff

3

0   500   1000   1500   1999

1992 projection 11.5 billion by 2150

Current projection 9.8 billion by 2150

6 billion Reached Oct. 12, 1999

5 billion Reached in 1987

4 billion Reached in 1974

3 billion Reached in 1960

2 billion Reached in 1927

1 billion Reached in 1804

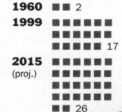

4. T / F   The world's birthrate has been rising in recent years.

5. T / F   The world's death rate has been decreasing in recent years.

6. What is the authors' opinion of the way that industrialized nations have developed their economies?

   a. positive

   b. negative

   c. no stated opinion

7. What dangers of increased population does the author mention?

8. T / F   On the map, light and dark colors are used to show different rates of population growth.

Graphic 2: Table and Pie Chart

9. T / F   The population in China will increase between now and 2050.

10. T / F   Graphic 2 shows that Russia and Japan will have decreases in population between 1999 and 2050.

11. Which continent has the greatest rate of population growth now?

12. Match each region listed below with the change that is predicted for its population.

   _____ Europe   a. increase greatly

   _____ North America   b. decrease

   _____ Africa   c. increase slightly

13. T / F   The population is increasing fastest in highly industrialized countries with large cities.

14. T / F   Generally speaking, the nations with the highest rates of population increase are the same countries that even today find it difficult to feed all their people.

Graphic 3: Chart

15. What is a megacity?

16. Which cities do you think were megacities in 1999?

17. T / F   The number of large cities in the world is projected to increase by 2015.

Graphic 4: Line Graph

18. T / F   The world population will probably stop increasing in 2150.

19. Look at graphic 4. Why are the lines at the top right broken rather than solid lines? Why are there two lines there instead of one?

20. Working with your classmates, make as many generalizations about population growth as you can based on graphic 4.

Critical Reading

1. The population growth rate depends on the fertility rate and the mortality rate. Why have these rates changed in the past? What might make them change in the future?

2. In the 1970s, according to a United Nations report, the world growth rate was 2 percent per year, and some population experts warned that world population might be more than 12 billion by 2100. How do those figures compare with numbers given in this article? Do you believe it's possible to make accurate predictions about population?

Discussion/Composition

1. What specific challenges will we face as world population grows? Consider economic, political, environmental, and/or personal challenges. Where possible, support your ideas with information from this article.

2. Imagine you are the minister of health in a country whose population is growing. What actions, if any, would you take to respond to the growing population? Prepare a speech to present to government leaders supporting your position. You might want to comment on some of the following approaches to the problem.

   • It is not the role of government to attempt to control population.

   • The government should plan for population growth through economic development.

   • The government should take a role in controlling population growth through measures such as educational campaigns or financial incentives for small families.

   • The government should control population by prohibiting families from having more than one child.

3. Write a brief paragraph that explains graphic 4. Imagine you will include this paragraph, next to graphic 4, in a report you are writing for one of your classes on how world population growth has changed over time. Do not simply repeat dates and numbers. Try to summarize the information shown in the graphic in an accurate and interesting way. Begin your paragraph with the following phrase: "As can be seen in graphic 4, . . ."

News magazines, targeted at a general audience, often present information about current economic issues and their impact on our lives. "The World Turns Gray" addresses changes in world population from an international perspective.

Before You Begin   1. When you walk down the street in your community, do you see more young people or more old people? How would your life be different if the numbers were reversed?

2. Based on the title of the article, "The World Turns Gray," what do you expect this article to be about?

Overview

Skim* "The World Turns Gray" to get a general understanding of the article and of the map. Then answer the following questions. Do not read every word and do not be concerned if you don't know the meanings of some words. Your teacher may want to set a time limit to encourage you to read quickly.

1. What is the main idea of this article?

2. Do you think this article will give you information about your country? If so, where?

3. Where would you look if you wanted to find information quickly about the changes predicted for Western Europe?

4. Why are the countries on the map shown in different colors?

5. a. What do the two long lines going across the map represent?

   b. What does it mean when they cross?

6. a. What do the brown and orange lines in the graphs (left side of the map) mean?

   b. Do the brown and orange lines on the bar charts (right side of the map) mean the same thing?

Now, read "The World Turns Gray" carefully. Your teacher may want you to do Vocabulary from Context exercise 1 on page 215 before you begin reading.

---

*For an introduction to skimming, see Unit 1.

The World Turns Gray

How global aging will challenge the world's economic well-being

by Phillip J. Longman

1 Worldwide, as recently as 1972, a woman gave birth to an average of 5.6 children over her lifetime. Global population, as a result, was doubling every generation. Citing the trend, a group of intellectuals known as the Club of Rome issued an influential study, titled "The Limits to Growth," that told what it all meant. The 21st century, said the club, would inevitably be marked by declining standards of living as human population exceeded the "carrying capacity" of the Earth, leading to mass famine and energy shortages.

2 But in the years since this Malthusian prophecy, a change has occurred in human behavior that is as revolutionary as it is unheralded. Around the world, fertility rates are plummeting. Today, women on average have just half the number of children they did in 1972. In 61 countries, accounting for 44 percent of the Earth's population, fertility rates are now at or below replacement levels.

3 That doesn't mean the Earth's population will fall anytime soon. Thanks to the high fertility rates of the past, a large percentage of the world's population is still of childbearing age. Life expectancy is also up. Globally, the average life span has jumped from 49.5 years in 1972 to more than 63 years. Consequently, according to projections by the United Nations, the world's population will slowly increase at an average rate of 1.3 percent a year during the next 50 years, and it could decline by midcentury if fertility continues to fall.

BIRTH DEARTH

4 So the world has a new problem. Global aging. In 2000, for the first time in history, people over 60 outnumbered kids 14 or younger in industrial countries. Even more

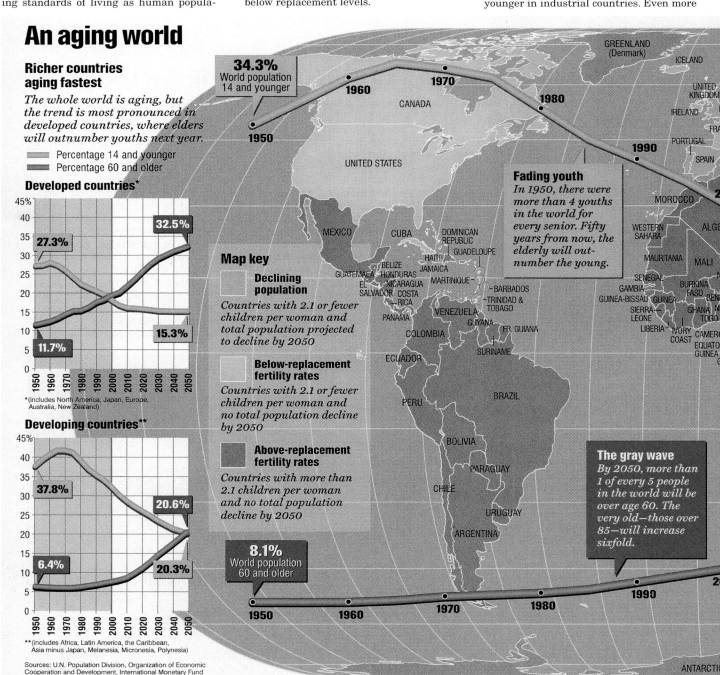

An aging world

Richer countries aging fastest

The whole world is aging, but the trend is most pronounced in developed countries, where elders will outnumber youths next year.

Percentage 14 and younger
Percentage 60 and older

Developed countries*

27.3%
32.5%
11.7%
15.3%

45% 40 35 30 25 20 15 10 5 0
1950 1960 1970 1980 1990 2000 2010 2020 2030 2040 2050

*(includes North America, Japan, Europe, Australia, New Zealand)

Developing countries**

37.8%
20.6%
6.4%
20.3%

45% 40 35 30 25 20 15 10 5 0
1950 1960 1970 1980 1990 2000 2010 2020 2030 2040 2050

**(includes Africa, Latin America, the Caribbean, Asia minus Japan, Melanesia, Micronesia, Polynesia)

Sources: U.N. Population Division, Organization of Economic Cooperation and Development, International Monetary Fund

34.3%
World population 14 and younger

1950 1960 1970 1980 1990

Map key

Declining population
Countries with 2.1 or fewer children per woman and total population projected to decline by 2050

Below-replacement fertility rates
Countries with 2.1 or fewer children per woman and no total population decline by 2050

Above-replacement fertility rates
Countries with more than 2.1 children per woman and no total population decline by 2050

Fading youth
In 1950, there were more than 4 youths in the world for every senior. Fifty years from now, the elderly will outnumber the young.

The gray wave
By 2050, more than 1 of every 5 people in the world will be over age 60. The very old—those over 85—will increase sixfold.

8.1%
World population 60 and older

1950 1960 1970 1980 1990

startling, the population of the Third World, while still comparatively youthful, is aging faster than that of the rest of the world. In France, for example, it took 140 years for the proportion of the population age 65 or older to double from 9 percent to 18 percent. In China, the same feat will take just 34 years. In Venezuela, 22. "The developed world at least got rich before it got old," notes Neil Howe, an expert on aging. "In the Third World the trend is reversed."

5 And that means trouble. For one thing, the cost of supporting a burgeoning elderly population will place enormous strains on the world's economy. Instead of there being more workers to support each retiree—as was the case while birthrates were still rising—there will be fewer. Instead of markets growing, they will shrink, at least in large parts of the globe.

PRODUCTIVITY PROBLEM

6 For the developed world, fiscal consequences of these trends are dire. Over the next 25 years, the number of persons of pensionable age (65 and over) in industrial countries will rise by 70 million, predicts the Organization for Economic Cooperation and Development (OECD), while the working-age population will rise by only 5 million. Today, working taxpayers outnumber nonworking pensioners in the developed world by 3 to 1. By 2030, absent increases in retirement ages, this ratio will fall to 1.5 to 1. In Italy and other places, it will drop to 1 to 1 or lower.

7 Of course, there will be fewer children to feed and educate. But most experts agree that while aging societies may be able to divert some resources that now go to the young, the increasing cost of supporting the elderly is almost certain to consume these savings many times over. Throughout the developed world, total public spending per old person is two to three times as great as public spending per child. And in the future, that gap will probably widen. The elderly consume far more health care resources than do children, and new technologies to extend life are bound to escalate health care costs.

8 Who will pay the bills? One option is to raise taxes on the diminishing number of workers. But according to official projections, doing so would require increasing the total tax burden on workers by the equivalent of 25 to 40 percent of their taxable wages, an unthinkable prospect in industrial countries, where payroll tax rates already sometimes exceed 40 percent.

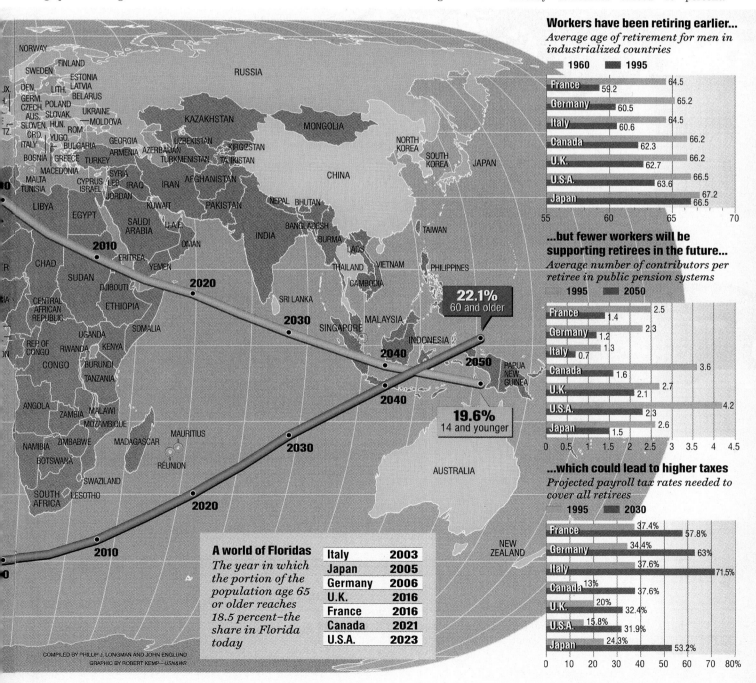

A world of Floridas
The year in which the portion of the population age 65 or older reaches 18.5 percent–the share in Florida today

Italy	2003
Japan	2005
Germany	2006
U.K.	2016
France	2016
Canada	2021
U.S.A.	2023

Workers have been retiring earlier...
Average age of retirement for men in industrialized countries

■ 1960   ■ 1995

Country	1960	1995
France	59.2	64.5
Germany	60.5	65.2
Italy	60.6	64.5
Canada	62.3	66.2
U.K.	62.7	66.2
U.S.A.	63.6	66.5
Japan	66.5	67.2

...but fewer workers will be supporting retirees in the future...
Average number of contributors per retiree in public pension systems

■ 1995   ■ 2050

Country	1995	2050
France	2.5	1.4
Germany	2.3	1.2
Italy	1.3	0.7
Canada	3.6	1.6
U.K.	2.7	2.1
U.S.A.	4.2	2.3
Japan	2.6	1.5

...which could lead to higher taxes
Projected payroll tax rates needed to cover all retirees

■ 1995   ■ 2030

Country	1995	2030
France	37.4%	57.8%
Germany	34.4%	63%
Italy	37.6%	71.5%
Canada	13%	37.6%
U.K.	20%	32.4%
U.S.A.	15.8%	31.9%
Japan	24.3%	53.2%

22.1% 60 and older

19.6% 14 and younger

COMPILED BY PHILLIP J. LONGMAN AND JOHN ENGLUND
GRAPHIC BY ROBERT KEMP—USN&WR

Another option would be to cut benefits, but given the political and ethical obstacles, this approach is likely to be put off for as long as possible.

9   That leaves borrowing. As aging nations attempt to avoid hard choices, they are likely to rack up mountains of debt. And, at some point, that could destabilize the world economy. For example, with neither tax increases nor benefit cuts, Japan will have to increase its public-debt levels from a little more than 20 percent of Gross Domestic Product (GDP) today to over 100 percent by 2050, according to OECD. In Europe, public indebtedness would have to rise from under 60 percent of GDP to nearly 110 percent.

LOOK TO BRAZIL

10 Like all Latin American countries, Brazil has seen a dramatic decline in its fertility rate over the last generation. In 1960, a Brazilian woman on average had more than six children over her lifetime; today, her counterpart has just 2.3 children. As a result, in a land once known for its celebration of dental-floss bikinis and youthful *carnaval* exuberance, pension debt has become the public's central preoccupation.

11 China also is struggling with pension and health care bills it can't afford. The large generation born in the first half of the 1950s will become elderly within the next two decades. Yet because of China's one-family/one-child policy, begun in the late 1970s, the number of workers is shrinking dramatically. Increasingly, the typical family pattern in China today is the "one-two-four household," with one child supporting two parents and four grandparents.

12 Other parts of Asia are aging even faster than China. Over the next decade, Japan, for example, will suffer a 25 percent drop in the number of workers under age 30.

13 Aside from the Muslim countries of North Africa and the Middle East, it's hard to find any part of the world that isn't aging. For many Third World countries, the challenge of supporting a growing elderly population is compounded by huge out-migrations of younger people. The nations of the Caribbean, for example, have lost 5.6 million mostly working-age citizens to emigration since 1950. This trend, combined with falling fertility rates and increasing life expectancy among the elderly, has given countries like Martinique, Barbados, and Aruba populations that are nearly as old as that of the United States.

14 Even Africa, the world's youngest continent, is more and more burdened by aging issues. Indeed, because of migration and the ravages of the AIDS epidemic, the number of working-age persons in sub-Saharan Africa available to support each elder is shrinking, causing enormous societal strains.

15 The plight of Grace Ngondo of Zimbabwe provides a good case study. Like millions of aging Africans these days, Ngondo must work to eat. Two of her sons have died of diseases Ngondo says had AIDS-like symptoms. A third son has moved away. Following the death of her husband and a brother-in-law, Ngondo now finds herself responsible for supporting more than a dozen grandchildren, nieces, and nephews. To make ends meet, she toils in the fields until the heat of the day overcomes her. Then she walks to the local school to sell ice cream to the departing children.

16 Like their African counterparts, the elderly in even the richest countries will most likely be called upon to work much later in life and to take more of a role in rearing the next generation. That may dash some people's dreams of an early retirement to the golf course or fishing hole, but in exchange for longer lives in a less crowded world, it may be a fair price to pay. ■

Comprehension

Answer the following questions. Your teacher may want you to answer orally, in writing, or by underlining appropriate portions of the text. True/False items are indicated by a T / F preceding the statement. Some items may have more than one correct answer.

1. T / F   The main problem discussed in this article is the world's high birthrate.

2. T / F   The Club of Rome predicted that in the 21st century, there would be so many people on Earth that there would not be enough food for all of them.

3. T / F   The average birthrate in the world has decreased since 1972.

4. Why is the world population still growing in some countries where the birthrate is only at or below replacement level? _____

_____

5. What does *global aging* mean? _____

_____

6. T / F   The countries aging fastest are those countries that are most industrialized.

_____

Note for paragraph 2: A Malthusian prophecy refers to a prediction made by Thomas Malthus (1766–1834), an English economist who believed that world population will always increase faster than the ability of the Earth to support it. Because the Earth would always have too many people, he believed that war, starvation, and illness were inevitable.

7. What are some negative effects of global aging? _____

_____

8. In paragraphs 8 and 9, there are three suggestions for how a country can get more money to care for its elderly retired people. What are they?

    a. _____

    b. _____

    c. _____

9. T / F   A "one-two-four" household has more young people than old people.

10. T / F   The Muslim countries of the Middle East are aging countries.

11. What is *out-migration* (in paragraph 13), and what economic effects does it have on some

    countries? _____

    _____

Questions 12 through 21 are based on information in the map on pages 210 and 211.

12. T / F   In 1950, about one-third of the world's population was 14 or younger.

13. T / F   Since 1950, the percent of the world's population that is 14 or younger has been steadily decreasing.

14. When will there be more old people than young people in the world? _____

    _____

15. Name a country whose population will decline by 2050. Name a country where the birthrate is

    relatively high. What is happening in your country? _____

    _____

16. Which industrialized country had the lowest average retirement age for men in 1995?

    _____

17. T / F   On average, men in industrialized countries retired later in 1960 than in 1995.

18. T / F   In Canada, in 1995, the ratio of workers to retirees was 3.6 to 1.0.

19. In 2050, which one of the industrialized countries listed in the bar chart on page 211 will have

    the fewest workers supporting each retiree? _____

20. In 1995, which three of the industrialized countries listed in the bar chart on page 211 had the highest payroll tax rates?

a. _____

b. _____

c. _____

21. T / F   By 2030, workers in several industrialized countries may be taxed more than half of what they earn.

Critical Reading

1. In paragraph 4, Neil Howe is quoted as saying, "The developed world at least got rich before it got old. In the Third World the trend is reversed." What does he mean?

2. Look at the "Map key." What does *replacement fertility rate* mean? How can a country have a below-replacement fertility rate and not have a declining population?

3. According to the map in this article, which are the "developed countries"? How do you feel about the terms *developed, developing,* and *Third World*?

4. Does the author think the problems caused by global aging are worse than problems that would be caused by a rapidly increasing world population?

Discussion/Composition

1. According to "The World Turns Gray," taking care of elderly retired people will become economically more difficult in the coming years. Two possible ways to provide for the elderly that were mentioned in the article are the following: raising the retirement age, so that people work longer than they do now; and raising taxes on working people to provide more money to support retired people. Which approach would you recommend? What effects would that approach have on both young people and old people?

2. Who should have the main responsibility for taking care of the elderly? The national government? The local community? Family members? Religious organizations?

3. Imagine you are a community leader in a country where the population is declining. What actions would you recommend that your country take to respond to the crisis of falling population? Prepare a speech or write a position paper in which you make recommendations. You might want to focus your recommendations on one or more of the following aspects of this topic.

   • what role, if any, the government should play in telling people what size family to have

   • the positive and negative effects of immigration on a country

   • whose responsibility it should be to care for the elderly in your country

   • the economic effects of changes in retirement age and tax policies

   • the social effects of changes in retirement age and tax policies

Vocabulary from Context

Exercise 1

Both the ideas and the vocabulary in the following passage are taken from "The World Turns Gray." Use the context provided to determine the meanings of the italicized words. Write a definition, synonym, or description of each of the italicized vocabulary items in the space provided.

1. _____

2. _____

3. _____

4. _____

5. _____

6. _____

7. _____

8. _____

9. _____

10. _____

11. _____

The rapidly increasing number of older people is creating a *challenge* for nations around the world, and it seems as though this pattern will continue. This *trend* of increased "graying" creates financial problems for rich and poor nations alike. Around the globe, nations are facing *fiscal* challenges as fewer and fewer young people must find ways to pay for the needs of the old. With increased costs of caring for the old, and fewer people to pay these costs, older people may find that they can no longer stop working as early as they once expected. Early *retirement* with enough money to live on may become a thing of the past. It may take longer to earn retirement *pensions* from employers. And, even so, nations may have to borrow money to support the large number of workers who are reaching *pensionable* age. This so-called pension *debt* will not only have serious fiscal consequences but will also create serious *ethical* challenges. Is it moral or fair for young people to have to borrow against their future to pay for the needs of the old? Will the debt prove an *obstacle* that stands in the way of their futures? Is it ethical or fair to make older people wait longer to retire when they were promised something better? There are no easy answers to these questions, but we do know that things are much better than they could be. Forty years ago, economists were predicting that the population would continue to grow so rapidly that the Earth wouldn't have the *capacity* to support all those people, that there would not be enough food for anyone. The prediction of worldwide *famine* has not come to pass. But people may have to work longer in a less-crowded world.

Exercise 2

This exercise is designed to give you additional clues to determine the meanings of unfamiliar vocabulary items in context. In the paragraph of "The World Turns Gray" indicated by the number in parentheses, find the word or phrase that best fits the meaning given. Your teacher may want to read these aloud as you quickly scan the paragraph to find the answer.

1. (1, second half of the paragraph) Which word means *unavoidably; definitely*?

2. (3) What phrase means *because of; due to; as a result of*?

3. (3) What phrase means *birthrates*?

4. (4, subhead of the paragraph) Which word means *shortage; lack; deficiency*?

5. (4, second half of the paragraph) Which word means *a remarkable act; an amazing achievement; a great accomplishment*?

6. (6) Which word means *terrible; very negative; awful; dreadful; horrifying*?

7. (6, second half of the paragraph) Which word means *without; unless there are*?

8. (7, first half of the paragraph) Which word means *turn in a different direction; use for another purpose*?

9. (7, second half of the paragraph) Which word means *a difference; the space between two things*?

10. (7, second half of the paragraph) What phrase means *will certainly; can't help but*?

11. (10, second half of the paragraph) Which word means *enthusiasm; excitement*?

12. (14) Which word means *damage; destruction; ruin*?

Exercise 3

This exercise should be done after you have finished reading "The World Turns Gray." The exercise is designed to give you practice using context clues to guess the meaning of unfamiliar vocabulary. Give a definition, synonym, or description of each of the words below. The number in parentheses indicates the paragraph in which the word can be found. Your teacher may want you to do these orally or in writing.

1. plummeting (2) _____

2. strains (5) _____

3. shrink (5) _____

4. escalate (7, second half of the paragraph) _____

5. diminishing (8) _____

6. exceed (8) _____

7. compounded (13) _____

8. toils (15, second half of the paragraph) _____

Figurative Language and Idioms

In the paragraph indicated by the number in parentheses, find the phrase that best fits the meaning given. Your teacher may want to read these aloud as you quickly scan the paragraph to find the answer.

1. (9) What phrase means *to come to owe large amounts of money*?

2. (10) What phrase refers to *very small bathing suits*?

3. (15) What phrase means *to support oneself; to earn enough money to live?*

4. (16) What phrase means *be required to; be depended upon to?*

Stems and Affixes

Both the ideas and the italicized words in the sentences below are taken from "The World Turns Gray." Beneath the sentences is a list of synonyms and definitions. Use your knowledge of stems and affixes* and the context to match each italicized word with its definition by placing the appropriate letter on the line before each sentence.

_____ 1. Overpopulation can lead to energy *shortages.*

_____ 2. Overpopulation can also cause a nation's overall standard of living to *decline.*

_____ 3. For the first time in history, older people *outnumber* younger ones.

_____ 4. The populations of the poorer countries are still *comparatively* young.

_____ 5. According to the *projections,* workers will soon have to work longer before retiring.

_____ 6. This *prospect* of later retirement may face political obstacles.

_____ 7. In China the typical child must *support* two parents and four grandparents.

_____ 8. It's easy to become *preoccupied* with these difficult issues.

_____ 9. Poorer countries face the problem of a large *out-migration* of younger people.

a. occupied with thoughts; lost in thought; worried

b. hold up; take care of

c. in comparison to others; relatively

d. having less than the amount needed

e. forecasts; predictions

f. people leaving the country; exodus

g. slope downward; decrease

h. exceed in number

i. looking forward; possibility

_____

*For an introduction to stems and affixes, see Unit 1.

Many words have more than one meaning. When you use a dictionary to discover the meaning of an unfamiliar word or phrase, you need to use the context to determine which definition is appropriate. The sentences below are based on "The World Turns Gray." Use the portions of the dictionary provided to select the best definition for each of the italicized words. Write the number of the definition in the space provided.

_____ 1. By 2030, *absent* increases in retirement ages, this ratio will fall from 1.5 to 1.

_____ 2. The elderly *consume* far more health resources than do children.

_____ 3. Who will pay the bills? One option is to raise taxes. Another option is to cut workers' *benefits,* but given the political problems, this approach is likely to be put off as long as possible.

_____ 4. Over the next decade, Japan, for example, will *suffer* a 25 percent drop in the number of workers under age 30.

_____ 5. The elderly in even the richest countries will most likely need to work much later in life and take more of a role in *rearing* the next generation.

_____ 6. Having to rear the next generation may *dash* some people's dreams of an early retirement.

---

ab•sent (ăb′sənt) *adj.* **1.** Not present; missing: *absent friends.* **2.** Not existent; lacking: *Morality is absent.* **3.** Exhibiting or feeling inattentiveness: *an absent nod.* — *tr.v.* (ăb-sĕnt′) **-sent•ed, -sent•ing, -sents.** To keep (oneself) away: *They absented themselves from the debate.* — *prep.* Without. [ME < OFr. < Lat. *absēns, absent-,* pr.part. of *abesse,* to be away : *abs-, ab-,* away; see AB-1 + *esse,* to be; see ES-*.] — **ab′-sent•ly** *adv.*

con•sume (kən-sōom′) *v.* **-sumed, -sum•ing, -sumes.** — *tr.* **1.** To eat or drink up; ingest. **2.a.** To expend; use up. **b.** To purchase (goods or services) for direct use or ownership. **3.** To waste; squander. **4.** To destroy totally: *flames that consumed the house.* **5.** To absorb; engross: *consumed with jealousy.* — *intr.* **1.** To be destroyed, expended, or wasted. **2.** To purchase economic goods and services. [ME *consumen* < Lat. *cōnsūmere* : *com-,* com- + *sūmere,* to take; see **em-*.]

ben•e•fit (bĕn′ə-fĭt) *n.* **1.a.** Something that promotes or enhances well-being; an advantage. **b.** Help; aid. **2.** A payment made or an entitlement available in accordance with a wage agreement, an insurance policy, or a public assistance program. **3.** A public entertainment or social event held to raise funds for a cause. **4.** *Archaic.* A kindly deed. — *v.* **-fit•ed, -fit•ing, -fits** also **-fit•ted, -fit•ting, -fits.** — *tr.* To be helpful or useful to. — *intr.* To derive benefit. [ME < OFr. *bienfait,* good deed < Lat. *benefactum* < *benefacere,* to do a service. See BENEFACTION.]

suf•fer (sŭf′ər) *v.* **-fered, -fer•ing, -fers.** — *intr.* **1.** To feel pain or distress; sustain loss, injury, harm, or punishment. **2.** To tolerate or endure evil, injury, pain, or death. See Syns at **bear**1. **3.** To appear at a disadvantage. — *tr.* **1.** To undergo or sustain (something painful, injurious, or unpleasant). **2.** To experience; undergo. **3.** To endure or bear; stand. **4.** To permit; allow. [ME *suffren* < OFr. *sufrir* < VLat. **sufferīre* < Lat. *sufferre* : *sub-,* sub- + *ferre,* to carry; see **bher-1*.] — **suf′fer•er** *n.* — **suf′fer•ing•ly** *adv.*

rear1 (rîr) *n.* **1.** A hind part. **2.** The point or area farthest from the front. **3.** The part of a military deployment usu. farthest from the fighting front. **4.** *Informal.* The buttocks. — *adj.* Of, at, or located in the rear. [ME *rere,* rear of an army, short for *rerewarde,* rear guard. See REARWARD2.]
rear2 (rîr) *v.* **reared, rear•ing, rears.** — *tr.* **1.** To care for (children or a child) during the early stages of life; bring up. **2.** To lift upright; raise. See Syns at **lift. 3.** To build; erect. **4.** To tend (growing plants or animals). — *intr.* **1.** To rise on the hind legs, as a horse. **2.** To rise high in the air; tower. [ME *reren,* to raise < OE *rǣran.*] — **rear′er** *n.*

dash1 (dăsh) *v.* **dashed, dash•ing, dash•es.** — *tr.* **1.** To break or smash by striking violently. **2.** To hurl, knock, or thrust with sudden violence. **3.** To splash; bespatter. **4.** To perform or complete hastily: *dash off a letter.* **5.a.** To add an enlivening or altering element to. **b.** To affect by adding an element to. **6.a.** To destroy or wreck. **b.** To confound; abash. — *intr.* **1.** To strike violently; smash. **2.** To move with haste; rush. — *n.* **1.** A swift, violent blow or stroke. **2.a.** A splash. **b.** A small amount of an added ingredient. **3.** A quick stroke, as with a pencil or brush. **4.** A sudden movement; a rush. **5.** *Sports.* A short footrace run at top speed. **6.** A spirited quality; verve. **7.** A punctuation mark (—) used in writing. **8.** In Morse code, the long sound or signal used with the dot and silent intervals to represent letters or numbers. **9.** A dashboard. [ME *dashen,* prob. of Scand. orig.; akin to Dan. *daske,* to beat.]
dash2 (dăsh) *tr.v.* **dashed, dash•ing, dash•es.** To damn. [Alteration of DAMN.]

From *The American Heritage College Dictionary,* 3d ed. (Boston: Houghton Mifflin, 2000).

Vocabulary Review

Exercise 1

Five of the words below, generally speaking, mean to get larger *or* to be larger than. *The other five words refer to becoming smaller. Place an L next to terms that are related to getting larger; place an S next to terms that refer to getting smaller.*

_____ declining   _____ plummeting   _____ shrinking

_____ diminishing   _____ compounding   _____ outnumbering

_____ burgeoning   _____ escalating   _____ exceeding

_____ cutting

Exercise 2

This exercise is designed to show the related uses of vocabulary items you've studied in "The World Turns Gray." For each set below, complete each sentence with the same word. Make sure your answer fits into every sentence in the set.

1. a. The student was _____ from school because he was sick.

    b. The population in Japan will decline, _____ an increase in the immigration rate.

2. a. Susan _____ her finger on the knife.

    b. The new governor promised to _____ taxes.

3. a. It is difficult to _____ a family with just one income.

    b. Mary has to _____ herself through college because her parents do not have money to give her.

    c. The bridge is _____ed by steel columns.

4. a. Sarah _____ed her back lifting her suitcase.

    b. Working long hours every day can put a lot of _____ on a person's family life.

5. a. There is a _____ between my two front teeth.

    b. The _____ between the rich and the poor is growing in many countries.

Each of the words or phrases in the following list is a synonym for one of the italicized items in the paragraph below. Place the appropriate word or phrase on the line provided. Do not use any word or phrase more than once.

challenge	rear	rapidly increasing
greatly diminished	increasing	fertility of a population
projections	burdened	exceed
declining	consumes	preoccupied

John is an optimist. He always sees the good side of things. When other people see their salaries *shrinking,* he notices that his interesting tasks now *outnumber* his boring tasks. When other people see *escalating* electric bills, he notices that the amount of unnecessary electricity he *uses* has *plummeted.* When other people feel *strained* by increased responsibilities, John appreciates the *invitation to test himself.* And John never worries about world events. If other people are *worried* with news about the *burgeoning birthrate,* John notices *predictions* about higher standards of living for all and looks forward to an opportunity to help *raise* his grandchildren. For John, the glass is always half full. We would all probably be happier if we were more like John.

1. shrinking: _____

2. outnumber: _____

3. escalating: _____

4. uses: _____

5. plummeted: _____

6. strained: _____

7. invitation to test himself: _____

8. worried: _____

9. burgeoning: _____

10. birthrate: _____

11. predictions: _____

12. raise: _____

Reading Selection 2
Magazine Article

Before You Begin

1. Why do people laugh? Do people laugh for different reasons?

2. Are there cultural differences that affect when and why people laugh?

3. Do you find jokes in English funny?

The following magazine article attempts to summarize scientific research for the general public. The author of the article below draws from the work of a number of experts in presenting an explanation for why we laugh.

First skim* the article. In order to facilitate skimming, your teacher may want to read first (and sometimes second or last) lines of each paragraph aloud to you. Then complete Comprehension exercise 1. Read the article a second time, more carefully, before completing the other exercises that follow. Your teacher may want you to do Vocabulary from Context exercise 1 on pages 225–26 before you begin reading.

Why We Laugh

Are you a quiet giggler? Or can you let loose with hearty laughter? Your ability to laugh may mean more than you think.

by Janet Spencer

1 **P**icture this cartoon: A man is watering his lawn just as an attractive blonde walks by. As he ogles her, he accidentally turns the hose on his dowdy wife, who is sitting on the porch.

2 Men usually think the cartoon is funny. Women do not. And there's a good reason for the difference in opinion.

3 We start finding things laughable—or not laughable—early in life. An infant first smiles at approximately eight days of age. Many psychologists feel this is an infant's first sign of simple pleasure—food, warmth and comfort.

At six months or less, the infant laughs to express complex pleasures—such as the sight of Mother's smiling face.

4 In his book *Beyond Laughter,* psychiatrist Martin Grotjahn says that the earlier infants begin to smile and laugh, the more advanced is their development. Studies revealed that children who did not develop these responses (because they lacked an intimate, loving relationship) "developed a schizophrenic psychosis in later life, or simply gave up and died."

5 Between the ages of six months and one year, babies learn to laugh for essentially the same reasons they will laugh throughout their lives, says Dr. Jacob Levine, associate professor of psychology at Yale University. Dr. Levine says that people laugh to express mastery over an anxiety. Picture what happens when parents toss children into the air. The children will probably laugh—but not the first time. In spite of their enjoyment of "flying," they are too anxious to laugh. How do they know Mommy or Daddy will catch them? Once the children realize they will be caught, they are free to enjoy the game. But more importantly, says Dr.

"Why We Laugh" by Janet Spencer from *Ladies' Home Journal.*
*For an introduction to skimming, see Unit 1.

Levine, the children laugh because they have mastered an anxiety.

6 Adult laughter is more subtle, but we also laugh at what we used to fear. The feeling of achievement, or lack of it, remains a crucial factor. Giving a first dinner party is an anxious event for newlyweds. Will the food be good? Will the guests get along? Will they be good hosts? All goes well; the party is over. Now they laugh freely. Their pleasure from having proved their success is the foundation for their pleasure in recalling the evening's activities. They couldn't enjoy the second pleasure without the first, more important one—their mastery of anxiety.

7 Laughter is a social response triggered by cues. Scientists have not determined a brain center for laughter, and they are perplexed by patients with certain types of brain damage who go into laughing fits for no apparent reason. The rest of us require company, and a reason to laugh.

8 When we find ourselves alone in a humorous situation, our usual response is to smile. Isn't it true that our highest compliment to a humorous book is to say that "it made me laugh out loud"? Of course, we do occasionally laugh alone; but when we do, we are, in a sense, socializing with ourselves. We laugh at a memory, or at a part of ourselves.

9 Practically every philosopher since Plato has written on how humor and laughter are related, but Sigmund Freud was the first to evolve a conclusive theory. Freud recognized that we all repress certain basic but socially "unacceptable" drives, such as sex and aggression. Jokes, not accidentally, are often based on either sex or aggression, or both. We find these jokes funny because they provide a sudden release of our normally suppressed drives. We are free to enjoy the forbidden, and the energy we normally use to inhibit these drives is discharged in laughter.

10 Another reason laughter is pleasurable is because of the physical sensations involved. Laughter is a series of minor facial and respiratory convulsions that stimulates our respiratory and circulatory systems. It activates the secretion of adrenalin and increases the blood flow to the head and brain. The total effect is one of euphoria.

11 Of course, we don't always need a joke to make us laugh. People who survive frightening situations, such as a fire or an emergency plane landing, frequently intersperse their story of the crisis with laughter. Part of the laughter expresses relief that everything is now all right. During a crisis, everyone mobilizes energy to deal with the potential problem. If the danger is averted, we need to release that energy. Some people cry; others laugh.

12 Part of the integral pleasure of a joke *is* getting the point. But if the sexual or aggressive element of the joke is too thinly disguised, as in "sick" humor, the joke will leave us feeling guilty instead of amused. We may laugh—but in embarrassment. According to Dr. Grotjahn, "The disguise must go far enough to avoid guilt," but "not so far that the thrill of aggression is lost."

13 Which brings us to why women may not have found the joke about the man watering his wife very funny—because they get the point only too well. Many psychiatrists agree that the reason women aren't amused by this kind of joke is that most sex jokes (a hefty percentage of all jokes) employ women as their target.

14 When we are made the butt of a joke either on a personal or impersonal level, we are emotionally involved in it. Consequently, we won't be able to laugh (except as a pretense). While we are feeling, we cannot laugh. The two do not mix. French essayist Henri Bergson

called laughter a "momentary anesthesia of the heart." We call it comic relief.

15 Knowing that laughter blunts emotion, we can better understand why we sometimes laugh when nothing is funny. We laugh during moments of anxiety because we feel no mastery over the situation, claims Dr. Levine. He explains, "Very often compulsive laughter is a learned response. If we laugh, it expresses good feelings and the fact that we are able to cope. When we're in a situation in which we *can't* cope, we laugh to reassure ourselves that we *can!*"

16 How often have we laughed at a funeral or upon hearing bad news? We laugh to deny an unendurable reality until we are strong enough to accept it. Laughter also breaks our tension. However, we may also be laughing to express relief that the tragedy didn't happen to us. We laugh before giving a big party, before delivering a speech, or while getting a traffic ticket, to say, "This isn't bothering me. See? I'm laughing."

17 But if we sometimes laugh in sorrow, more often we laugh with joy. Laughter creates and strengthens our social bonds. And the ability to share a laugh has guided many marriages through hard periods of adjustment.

18 According to Dr. Levine, we can measure our adjustment to the world by our capacity to laugh. When we are secure about our abilities, we can poke fun at our foibles. If we can laugh through our anxieties, we will not be overpowered by them.

19 The ability to laugh starts early, but it takes a lifetime to perfect. Says Dr. Grotjahn, "When social relationships are mastered, when individuals have mastered . . . a peaceful relationship with themselves, then they have . . . a sense of humor." And then they can throw back their heads and laugh.

Comprehension

Indicate if each statement is true (T) or false (F) according to your understanding of the article.

1. _____ We laugh as a release for our normally repressed drives.

2. _____ Laughter strengthens social bonds.

3. _____ We laugh to express mastery over anxiety.

4. _____ We laugh to release energy after a crisis.

5. _____ We laugh at jokes of which we are the target.

6. _____ We never laugh when we are alone because we require company to laugh.

7. _____ We laugh immediately at birth.

8. _____ We sometimes laugh in times of sorrow.

9. _____ We sometimes laugh when nothing is funny.

10. _____ The ability to laugh takes a lifetime to perfect.

11. _____ We laugh to break tension.

12. _____ Laughter is an unpleasant physical sensation.

13. _____ A sense of humor is a result of the mastery of human relationships.

14. _____ We always laugh when we understand a joke.

Now read the article again and complete the exercises that follow.

Exercise 2

The sentences in exercise 1 are general statements about laughter. Often authors will give specific examples to make an argument stronger or clearer. Following is a list of situations that the author of this article uses to illustrate some of the true statements in exercise 1. Match each of the examples below with the number of the appropriate general statement from the previous exercise. Some items have more than one possible answer. Choose what you feel to be the best answer. Be prepared to defend your choice.

Example | _3_   Children laugh when their parents throw them in the air.

1. _____ A newlywed couple laughs after they give their first successful dinner party.

2. _____ People who survive an emergency plane landing intersperse their story with laughter.

3. _____ We laugh before delivering a speech.

4. _____ We sometimes laugh at a funeral or when we hear bad news.

5. _____ We laugh at a sexual joke.

6. _____ Married couples laugh through hard periods of social adjustment.

Critical Reading

Exercise 1

In order to evaluate an author's arguments, it is important to notice whom she quotes to support her statements. A number of experts are cited in this article. Next to each name below, write the person's profession.

Example | Sigmund Freud __psychiatrist__

1. Henri Bergson _____

2. Martin Grotjahn _____

3. Jacob Levine _____

4. Plato _____

Exercise 2

When an article combines information from many sources, it is sometimes difficult to determine the source of an individual piece of information. In this article it is especially difficult to determine if individual statements are those of the author or are based on the work of the experts cited.

Following is a list of statements made in the article. Indicate if each one has been made by the author or one of her sources.

Example | _____Levine_____ We laugh to express mastery over anxiety.

1. _____ We laugh as a release for our normally repressed drives.

2. _____ Laughter strengthens social bonds.

3. _____ We laugh to release energy after a crisis.

4. _____ A sense of humor is a result of the mastery of human relationships.

5. _____ We sometimes laugh when nothing is funny.

6. _____ Laughter is a pleasurable physical sensation.

Exercise 3

Now that you have examined the experts and information cited by the author, what is your opinion of the article? Why are the experts cited? How could this article be made more persuasive?

Discussion/Composition

1. Tell a joke that you enjoy. How was your joke received? Are there ideas from the article that explain your classmates' reactions?

2. This article discusses situations that bring about laughter in the United States. Which situations given are similar to those in your community or your country? Which are different? Which elements of laughter do you think are the same for all people?

Vocabulary from Context

Exercise 1

Use the context provided to determine the meanings of the italicized words. Write a definition, synonym, or description of each of the italicized vocabulary items in the space provided.

1. _____
2. _____
3. _____
4. _____
5. _____

Some people feel very nervous when they try something new. No matter how hard they try, they cannot lower their *anxiety.* Some of them enjoy talking about their fears, while others *resent* being asked to discuss their personal feelings. Many are aware that they feel anxious, but only a few are *conscious* of the way they express their *tension.* Some people try to hide their nervousness; they try to *disguise* their anxiety by telling jokes. Others become loud and *aggressive,* attacking people by making them the *butt* of cruel jokes.

6. _____

7. _____

8. _____

Sometimes making someone else the *target* of jokes is an attempt to control one's own fears—to *master* anxiety.

9. _____

10. _____

A number of *factors* can be mentioned as important in explaining why some people have a fear of new experiences: early childhood experiences, general level of security, level of trust in others,

11. _____

etc., but the *crucial* factor seems to be a need to be in control.

12. _____

Usually, we are able to *suppress* our feelings so that they do not affect our behavior.

13. _____ By smiling foolishly and talking loudly, we are able to *repress* the rising feeling of fear so that it does not affect the way we behave.

14. _____ Most of us learn very young in life to control basic *drives* such as sex, hunger, and aggression.

15. _____ Sometimes the tension produced by our fears is so great that we cannot suppress it. At such times we need to *discharge* the tension by laughing or crying.

16. _____ The memory of a bad experience can sometimes *trigger* the same fear caused by that experience. Thus, a child might be frightened by the sight of a dog even though he is safe, merely because he once had a bad experience with a dog. A bad experience can be

17. _____ the *cue* that triggers our fears.

18. _____ Everyone experiences fear during major *crises*—such as fires, automobile accidents, etc.—but some people are even afraid of the dark.

19. _____ At the time of the crime, the man felt no emotion, but later he began to feel *guilty,* so he went to the police and told them the whole story.

20. _____ Because it is necessary to recognize a problem before it can be solved, admitting that we are afraid is an *integral* part of the process of mastering our fears.

Exercise 2

The following groups of sentences have been adapted from the article "Why We Laugh." Use context clues to determine the meanings of the italicized words. Write a definition, synonym, or description of each of the italicized vocabulary items in the space provided.

1. People who survive frightening situations frequently *intersperse* their story of the crisis with laughter. Part of the laughter expressed is relief that everything is all right. During a crisis, everyone mobilizes energy to deal with the potential problem. If the danger is avoided we need to release that energy. For example, if a pilot *averts* a plane crash by making a safe emergency landing, he may laugh as he describes his experience.

   intersperse: _____

   averts: _____

2. We find these jokes funny because they provide a sudden release of our normally suppressed drives. We are free to enjoy the forbidden, and the energy we normally use to *inhibit* these drives is discharged as laughter.

   inhibit: _____

3. When we are secure about our abilities, we can joke about our *foibles*. If we can laugh at our small faults, we will not be overpowered by them.

foibles: _____

4. A man is watering his lawn just as an attractive, well-dressed blond walks by. As he *ogles* her, he accidently turns the hose on his ugly, *dowdy* wife.

ogle: _____

dowdy: _____

Vocabulary Review

Two of the words in each line below are similar or related in meaning. Circle the word that does not belong.

1. cue   butt   target

2. inhibit   suppress   trigger

3. resent   release   discharge

4. crucial   conscious   integral

5. aggression   repression   suppression

Reading Selection 3
Short Story

Before You Begin   1. What is a lottery?

2. Why do you think lotteries have become popular throughout the world?

When "The Lottery" first appeared in the *New Yorker* in 1948, letters flooded the magazine expressing admiration, anger, and confusion at the story. For a long time, Shirley Jackson refused to discuss the story, apparently believing that people had to make their own evaluation of it and come to a personal understanding of its meaning. Whatever people may think of it, they all agree that it is unusual.

Read "The Lottery" carefully and make your own judgment. Your teacher may want you to do Vocabulary from Context exercise 1 on page 236 before you begin reading.

The Lottery

Shirley Jackson

1   The morning of June 27th was clear and sunny, with the fresh warmth of a full-summer day; the flowers were blossoming profusely, and the grass was richly green. The people of the village began to gather in the square, between the post office and the bank, around ten o'clock; in some towns there were so many people that the lottery took two days and had to be started on June 26th, but in this village, where there were only about three hundred people, the whole lottery took only about two hours, so it could begin at ten o'clock in the morning and still be through in time to allow the villagers to get home for noon dinner.

2   The children assembled first, of course. School was recently over for the summer, and the feeling of liberty sat uneasily on most of them; they tended to gather together quietly for a while before they broke into boisterous play, and their talk was still of the classroom and the teacher, of books and reprimands. Bobby Martin had already stuffed his pockets full of stones, and the other boys soon followed his example, selecting the smoothest and roundest stones; Bobby and Harry Jones and Dickie Delacroix—the villagers pronounced the name "Dellacroy"—eventually made a great pile of stones in one corner of the square and guarded it against the raids of the other boys. The girls stood aside, talking among themselves, looking over their shoulders at the boys,

Reprinted from *The Lottery* by Shirley Jackson (New York: Farrar, Straus and Giroux).

and the very small children rolled in the dust or clung to the hands of their older brothers or sisters.

3   Soon the men began to gather, surveying their own children, speaking of planting and rain, tractors and taxes. They stood together, away from the pile of stones in the corner, and their jokes were quiet, and they smiled rather than laughed. The women, wearing faded house dresses and sweaters, came shortly after their menfolk. They greeted one another and exchanged bits of gossip as they went to join their husbands. Soon the women, standing by their husbands, began to call to their children, and the children came reluctantly, having to be called four or five times. Bobby Martin ducked under his mother's grasping hand and ran, laughing, back to the pile of stones. His father spoke up sharply, and Bobby came quickly and took his place between his father and his oldest brother.

4   The lottery was conducted—as were the square dances, the teen-age club, the Halloween program—by Mr. Summers, who had time and energy to devote to civic activities. He was a round-faced, jovial man, and he ran the coal business; and people were sorry for him, because he had no children and his wife was a scold. When he arrived in the square, carrying the black wooden box, there was a murmur of conversation among the villagers, and he waved and called, "Little late today, folks." The postmaster, Mr. Graves, followed him, carrying a three-legged stool; and the stool was put in the center of the square, and Mr. Summers set the black box down on it. The villagers kept their distance, leaving a space between themselves and the stool, and when Mr. Summers said, "Some of you fellows want to give me hand?" there was a hesitation before two men, Mr. Martin and his oldest son, Baxter, came forward to hold the box steady on the stool while Mr. Summers stirred up the papers inside it.

5   The original paraphernalia for the lottery had been lost long ago, and the black box now resting on the stool had been put into use even before Old Man Warner, the oldest man in town, was born. Mr. Summers spoke frequently to the villagers about making a new box, but no one liked to upset even as much tradition as was represented by the black box. There was a story that the present box had been made with some pieces of the box that had preceded it, the one that had been constructed when the first people settled down to make a village here. Every year, after the lottery, Mr. Summers began talking again about a new box, but every year the subject was allowed to fade off without anything's being done. The black box grew shabbier each year; by now it was no longer completely black but splintered badly along one side to show the original wood color, and in some places faded or stained.

6   Mr. Martin and his oldest son, Baxter, held the black box securely on the stool until Mr. Summers had stirred the papers thoroughly with his hand. Because so much of the ritual had been forgotten or discarded, Mr. Summers had been successful in having slips of paper substituted for the chips of wood that had been used for generations. Chips of wood, Mr. Summers had argued, had been all very well when the village was tiny, but now that the population was more than three hundred and likely to keep on growing, it was necessary to use something that would fit more easily into the black box. The night before the lottery, Mr. Summers

and Mr. Graves made up the slips of paper and put them into the box, and it was then taken to the safe of Mr. Summers's coal company and locked up until Mr. Summers was ready to take it to the square next morning. The rest of the year, the box was put away, sometimes one place, sometimes another; it had spent one year in Mr. Graves's barn and another year underfoot in the post office, and sometimes it was set on a shelf in the Martin grocery and left there.

7   There was a great deal of fussing to be done before Mr. Summers declared the lottery open. There were the lists to make up—of heads of families, heads of households in each family, members of each household in each family. There was the proper swearing-in of Mr. Summers by the postmaster, as the official of the lottery; at one time, some people remembered, there had been a recital of some sort, performed by the official of the lottery, a perfunctory, tuneless chant that had been rattled off duly each year; some people believed that the official of the lottery used to stand just so when he said or sang it; others believed that he was supposed to walk among the people; but years and years ago this part of the ritual had been allowed to lapse. There had been also a ritual salute, which the official of the lottery had had to use in addressing each person who came up to draw from the box, but this also had changed with time, until now it was felt necessary only for the official to speak to each person approaching. Mr. Summers was very good at all this; in his clean white shirt and blue jeans, with one hand resting carelessly on the black box, he seemed very proper and important as he talked interminably to Mr. Graves and the Martins.

8   Just as Mr. Summers finally left off talking and turned to the assembled villagers, Mrs. Hutchinson came hurriedly along the path to the square, her sweater thrown over her shoulders, and slid into place in the back of the crowd. "Clean forgot what day it was," she said to Mrs. Delacroix, who stood next to her, and they both laughed softly. "Thought my old man was out back stacking wood," Mrs. Hutchinson went on, "and then I looked out the window and the kids was gone, and then I remembered it was the twenty-seventh and came a-running." She dried her hands on her apron, and Mrs. Delacroix said, "You're in time, though. They're still talking away up there."

9   Mrs. Hutchinson craned her neck to see through the crowd and found her husband and children standing near the front. She tapped Mrs. Delacroix on the arm as a farewell and began to make her way through the crowd. The people separated good-humoredly to let her through; two or three people said, in voices just loud enough to be heard across the crowd, "Here comes your Mrs., Hutchinson," and "Bill, she made it after all." Mrs. Hutchinson reached her husband, and Mr. Summers, who had been waiting, said cheerfully, "Thought we were going to have to get on without you, Tessie." Mrs. Hutchinson said, grinning, "Wouldn't have me leave m'dishes in the sink, now, would you Joe?" and soft laughter ran through the crowd as the people stirred back into position after Mrs. Hutchinson's arrival.

10   "Well, now," Mr. Summers said soberly, "guess we better get started, get this over with, so's we can go back to work. Anybody ain't here?"

"Dunbar," several people said. "Dunbar, Dunbar."

Mr. Summers consulted his list. "Clyde Dunbar," he said. "That's right. He's broke his leg, hasn't he? Who's drawing for him?"

11   "Me, I guess," a woman said, and Mr. Summers turned to look at her. "Wife draws for her husband," Mr. Summers said. "Don't you have a grown boy to do it for you, Janey?" Although Mr. Summers and everyone else in the village knew the answer perfectly well, it was the business of the official of the lottery to ask such questions formally. Mr. Summers waited with an expression of polite interest while Mrs. Dunbar answered.

"Horace's not but sixteen yet," Mrs. Dunbar said regretfully. "Guess I gotta fill in for the old man this year."

"Right," Mr. Summers said. He made a note on the list he was holding. Then he asked, "Watson boy drawing this year?"

12   A tall boy in the crowd raised his hand, "Here," he said. "I'm drawing for m'mother and me." He blinked his eyes nervously and ducked his head as several voices in the crowd said things like "Good fellow, Jack," and "Glad to see your mother's got a man to do it."

"Well," Mr. Summers said, "guess that's everyone. Old Man Warner make it?"

"Here," a voice said, and Mr. Summers nodded.

13   A sudden hush fell on the crowd as Mr. Summers cleared his throat and looked at the list. "All ready?" he called. "Now, I'll read the names—heads of families first—and the men come up and take a paper out of the box. Keep the paper folded in your hand without looking at it until everyone has had a turn. Everything clear?"

14   The people had done it so many times that they only half listened to the directions; most of them were quiet, wetting their lips, not looking around. Then Mr. Summers raised one hand high and said, "Adams." A man disengaged himself from the crowd and came forward. "Hi, Steve," Mr. Summers said, and Mr. Adams said, "Hi, Joe." They grinned at one another humorlessly and nervously. Then Mr. Adams reached into the black box and took out a folded paper. He held it firmly by one corner as he turned and went hastily back to his place in the crowd, where he stood a little apart from his family, not looking down at his hand.

"Allen," Mr. Summers said. "Anderson . . . Bentham."

15   "Seems like there's no time at all between lotteries any more," Mrs. Delacroix said to Mrs. Graves in the back row. "Seems like we got through with the last one only last week."

"Time sure goes fast," Mrs. Graves said.

"Clark . . . Delacroix."

"There goes my old man," Mrs. Delacroix said. She held her breath while her husband went forward.

"Dunbar," Mr. Summers said, and Mrs. Dunbar went steadily to the box while one of the women said, "Go on, Janey," and another said, "There she goes."

16   "We're next," Mrs. Graves said. She watched while Mr. Graves came around from the side of the box, greeted Mr. Summers gravely, and selected a slip of paper from the box. By now, all through the crowd there were men holding the small folded papers in their large hands, turning them over and over nervously.

Mrs. Dunbar and her two sons stood together, Mrs. Dunbar holding the slip of paper.

"Harburt . . . Hutchinson."

"Get up there, Bill," Mrs. Hutchinson said, and the people near her laughed.

"Jones."

17 "They do say," Mr. Adams said to Old Man Warner, who stood next to him, "that over in the north village they're talking of giving up the lottery."

Old Man Warner snorted. "Pack of crazy fools," he said. "Listening to the young folks, nothing's good enough for them. Next thing you know, they'll be wanting to go back to living in caves, nobody work any more, live *that* way for a while. Used to be a saying about 'Lottery in June, corn be heavy soon.' First thing you know, we'd all be eating stewed chickweed and acorns. There's always been a lottery," he added petulantly. "Bad enough to see young Joe Summers up there joking with everybody."

18 "Some places have already quit lotteries," Mrs. Adams said.

"Nothing but trouble in that," Old Man Warner said stoutly. "Pack of young fools."

"Martin." And Bobby Martin watched his father go forward. "Overdyke . . . Percy."

"I wish they'd hurry," Mrs. Dunbar said to her older son. "I wish they'd hurry."

"They're almost through," her son said.

"You get ready to run tell Dad," Mrs. Dunbar said.

19 Mr. Summers called his own name and then stepped forward precisely and selected a slip from the box. Then he called, "Warner."

"Seventy-seventh year I been in the lottery," Old Man Warner said as he went through the crowd. "Seventy-seventh time."

"Watson." The tall boy came awkwardly through the crowd. Someone said, "Don't be nervous, Jack," and Mr. Summers said, "Take your time, son."

"Zanini."

20 After that, there was a long pause, a breathless pause, until Mr. Summers, holding his slip of paper in the air, said, "All right, fellows." For a minute, no one moved, and then all the slips of paper were opened. Suddenly, all the women began to speak at once, saying, "Who is it?" "Who's got it?" "Is it the Dunbars?" "Is it the Watsons?" Then the voices began to say, "It's Hutchinson. It's Bill. Bill Hutchinson's got it."

"Go tell your father," Mrs. Dunbar said to her older son.

21 People began to look around to see the Hutchinsons. Bill Hutchinson was standing quiet, staring down at the paper in his hand. Suddenly, Tessie Hutchinson shouted to Mr. Summers, "You didn't give him time enough to take any paper he wanted. I saw you. It wasn't fair!"

"Be a good sport, Tessie," Mrs. Delacroix called, and Mrs. Graves said, "All of us took the same chance."

"Shut up, Tessie," Bill Hutchinson said.

22 "Well, everyone," Mr. Summers said, "that was done pretty fast, and now we've got to be hurrying a little more to get done in time." He consulted his next

list. "Bill," he said, "you draw for the Hutchinson family. You got any other households in the Hutchinsons?"

"There's Don and Eva," Mrs. Hutchinson yelled. "Make *them* take their chance!"

"Daughters draw with their husbands' families, Tessie," Mr. Summers said gently. "You know that as well as anyone else."

"It wasn't *fair!*" Tessie said.

23 "I guess not, Joe," Bill Hutchinson said regretfully. "My daughter draws with her husband's family. That's only fair. And I've got no other family except the kids."

"Then, as far as drawing for families is concerned, it's you," Mr. Summers said in explanation, "and as far as drawing for households is concerned, that's you, too. Right?"

"Right," Bill Hutchinson said.

"How many kids, Bill?" Mr. Summers asked formally.

"Three," Bill Hutchinson said. "There's Bill, Jr., and Nancy, and little Dave. And Tessie and me."

"All right, then," Mr. Summers said. "Harry, you got their tickets back?"

24 Mr. Graves nodded and held up the slips of paper. "Put them in the box, then," Mr. Summers directed. "Take Bill's and put it in."

"I think we ought to start over," Mrs. Hutchinson said, as quietly as she could. "I tell you it wasn't *fair.* You didn't give him time enough to choose. *Everybody* saw that."

Mr. Graves had selected the five slips and put them in the box, and he dropped all the papers but those onto the ground, where the breeze caught them and lifted them off.

"Listen, everybody," Mrs. Hutchinson was saying to the people around her.

"Ready, Bill?" Mr. Summers asked, and Bill Hutchinson, with one quick glance around at his wife and children, nodded.

25 "Remember," Mr. Summers said, "take the slips and keep them folded until each person has taken one. Harry, you help little Dave." Mr. Graves took the hand of the little boy, who came willingly with him up to the box. "Take a paper out of the box, Davy," Mr. Summers said. Davy put his hand into the box and laughed. "Take just one paper," Mr. Summers said. "Harry, you hold it for him." Mr. Graves took the child's hand and removed the folded paper from the right fist and held it while little Dave stood next to him and looked up at him wonderingly.

26 "Nancy next," Mr. Summers said. Nancy was twelve, and her school friends breathed heavily as she went forward, switching her skirt, and took a slip daintily from the box. "Bill, Jr.," Mr. Summers said, and Billy, his face red and his feet overlarge, nearly knocked the box over as he got a paper out. "Tessie," Mr. Summers said. She hesitated for a minute, looking around defiantly, and then set her lips and went up to the box. She snatched a paper out and held it behind her.

27 "Bill," Mr. Summers said, and Bill Hutchinson reached into the box and felt around, bringing his hand out at last with the slip of paper in it.

The crowd was quiet. A girl whispered, "I hope it's not Nancy," and the sound of the whisper reached the edges of the crowd.

"It's not the way it used to be," Old Man Warner said clearly. "People ain't the way they used to be."

"All right," Mr. Summers said. "Open the papers. Harry, you open little Dave's."

28   Mr. Graves opened the slip of paper, and there was a general sigh through the crowd as he held it up and everyone could see that it was blank. Nancy and Bill, Jr., opened theirs at the same time, and both beamed and laughed, turning around to the crowd and holding their slips above their heads.

"Tessie," Mr. Summers said. There was a pause, and then Mr. Summers looked at Bill Hutchinson, and Bill unfolded his paper and showed it. It was blank.

"It's Tessie," Mr. Summers said, and his voice was hushed. "Show us her paper, Bill."

29   Bill Hutchinson went over to his wife and forced the slip of paper out of her hand. It had a black spot on it, the black spot Mr. Summers had made the night before with the heavy pencil in the coal-company office. Bill Hutchinson held it up, and there was a stir in the crowd.

"All right, folks," Mr. Summers said, "Let's finish quickly."

30   Although the villagers had forgotten the ritual and lost the original black box, they still remembered to use stones. The pile of stones the boys had made earlier was ready; there were stones on the ground with the blowing scraps of paper that had come out of the box. Mrs. Delacroix selected a stone so large she had to pick it up with both hands and turned to Mrs. Dunbar. "Come on," she said. "Hurry up."

Mrs. Dunbar had small stones in both hands, and she said, gasping for breath, "I can't run at all. You'll have to go ahead and I'll catch up with you."

31   The children had stones already, and someone gave little Davy Hutchinson a few pebbles.

Tessie Hutchinson was in the center of a cleared space by now, and she held her hands out desperately as the villagers moved in on her. "It isn't fair," she said. A stone hit her on the side of the head.

Old Man Warner was saying, "Come on, come on, everyone." Steve Adams was in the front of the crowd of villagers, with Mrs. Graves beside him.

"It isn't fair, it isn't right," Mrs. Hutchinson screamed, and then they were upon her.

Comprehension

Exercise 1

Without referring to the story, indicate if each statement below is true (T) or false (F).

1. _____ The lottery was always held in summer.

2. _____ The lottery had not changed for many generations.

3. _____ The villagers were angry at Mrs. Hutchinson for being late.

4. _____ In the first drawing, only one person from each family drew a paper from the black box.

5. _____ The lottery was a custom only in this small village.

6. _____ Bill Hutchinson thought the first drawing was unfair.

7. _____ Tessie Hutchinson drew the paper with the black dot in the final drawing.

8. _____ The people wanted to finish in a hurry because they didn't like Tessie.

9. _____ The lottery was a form of human sacrifice.

Exercise 2

The following exercise requires a careful reading of "The Lottery." Indicate if each statement below is true (T) or false (F) according to your understanding of the story. Use information in the passage and inferences that can be drawn from the passage to make your decisions. You may refer to the story if necessary.

1. _____ Old Man Warner believed that the lottery assured the prosperity of the village.

2. _____ The date of the lottery was not rigidly fixed but occurred any time in summer when all of the villagers could be present.

3. _____ Mr. Summers never managed to make a new box for the lottery because people were unwilling to change the traditions that remained from the past.

4. _____ A family might contain several households.

5. _____ Mr. Warner felt that stopping the lottery would be equal to returning to prehistoric times.

6. _____ Only Mr. Warner remembered when the lottery was started.

7. _____ The villagers were hesitant to take part in the final step in the lottery.

Drawing Inferences

1. When did you first realize that this was a strange lottery? That winning the lottery was not desirable?

2. What details did the author add to make the lottery seem like a "normal" lottery? What details indicate that the lottery was strange? What details have double meanings?

3. Why do you think everyone had to take part in the final step of the lottery?

4. What was Mr. Warner's attitude toward the lottery? In what way and why did his attitude differ from those of other members of the community? What group in every society does Mr. Warner represent?

5. Why did Tessie want to include Don and Eva in the final drawing?

6. Which aspects of the lottery have changed? Which have not changed?

Discussion

1. How do you think the lottery began? Why was it started? Why does it take place at that time of year?

2. Why do you think the community continues the lottery?

3. Would you take part in the lottery if you were a member of the community?

4. This story is about a physical sacrifice in which a person is killed. Sacrifice is characterized by the suffering of one member of a group for the benefit of the group as a whole and by a sense of relief when one realizes that he or she has not been selected. This relief is so great that it leads to unconcern toward the fate of the person(s) to be sacrificed. Using this definition, can you think of specific institutions in modern societies in which sacrifices take place? Aside from physical sacrifice, what other types of sacrifice are possible?

Discussion/Composition

Was the lottery fair?

Vocabulary from Context

Exercise 1

Use the context provided to determine the meanings of the italicized words. Write a definition, synonym, or description of each of the italicized vocabulary items in the space provided.

1. _____

2. _____

3. _____

4. _____

5. _____

6. _____

7. _____

8. _____

     I like any game of chance, but I most enjoy taking part in a lottery. The lottery is like an unchanging religious ceremony, and it is perhaps this *ritual* quality of the lottery that people enjoy. Unlike other games of chance, a lottery does not require a great deal of *paraphernalia*. The only equipment needed is a bowl filled with slips of paper. I enjoy the excitement of watching the official pick the winning number. The moment before the *drawing* is very serious. The judge *gravely* approaches the bowl and looks at the crowd *soberly*. The crowd is quiet except for the low *murmur* of excitement. Suddenly the winner is selected. After the lottery is over, everyone but the winner throws away his or her piece of paper, and the *discarded* slips are soon blown away by the wind. People begin to *disengage* themselves from the crowd and the lottery is over.

Exercise 2

This exercise is designed to give you additional clues to determine the meanings of unfamiliar vocabulary items in context. In the paragraph of "The Lottery" indicated by the number in parentheses, find the word that best fits the meaning given. Your teacher may want to read these aloud as you quickly scan* the paragraph to find the answer.

*For an introduction to scanning, see Unit 1.

1. (2) Which word means *noisy and excited*?

2. (2) Which word means *criticisms; severe or formal scoldings*?

3. (3) Which word means *information, usually about other people, not always factual*?

4. (7) Which word at the beginning of the paragraph means *taking care of details*?

5. (7) Which word at the bottom of the paragraph means *endlessly*?

Exercise 3

This exercise should be done after you have finished reading "The Lottery." The exercise is designed to give you practice using context clues to guess the meaning of unfamiliar vocabulary. Give a definition, synonym, or description of each of the words and phrases below. The number in parentheses indicates the paragraph in which the word can be found. Your teacher may want you to do these orally or in writing.

1. devote (first sentence, paragraph 4) _____

2. stirred up (last sentence, paragraph 4) _____

3. fade off (bottom, paragraph 5) _____

4. shabbier (last sentence, paragraph 5) _____

5. lapse (middle, paragraph 7) _____

6. craned (first sentence, paragraph 9) _____

7. tapped (second sentence, paragraph 9) _____

8. consulted (paragraph 10) _____

Nonprose Reading
Bus Schedule

The United States is a country that has depended heavily on the automobile. In recent years, because of concern about oil resources and the pollution caused by auto emissions, large cities have tried to change commuter habits by encouraging people to ride buses rather than drive their cars. Bus schedules such as the one that follows are a part of this effort.

Before You Begin   If you are familiar with bus travel in a country other than the United States, reflect on that experience.

1. How convenient is the bus service? How often do the buses run? Are there many buses to choose from?

2. Do buses serve small towns as well as cities? Rural areas as well as urban areas? Do many people ride buses?

3. Do drivers adhere to a strict schedule? Do drivers wait for passengers who are running to catch the bus?

4. How do you find out about the buses? Do you use printed schedules to find the appropriate bus routes and times?

Consider bus travel in the U.S.

1. In the U.S., bus travelers rely on printed bus schedules. Why do you think this might be?

2. Imagine you are visiting a very large city in the United States for the first time. You plan to take city buses to see some of the city's parks, museums, and important landmarks. What would you need to know about the city's bus system in order to plan your tour?

Bus schedules are often difficult to read.* Following are pages of a Denver, Colorado, bus schedule. The accompanying exercises are designed to help you solve typical problems encountered by bus travelers.

---

*For an explanation of nonprose reading, see Unit 1.

Exercise 1

At the top of page 242 are the cover pages of a Denver bus schedule. Skim* them to get a general idea of the kinds of information they provide. Then use questions 1 through 8 to guide you in finding specific information.

1. Within the Denver bus system there are many different bus routes. Each route, or line, has a different name and a separate printed schedule. What bus route is this schedule for?

   _____

2. Do you know if this bus goes to the campus of the University of Colorado at Denver? To the Denver Museum of Natural History?

   _____

3. What are "peak hours"? Why is it important to know if your bus is traveling during peak hours?

   _____

   _____

4. How much would it cost two adults and a 5-year-old child to take a local bus ride on a Saturday?

   _____

5. Suppose that all you have is a five-dollar bill. Will you need to get change before you board the bus?

   _____

6. If you left your umbrella on a Denver bus, what number would you call to see if it had been found?

   _____

7. If you have questions about bus routes, what number should you call?

   _____

8. How much would it cost a handicapped passenger (with proper RTD identification) to ride a bus at noon on a Monday?

   _____

Exercise 2

The map on the bottom of page 242 shows the routes followed by eastbound and westbound 20th Avenue buses. Use the map to answer the following questions. True/False items are indicated by a T / F preceding the statement.

1. Can you connect to a route 76 bus from a route 20 bus? _____

2. T / F   The westbound bus passes Precedent Health Center.

_____

*For an introduction to skimming, see Unit 1.

3. T / F   The eastbound bus stops in front of Children's Hospital.

4. You want to meet a friend at Fitzsimons PX. Does the 20th Avenue bus go directly there?

_____

Exercise 3

Within the 20th Avenue bus schedule, there are separate timetables for buses that travel east and buses that travel west. On page 243 are the timetables for the eastbound 20th Avenue buses. Suppose that you are staying near the Denver West Marriott Hotel. Use the timetables to answer the following questions. For some questions you may want to use the map at the bottom of page 242 as well as the timetables.

1. T / F   It costs more to take the 8:56 A.M. weekday bus from the Marriott than to take the 9:58 A.M. bus.

2. If you use a wheelchair, which 20th Avenue bus would you take? _____

3. If you wanted to meet a friend at Mile High Stadium at 10:00 A.M. on a Wednesday, what bus

   would you need to catch from the hotel? _____

4. It's Friday. You want to meet a friend for an 8:00 P.M. dinner at a restaurant on the corner of

   E. 17th and York. What is the latest bus you could catch from your hotel? _____

5. How many buses go from the Marriott Hotel to Union Station? _____

6. T / F   The Marriott is a convenient place to stay if you want to visit downtown Denver on the weekend.

7. T / F   20th Avenue buses do not run on Christmas Day.

8. T / F   The bus schedule is bilingual.

_____

Bus schedule from Regional Transportation District, Denver, Colorado.

10 January 1999

20

RTD · **20th Avenue**

X Stops

Service to:
Children's Hospital
City Park
Denver Museum of Natural History
Denver West Marriott
Downtown Denver
Fitzsimons
Kaiser Permanente
McNichols Arena
Mile High Stadium
National Renewable
     Energy Laboratory
Precedent Health Center
Provenant St. Anthony
     Hospital Central
Sloan's Lake
St. Joseph's Hospital
Union Station

For information call:
303.299.6000 or 1.800.366.7433
www.RTD-Denver.com

Fares/Tarifas

Type of Service		Monthly Passes		
	Peak	Off-Peak	Regular	Elderly-Handicapped Youth (6-19 yrs.)
Mail Shuttle	free	free	–	–
Circulator	.70	.70	$18.00	$12.00
Boulder City	$1.00	.70	$25.00	$16.00
Local/Ltd	$1.50	.70	$32.00	$24.00
Express	$2.00	$2.00	$54.00	$36.00
Regional long distance	$3.50	$3.50	$90.00	$60.00
Transfers	free	free		

Peak Hours are 6:00-9:00 AM and 4:00-6:00 PM weekdays only.

Off-Peak Hours are all other times including holidays.

Exact Fare, Token or Monthly Pass Only! Drivers carry no change.

Transfers are intended for one continuous trip in the same direction. Request transfers at the time a fare is paid by cash or token.

Passes and Tokens are available at selected RTD offices and all King Soopers and Safeway stores. Tokens are sold at all Albertsons stores. Charge your pass or tokens by the roll to your MasterCard or Visa Card at selected RTD locations, by mail or by phone. To charge by phone, call 777-8893 seven days a week, 24 hours a day.

Elderly (65+), Handicapped and Youth pass discounts are available at selected RTD locations. Youth show proof of age. Elderly show a Medicare card, driver's license or Colorado ID. Handicapped show an authorized RTD identification card available through RTD, call 777-8600. To receive discounted passes by mail, initial eligibility must be established at an RTD location.

Elderly and Handicapped passengers ride for just 5¢ during off-peak hours by showing identification noted above for pass discounts.

Children 5 and under ride free if accompanied by adult passenger (limit 3).

RTD's Downtown Information Center is located at Civic Center Station, Broadway and Colfax. Passes, tokens and customer schedules are available here. Hours are from 8:00 AM-6:00 PM Monday-Friday.

RTD's Customer Service is located at Civic Center Station, Broadway and Colfax. For compliments or concerns call 573-2343. Hours are from 8:00 AM-5:00 PM Monday-Friday.

Lost and Found articles can be reclaimed at the following locations:

    Denver: Civic Center Station, Broadway and Colfax
    Hours: 8:00 AM-5:00 PM Monday-Friday. Call 573-2288

    Boulder: Boulder Transit Center, 14th and Walnut
    Hours: 7:00 AM-7:00 PM Monday-Friday. Call 442-7332

    Longmont: Longmont Terminal, 815 South Main
    Hours: 8:00 AM-5:00 PM Monday-Friday. Call 776-4141

Notice: Although RTD makes every effort to operate its service as scheduled, bus schedules may vary because of road, traffic, equipment, and other conditions. RTD makes no warranty or guarantee, express or implied, that bus service will be provided as scheduled. The RTD's liability is limited to the value of the fare for a one-way ride.

For information call: 303-299-6000 or 1-800-366-7433, 5:00 AM to 10:00 PM Mon-Fri and 7:00 AM to 10:00 PM Sat/Sun/Holiday.

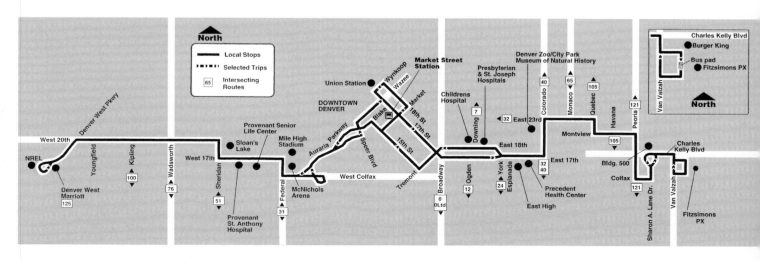

Monday - Friday

NREL Visitors Center	Denver West Marriott	West 20th - Youngfield	West 20th - Wadsworth	West 17th - Sheridan	West 17th - Federal	Wynkoop - 17th (Union Station)	17th - Blake	17th - Champa*	East 17th - Ogden	East 17th - York	Colorado - East 17th	East 23rd - Monaco	Montview - Havana	Fitzsimons PX	Bldg. 500
518A	519	523	533	538	543	—	551	555	602	605	609	615	623	631	—
603	604	608	618	623	628	—	617	621	628	632	636	642	650	658	—
—	—	—	—	—	—	616	—	—	—	—	—	—	—	—	—
630	631	635	646	653	658	—	652	656	703	707	711	717	725	733	—
—	—	—	—	—	—	651	—	—	—	—	—	—	—	—	—
—	—	—	—	—	—	—	707	711	718	722	726	732	740	748	—
700	701	705	716	723	728	—	722	726	733	737	741	747	755	803	—
—	—	—	—	—	—	721	—	—	—	—	—	—	—	—	—
730	731	735	746	753	758	—	737	741	748	752	756	802	810	818	—
—	—	—	—	—	—	—	807	811	818	822	826	832	840	848	—
800	801	805	816	823	828	—	822	826	833	837	841	847	855	903	—
—	—	—	—	—	—	821	—	—	—	—	—	—	—	—	—
—	—	—	—	—	—	—	837	841	848	852	856	902	910	918	—
835	836	840	851	858	903	—	852	856	903	907	911	917	925	933	—
—	—	—	—	—	—	851	—	—	—	—	—	—	—	—	—
855	856	900	911	918	923	—	932	936	943	947	951	957	1005	1013	—
—	—	—	—	—	—	951	952	956	1003	1007	1011	1017	1026	1034	—
957	958	1003	1013	1019	1024	—	1012	1016	1023	1027	1031	1037	1046	1054	—
—	—	—	—	—	—	1011	—	—	—	—	—	—	—	—	—
—	—	—	—	—	—	—	1032	1036	1043	1047	1051	1057	1106	1114	—
—	—	—	—	—	—	1051	1052	1056	1103	1107	1111	1117	1126	1134	—
1057	1058	1103	1113	1119	1124	—	1112	1116	1123	1127	1131	1137	1146	1154	—
—	—	—	—	—	—	1111	—	—	—	—	—	—	—	—	—
—	—	—	—	—	—	—	1132	1136	1143	1147	1151	1157	1206P	1214	—
—	—	—	—	—	—	1151	1152	1156	1203P	1207	1211	1217	1226	1234	—
1156	1157	1202P	1212	1218	1223	—	1212	1216	1223	1227	1231	1237	1246	1254	—
—	—	—	—	—	—	1211P	—	—	—	—	—	—	—	—	—
—	—	—	—	—	—	—	1232	1236	1243	1247	1251	1257	106	114	—
—	—	—	—	—	—	1251	1252	1256	103	107	111	117	126	134	—
1256P	1257	102	112	118	123	—	112	116	123	127	131	137	146	154	—
—	—	—	—	—	—	111	—	—	—	—	—	—	—	—	—
—	—	—	—	—	—	—	132	136	143	147	151	157	206	214	—
—	—	—	—	—	—	151	152	156	203	207	211	217	226	234	—
—	—	—	—	—	—	206	207	211	218	222	226	232	242	250	—
—	—	—	—	—	—	221	222	226	233	237	241	247	257	305	—
200	201	206	216	223	228	—	237	241	248	252	256	302	312	320	—
—	—	—	—	—	—	—	—	—	—	—	257**	305**	316**	—	—
—	—	—	—	—	—	251	252	256	303	307	311	327	335	346	—
259	300	305	315	322	327	—	307	311	318	322	327	342	350	401	409
—	—	—	—	—	—	321	322	326	333	337	342	357	405	416	424
329	330	335	345	352	357	—	337	341	348	352	357	405	416	424	—
—	—	—	—	—	—	351	352	356	403	407	412	420	431	439	—
—	—	—	—	—	—	—	407	411	418	422	427	435	446	454	—
—	—	—	—	—	—	416	417	422	430	434	438	446	457	505	—
402	403	408	419	426	431	—	429	434	442	446	450	458	509	517	—
—	—	—	—	—	—	428	—	—	—	—	—	—	—	—	—
—	—	—	—	—	—	452	453	458	506	510	514	522	533	541	—
424	425	430	441	448	453	—	503	508	516	520	524	532	543	551	—
—	—	—	—	—	—	514	515	520	528	532	536	544	555	603	—
—	—	—	—	—	—	529	530	535	543	547	551	559	610	618	—
507	508	513	523	530	535	—	545	550	558	602	606	614	625	633	—
—	—	—	—	—	—	559	600	604	612	616	620	627	636	—	644
547	548	552	601	607	612	—	620	624	632	636	640	647	656	—	704
607	608	612	621	627	632	—	640	644	652	656	700	707	716	—	724
—	—	—	—	—	—	715	716	719	725	728	731	737	745	—	752
—	—	—	—	—	—	745	746	749	755	758	801	807	815	—	822
—	—	—	—	—	—	815	816	819	825	828	831	837	845	—	852
—	—	—	—	—	—	845	846	849	855	858	901	907	915	—	922
—	—	—	—	—	—	915	916	919	925	928	931	937	945	—	952
—	—	—	—	—	—	945	946	949	955	958	1001	1007	1015	—	1022
—	—	—	—	—	—	1015	1016	1019	1025	1028	1031	1037	1045	—	1052
—	—	—	—	—	—	1045	1046	1049	1055	1058	1101	1107	1115	—	1122
—	—	—	—	—	—	1115	1116	1119	1125	1128	1131	1137	1145	—	1152
—	—	—	—	—	—	1145	1146	1149	1155	1158	1201A	1207	1215	—	1222

"Night Meets" in Downtown Denver

For safe and easy connections, most bus routes with service after 7:00 P.M. have been scheduled to meet in Downtown Denver at stops on or close to California Street. Arrivals and departures are grouped around the "Night Meet" times of :15 and :45 minutes after each hour. Please check schedules of your individual routes for trip times.

PEAK HOUR FARE DURING THESE TIMES: MONDAY-FRIDAY 6AM-9AM, 4PM-6PM. OFF-PEAK HOURS ARE ALL OTHER TIMES.

* This route makes the folowing "X" stops on 17th Street
17th - Lawrence
17th - Champa
17th - Welton

Accessible Service: All local buses are wheelchair lift equipped.

Holidays: New Year's Day, Memorial Day, Independence Day, Labor Day, Thanksgiving Day and Christmas Day.

Safety is our first concern.
Times listed are approximate.

TDD Information service for patrons with hearing and speech impairments **only:** Call RTD 303.299.6089

**: This trip operates September-May, school days only, and is open to the general public.

Saturday

Wynkoop - 17th (Union Station)	17th - Blake	17th - Champa*	East 17th - Ogden	East 17th - York	Colorado - East 17th	East 23rd - Monaco	Montview - Havana	Fitzsimons PX	Bldg. 500
—	543A	546	550	554	557	603	611	619	—
642	643	646	650	654	657	703	711	719	—
712	713	716	720	724	727	733	741	749	—
742	743	746	750	754	757	803	811	819	—
812	813	816	820	824	827	833	841	849	—
842	843	846	851	855	858	904	912	921	—
912	913	916	921	925	928	934	942	951	—
942	943	946	951	955	958	1004	1012	1021	—
1011	1012	1016	1023	1027	1030	1037	1047	1055	—
1041	1042	1046	1053	1057	1100	1107	1117	1125	—
1111	1112	1116	1123	1127	1130	1137	1147	1155	—
1211P	1212	1216	1223	1227	1230	1237	1247	1255	—
1241	1242	1246	1253	1257	100	107	117	125	—
111	112	116	123	127	130	137	147	155	—
141	142	146	153	157	200	207	217	225	—
211	212	216	223	227	230	237	247	255	—
241	242	246	253	257	300	307	317	325	—
311	312	316	323	327	330	337	347	355	—
341	342	346	353	357	400	407	417	425	—
411	412	416	423	427	430	437	447	455	—
441	442	446	453	457	500	507	517	525	—
511	512	516	523	527	530	537	547	555	—
541	542	546	553	557	600	607	617	624	—
611	612	616	623	627	630	637	647	—	654
641	642	646	653	657	700	707	717	—	724
715	716	719	725	728	731	737	745	—	752
745	746	749	755	758	801	807	815	—	822
815	816	819	825	828	831	837	845	—	852
845	846	849	855	858	901	907	915	—	922
915	916	919	925	928	931	937	945	—	952
945	946	949	955	958	1001	1007	1015	—	1022
1015	1016	1019	1025	1028	1031	1037	1045	—	1052
1045	1046	1049	1055	1058	1101	1107	1115	—	1122
1115	1116	1119	1125	1128	1131	1137	1145	—	1152

Sunday/Holidays

Wynkoop - 17th (Union Station)	17th - Blake	17th - Champa*	East 17th - Ogden	East 17th - York	Colorado - East 17th	East 23rd - Monaco	Montview - Havana	Fitzsimons PX	Bldg. 500
628A	629	631	636	639	642	648	656	703	—
658	659	701	706	709	712	718	726	733	—
738	739	741	746	749	752	758	806	813	—
814	815	817	822	825	828	834	842	849	—
844	845	847	852	855	858	904	912	919	—
914	915	917	922	925	928	934	942	949	—
944	945	947	952	955	958	1004	1012	1019	—
1014	1015	1017	1022	1025	1028	1034	1042	1049	—
1044	1045	1047	1052	1055	1058	1104	1112	1119	—
1114	1115	1117	1122	1125	1128	1134	1142	1149	—
1144	1145	1147	1152	1155	1158	1204P	1212	1219	—
1214P	1215	1217	1222	1225	1228	1234	1242	1249	—
1244	1245	1247	1252	1255	1258	104	112	119	—
114	115	117	122	125	128	134	142	149	—
144	145	148	153	156	159	205	213	220	—
214	215	218	223	226	229	235	243	250	—
244	245	248	253	256	259	305	313	320	—
314	315	318	323	326	329	335	343	350	—
344	345	348	353	356	359	405	413	420	—
414	415	418	423	426	429	435	443	450	—
444	445	448	453	456	459	505	513	520	—
514	515	518	523	—	528	534	542	549	—
544	545	548	553	555	558	604	612	619	—
615	616	619	624	626	629	635	643	—	650
645	646	649	654	656	659	705	713	—	720
715	716	719	724	726	729	735	743	—	750
745	746	749	754	756	759	805	813	—	820
815	816	818	823	825	828	833	840	—	846
845	846	848	853	855	858	903	910	—	916
915	916	918	923	925	928	933	940	—	946
945	946	948	953	955	958	1003	1010	—	1016
1015	1016	1018	1023	1025	1028	1033	1040	—	1046
1045	1046	1048	1053	1055	1058	1103	1110	—	1116
1115	1116	1118	1123	1125	1128	1133	1140	—	1146

Word Study
Stems and Affixes

Below is a list of some commonly occurring stems and affixes.* Study their meanings, and then do the exercises that follow. Your teacher may ask you to give examples of other words you know that are derived from these stems and affixes.

Prefixes		
by-	aside or apart from the common, secondary	bypass, by-product
de-	down from, away	descend, depart
dia-	through, across	diameter, diagonal
epi-	upon, over, outer	epidermis
hyper-	above, beyond, excessive	hypersensitive
hypo-	under, beneath, down	hypothesis, hypothermia

Stems		
-capit-	head, chief	captain, cap, decapitate
-corp-	body	corporation, incorporate
-derm-	skin	epidermis, dermatology
-geo-	earth	geology, geography
-hydr-, -hydro-	water	hydrogen, hydrology
-ortho-	straight, correct	orthodox, orthography
-pod-, -ped-	foot	podiatrist, pedestrian
-son-	sound	sound, sonic
-therm-, -thermo-	heat	thermal, hypothermia
-ver-	true	verity, veritable

Suffixes		
-ate	to make	activate
-fy	to make	liquify
-ize	to make	crystallize

*For a list of all stems and affixes taught in *Reader's Choice,* see the Appendix.

Word analysis can help you to guess the meanings of unfamiliar words. For each item, using context clues and what you know about word parts, write a synonym, description, or definition of the italicized word or phrase.

1. _____ Adam is employed at a *hydroelectric* power plant.

2. _____ Before Cindy gets dressed in the morning, she looks at the *thermometer* hanging outside her kitchen window.

3. _____ Some doctors prescribe medication to calm *hyperactive* children.

4. _____ I'm not sure if that information is correct, but I'll look in our records to *verify* it.

5. _____ Susan wants to replace the *pedals* on her bicycle with a special kind that racers use.

6. _____ After spending so many days lost in the desert, he was suffering from severe *dehydration*.

7. _____ June's father's hobby is photography, so she bought him a top-quality *tripod* for his birthday.

8. _____ He will never learn how to improve his writing unless he stops being so *hypersensitive* to criticism.

9. _____ Dr. Robinson said that just the sight of a *hypodermic* needle is enough to frighten many of his patients.

10. _____ Although she finished her degree in dentistry in 1995, she wants to go back to school next year to specialize in *orthodontics*.

11. _____ The immigration authorities *deported* Bob Jensen because he did not have a legal passport.

12. _____ The average *per capita* annual income in this country for people between the ages of sixteen and sixty-five has risen dramatically in the last ten years.

13. _____ Sam Thompson made an appointment with a *dermatologist* because he noticed small red spots on his hands.

14. _____ Scientists have developed a sensitive instrument to measure *geothermal* variation.

15. _____ Anthropologists say that bipedalism played an important role in the cultural evolution of the human species. Because early humans were *bipedal,* their hands were free to make and use tools.

16. _____ They doubted the *veracity* of his story.

17. _____ The Concorde, which flies at *supersonic* speed, can cross the Atlantic in about three hours.

Following is a list of words containing some of the stems and affixes introduced in this unit and the previous ones. Definitions of these words appear on the right. Put the letter of the appropriate definition next to each word.

1. ___ hyperbole
2. ___ hypodermis
3. ___ epicenter
4. ___ epidermis
5. ___ epigraph

a. the tissue immediately beneath the outer layer of the tissue of plants
b. a quotation printed at the beginning of a book or chapter to suggest its theme
c. the outer layer of skin of some animals
d. an exaggeration; a description that is far beyond the truth
e. the part of the Earth's surface directly above the place of origin of an earthquake

6. ___ orthography
7. ___ hydrate
8. ___ decapitate
9. ___ orthodox
10. ___ hydrophobia
11. ___ corpulent

a. fear of water
b. agreeing with established beliefs
c. fat; having a large body
d. to cut off the head of
e. correct spelling; writing words with the proper, accepted letters
f. to cause to combine with water

12. ___ bypass
13. ___ pedestrian
14. ___ by-product
15. ___ corporeal
16. ___ corpse
17. ___ podiatry

a. of or related to walking; a person who walks
b. a dead body
c. a passage to one side; a route that goes around a town
d. a secondary and sometimes unexpected result; something produced (as in manufacturing) in addition to the principal product
e. the care and treatment of the human foot in health and disease
f. bodily; of the nature of the physical body; not spiritual

18. ___ deflect
19. ___ decentralize
20. ___ diaphanous
21. ___ verisimilitude
22. ___ geomorphic

a. to turn aside from a fixed course
b. of or relating to the form of the Earth or its surface features
c. to divide and distribute what has been concentrated or united
d. the quality of appearing to be true
e. characterized by such fineness of texture that one can see through it

Sentence Study
Comprehension

Read these sentences carefully.* The questions that follow are designed to test your comprehension of complex grammatical structures. Select the *best* answer.

1. Like physical anthropology, orthodontics (dentistry dealing with the irregularities of teeth) tries to explain how and why people are different; unlike anthropology, it also tries to correct those differences for functional or aesthetic reasons.

   How does orthodontics differ from physical anthropology?

   _____ a. Physical anthropology is concerned with aesthetics; orthodontics is not.

   _____ b. Physical anthropology deals with the irregularities of teeth.

   _____ c. Orthodontics tries to explain why people are different, anthropology does not.

   _____ d. Anthropology does not try to correct differences among people; orthodontics does.

2. What is most obvious in this book are all those details of daily living that make Mary Richards anything but common.

   According to this statement, what kind of person is Mary Richards?

   _____ a. She is very obvious.

   _____ b. She is an unusual person.

   _____ c. She is anything she wants to be.

   _____ d. She is quite ordinary.

3. A third island appeared gradually during a period of volcanic activity that lasted over four years. Later, the 1866 eruptions, which brought to Santorin those volcanologists who first began archaeological work there, enlarged the new island through two new crater vents.

   What enlarged the third island?

   _____ a. the eruptions of 1866

   _____ b. a four-year period of volcanic activity

   _____ c. the activities of the people who came to study volcanoes

   _____ d. archaeological work, which created two new crater vents

---

*For an introduction to sentence study, see Unit 3.

4. Just before his tenth birthday Juan received a horse from his father; this was the first of a series of expensive gifts intended to create the impression of a loving parent.

Why did Juan receive the horse?

_____ a. because he was ten

_____ b. because his father loved him

_____ c. because his father wanted to seem loving

_____ d. because his father wouldn't be able to give him expensive gifts in the future

5. Since industry and commerce are the largest users of electrical energy, using less electricity would mean a reduced industrial capacity and fewer jobs in the affected industries and therefore an unfavorable change in our economic structure.

According to this sentence, decreasing the use of electricity _____

_____ a. must begin immediately.   _____ c. will cause difficulties.

_____ b. isn't important.   _____ d. won't affect industry.

6. The medical journal reported that heart attack victims who recover are approximately five times as likely to die within the next five years as those people without a history of heart disease.

What did this medical journal say about people who have had a heart attack?

_____ a. They are more likely to die in the near future than others.

_____ b. They will die in five years.

_____ c. They are less likely to die than people without a history of heart disease.

_____ d. They are likely to recover.

7. Few phenomena in history are more puzzling than this one: that men and women with goals so vague, with knowledge so uncertain, with hopes so foggy still would have risked dangers so certain and tasks so great.

What historical fact is puzzling?

_____ a. that people had such vague goals

_____ b. that people took such great risks

_____ c. that people had foggy hopes and uncertain knowledge

_____ d. that people completed such great tasks

8. Next he had to uncover the ancient secret—so jealously guarded by the ancients that no text of any kind, no descriptive wall painting, and no tomb inscriptions about making papyrus are known to exist.

What secret did this man want to discover?

_____ a. how to understand wall paintings

_____ b. how to read tomb inscriptions

_____ c. how to read the ancient texts

_____ d. how to produce papyrus

9. Alexis, ruler of a city where politics was a fine art, concealed his fears, received the noblemen with extravagant ceremonies, impressed them with his riches, praised them, entertained them, bribed them, made promises he had no intention of keeping—and thus succeeded in keeping their troops outside his city walls.

Why did Alexis give money and attention to the noblemen?

_____ a. because they praised him

_____ b. in order to prevent their armies from entering the city

_____ c. in order to impress them with his riches

_____ d. because they were his friends

Paragraph Reading
Restatement and Inference

This exercise is similar to the one found in Unit 5. Each paragraph below is followed by five statements. The statements are of four types.

1. Some of the statements are restatements of ideas in the original paragraph. They give the same information in a different way.

2. Some of the statements are inferences (conclusions) that can be drawn from the information given in the paragraph.

3. Some of the statements are false based on the information given.

4. Some of the statements cannot be judged true or false based on information given in the original paragraph.

Put a check (✔) next to all restatements and inferences (types 1 and 2). *Note:* do not check a statement that is true of itself but cannot be inferred from the paragraph.

Paragraph 1

It was the weekend before the exam. We were at the Walkers' house and it was pouring rain. Jack came in late, drenched to the skin. He explained that a car had broken down on the road and he had stopped to help push it onto the shoulder and out of the traffic. I remember thinking then how typical that was of Jack. So helpful, so accommodating.

_____ a. Jack came in late because it was raining.

_____ b. Jack came in late because his car had broken down.

_____ c. The narrator thinks Jack is typical.

_____ d. The narrator bases his opinion of Jack on this one experience.

_____ e. Jack often helps other people.

Paragraph 2

The illustrations in books make it easier for us to believe in the people and events described. The more senses satisfied, the easier is belief. Visual observation tends to be the most convincing evidence. Children, being less capable of translating abstractions into actualities, need illustration more than adults. Most of us, when we read, tend to create only vague and ghostlike forms in response to the words. Illustrators, when they read, must see. Great illustrators see accurately.

_____ a. Illustrations help us to believe events described in words.

_____ b. When most people read, they do not picture events as accurately as can a great illustrator.

_____ c. Children are less able than adults to visualize events described in books.

_____ d. The author believes illustrators are especially able to imagine visual details described with words.

_____ e. The author believes all illustrators see accurately.

Paragraph 3 | The gourd plant has been described as one of nature's greatest gifts to humankind. Of all the known plants, the gourd is the only one experts believe spanned the entire globe in prehistoric times. It appears as one of the first cultivated plants in regions throughout the world and was used by every known culture in the Temperate and Tropical Zones. Gourds played an important role in the changes that took place as humans became tool users and masters of their environment. Evidence from Florida and the Ocampo Caves in Mexico indicates that gourds were used as containers long before baskets or pottery served that purpose. Samples of the oldest known pottery imitate the familiar shapes of bottle gourds, suggesting that the bottle gourd was familiar to, and most likely used by, the earliest cultures not only in Africa and North America, but in Asia, too.

_____ a. It appears that gourds were used around the globe in every human culture.

_____ b. While used in Africa and North America, bottle gourds were probably not familiar to early cultures in Asia.

_____ c. Gourds were the only prehistoric plant used around the globe in the Temperate and Tropical Zones.

_____ d. Finding baskets in the shape of bottle gourds suggests that basket makers were familiar with gourds.

_____ e. Making gourd containers was the first use of tools.

Paragraph 3 adapted from _The Complete Book of Gourd Craft_ by Ginger Summit and Jim Widess (New York: Lark Books, 2000).

Paragraph 4 | The dusty book room whose windows never opened, through whose panes the summer sun sent a dim light where gold specks danced and shimmered, opened magic windows for me through which I looked out on other worlds and times than those in which I lived. The narrow shelves rose halfway up the walls, their tops piled with untidy layers that almost touched the ceiling. The piles on the floor had to be climbed over, columns of books flanked the window, falling at a touch.

_____ a. The room is dusty and shadowy, filled with books from floor to ceiling.

_____ b. The sun never enters the room.

_____ c. The author spent time in this room as a child.

_____ d. The author did not like the room.

_____ e. Through the windows in the room, the author saw worlds other than those in which he lived.

Paragraph 5 | By voting against mass transportation, voters have chosen to continue on a road to ruin. Our interstate highways, those much praised golden avenues built to whisk suburban travelers in and out of downtown, have turned into the world's most expensive parking lots. That expense is not only economic—it is social. These highways have created great walls separating neighborhood from neighborhood, disrupting the complex social connections that help make a city livable.

_____ a. Interstate highways have created social problems.

_____ b. Highways create complex social connections.

_____ c. By separating neighborhoods, highways have made cities more livable.

_____ d. The author supports the idea of mass transportation.

_____ e. The author agrees with a recent vote by the citizens.

Discourse Focus
Careful Reading / Drawing Inferences

This exercise is similar to the one found in Unit 5. Once again you must match wits with the great Professor Fordney. Solve the following mysteries, drawing inferences from the clues provided. Your teacher may want you to work with your classmates to answer the question following each mystery. Be prepared to defend your solution with details from the passage.

Mystery 1: Murder on Board

During a lull in the storm which tossed and rocked the sturdy little steamer *Dauntless*, a shot rang out on A deck.

Professor Fordney threw down the detective story he was somewhat unsuccessfully trying to read and hastened into the companionway. Where it turned at the far corner, he found Steward Mierson bending over the body of a man who had been instantly killed. Just then the heavens opened; lightning flashed and thunder boomed as if in ghoulish mockery.

The dead man's head bore powder burns. Captain Larson and the criminologist started checking the whereabouts of everyone aboard, beginning with those passengers nearest where the body was discovered.

The first questioned was Nathan Cohen, who said he was just completing a letter in his cabin when he heard the shot.

"May I see it?" Larson asked.

Looking over the captain's shoulder, Fordney saw the small, precise handwriting, on the ship's stationery. The letter was apparently written to a woman.

The next cabin was occupied by Miss Margaret Millsworth. On being questioned regarding what she was doing at the time, Miss Millsworth became excited and nervous. She stated that she had become so frightened by the storm, that about fifteen minutes before the shot was fired she had gone to the cabin of her fiancée, James Montgomery, directly opposite. The latter corroborated her statement, saying they hadn't rushed into the passageway because it would have looked compromising were they seen emerging together at that hour. Fordney noticed a dark red stain on Montgomery's dressing gown.

The whereabouts of the rest of the passengers and crew were satisfactorily checked.

Whom did the captain hold on suspicion? Why? _____

_____

_____

From *Minute Mysteries* by Austin Ripley (New York: Pocket Books).

While hunting in the Adirondacks, Fordney was informed of a tragedy at one of the camps. Thinking he might be of some help, he went over and introduced himself and was told of the accident by Wylie, the victim's companion.

"When Moore hadn't returned to camp at nine o'clock last night, I was a bit worried, because he didn't know these mountains. There wasn't a star out and it was dark and moonless, so I decided to look around for him. We're five miles out from anyone, you know.

"Putting more wood on the fire, I set out. After searching for an hour I was coming up the slope of a ravine when I saw a pair of eyes shining at me.

"Calling twice, and getting no answer, I fired, thinking it was a mountain lion. Imagine my horror when I reached the spot, struck a match, and saw I had nearly blown off Moore's head. A terrible experience!"

"I carried him back to camp and then walked to the nearest house to report the accident."

"How far from camp did you find him?"

"About a quarter of a mile."

"How did you manage to shoot with your right hand bandaged?"

"Oh—I use either hand."

"Mind if I look at the gun?"

"Not at all." Wylie handed it over.

"H'mmmmmmm. European make. Had it long?"

"No. It's rather new."

"Why did you deliberately murder Moore?" Fordney abruptly demanded. "For that's what you did!"

How did he know? _____

_____

Mystery 3:
Case # 194

Rudolph Mayer stumbled into the police station of the little village of Monroe, shook water from his clothes, and collapsed. A local physician was summoned and brought Mayer around. He told the following story.

"My wife and I, fond of winter sports, registered at the Fox Head Resort this afternoon—I've spent several vacations here. Shortly before dusk we decided to go skating on Lake Howard. We'd been out probably twenty minutes, as nearly as I can figure it, when my wife, who was about ten yards in front of me, suddenly dropped into the water through a large hole. Someone must have been cutting ice. I swerved, took off my skates, and jumped in after her. Despite my efforts, however, I couldn't locate her. I was barely able to pull myself out, and as I called and there was no help at hand, made my way here, somehow. It's about half a mile, I guess, and I didn't think I'd be able to do it. For God's sake send someone out there!"

Again the man fainted but was revived in a few minutes, mumbling incoherently about skates.

Two constables were dispatched through the ten below zero weather to the scene and returned with Mayer's skates found on the edge of a large hole where a local concern had been cutting ice. At the sight of them Mayer again collapsed.

Professor Fordney read no further in the above newspaper account.

"Mayer is certainly lying," he said to himself.

How did he know? _____

_____

Four tough prisoners in the county jail tore plumbing from the wall, beat two guards with iron pipes, brutally killing one, and escaped through a hole in the wall, after arming themselves with guns and ammunition. They were Dan Morgan, Sam Chapin, Louis Segal and Anton Kroll, all being held for armed robbery.

A posse was quickly organized and the gang surrounded in a small valley fifteen miles from the jail. Two of the mob were wounded and all captured, but not before one of the gang killed State Trooper Don Burton with a bullet through his head.

Professor Fordney interrogated the sullen four separately but each refused any information concerning himself or the others. From outside sources, however, the criminologist learned the following facts.

1. A dancer, one of the four, acted as leader of the gang. He spoke several languages fluently.
2. For some time the ugly Segal and the handsome leader had been suspicious of each other.
3. A week before their arrest, Sam Chapin and the leader won $4,000 each in a crap game at Anton Kroll's lake cabin. Kroll does not gamble.
4. The leader and the prisoner who killed Trooper Don Burton are good friends. They once ran a gambling house in Cuba.
5. Anton Kroll and the killer have been going with twin sisters who knew nothing of their criminal backgrounds.

Fordney sat in his study evaluating the above data. After a few moments he reached for the phone, called the prosecuting attorney and advised him to issue a murder warrant for . . . .

Who killed trooper Don Burton? _____

_____

 Science Reporting

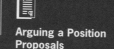 Arguing a Position
Proposals

 Poetry

 Short Story

 Analogy
Fiction

10

Reading Selections 1A–1B
Science Reporting

Following are two magazine articles that discuss genetically engineered (GE) crops, also called genetically modified (GM) crops. These are agricultural plants that have been "improved" by scientists. Their genes have been changed in order to create plants with desirable characteristics, for example, plants that are resistant to insect pests or that can grow with very little rainfall.

Before You Begin

1. What do you already know about GM crops? Is your impression positive or negative?

2. GM crops are very controversial. Why do you think some people think these crops will save the world? Why do you think some people oppose them just as strongly?

3. Have you ever eaten any GM food? How do you know?

Selection 1A   Popular Science

Overview

First, look at the title of the article and the bold print below it.

1. T / F   The purpose of this article is to convince you to agree with the author's opinion of GM foods.

2. What kinds of information do you expect to find in this article?

As you probably predicted, "Grains of Hope" presents arguments for and against genetically engineered crops. Read the article to get a sense of the arguments presented. Then do the tasks below. Your teacher may want you to do Vocabulary from Context exercise 1 on pages 262–63 before you begin reading.

Grains of Hope

Genetically engineered crops could revolutionize farming. Protesters fear they could also destroy the ecosystem. You decide.

By J. Madeleine Nash

1 At first, the grains of rice that Ingo Potrykus held in his fingers did not seem at all special, but inside, these grains were not white, as ordinary rice is, but a very pale yellow—thanks to beta-carotene, a building block for vitamin A.

2 Potrykus was elated. For more than a decade he had dreamed of creating a golden rice that could improve the lives of millions of the poorest people in the world, strengthening their eyesight and their resistance to disease.

3 He saw his rice as the start of a new green revolution in which ancient food crops would gain all sorts of useful properties: bananas that wouldn't rot on the way to market; corn that could supply its own fertilizer; wheat that could grow even during a drought.

4 But imagining golden rice was one thing and creating one quite another. Year after year, Potrykus and his colleagues ran into one obstacle after another until success finally came in the spring of 1999.

5 At that point, he tackled an even greater challenge. The golden grains contained pieces of DNA borrowed from bacteria and flowers. It was what some would call *Frankenfood,* a product of genetic engineering. As such, it was caught in a web of hopes and fears.

6 Golden grain has brought attention to a growing public debate. Are genetically modified crops (GM crops) a technological leap forward that will have extraordinary benefits for the world and its people? Or do they represent a dangerous step towards ecological and agricultural ruin? Is genetic engineering just a more efficient way of doing traditional crossbreeding? Or does the ability to mix the genes of any species—even plants and animals—give humans more power than they should have?

7 The debate began the moment genetically engineered crops were first sold in the 1990s, and it has escalated ever since. First to start major protests against biotechnology were European environmentalists and consumer-advocacy groups. They were soon followed by their U.S. counterparts.

8 The hostility is understandable. Most of the GM crops introduced so far have been developed for one of two purposes: either to produce a plant resistant to insect pests or a plant resistant to the chemicals that farmers use to kill weeds

HOW TO MAKE GOLDEN RICE

A four-step process to feed the poor

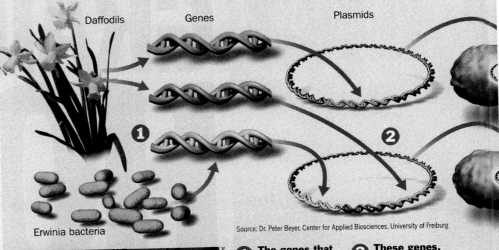

Daffodils   Genes   Plasmids

1

2

Erwinia bacteria

Source: Dr. Peter Beyer, Center for Applied Biosciences, University of Freiburg

1 The genes that give golden rice its ability to make beta-carotene in its endosperm (the interior of the kernel) come from daffodils and a bacterium called *Erwinia uredovora*

2 These genes, along with promoters (segments of DNA that activate genes), are inserted into plasmids (small loops of DNA) that occur inside a species of bacterium known as *Agrobacterium tumefaciens*

PETER BEYER

DAFFODIL MAN: Expert on the biochemistry of this gaily colored flower, he provided the genes for making beta-carotene

FROM THE TRANSGENIC GARDEN

COTTON

BEAUTIFUL BOLL: This plant has been given a bacterial gene to help it fight off worms that infest cotton crops

CORN

HEALTHY KERNEL: These corn seeds are protected by the same bacterial gene, one that ecologists fear could harm butterflies

PAPAYA

VIRAL RESISTANCE: Fruit carrying a gene from the ringspot virus are better able to withstand ringspot outbreaks

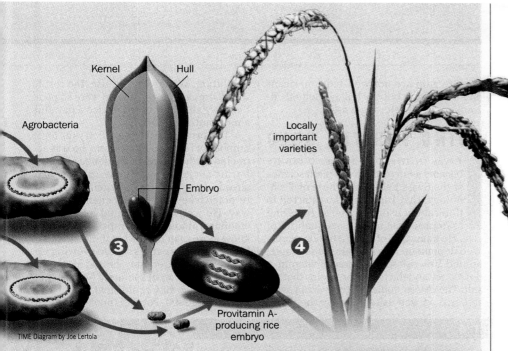

Kernel Hull

Agrobacteria

Embryo

Locally important varieties

③

④

Provitamin A-producing rice embryo

TIME Diagram by Joe Lertola

③ These agrobacteria are then added to a Petri dish containing rice embryos. As they "infect" the embryos, they also transfer the genes that encode the instructions for making beta-carotene

④ The transgenic rice plants must now be crossed with strains of rice that are grown locally and are suited to a particular region's climate and growing conditions

INGO POTRYKUS

GENE JOCKEY: His dream of creating a rice that would help hungry children came true just days before his scheduled retirement

MARKUS BUHLER—LOOKAT PHOTOS FOR TIME

CANOLA

PROBLEM POLLEN: When transgenic seeds contaminated a nontransgenic shipment from Canada, European farmers cried foul

SOYBEANS

ROUNDUP READY: Will crops designed to take frequent spraying with Monsanto's top weed killer lead to Roundup-resistant weeds?

CHARLTON PHOTOS; INGA SPENCE—CHARLTON PHOTOS

in their fields. These genetically engineered crops are often sold by the same large, multinational corporations that produce and sell the weed-killing chemicals that farmers spray on their fields. Consumers have become suspicious. Why use a strange new technology that might cause ecological damage, they ask, when the benefits of doing so seem small?

9   The benefits did seem small until golden rice was developed. It is the first strong example of a GM crop that may benefit not just the farmers who grow it but also the consumers who eat it. In this case, the consumers include at least a million children who die every year because they are weakened by vitamin-A deficiency and an additional 350,000 who go blind.

10   Many people worried about poverty and hunger look at golden rice and see it as evidence that GM crops can be made to serve the greater public good. They see a critical role for GM crops in feeding the world's ever-increasing population. As former U.S. President Jimmy Carter put it, "Responsible biotechnology is not the enemy; starvation is."

11   Indeed by the year 2020, the demand for grain is projected to go up by nearly half, while the amount of land available for farming will probably decrease. Also, there will be a greater need to conserve water and reduce polluting chemicals. The challenges are enormous.

12   In order to meet them, believes Gordon Conway, the agricultural ecologist who heads the Rockefeller Foundation, 21st century farmers will have to take advantage of everything available to them to produce more food, including genetic engineering. And contrary to what the public believes, he says, those who have the least to lose and the most to gain are not well-fed Americans and Europeans but hungry citizens of the developing world.

Weighing the Perils

13   Even proponents of agricultural biotechnology agree, though, that there are a number of real concerns about GM foods. First, all foods, including GM foods, are potential sources of allergens. That's because genes transferred in the process of making GM foods contain instructions for making proteins. Some—those in peanuts, for example— are well known for causing allergic reactions. To many, the possibility that golden rice might cause such a problem seems extremely unlikely, but it still needs to be considered.

14   Then there is the problem of "genetic pollution," as opponents of biotechnology term it. Pollen from wind-pollinated plants, such as corn and canola, is carried far and wide. Genetically-modified canola grown in one field, for example, can very easily pollinate non-GM plants grown in another field. This alarmed European farmers and led to protests when it was discovered that canola seeds from Canada—unknowingly planted by European farmers—contained transgenic contaminants.

15   Other arguments center around Bt corn and cotton—now grown in the U.S., Argentina, and China. Bt stands for a common soil bacteria, *Bacillus thuringiensis*. Bt produces poisons that affect certain insects. Monsanto and other companies have produced crops that are resistant to these insects by transferring into them the bacterial genes that produce specific insect poisons. Some ecologists worry, though, that planting these Bt crops will lead to the development of insects that have a resistance to Bt. That would be unfortunate, they say, because Bt is a safe and effective natural insecticide that is popular with organic farmers.

16   Even more worrisome are ecological concerns. In his laboratory in 1999, Cornell University entomologist John Losey dusted Bt corn pollen on plants populated by monarch-butterfly caterpillars. Many of the caterpillars died. Could what happened in Losey's laboratory happen in cornfields across the Midwest?

17   Although there have been studies done, there is as yet no clear answer to this question. Losey himself is not yet convinced that Bt corn is harmful to North America's monarch butterfly population, but he does think the issue deserves attention.

18   And others agree. "I'm not anti-biotechnology *per se*," says biologist Rebecca Goldberg, a senior scientist with the Environmental Defense Fund, but she would like there to be stronger laws regarding these crops and more study of them before they are sold.

19   Are there more potential problems? One is the possibility that pollen drifting from GM crops will fertilize wild plants, making stronger weeds that are even more difficult to control. No one knows how likely this is to happen, but Margaret Mellon, director of the Union of Concerned Scientists' agriculture and biotechnology program, and others like her believe that it's time we find out. Says she: "People should be responding to these concerns with experiments, not assurances."

20   And that is beginning to happen, although—contrary to expectations—the reports coming in are not that scary. For three years now, University of Arizona entomologist Bruce Tabashnik has been monitoring fields of Bt cotton that farmers have planted in his state. And in this instance, he says, "the environmental risks seem minimal, and the benefits seem great." Tabashnik says that Arizona farmers have reduced their use of chemical insecticides 75%. So far, there is no evidence that insects have become resistant to Bt either.

Assessing the Promise

21   Are the critics of agricultural biotechnolgy right? Are the supposed benefits of biotechnology just corporate advertising? Papaya growers in Hawaii disagree. In 1992 a virus threatened to destroy the state's papaya industry. By 1994, nearly half the state's papaya crop had been infected. But then help arrived, in the form of a virus-resistant GM papaya developed by Cornell University plant pathologist Dennis Gonsalves.

22   In 1995, scientists planted a trial field of regular papaya plants and two types of transgenic papaya. The regular papaya plants in the field trial failed to grow, but the GM plants were healthy. In 1998, the papaya growers switched to the GM seeds.

"Consumer acceptance has been great," reports Rusty Perry, who runs a papaya farm near Puna. "We've found that customers are more concerned with how the fruits look and taste than with whether they are transgenic or not."

23   In Africa, viral diseases and insects are major causes of crop loss. Kenyan plant scientist Florence Wambugu hopes to improve the sweet potato crop yield there by introducing a GM sweet potato that is resistant to the feathery mottle virus. To Wambugu, the argument in the U.S. and Europe about GM crops seems almost ridiculous. In Africa, she notes, nearly half the fruit and vegetable harvest is lost because it rots on the way to market. "If we had a transgenic banana that ripened more slowly," she says, "we could have 40% more bananas than now." Wambugu also dreams of getting herbicide-resistant crops. Says she: "We could liberate so many people if our crops were resistant to herbicides that we could then spray on the surrounding weeds. Weeding enslaves Africans; it keeps children from school."

24   The popular belief that agricultural biotechnology is bad for the environment puzzles the Rockefeller Foundation's Conway. He sees genetic engineering as an important tool for achieving a "doubly green revolution." If technology can increase a plant's natural defenses against weeds and viruses, if it can make crops grow using only small amounts of chemical fertilizers or in drought-ridden land, then what's wrong with it? ■

Comprehension

1.   "Grains of Hope" attempts to summarize scientific research for the general public. The author cites a number of individuals and groups as spokespeople for particular points of view. A first step in determining one's own point of view is to understand the perspectives of others. Following, you will find a list of names cited in "Grains of Hope"; the number in parentheses indicates the paragraph number in the article in which each name appears. Place each of these names in one of the charts below: in table 1 for those who support GM crops or in table 2 for those who oppose them. Also indicate the person/group's position and organization (if provided) and the reason given or implied for their point of view. You may decide that for some of the names, you do not have enough information to know whether they support or oppose GM crops. If you decide you don't have enough information, just circle those names on the list below. There will not always be a single correct answer, and sometimes you will have to draw inferences. Your teacher may want you to work in pairs or in groups. The first name on the list has been put in table 1 as an example.

Ingo Potrykus (1–5)

European environmentalists and
   consumer-advocacy groups (7)

Jimmy Carter (10)

Gordon Conway (12, 24)

European farmers (14)

Monsanto (15)

John Losey (16, 17)

Rebecca Goldberg (18)

Margaret Mellon (19)

Bruce Tabashnik (20)

Dennis Gonsalves (21)

Rusty Perry (22)

Florence Wambugu (23)

TABLE 1. People and Organizations Who Are "for" GM Crops and the Reasons They Give for Supporting Their Use

Name	Job/Position	Reason for Supporting GM Crops
Ingo Potrykus	Creator of a GM crop, golden rice	Way to improve health of poor people in the world

TABLE 2. People and Organizations Who Are "against" GM Crops and the Reasons They Give for Opposing Their Use

Name	Job/Position	Reason for Opposing GM Crops

2. Look at the names that you circled on the list in question 1. Compare the names you circled with those your classmates circled. Discuss any differences you find in your lists.

3. Do you recall other arguments against GM foods that were mentioned in "Grains of Hope" but that do not appear in table 2? Skim* the article and make a list of other arguments against GM foods that were mentioned in the article.

Critical Reading

1. Look at the charts you've just produced along with your answers to Comprehension question 3. For you, what are the most convincing arguments for GM food? What are the most convincing arguments against it?

2. No point of view is completely neutral. We all have an "interest" in (a share in; a benefit from) one point of view over another. This is our self-interest. Look again at the charts. Put a plus (+) in the job/position column for those people/groups for whom GM crops would be in their interest. Put a minus (−) for those people/groups for whom not having GM crops would be in their interest. Put a zero (0) for those whom you feel have no interest in the outcome of this debate. Do you see a pattern to the pluses and minuses? Does this affect how you feel about the research cited in the article? Do you believe that the knowledge produced by this article is "interested knowledge," that is, knowledge that serves some people's interests and does not benefit others? Again, there is no single correct answer.

3. What is your position on GM food? Is there additional information you'd like to have about GM food? Where might you get it?

Composition

Write a paper describing your position on the issue of whether or not genetically engineered crops should be grown. Make sure to state your view clearly and to support your opinions with strong reasons and good examples. Use information from "Grains of Hope," from class discussions, and from your own readings and experience to support your opinions. Another source of information is "The Global Food Fight" on pages 268–69.

Vocabulary from Context

Exercise 1

Both the ideas and the vocabulary in the following exercise are taken from "Grains of Hope." Use the context provided to determine the meanings of the italicized words. Write a definition, synonym, or description of each of the italicized vocabulary items in the space provided.

---

*For an introduction to skimming, see Unit 1.

1. _____

2. _____

3. _____

4. _____

5. _____

6. _____

7. _____

8. _____

9. _____

10. _____

11. _____

12. _____

13. _____

14. _____

15. _____

16. _____

17. _____

18. _____

19. _____

20. _____

21. _____

GM crops are controversial. On the one hand, some farmers and scientists feel that GM crops can make the world a better place. If bioengineers can create crops that are *resistant to* insects, for example, then they won't have to worry about insects destroying plants. In the absence of insect *damage,* crops can grow to feed the poor and hungry. Genetic engineering can create plants with other desirable *properties* as well. Plants that don't require much water, that can live even in times of *drought,* can help prevent the widespread *starvation* that would occur if people have nothing to eat. It's easy to see why many people believe that GM crops will help the world meet the difficult *challenges* that it will face as more and more people need to be fed.

But not everyone thinks bioengineering is a good idea. Other people are *suspicious.* They mistrust the claims made and don't believe that biotechnology is without *risks.* The possible dangers include harming the *ecosystem*—the interrelated community of plants and animals and bacteria that makes up the Earth. They worry that changing plants can harm our *environment,* and damage to our surroundings can hurt us. One danger is that GM crops can transfer their characteristics to other plants. Plants that reproduce by spreading their *pollen* in the wind can possibly *fertilize* wild plants, making them more difficult to control. Another worry is that GM plants might be a source of *allergens.* This seems unlikely, but in the process of making GM foods, genes are transferred that are known to cause problems for some people. Allergic reactions can range from coughing and sneezing to death.

Indeed, people hold very different opinions about bioengineering. While some people look forward to crops that will not rot during the trip to market, others worry that we will *ruin* our cropland and destroy what we are trying to save. While some people look forward to crops that can withstand droughts, others worry that contact with GM plants can *contaminate* and *pollute* other crops, making them impure and unfit for use. For some people, GM crops are the hope of the future; for others, they are a *poison* that will harm or destroy our farmland.

Thus, for people concerned with protecting our ecosystem, the risks are too high. Some *ecologists* remind us that our environment is made up of a *web* of interconnecting parts. They argue that the *benefits* of biotechnology are not as great as the risks. Over the coming years they will be watching and checking the effects of GM crops, *monitoring* whether there are any unexpected effects. And around the world, farmers and scientists alike will be hoping for the best results possible.

Exercise 2

This exercise is designed to give you additional clues to determine the meanings of unfamiliar vocabulary items in context. In the paragraph of "Grains of Hope" indicated by the number in parentheses, find the word or phrase that best fits the meaning given. Your teacher may want to read these aloud as you quickly scan* the paragraph to find the answer.

1. (2)   Which word means *extremely happy; overjoyed; ecstatic; thrilled*?

2. (3)   Which word means *characteristics*?

3. (3, 23) Which word means *spoil; go bad; become damaged or useless*?

4. (6)   What phrase means *an advance; an innovation; an improvement*?

5. (7)   What phrase means *groups who represent the interests of the general public*?

6. (10)   Which word means *very important; fundamental; essential; significant*?

7. (11)   Which word means *save; protect; preserve*?

8. (12)   What phrase means *make use of; make the most of*?

9. (16)   Which word means *a scientist who studies insects*?

10. (19)   Which word means *traveling; moving away; carried along, as by the wind*?

11. (21)   Which word means *a scientist who studies illnesses/diseases*?

12. (24)   What phrase means *a great change that will help the environment*?

13. (24)   What phrase means *a location that hasn't had rainfall for a long time*?

Exercise 3

This exercise should be done after you have finished reading "Grains of Hope." The exercise is designed to give you practice using context clues to guess the meaning of unfamiliar vocabulary. Give a definition, synonym, or description of each of the words and phrases below. The number in parentheses indicates the paragraph in which the word or phrase can be found. Your teacher may want you to do these orally or in writing.

1. Frankenfood (5) is an invented term, constructed by combining *Frankenstein* and *food*. What do you think the term means? _____

2. escalated (7) _____

3. protests (7, 14) _____

4. insect pests (8) _____

5. projected (11) _____

---

*For an introduction to scanning, see Unit 1.

6. proponents (13) _____

7. alarmed (14, second half of the paragraph) _____

8. transgenic contaminants (14, second half of the paragraph) _____

9. weeds (23, second half of the paragraph) _____

Stems and Affixes

The sentences below are adapted from "Grains of Hope." Use your knowledge of stems and affixes* and the context to match the italicized words (reprinted in a column on the left), with their definitions (on the right).

1. Is genetic engineering just a more efficient way of doing traditional *crossbreeding,* or does the ability to mix genes of plants and animals give human beings too much power?

2. European environmentalists protested against genetically engineered crops; they were soon followed by their U.S. *counterparts.*

3. In 1995, scientists planted a trial field of regular papaya and two types of *transgenic* papaya, which were virus resistant.

4. Some farmers worry that transgenic crops will create insects that are resistant to natural *insecticides.*

1. ____ crossbreeding	a.	corresponding person in another group; complement
2. ____ counterparts	b.	having genes borrowed from other species; bioengineered
3. ____ transgenic	c.	something that kills insects
4. ____ insecticide	d.	reproduce by mixing different plants or animals

Vocabulary Review

Exercise 1

Three of the words in each line below are similar or related in meaning. Circle the word that does not belong.

1. ecosystem   environment   escalate   ecology

2. contamination   pollution   poison   proponent

3. pathologist   consumer advocate   entomologist   bioengineer

---

*For an introduction to stems and affixes, see Unit 1.

Use a correct form of each of the words on the left to complete the sentences on the right.

1. resist   a. Ingo Potrykus wanted to create a golden rice that would strengthen people's _____ to disease.

               b. Other scientists have worked to create a plant that is _____ to insect pests.

2. ecology   a. Will GM crops have extraordinary benefits for people, or do they represent a dangerous step toward _____ ruin?

               b. Gordon Conway, an agricultural _____, believes farmers will need to take advantage of genetic engineering.

3. environment   a. European _____ were the first to protest against biotechnology.

               b. Bruce Tabashnik, an entomologist, says, "The _____ risks seem minimal, and the benefits seem great."

4. pollute   a. By the year 2020, there will be a greater need to conserve water and reduce _____ chemicals.

               b. People disagree strongly as to whether GM crops will contribute to or help solve the problem of _____.

5. allergy   a. A real concern about GM foods is that they are a potential source of _____.

               b. Genes transferred in the process of making GM foods make proteins, some of which are well known for causing _____ reactions.

6. contaminate   a. Some people worry that pollen from GM crops will travel to other crops and _____ them.

               b. Farmers worry that they will unknowingly plant seeds that contain transgenic _____.

7. pollen   a./b. _____ from wind-_____ plants can travel widely and contaminate other crops.

Authors sometimes use graphics (such as graphs, tables, charts, and maps) in order to present detailed information clearly, concisely, and in an attractive format. The map on the following pages provides readers with information about how different countries around the world feel about genetically modified (GM) food. GM food comes from plants whose genes have been changed by bioengineers in order to improve them in some way. For example, scientists may want to create a fruit that takes a long time to spoil once it is picked.

Before You Begin   1. How would you describe your country's attitude toward GM food?

2. Why do you think some countries would be in favor of using GM foods? Why do you think others would not be?

3. Without looking at the map, which countries do you predict would support using GM foods? Which do you predict would oppose using them?

Overview

Skim* "The Global Food Fight" to get a general understanding of this magazine graphic. Pay attention to the bold print, the key, and the symbols. Do not read every word and do not be concerned if you don't know the meanings of some words. Your teacher may want to set a time limit to encourage you to read quickly. Then answer the comprehension questions that follow in exercise 1.

Comprehension

Exercise 1

1. What do the colors on the map mean? _____

_____

2. What do the numbers on the map refer to? _____

_____

3. In the circular pie chart for each country, what does the shaded area represent? _____

_____

---

*For an introduction to skimming, see Unit 1.
"The Global Food Fight" from *Time,* July 31, 2000. © 2000 Time, Inc. Reprinted by permission.

THE GLOBAL FOOD FIGHT

1 BRUSSELS, 1998 France, Italy, Greece, Denmark and Luxembourg team up to block introduction of all new GM products in the European Union— including those approved by E.U. scientific advisory committees and even a few developed in these five countries. Several E.U. countries have also banned the importation and use of 18 GM crops and foods approved before the blockade went into effect. New safety rules could eventually break this logjam.

2 SEATTLE, NOVEMBER 1999 Taking to the streets to protest the spread of "Frankenfoods," among other issues, demonstrators trying to disrupt the World Trade Organization summit are tear-gassed and beaten by police.

3 MIDWESTERN U.S., 1999 A coalition of agricultural groups calls for a freeze on government approval of new GM seeds in light of dwindling markets in anti-GM European countries. Planting of GM corn drops from 25 million acres (10 million hectares) in 1999 to 19.9 million acres (8 million hectares) in 2000.

4 MONTREAL, JANUARY 2000 130 nations, including Mexico, Australia and Japan, sign the Cartagena Protocol on Biosafety, which requires an exporting country to obtain permission from an importing country before shipping GM seeds and organisms and to label such shipments with warnings that they "may contain" GM products.

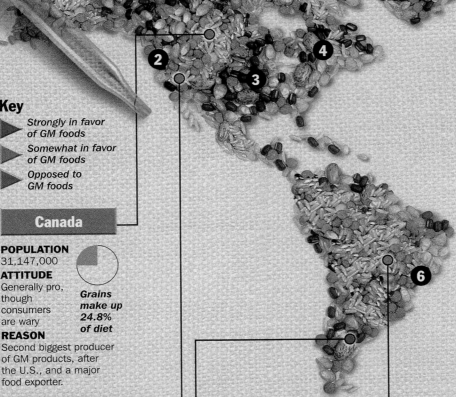

Key

► **Strongly in favor of GM foods**

► **Somewhat in favor of GM foods**

► **Opposed to GM foods**

Canada

POPULATION
31,147,000

ATTITUDE
Generally pro, though consumers are wary

Grains make up 24.8% of diet

REASON
Second biggest producer of GM products, after the U.S., and a major food exporter.

–By Michael D. Lemonick. With reporting by Yudhijit Bhattacharjee and Max Rust/New York, with other bureaus

U.S.

POPULATION
278,357,000

ATTITUDE
Cautiously pro

REASON
As a major food exporter and home to giant agribiotech businesses, led by Monsanto, the country stands to reap huge profits from GM foods.

Grains make up 23.6% of diet

Argentina

POPULATION
37,031,000

ATTITUDE
Pro

REASON
Third largest producer of biotech crops in the world, after the U.S. and Canada.

Grains make up 29.5% of diet

Brazil

POPULATION
170,116,000

ATTITUDE
Very cautiously pro

REASON
The country is eager to participate in the potentially profitable biotech revolution but is worried about alienating anti-GM customers in Europe.

Grains make up 30.9% of diet

Britain

POPULATION
58,830,000

ATTITUDE
Strongly anti

REASON
"Mad cow" disease in beef and a report that GM potatoes caused immune-system damage in rats have alarmed most Brits. Markets ban GM foods, and experiments are tightly controlled.

Grains make up 22.8% of diet

France

POPULATION
59,079,000

ATTITUDE
Strongly anti

REASON Like Britain, France has been stung by incidents with tainted food. Its attitude is also colored by hostility to U.S. imports and a desire to protect French farmers.

Grains make up 24.3% of diet

⑤ COLOMBO, SRI LANKA, FEBRUARY 2000
The government bans GM foods pending further research.

⑥ RIO DE JANEIRO, FEBRUARY 2000
A U.S. ship suspected of carrying GM corn is turned away by a Brazilian meat producer. The nation as a whole prohibits the importation of GM foods unless they've been proved safe; earlier this month, a federal court upheld that policy despite a statement from the Cabinet that Brazil "cannot be left out of this technology."

⑦ NEW DELHI, MAY 2000
The government approves large-scale field trials of Bollgard, Monsanto's pest-resistant GM cotton. Two years earlier, activists and angry farmers had burned fields planted with transgenic cotton.

⑧ BEIJING, JULY 2000
While still receptive to GM foods, the government passes a law requiring the labeling of GM seeds.

⑨ TOKYO, 2001
New rules will go into effect requiring GM foods to be labeled as such and tested for safety—although the government is also promoting the export of Japanese GM expertise and technology to Third-World nations. Meanwhile, a small anti-GM movement is growing stronger.

India

POPULATION
1,013,661,000

ATTITUDE
Cautiously pro

REASON
Needs to find the most efficient ways to feed and clothe its enormous, rapidly growing population.

Grains make up 62.6% of diet

China

POPULATION
1,277,558,000

ATTITUDE
Pro

REASON
Needs to feed and clothe a large population; rural hunger brought about a revolution 50 years ago, and leaders don't want another one.

Grains make up 54.7% of diet

Japan

POPULATION
126,714,000

ATTITUDE
Cautiously pro, but heading toward anti

REASON
Japan has a national obsession with food quality, enhanced by several recent food-poisoning incidents, and a tradition of protectionism for Japanese farmers.

Grains make up 40.7% of diet

Now scan* "The Global Food Fight" and use information from the graphic to answer the following questions. For statements preceded by T / F / N, circle *T* if the statement is true, *F* if the statement is false, and *N* if there is not enough information in the magazine graphic to know whether the statement is true or false. Your teacher may want to read these questions aloud to you as you scan for the answers.

1. Which countries mentioned on the map are most opposed to GM food?

2. Which countries mentioned on the map are most supportive of GM food?

3. T / F / N   Mexico supports using GM food.

4. T / F / N   There is no GM food used in the Middle East.

5. Which three countries named on this map are the largest producers of GM foods?

6. What event related to GM food occurred in Canada in 2000?

7. T / F / N   People in Japan are unified in their attitude toward GM food.

8. T / F / N   French farmers might be hurt economically by the introduction of genetically modified crops.

9. T / F / N   The British are angry at their cows. ;-)

Critical Reading

1. Why do you think that the authors of this magazine graphic included information about the diets in various countries? Do you see any relationship between a country's diet and its attitude toward genetically modified food?

2. What are some characteristics of countries that favor genetically modified food? What are some characteristics of countries opposed to GM food?

3. What is your opinion of GM food?

4. Where would you go to get more information about GM food? How would you decide if it was reliable information?

*For an introduction to scanning, see Unit 1.

Discussion/Composition

What actions, if any, should be taken in relation to the production, use, and sale of genetically modified foods? Write a position paper to present to government leaders describing and supporting your position. You might want to address one or more of the following viewpoints.

- It is not the role of government to attempt to control what farmers grow.

- The government should protect people's health by strictly controlling what types of foods can be planted and sold.

- The government should require labels on all GM foods that are sold in the country so that people know what they are buying.

- The government should fund research in and development of GM foods.

Web Work

Large corporations often use their own Web sites to present information about themselves and their points of view. Search the Web to locate a Web site of a company that produces GM foods (e.g., the Monsanto site, **http://www.monsanto.com**). What is the company's position on GM food? What kind of arguments and evidence does this Web site present? Do you find these arguments persuasive? Why or why not? Give specific examples from your Web search to support your views.

Vocabulary from Context

Exercise 1

As you have learned from "The Global Food Fight," there is a wide variety of opinion about GM food. Some nations oppose it, while others support its use. This exercise is designed to give you additional practice recognizing vocabulary items that indicate positive and negative opinions and actions. The questions below refer either to the numbered paragraphs in "The Global Food Fight" or to the descriptions of nations. In the paragraphs indicated in parentheses, find the words that fit the meaning given. Your teacher may want to read these aloud as you quickly scan the paragraphs to find the answers. After you have finished, you may want to work with classmates to determine the specific differences among these generally negative and positive terms. Feel free to use your dictionaries.

1. (1: 4 items, 3, 5, 6) Which words refer to *stopping or keeping something out*?

2. (7, 8, 9) Which words refer to *positive feelings or actions*?

3. (Brazil, Britain, France) Which words refer to *negative feelings*?

4. (France, Japan) What phrases refer to *spoiled or polluted food*?

Exercise 2

This exercise should be done after you have finished reading "The Global Food Fight." The exercise is designed to give you practice using context clues to guess the meaning of unfamiliar vocabulary. Give a definition, synonym, or description of each of the words below. The country in parentheses indicates the paragraph of "The Global Food Fight" in which the word can be found. Your teacher may want you to do these orally or in writing.

1. (Canada) wary _____

2. (U.S.) reap _____

3. (Brazil) eager _____

4. (Brazil) alienating _____

5. (Britain) alarmed _____

Vocabulary Review

Three of the words in each line below are similar or related in meaning. Circle the word that does not belong.

1. block   promote   ban   freeze

2. prohibiting   approving   receptive   promoting

Reading Selection 2
Poetry

In Units 1, 3, and 7 you read poems to determine the main ideas, to discover what the poems were about. But poetry can be enjoyed on many levels and read in many ways. You can read a poem once, simply to enjoy the language or the main message of the poem. Or you can decide to experience a poem more fully by reading it several times for different purposes or meanings. The two poems that follow describe this process of intense discovery.

How to Eat a Poem

1 Don't be polite.
Bite in.
Pick it up with your fingers and lick the juice that
    may run down your chin.
5 It is ready and ripe now, whenever you are.

6 You do not need a knife or fork or spoon
or plate or napkin or tablecloth.

8 For there is no core
or stem
or rind
or pit
12 or seed
or skin
to throw away.

Eve Merriam

Unfolding Bud

1 One is amazed
By a water-lily bud
Unfolding
With each passing day,
Taking on a richer color
6 And new dimensions.

7 One is not amazed,
At a first glance,
By a poem,
Which is as tight-closed
11 As a tiny bud.

12 Yet one is surprised
To see the poem
Gradually unfolding,
15 Revealing its rich inner self,
As one reads it
Again
18 And over again.

Naoshi Koriyama

"How to Eat a Poem" by Eve Merriam, from *Jamboree: Rhymes for All Times* (New York: Dell); "Unfolding Bud" by Naoshi Koriyama, *Christian Science Monitor.*

Comprehension

Answer the following questions. Your teacher may want you to discuss these questions as a class, in small groups, or in pairs.

1. Eve Merriam, the author of "How to Eat a Poem," compares the process of reading a poem to eating a fruit. What does she mean?

    a. In what ways is reading a poem like eating?

    b. What does the author mean when she advises us, "Don't be polite"?

    c. Why don't you need a plate or a napkin in order to eat a poem?

    d. Why do you think the author chose eating a fruit instead of eating a piece of bread for her analogy?

    e. The author gives us a model for reading poetry. Are there other things that you read in this way?

2. Naoshi Koriyama compares poetry to an unfolding bud. What does she mean?

    a. In what ways is a poem like a water-lily bud?

    b. According to Koriyama, what is a difference between our reaction to a water lily and to a poem?

3. What are the similarities and differences in these two poets' views of reading poetry?

The three selections that follow will give you an opportunity to eat poems, to watch them unfold. Read each poem once. Then work with your classmates to answer the questions that follow. Because so much of poetry depends upon individual response, there is no single correct answer to many of these questions. Your teacher may want you to discuss these questions as a class, in small groups, or in pairs.

This is Just to Say

1 I have eaten
the plums
that were in
the icebox

5 and which
you were probably
saving
for breakfast

9 Forgive me
they were delicious
so sweet
and so cold.

William Carlos Williams

Comprehension

1. Some people think this is a wonderful poem; others don't think it is a poem at all. What do you think accounts for these different reactions?

2. The poem seems to be in the form of a note. Did this note need to be written? Do you think the writer believes that the reader will be angry with him? Is this really an apology?

3. Consider the relationship between the writer and the addressee of the note. Do they live together? Are they close? What is their relationship?

4. Why do you think this poem/note was written?

5. Do you think this is a poem? If you had found it in your kitchen, would you experience it as a poem?

The poet e. e. cummings is noted for his unusual placement of words on the page and his lack of capital letters. Your teacher will read the poem on page 276 aloud to show the effects achieved by this unusual spacing.

"This is Just to Say" by William Carlos Williams, from *Collected Poems: 1909–1939, Volume 1* (New York: New Directions).

in Just-

1   in Just-
    spring   when the world is mud-
    luscious the little
    lame balloonman

5   whistles   far   and wee
    and eddieandbill come
    running from marbles and
    piracies and it's
    spring

10   when the world is puddle-wonderful

    the queer
    old balloonman whistles
    far   and   wee
    and bettyandisbel come dancing

15   from hop-scotch and jump-rope and

    it's
    spring
    and
      the

20   goat-footed

    balloonMan   whistles
    far
    and
    wee

e. e. cummings

Comprehension

1. This poem describes spring. What aspects of springtime does it mention?

2. What are the names of the children?

3. Cummings is also noted for inventing words. In this poem, the words *mud-luscious* and *puddle-wonderful* have been created by combining common English words. What do you think each of these means? Do you find cummings's unusual spacing and invented words effective?

4. What is e. e. cummings's attitude toward spring? Toward the balloonman? What is the spirit or mood of the poem? Is it happy? Sad? Threatening? Use evidence from the poem to support your position.

5. Both Williams and cummings use the word *just.* Is this *just* spring? Was Williams's poem *just* an apology?

"in Just-" by E. E. cummings, from *Complete Poems: 1904–1962* by E. E. cummings, edited by George J. Firmage (New York: Liveright, 1976).

Spring and Fall:
To a Young Child

1 Margaret, are you grieving
Over Goldengrove unleaving?
Leaves, like the things of man, you
With your fresh thoughts care for, can you?
5 Ah! as the heart grows older
It will come to such sights colder
By and by, nor spare a sigh
Though worlds of wanwood leafmeal lie;
And yet you will weep and know why.
10 Now no matter child, the name:
Sorrow's springs are the same.
Nor mouth had, no nor mind, expressed
What heart heard of, ghost guessed:
It is the blight man was born for,
15 It is Margaret you mourn for.

Gerard Manley Hopkins

Comprehension

1. This poem begins with a question: Why is Margaret grieving? The poem unfolds in a way that answers this question. To discover the answer, first we must untangle some unusual syntax.

   a. Rearrange the words in lines 3 and 4 so that the word order is closer to standard English.

   _____

   _____

   b. Change lines 12 and 13 so that they too are closer to standard English. In this case you may want to change or add words; for example, *neither* usually precedes *nor*.

   _____

   _____

"Spring and Fall: To a Young Child" by Gerard Manley Hopkins, from *Poetry: From Statement to Meaning* (New York: Oxford University Press).

2. In this poem, Hopkins has invented a number of new words. These have been created by combining words or word forms. What do you think is the meaning of each of the following? Feel free to use your dictionary to look up the meanings of parts of these compound words.

Goldengrove (line 2) _____

unleaving (line 2) _____

wanwood (line 8) _____

leafmeal (line 8) _____

3. Now that you have looked more closely at the language of the poem, read it through once again. Why is Margaret grieving?

Reading Selection 3
Short Story

Before You Begin   There is a saying in English: "Be careful, or your wishes will come true."

   1. What does this mean?

   2. Do you believe there is wisdom in this saying?

Alan Austen is a troubled young man. Luckily, he finds a strange old man who can help him. There's just one problem. . . .

   Read this classic short story, then do the exercises that follow. Your teacher may want you to do Vocabulary from Context exercise 1 on page 283 before you begin reading.

The Chaser

John Collier

1   Alan Austen, as nervous as a kitten, went up certain dark and creaky stairs in the neighborhood of Pell Street and peered about for a long time on the dim hallway before he found the name he wanted written obscurely on one of the doors.

2   He pushed open this door, as he had been told to do, and found himself in a tiny room, which contained no furniture but a plain kitchen table, a rocking-chair, and an ordinary chair. On one of the dirty buff-coloured walls were a couple of shelves, containing in all perhaps a dozen bottles and jars.

3   An old man sat in the rocking chair, reading a newspaper. Alan, without a word, handed him the card he had been given. "Sit down, Mr. Austen," said the old man very politely. "I am glad to make your acquaintance."

4   "Is it true," asked Alan, "that you have a certain mixture that has-er-quite extraordinary effects?"

   "My dear sir," replied the old man, "my stock in trade is not very large—I don't deal in laxatives and teething mixtures—but such as it is, it is varied. I think nothing I sell has effects which could be precisely described as ordinary."

   "Well, the fact is . . ." began Alan.

5   "Here, for example," interrupted the old man, reaching for a bottle from the shelf. "Here is a liquid as colourless as water, almost tasteless, quite imperceptible in coffee, wine, or any other beverage. It is also quite imperceptible to any known method of autopsy."*

6   "Do you mean it is a poison?" cried Alan, very much horrified.

   "Call it a glove-cleaner if you like," said the old man indifferently. "Maybe it will clean gloves. I have never tried. One might call it a life-cleaner. Lives need cleaning sometimes."

"The Chaser" by John Collier. Originally published in the *New Yorker.*
*autopsy: the examination of a dead body to determine the cause of death

7 "I want nothing of that sort," said Alan.

"Probably it is just as well," said the old man. "Do you know the price of this? For one teaspoonful, which is sufficient, I ask five thousand dollars. Never less. Not a penny less."

"I hope all your mixtures are not as expensive," said Alan apprehensively.

8 "Oh dear, no," said the old man. "It would be no good charging that sort of price for a love potion, for example. Young people who need a love potion very seldom have five thousand dollars. Otherwise they would not need a love potion."

"I am glad to hear that," said Alan.

9 "I look at it like this," said the old man. "Please a customer with one article, and he will come back when he needs another. Even if it is more costly. He will save up for it, if necessary."

"So," said Alan, "you really do sell love potions?"

10 "If I did not sell love potions," said the old man, reaching for another bottle, "I should not have mentioned the other matter to you. It is only when one is in a position to oblige that one can afford to be so confidential."

"And these potions," said Alan. "They are not just-just-er-"

11 "Oh, no," said the old man. "Their effects are permanent, and extend far beyond the mere casual impulse. But they include it. Oh, yes, they include it. Bountifully, insistently. Everlastingly."

"Dear me!" said Alan, attempting a look of scientific detachment. "How *very* interesting!"

12 "But consider the spiritual side," said the old man.

"I do, indeed," said Alan.

"For indifference," said the old man, "they substitute devotion. For scorn, adoration. Give one tiny measure of this to the young lady—its flavour is imperceptible in orange juice, soup, or cocktails—and however gay and giddy she is, she will change altogether. She will want nothing but solitude and you."

13 "I can hardly believe it," said Alan. "She is so fond of parties."

"She will not like them *any* more," said the old man. "She will be afraid of the pretty girls you may meet."

"She will actually be jealous?" cried Alan in a rapture. "Of me?"

"Yes, she will want to be everything to you."

"She is, already. Only she doesn't care about it."

14 "She will, when she has taken this. She will care intensely. You will be her sole interest in life."

"Wonderful!" cried Alan.

"She will want to know *all* you do," said the old man. "*All* that has happened to you during the day. *Every* word of it. She will want to know what you are thinking about, why you smile suddenly, why you are looking sad."

"That is love!" cried Alan.

15   "Yes," said the old man. "How carefully she will look after you! She will never allow you to be tired, to sit in a draught, to neglect your food. If you are an hour late, she will be terrified. She will think you are killed, or that some siren has caught you."

"I can hardly imagine Diana like that!" cried Alan, overwhelmed with joy.

16   "You will not have to use your imagination," said the old man. "And, by the way, since there are always sirens, if by any chance you *should*, later on, slip a little, you need not worry. She will forgive you, in the end. She will be terribly hurt, of course, but she will forgive you—in the end."

"That will not happen," said Alan fervently.

17   "Of course not," said the old man. "But, if it did, you need not worry. She would never divorce you. Oh, no! And, of course, she will never give you the least, the very least, grounds for—uneasiness."

"And how much," said Alan, "is this wonderful mixture?"

"It is not as dear," said the old man, "as the glove-cleaner, or life-cleaner, as I sometimes call it. No. That is five thousand dollars, never a penny less. One has to be older than you are to indulge in that sort of thing. One has to save up for it."

18   "But the love potion?" said Alan.

"Oh, that," said the old man, opening the drawer in the kitchen table, and taking out a tiny, rather dirty-looking phial. "That is just a dollar."

"I can't tell you how grateful I am," said Alan, watching him fill it.

19   "I like to oblige," said the old man. "Then customers come back, later in life, when they are better off, and want more expensive things. Here you are. You will find it very effective."

"Thank you again," said Alan. "Good-bye."

"*Au revoir*,"* said the old man.

Comprehension

Answer the following questions. Your teacher may want you to do this exercise orally, in writing, or by underlining appropriate parts of the text. True/False items are indicated by a T / F preceding the statement.

1. T / F   Alan Austen accidentally discovered the old man's room.

2. T / F   The old man sold a large number of mixtures commonly found in pharmacies.

3. What did the old man call the $5,000 mixture? _____

4. What was the $5,000 mixture? _____

---

au revoir: (French) good-bye; until we meet again

5. T / F   Alan Austen loved Diana more than she loved him.

6. How would you describe Diana? _____

   _____

7. According to the old man, what effect would the love potion have on Diana? _____

   _____

8. T / F   Alan felt that he could never love anyone but Diana.

9. A chaser is a drink taken to cover the unpleasant taste of a preceding drink. What is the first
   drink in this story? What is its unpleasant "taste"? What is the chaser? _____

   _____

10. How could the old man make enough money to live if he sold his love potion for only one dollar?

    _____

    _____

Drawing Inferences

In part, what makes "The Chaser" an interesting story is the fact that the author and the reader share a secret: they know something that Alan Austen doesn't know. Each reader will discover the meaning of the title, "The Chaser," at a different moment in the story. However, even if you finished the story before you realized the real meaning of the old man's words, you were probably able to go back and find double meanings in many of the passages in the story.

The following quotations are taken from "The Chaser." Read each one; then give two possible meanings: (1) the meaning Alan Austen understands and (2) what you consider to be the real meaning. The number in parentheses indicates the paragraph where the quotation can be found. Your teacher may want you to do this exercise orally or in writing.

1. (14) "She will want to know *all* you do," said the old man. "*All* that has happened to you during the day. *Every* word of it. She will want to know what you are thinking about, why you smile suddenly, why you are looking sad."

2. (17) ". . . you need not worry. She would never divorce you."

3. (19) "I like to oblige," said the old man. "Then customers come back, later in life, when they are better off, and want more expensive things."

4. (19) "Thank you again," said Alan. "Good-bye."
   "*Au revoir,*" said the old man.

Discussion/Composition

1. This short story suggests that love potions require an antidote. By this logic, are there other desires that, if fulfilled, require an antidote? What are some of these?

2. Write a scene between Alan and the old man or Alan and Diana that takes place in the future.

Vocabulary from Context

Exercise 1

Use the context provided to determine the meanings of the italicized words. Write a definition, synonym, or description of each of the italicized vocabulary items in the space provided.

1. _____ The doctor said that if a person ate even one leaf of the hemlock plant, he or she would die because the plant is a deadly *poison.*

2. _____ The murderer had developed a poison that could not be tasted or smelled when mixed with food. Because it was *imperceptible,* he was able to murder a number of people without being caught.

3. _____ "When making this mixture," the man said, "you don't need two teaspoons of salt, because one teaspoon is *sufficient.*"

4. _____ "Since you are my best friend, and because I can trust you, I know I can be *confidential* with you. Listen carefully, because what I am going to tell you is a secret," said Henry.

5. _____ "I am able to *oblige* you, sir; I can give you the item you wanted so badly."

6. _____ There are times when one wants to be surrounded by people, and there are times when one needs *solitude.*

7. _____ The husband was so *jealous* that he would not allow his wife to talk to other men.

Exercise 2

This exercise is designed to give you additional clues to determine the meanings of unfamiliar vocabulary items in context. In the paragraph of "The Chaser" indicated by the number in parentheses, find the word that best fits the meaning given. Your teacher may want to read these aloud as you quickly scan* the paragraph to find the answer.

1. (1)   Which word means *poorly lighted; dark?*

2. (4)   Which word means *objects for sale; items kept for sale?*

3. (7)   Which word means *worriedly; with alarm or concern?*

4. (10) Which word means *to perform a service; to please or help someone?*

5. (16) Which word means *women who attract, seduce, lure men?*

6. (17) Which word means *reason; basis; foundation?*

---

*For an introduction to scanning, see Unit 1.

Exercise 3

This exercise should be done after you have finished reading "The Chaser." The exercise is designed to give you practice using context clues to guess the meaning of unfamiliar vocabulary. Give a definition, synonym, or description of each of the words and phrases below. The number in parentheses indicates the paragraph in which the word or phrase can be found. Your teacher may want you to do these orally or in writing.

1. (1) peered _____

2. (8) potion _____

3. (16) slip a little _____

4. (17) dear _____

5. (19) better off _____

Nonprose Reading
Road Map

If you travel by car in an English-speaking country, you will need to read road maps in English. This exercise is designed to give you practice in many aspects of map reading.*

Before You Begin   Reflect on road travel in your country or region.

1. If you are traveling to an unfamiliar area, how do you find out about the route? Do you ever rely on road maps?

2. Why do you think road maps are important to travel in the United States?

Introduction

Exercise 1

Examine the parts of the map you will need to use in order to answer the questions below.

1. On page 289 is a section of a *map* in Tennessee (TN) and Kentucky (KY), two states of the United States.

   Find the Kentucky-Tennessee border.

2. On page 288 is a section of the *Tennessee City and Town Index.* This lists the larger cities and towns in Tennessee with coordinates to help you find the names of these cities and towns on the map.

   a. What are the coordinates of Clarksville, TN? _____

   b. Locate Clarksville on the map on page 289.

---

*For an explanation of nonprose reading, see Unit 1.

3. On page 290 is an *inset* (a larger, more detailed reproduction) of Nashville, TN. You will need to use the inset of Nashville to find information about major roads and landmarks within Nashville.

Tennessee State University (on the west side of the city) is located near the intersection of which two streets?

_____

4. On page 291 is a *legend,* that is, a list of symbols to help you interpret the map on page 289. On the legend is the *distance scale,* which tells you the relationship of both miles and kilometers to inches on the map. Examine the legend carefully to see if you have any questions.

   a. Using the distance scale, estimate the distance in both miles and kilometers from Bowling Green, KY (coordinates: J-13) to the KY-TN border.

   _____

   b. What is the difference between the two roads, Route 31W and Route 65, that connect Bowling Green to Nashville?

   _____

5. Finally, on page 291 you will find a *driving distance map.* This map will tell you the exact distance in miles between many of the large cities in Kentucky, Tennessee, and surrounding states. It also estimates the driving time from city to city.

   What is the distance between Bowling Green, KY, and Nashville, TN? _____

Exercise 2

This exercise is designed to give you practice in deciding where to look for specific pieces of information. Below are questions you might ask if you needed to find information from a map. Read each question, and then decide if you would look for the answer on the map itself, in the Tennessee City and Town Index, on the inset of Nashville, on the legend, or on the driving distance map. Put the appropriate letter in the blank provided.

a. map

b. city and town index

c. inset

d. legend

e. driving distance map

Where should you look to find the following?

1. _____ the distance between Bowling Green, KY, and Cincinnati, Ohio?

2. _____ the coordinates of McMinnville, TN?

3. _____ the best route from Ashland City, TN, to Murfreesboro, TN?

4. _____ the location in Nashville of the Country Music Hall of Fame and Museum?

5. _____ what the symbol 𝘈 means?

6. _____ how to get to Vanderbilt University in Nashville from Interstate Highway 65?

Map Reading

Use all the information provided on pages 288–91 to do the exercises that follow.

Exercise 1

Indicate if each statement below is true (T) or false (F). Work as quickly as you can.

1. _____ There is a direct route going northwest between Nashville and Clarksville, TN.

2. _____ Franklin, located north of Nashville, is in Tennessee.

3. _____ Cincinatti, Ohio, is about 300 miles driving distance from Nashville, TN.

4. _____ In southwest Nashville, Route 70S will take you directly to the Belle Meade Plantation.

5. _____ There is a passenger service airport near Nashville, TN.

6. _____ Going toward downtown Nashville from the southeast, you can get onto Route 40 from Route 24.

7. _____ Northwest of Nashville, a state highway connects Ashland City and Clarksville.

8. _____ Bellwood, TN, is west of Bellsburg, TN.

9. _____ Ashland City, TN, northwest of Nashville, is less than 14 miles/22.4 kilometers from Bellsburg.

10. _____ Nashville is the capital of Tennessee.

11. _____ Coming into downtown Nashville from the north on Route 431 (Whites Creek Pike), you can exit directly onto Route 65.

Exercise 2

If you were to take a trip by car through Kentucky and Tennessee, you would have to solve problems such as the ones posed by the questions in this exercise. Answer each question as completely as possible. Often there is more than one correct answer. Your teacher may ask you to do these orally or in writing.

1. Could you leave Chattanooga, TN, at 8:00 A.M. and get to Bowling Green, KY, in time for a 12:00 lunch? How fast would you have to drive?

2. Which route would you take going northeast from Bowling Green to Mammoth Cave National Park?

_____

Can you spend the night at Mammoth Cave National Park? _____

3. Which route would you take from McMinnville, TN, to Nashville, TN, if you wanted to see the Edgar Evins State Park (north of McMinnville) and Cedars of Lebanon State Park (north of Murfreesboro)?

_____

TENNESSEE CITY AND TOWN INDEX

Acton....................R-7	Avoca............L-27,P-28	Buffalo Valley.........N-15	Centertown.............O-15	Coalfield..............N-20
Adair....................O-5	Bailey...................R-2	Buladeen...............P-29	Centerville............O-10	Coalmont..............Q-16
Adams...................L-12	Baileyton.............M-26	Bulls Gap..............M-24	Central.................N-5	Coble..................O-10
Adamsville..............Q-7	Bairds Mill...........N-14	Bumpus Mill.........D-3,L-9	Cerro Gordo...........Q-8	Coghill................Q-20
Aetna...................P-10	Bakerville..............N-9	Burke..................O-18	Chalk Level...........M-24	Cokercreek............Q-21
Alamo...................O-5	Bakewell..............Q-18	Burlison................P-2	Chanute................L-18	Coldwater.............R-13
Alcoa............M-49,O-22	Baneberry.............N-24	Burns..................N-11	Chapel Hill............P-13	Colesburg.............N-11
Alexandria.............N-14	Banner Hill.......N-27,R-28	Burrville...............M-19	Chapmansboro.........M-11	Collegedale...........R-18
Algood.................N-17	Banner Springs........M-18	Burwood...............O-12	Charleys Branch.......N-20	College Grove.........O-13
Allardt................M-19	Barfield...............O-13	Busby..................R-11	Charleston.............P-3	Collierville............R-3
Allens...................P-5	Bargerton..............O-6	Butler.................Q-29	Charleston............Q-19	Collinwood............Q-9
Allisona................O-12	Barkertown............Q-16	Bybee............K-55,N-24	Charlotte..............N-11	Colonial Heights.......I-49
Allons.................M-17	Barnesville............Q-10	Bybee..................O-15	Chaska.................L-21	Columbia..............P-12
Allred.................M-17	Barren Plains..........L-12	Byrdstown.............L-18	Chattanooga......R-18,R-42	Comfort...............R-16
Almaville...............O-13	Bartlett...........K-42,Q-3	Cades...................N-6	Cherokee Hills.........L-52	Como...................M-7
Alnwick..........M-49,O-21	Bath Springs...........Q-8	Cades Cove.............P-22	Cherry.................O-3	Conasauga.............R-19
Alpha..................N-23	Baxter.................N-16	Cainsville.............N-14	Cherry Valley..........N-14	Concord................O-13
Alpine.................M-17	Beacon.................P-8	Calderwood.......O-49,P-22	Chesney...............M-22	Concord...............O-21
Altamont...............Q-15	Beans Creek...........R-14	Calhoun................Q-19	Chesterfield...........P-7	Cookeville............N-16
Alto...................Q-15	Bean Station..........M-24	Camden.............G-2,N-8	Chestnut Hill......L-54,O-24	Coopertown...........L-12
Anderson...............R-15	Beardstown............O-9	Camelot................L-24	Chestnut Mound........N-16	Copperhill.............R-20
Andersonville.........N-21	Bear Spring............L-9	Campbellsville.........Q-11	Chewalla...............R-6	Corbin Hill............N-20
Annadel...............N-19	Beech Bluff............P-6	Camp Creek............N-26	Chic....................N-3	Cordova...............Q-2
Antioch................N-13	Beechgrove............P-14	Caney Branch.....K-56,N-25	Christiana.............P-14	Cornersville...........Q-12
Apison.................R-18	Beersheba Springs......P-16	Caneyspring............P-12	Christmasville.........N-6	Corryton..............N-22
Archer.................Q-12	Belfast.................Q-12	Capleville..............R-2	Chuckey...............M-26	Cosby............M-54,O-24
Archville..............R-20	Bell Buckle............P-14	Carlisle.................M-9	Church Hill............L-26	Cottage Grove..........M-7
Ardmore...............R-13	Belle Meade...........N-44	Carlock................Q-20	Churchton.............N-5	Cottontown...........M-13
Arlington...............Q-3	Belleville.............Q-13	Carson Springs........L-54	Clairfield..............L-22	Cottonwood Grove.....M-3
Armathwaite..........M-19	Bells...................O-5	Carter................P-29	Clarkrange............N-18	Coulterville...........Q-18
Arp....................O-3	Bellsburg.............M-11	Carthage..............M-15	Clarksburg.............O-7	Counce.................R-7
Arrington..............O-12	Bell Town.............N-11	Caryville..............M-21	Clarksville........G-45,L-10	Cove Creek Cascades...M-51,
Arthur.................L-22	Bellwood..............M-14	Cash Point............R-12	Clayton................L-4	O-22
Ashland City..........M-12	Belvidere..............R-14	Castalian Springs......M-14	Cleveland..............R-19	Covington..............P-3
Ashport................O-2	Benton.................R-19	Catlettsburg...........O-23	Clevenger.........K-54,N-24	Cowan.................R-15
Aspen Hill.............R-11	Buchanan..........E-1,L-8	Cavvia.................O-8	Clifton................Q-9	Crab Orchard..........O-19
Athens.................P-20	Buckeye...............M-21	Cedar Creek......K-57,N-25	Clifton Jct.............Q-8	Crabtree..............Q-29
Atoka...................P-2	Bucksnort..............O-9	Cedar Grove............O-6	Clifty..................O-18	Craggie Hope..........N-11
Atwood.................N-6	Buena Vista............N-8	Cedar Hill.............L-12	Clinton................N-21	
Auburntown............O-15	Buffalo.................O-9	Celina.................L-16	Clovercroft............O-12	McMinnville...........P-16
Austin Sprs......M-27,P-28	Buffalo Springs.........M-23	Center.................Q-10	Cloverport.............Q-5	Murfreesboro..........O-14
		Center Point..........R-11		

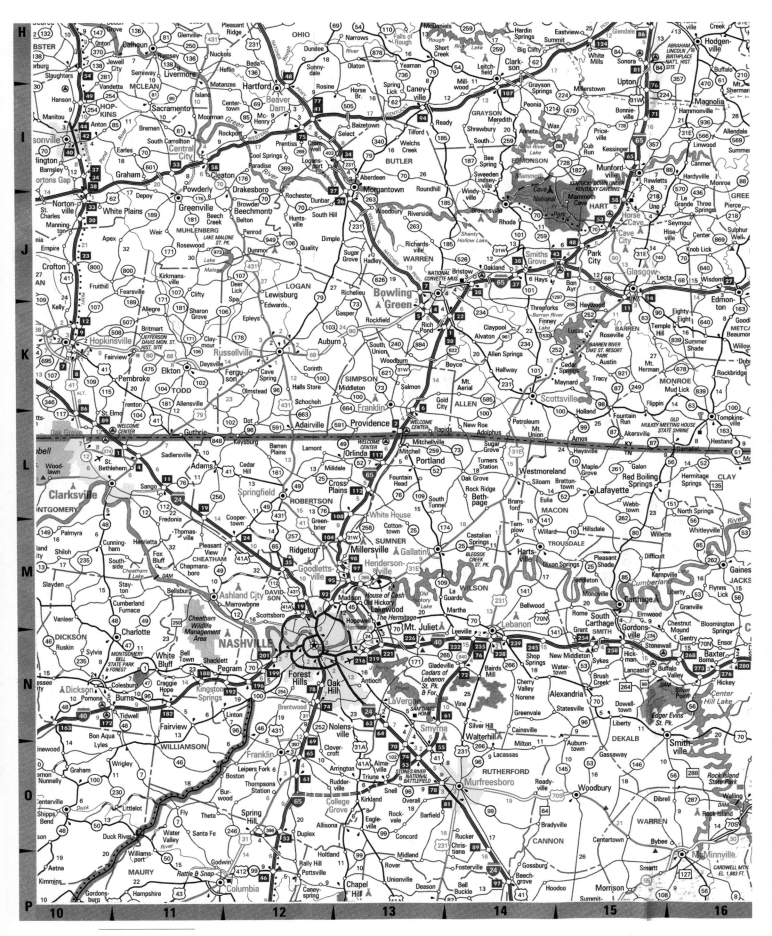

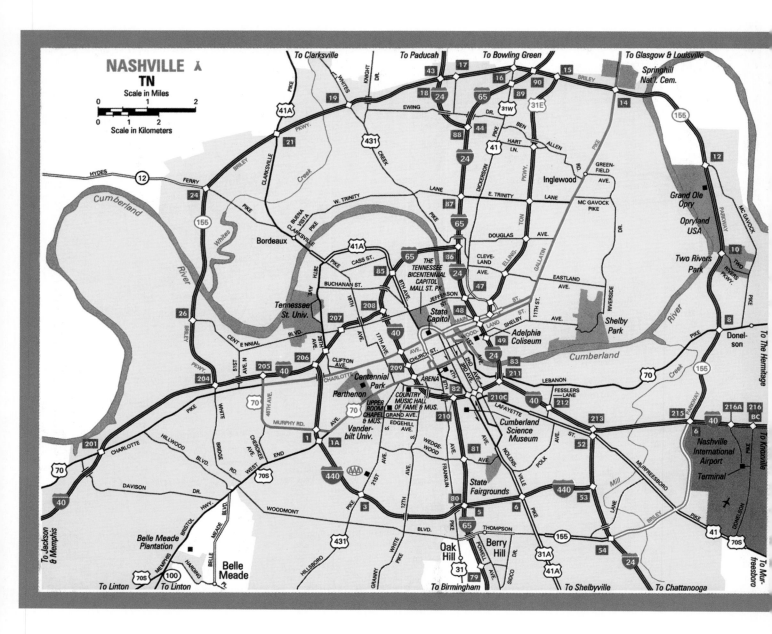

© AAA reproduced by permission.

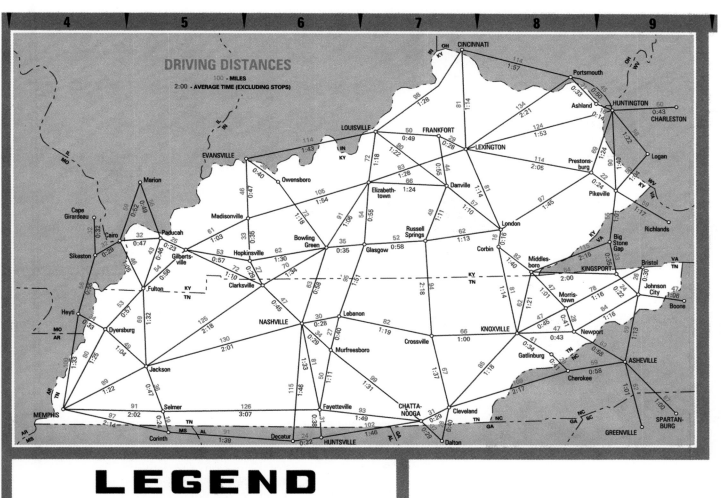

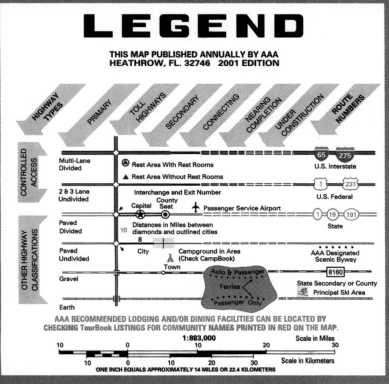

© AAA reproduced by permission.

Word Study
Context Clues

Exercise 1

In the following exercise, do NOT try to learn the italicized words. Concentrate on developing your ability to guess the meanings of unfamiliar words using context clues. Read each sentence carefully and write a definition, synonym, or description of the italicized word on the line provided.

1. _____ As he reached for the rock above him, his rope broke, and he hung *precariously* by one hand as the rescuers ran toward him.

2. _____ The tired soldiers *trudged* through knee-deep mud for hours before they found a dry place to sleep.

3. _____ In the past, the world seemed to run in an orderly way. Now, however, everything seems to be in a state of *turmoil.*

4. _____ Monkeys are well known for their *grooming* habits; they spend hours carefully cleaning bits of dirt and straw from their coats.

5. _____ *Matrimony* doesn't seem to agree with Liz—she's been unhappy ever since she got married.

6. _____ Using a long, slender instrument called a *probe,* doctors are able to locate and remove pieces of metal from a patient's wounds.

7. _____ The following Monday, when the president *convened* the second meeting of the committee, we all sat down quietly and waited for the meeting to begin.

8. _____ We think of plants in general as absorbing food; we think of animals as *ingesting* or "eating" it.

9. _____ Robben is considered an *autocratic* administrator because he makes decisions without seeking the opinions of others.

10. _____ There is an element of word magic here: entomology and *limnology* sound more important than merely insect biology and freshwater biology.

This exercise is designed to give you practice using context clues from a passage. Use your general knowledge along with information from the entire text below to write a definition, synonym, or description of the italicized word on the line provided. Read through the entire passage before making a decision. Note that some of the words appear more than once; by the end of the passage you should have a good idea of their meaning. Do not worry if your definition is not exact; a general idea of the meaning will often allow you to understand the meaning of a written text.

Major Personality Study Finds That Traits Are Mostly Inherited

Daniel Goleman

The *genetic* makeup of a child is a stronger influence on personality than child *rearing,* according to the first study to examine identical twins *reared* in different families. The *findings shatter* a widespread belief among experts and laypeople alike in the *primacy* of family influence and are sure to lead to fierce debate.

The *findings* are the first major results to emerge from a long-term project at the University of Minnesota in which more than 350 pairs of twins have gone through six days of extensive testing that has included analysis of blood, brain waves, intelligence, and allergies.

For most of the traits measured, more than half the variation was found to be due to *heredity,* leaving less than half determined by the influence of parents, home environment and other experiences in life.

The Minnesota *findings* stand in sharp contradiction to standard wisdom on nature vs. *nurture* in forming adult personality. Virtually all major theories since Freud have given far more importance to environment, or *nurture,* than to *genes* or nature.

genetic/genes: _____

rearing/reared: _____

findings: _____

shatter: _____

primacy: _____

heredity: _____

nurture: _____

From the *New York Times.*

Sentence Study
Restatement and Inference

This exercise is similar to the one found in Unit 7.* Each sentence below is followed by five statements. The statements are of four types.

1. Some of the statements are restatements of the original sentence. They give the same information in a different way.

2. Some of the statements are inferences (conclusions) that can be drawn from the information given in the original sentence.

3. Some of the statements are false based on the information given.

4. Some of the statements cannot be judged true or false based on the information given in the original sentence.

Put a check (✓) next to all restatements and inferences (types 1 and 2). *Note:* do not check a statement that is true of itself but cannot be inferred from the sentence given.

1. A favorite definition of joking has long been the ability to find similarity between dissimilar things—that is, hidden similarities.

   _____ a. Joking is the ability to find similarity in dissimilar things.

   _____ b. It takes a long time to develop the ability to tell good jokes.

   _____ c. This definition of joking is a new one in literary theory.

   _____ d. Many people define joking as the ability to find similarity in dissimilar things.

   _____ e. The author agrees with this definition.

2. After the Romantic period, most modern theory dealt with the peculiar act of the poet rather than the poet's product or its effect on the audience.

   _____ a. Most modern theory did not deal with the poem itself or its effect on the audience.

   _____ b. Most modern theory of poetry dealt with the act of the poet.

   _____ c. After the Romantic period, literary theory dealt with the effect of poetry on the reader.

   _____ d. The author believes that literary theory should deal only with the peculiar act of the poet.

   _____ e. Modern theory is considered to begin at the Romantic period.

_____

*For an introduction to sentence study, see Unit 3.

3. Although women still make up the majority of volunteer groups, male participation is reported on the rise nationwide as traditional distinctions between men's work and women's work fade.

_____ a. As traditional societal roles change, more men are becoming members of volunteer groups.

_____ b. Most members of volunteer groups are women.

_____ c. In the past, volunteer work was done mainly by women.

_____ d. Male participation in volunteer groups is increasing in all cities.

_____ e. The author believes there is a relationship between the changing societal roles and the increasing willingness of men to do work previously done by females.

4. The overall picture of this very early settled Peruvian population is that of a simple, peaceful people living in a small cultivable oasis by the sea; fishing; raising a few food crops; living in small, simple, nonmasonry houses and making the objects necessary for their economic and household life, with slight attention to art.

_____ a. This early Peruvian population had all the basic necessities of life available to it.

_____ b. We can assume that art only exists in very advanced societies.

_____ c. This society moved many times during the year.

_____ d. Because the people worked so hard they had no time for art.

_____ e. The author believes this society provides nothing of interest for historians.

5. Only a small number of scholars can be named who have entered at all deeply into the problems of jokes.

_____ a. Only a few scholars have studied jokes.

_____ b. The area of jokes is so complex that only a small number of people have been able to study it.

_____ c. Few scholars have studied the problem of jokes at all deeply.

_____ d. The author cannot remember the names of scholars who have studied jokes.

_____ e. It is not possible to name all those who have studied jokes at all deeply.

6. There is a question about the extent to which any one of us can be completely free of a prejudiced view in the area of religion.

_____ a. Probably all people are prejudiced in their views on religion.

_____ b. Any one of us can be free of prejudice in the area of religion.

_____ c. To some extent we can never be free of prejudice in the area of religion.

_____ d. A prejudiced view in the area of religion is undesirable.

_____ e. Because we can't be free of prejudice in the area of religion, we should not practice a religion.

7. Although the November election may significantly change the face of the county Board of Commissioners, the group will still have to confront the same old problems.

_____ a. The November election may give the Board of Commissioners a new building.

_____ b. The Board of Commissioners consists of several members.

_____ c. The November election may change the membership of the Board of Commissioners.

_____ d. Although board members may change, the problems will remain the same.

_____ e. The author does not believe that this election will change the difficulties facing the commissioners.

8. If this book begins with a familiar theme—the Native American experience of the last 120 years—the author brings to it great power and deep understanding.

_____ a. This book was written 120 years ago.

_____ b. The Native American experience of the last 120 years is a familiar experience, and nothing new can be written about it.

_____ c. The book lacks understanding of the Native American experience.

_____ d. The book begins with a familiar theme.

_____ e. The author of this sentence likes the book.

9. In this part of the world, the political and social changes of the past 20 years have by no means eliminated the old upper class of royalty and friends and advisers of royalty, the holders of state monopolies, the great landlords and lords of commercial fiefs, and tribal and village leaders.

_____ a. In this part of the world, political and social changes have eliminated great landlords, lords of commercial fiefs, and village leaders.

_____ b. In this part of the world, the upper class and their friends and advisers have not been eliminated by political and social change.

_____ c. No means can eliminate the old upper class of royalty in this part of the world.

_____ d. The upper class of royalty has not changed in the past 20 years in this part of the world.

_____ e. In this part of the world, village leaders hold as much power as the advisers of royalty.

10. People should and do choose their elected representatives partly on the basis of how well they believe these representatives, once in office, can convince them to do or support whatever needs to be done.

   ____ a. It is the author's belief that people should choose representatives whom they believe will convince them to take action.

   ____ b. People choose representatives on the basis of whether or not they believe the representatives can be convinced to do what needs to be done.

   ____ c. Although people should choose representatives whom they believe will convince them to take action, often they do not.

   ____ d. People choose representatives whom they believe will convince them to take action.

   ____ e. Representatives are elected only on the basis of their ability to take action.

Paragraph Analysis
Reading for Full Understanding

This exercise is similar to the one found in Unit 7. Read each paragraph carefully. Try to determine the author's main idea while attempting to remember important details. For each of the questions below, select the *best* answer. You may refer to the passage to answer the questions.

Paragraph 1

```
 1     Summers with my father were always enjoyable. Swimming, hiking,
 2   boating, fishing—the days were not long enough to contain all of our
 3   activities. There never seemed to be enough time to go to church,
 4   which disturbed some friends and relations. Accused of neglecting this
 5    part of our education, my father instituted a summer school for my
 6   brother and me. However, his summer course included ancient history,
 7   which Papa felt our schools neglected, and navigation, in which we first
 8   had a formal examination in the dining room, part of which consisted
 9   of tying several knots in a given time limit. Then we were each
10   separately sent on what was grandly referred to as a cruise in my
11   father's 18-foot knockabout, spending the night on board, and loaded
12   down, according to my mother, with enough food for a week. I
13   remember that on my cruise I was required to formally plot our course,
14   using the tide table, even though our goal was an island I could see
15   quite clearly across the water in the distance.
```

1. What was the original reason for holding the summer school?

   _____ a. Friends and relatives thought the children should learn religion.

   _____ b. The father wanted the children to learn more about religion.

   _____ c. The children got poor grades in their regular school.

   _____ d. The regular schoolteachers neglected the children.

2. The purpose of the cruise mentioned in the passage was to _____

   _____ a. have fun.

   _____ b. test the author's sailing ability.

   _____ c. reward the author for completing summer school.

   _____ d. get to the island.

From Sylvia Wright, Introduction to *Islandia*, by Austin Tappan Wright (New York: Rinehart and Co.).

3. Why did the author have to plot the course of her cruise?

_____ a. She had to demonstrate her ability to do so.

_____ b. She was afraid of getting lost.

_____ c. The coast was dangerous.

_____ d. The tides were strong.

4. How long did the author's cruise last?

_____ a. all summer   _____ c. overnight

_____ b. a week   _____ d. one day, morning till night

5. Apparently a knockabout is ___

_____ a. an island.   _____ b. a cruise.   _____ c. a boat.   _____ d. a seaman's knot.

Paragraph 2

1   The cicada exemplifies an insect
2   species which uses a combinatorial
3   communication system. In their life
4   cycle, communication is very impor-
5   tant, for only through the exchange of
6   sounds do cicadas know where to meet
7   and when to mate. Three different calls
8   are employed for this purpose. Because
9   of their limited sound producing
10 mechanisms, cicadas can make only
11 ticks and buzzes. The only way they
12 can distinguish between congregation
13 and courtship calls is by varying the
14 rate with which they make ticks and
15 buzzes. The congregation call consists
16 of 12 to 40 ticks, delivered rapidly, followed by a two-second buzz. It
17 is given by males but attracts cicadas of both sexes. Once they are all
18 together, the males use courtship calls. The preliminary call, a
19 prolonged, slow ticking, is given when the male notices a female near
20 him. The advanced call, a prolonged series of short buzzes at the same
21 slow rate, is given when a female is almost within grasp. The preliminary
22 call almost invariably occurs before the advanced call, although the
23 latter is given without the preliminary call occurring first if a female is
24 suddenly discovered very near by. During typical courtship, though,
25 the two calls together result in ticking followed by a buzzing—the
26 same pattern which comprises the congregation call but delivered at a
27 slower rate. In this way, cicadas show efficient use of their minimal
28 sound-producing ability, organizing two sounds delivered at a high rate
29 as one call and the same sounds delivered at a slow rate as two or
30 more calls.

From David McNeill, *The Acquisition of Language* (New York: Harper and Row).

1. The cicada congregation call _____

_____ a. attracts only males.

_____ c. is given only by males.

_____ b. is given by both sexes.

_____ d. attracts only females.

2. During typical courtship, when a male first notices a female near him, he gives _____

_____ a. the two courtship calls together.

_____ c. 12 to 40 rapid ticks.

_____ b. a series of slow ticks.

_____ d. a two-second buzz.

3. How does the congregation call differ from the two courtship calls together?

_____ a. It is delivered at a slower rate.

_____ c. The ticks precede the buzzes.

_____ b. It is delivered at a faster rate.

_____ d. The buzzes precede the ticks.

4. According to this passage, why is communication so important for cicadas?

_____ a. It helps them defend themselves against other insect species.

_____ b. It warns them of approaching danger.

_____ c. It separates the males from the females.

_____ d. It is necessary for the continuation of the species.

Paragraph 3

1 Robert Spring, a 19th century forger, was so good at his profession
2 that he was able to make his living for 15 years by selling false signa-
3 tures of famous Americans. Spring was born in England in 1813 and
4 arrived in Philadelphia in 1858 to open a bookstore. At first he pros-
5 pered by selling his small but genuine collection of early U.S. auto-
6 graphs. Discovering his ability at copying handwriting, he began
7 imitating signatures of George Washington and Ben Franklin and
8 writing them on the title pages of old books. To lessen the chance of
9 detection, he sent his forgeries to England and Canada for sale and
10 circulation.
11 Forgers have a hard time selling their products. A forger can't
12 approach a respectable buyer but must deal with people who don't
13 have much knowledge in the field. Forgers have many ways to make
14 their work look real. For example, they buy old books to use the aged
15 paper of the title page, and they can treat paper and ink with chemicals.
16 In Spring's time, right after the Civil War, Britain was still fond of the
17 Southern states, so Spring invented a respectable maiden lady known
18 as Miss Fanny Jackson, the only daughter of General "Stonewall"
19 Jackson. For several years Miss Fanny's financial problems forced her to
20 sell a great number of letters and manuscripts belonging to her famous
21 father. Spring had to work very hard to satisfy the demand. All this
22 activity did not prevent Spring from dying in poverty, leaving sharp-
23 eyed experts the difficult task of separating his forgeries from the originals.

From the *Michigan Daily.*

1. Why did Spring sell his false autographs in England and Canada?

_____ a. There was a greater demand there than in America.

_____ b. There was less chance of being detected there.

_____ c. Britain was Spring's birthplace.

_____ d. The prices were higher in England and Canada.

2. After the Civil War, there was a great demand in Britain for _____

_____ a. Southern money.

_____ b. signatures of George Washington and Ben Franklin.

_____ c. Southern manuscripts and letters.

_____ d. Civil War battle plans.

3. Robert Spring spent 15 years _____

_____ a. running a bookstore in Philadelphia.

_____ b. corresponding with Miss Fanny Jackson.

_____ c. as a forger.

_____ d. as a respectable dealer.

4. According to the passage, forgeries are usually sold to _____

_____ a. sharp-eyed experts.

_____ b. persons who aren't experts.

_____ c. book dealers.

_____ d. owners of old books.

5. Who was Miss Fanny Jackson?

_____ a. the only daughter of General "Stonewall" Jackson

_____ b. a little-known girl who sold her father's papers to Robert Spring

_____ c. Robert Spring's daughter

_____ d. an imaginary person created by Spring

Paragraph 4

1   In science the meaning of the word "explain" suffers with civilization's
2 every step in search of reality. Science cannot really explain electricity,
3 magnetism, and gravitation; their effects can be measured and predicted,
4 but of their nature no more is known to the modern scientist than to
5 Thales, who first speculated on the electrification of amber. Most con-
6 temporary physicists reject the notion that human beings can ever
7 discover what these mysterious forces "really" are. Electricity, Bertrand
8 Russell says, "is not a thing, like St. Paul's Cathedral; it is a way in
9 which things behave. When we have told how things behave when
10 they are electrified, and under what circumstances they are electrified,
11 we have told all there is to tell." Until recently scientists would have
12 disapproved of such an idea. Aristotle, for example, whose natural
13 science dominated Western thought for two thousand years, believed
14 that human beings could arrive at an understanding of reality by
15 reasoning from self-evident principles. He felt, for example, that it is
16 a self-evident principle that every-
17 thing in the universe has its proper
18 place; hence one can deduce that
19 objects fall to the ground because
20 that's where they belong, and
21 smoke goes up because that's
22 where it belongs. The goal of
23 Aristotelian science was to explain
24 *why* things happen. Modern
25 science was born when Galileo
26 began trying to explain *how* things
27 happen and thus originated the
28 method of controlled experiment
29 which now forms the basis of
30 scientific investigation.

1. The aim of controlled scientific experiments is _____

    _____ a. to explain why things happen.

    _____ b. to explain how things happen.

    _____ c. to describe self-evident principles.

    _____ d. to support Aristotelian science.

2. What principles most influenced scientific thought for two thousand years?

    _____ a. the speculations of Thales

    _____ b. the forces of electricity, magnetism, and gravity

    _____ c. Aristotle's natural science

    _____ d. Galileo's discoveries

3. Bertrand Russell's notion about electricity is _____

_____ a. disapproved of by most modern scientists.

_____ b. in agreement with Aristotle's theory of self-evident principles.

_____ c. in agreement with scientific investigation directed toward "how" things happen.

_____ d. in agreement with scientific investigation directed toward "why" things happen.

4. The passage says that until recently scientists disagreed with the idea _____

_____ a. that there are mysterious forces in the universe.

_____ b. that humankind cannot discover what forces "really" are.

_____ c. that there are self-evident principles.

_____ d. that we can discover why things behave as they do.

Paragraph 5		
	1	By about age 12, students who feel threatened by mathematics start
	2	to avoid math courses, do poorly in the few math classes they do take,
	3	and earn low scores on math-achievement tests. Some scientists have
	4	theorized that kids having little math aptitude in the first place justifiably
	5	dread grappling with numbers. However, it is not that simple, at least
	6	for college students, according to a study in the June *Journal of Experi-*
	7	*mental Psychology: General.* According to the study, people's intrusive
	8	worries about math temporarily disrupt mental processes needed for
	9	doing arithmetic and drag down math competence, report Mark H.
	10	Ashcraft and Elizabeth P. Kirk, both psychologists at Cleveland (Ohio)
	11	State University. Math anxiety exerts this effect by making it difficult to
	12	hold new information in mind while simultaneously manipulating it,
	13	the researchers hold. Psychologists regard this capacity, known as
	14	working memory, as crucial for dealing with numbers. "Math anxiety
	15	soaks up working memory resources and makes it harder to learn
	16	mathematics, probably beginning in middle school," Ashcraft says.

1. What did psychologists Ashcraft and Kirk find?

_____ a. Doing poorly in math causes math anxiety.

_____ b. College students learn math differently than 12 year olds do.

_____ c. Worrying about math makes it harder to do math.

_____ d. Students should take harder math classes starting in middle school.

Adapted from *Science News,* June 30, 2001.

2. What term is used to mean *remembering new information at the same time that you are working with it*?

_____ a. math anxiety

_____ b. math aptitude

_____ c. disruptive mental process

_____ d. working memory

3. What theory does the Ashcraft and Kirk study challenge?

_____ a. Math anxiety improves math performance.

_____ b. Math anxiety is a result of low math aptitude.

_____ c. Starting to study math at a young age improves math performance.

_____ d. The more math aptitude one has, the less working memory is needed.

4. What does *crucial for* mean (in the next-to-the-last sentence)?

_____ a. required for

_____ b. harmful to

_____ c. identical to

_____ d. ordinary in

5. The purpose of this passage is to _____

_____ a. report a study about math anxiety.

_____ b. describe how to teach math better.

_____ c. criticize the way math is taught.

_____ d. praise the work of Ashcraft and Kirk.

6. Which of the following is a reasonable inference to draw from this passage?

_____ a. Students who have math anxiety should not be forced to take math classes after middle school.

_____ b. Math aptitude cannot accurately be determined until middle school.

_____ c. Teachers should try to help students avoid worrying when they do math problems.

_____ d. Taking more difficult math classes will improve a student's working memory.

This exercise is similar to the one found in Unit 7. It is designed to give you practice in consciously developing and confirming expectations.

    Below is part of an article about the family. Read the article, stopping to respond to the questions that appear at several points throughout. Remember, you cannot always predict precisely what an author will do, but you can use clues from the text and your general knowledge to make good guesses. Work with your classmates on these items, defending your predictions with parts of the text. Do not worry about unfamiliar vocabulary.

The Changing Family

by Maris Vinovskis

1. Based on the title, what aspect of the family do you think this article will be about? List several possibilities.

   _____

   _____

   _____

Now read the opening paragraph to see what the focus of the article will be.

There is widespread fear among policymakers and the public today that the family is falling apart. Much of that worry stems from a basic misunderstanding of the nature of the family in the past and a lack of appreciation for its strength in response to broad social and economic changes. The general view of the family is that it has been a stable and relatively unchanging institution through history and is only now undergoing changes; in fact, change has always been characteristic of it.

The Family and Household in the Past

2. This article seems to be about the changing nature of the family throughout history. Is this what you expected?

From *LSA* magazine.

3. The introduction is not very specific, so you can only guess what changing aspects of the family will be mentioned in the next section. Using information from the introduction and your general knowledge, check (✔) those topics below that you think will be mentioned.

_____ a. family size   _____ f. the family throughout the world

_____ b. relations within the family   _____ g. the economic role of the family

_____ c. the definition of a family   _____ h. sex differences in family roles

_____ d. the role of the family in society   _____ i. the role of children

_____ e. different family customs   _____ j. sexual relations

Now read the next section, noting which of your predictions are confirmed.

In the last twenty years, historians have been re-examining the nature of the family and have concluded that we must revise our notions of the family as an institution, as well as our assumptions about how children were perceived and treated in past centuries. A survey of diverse studies of the family in the West, particularly in seventeenth-, eighteenth- and nineteenth-century England and America, shows something of the changing role of the family in society and the evolution of our ideas of parenting and child development. (Although many definitions of *family* are available, in this article I will use it to refer to kin living under one roof.)

4. Which aspects of the family listed above were mentioned in this section? _____

_____

_____

5. Which other ones do you predict will be mentioned further on in the article? _____

_____

6. What aspects of the text and your general knowledge help you to create this prediction?

_____

_____

7. Below is the topic sentence of the next paragraph. What kind of supporting data do you expect to find in the rest of the paragraph? How do you think the paragraph will continue?

_____

_____

_____

Although we have tended to believe that in the past children grew up in "extended households" including grandparents, parents, and children, recent historical research has cast considerable doubt on the idea that as countries became increasingly urban and industrial, the Western family evolved from extended to nuclear [i.e., parents and children only].

The rest of the paragraph is reprinted below. Read on to see if your expectations are confirmed.

Historians have found evidence that households in pre-industrial Western Europe were already nuclear and could not have been greatly transformed by economic changes. Rather than finding definite declines in household size, we find surprisingly small variations, which turn out to be a result of the presence or absence of servants, boarders, and lodgers, rather than relatives. In revising our nostalgic picture of children growing up in large families, Peter Laslett, one of the foremost analysts of the pre-industrial family, contends that most households in the past were actually quite small (mean household size was about 4.75). Of course, patterns may have varied somewhat from one area to another, but it seems unlikely that in the past few centuries many families in England or America had grandparents living with them.

8. Were your predictions confirmed?

9. Here is the list of topics you saw in question 3. Now skim* the rest of the article; check (✓) the topics that the author actually discusses.

_____ a. family size

_____ b. relations within the family

_____ c. the definition of a family

_____ d. the role of the family in society

_____ e. different family customs

_____ f. the family throughout the world

_____ g. the economic role of the family

_____ h. sex differences in family roles

_____ i. the role of children

_____ j. sexual relations

However, as Philip Aries has argued in his well-known *Centuries of Childhood*, the medieval family was nevertheless quite different from its modern counterpart, largely because the boundary between the household and the larger society was less rigidly drawn, and the roles of parents, servants, or neighbors in the socialization of children were more blurred. Relationships within the nuclear family were not much closer, it seems, than those with neighbors, relatives, or other friends.

Another difference, according to Lawrence Stone, was that within property-owning classes, as in sixteenth-century England, for example, a marriage was a collective decision, involving not only the immediate family, but also other kin. Protection of long-term interests of lineage and consideration for the needs of the larger kinship group were more important than individual desires for happiness or romantic love. In addition, because the strong sense of individual or family privacy had not yet developed, access to the household by local neighbors was relatively easy. But this type of family gave way in the late sixteenth century to a "restricted patriarchal nuclear family," which predominated

*For an introduction to skimming, see Unit 1.

from 1580 to 1640, when concern for lineage and loyalty to the local community declined, and allegiances to the State and Church and to kin within the household increased. The authority of the father, as head of the household, was enhanced and bolstered by State and Church support. This drive toward parental dominance over children was particularly characteristic of the Puritans and was not limited to the child's early years; upper-class parents, especially, sought to extend their control to their children's choices of both career and spouse.

By the mid-seventeenth century, the family was increasingly organized around the principle of personal autonomy and was bound together by strong ties of love and affection. The separation, both physical and emotional, between members of a nuclear family and their servants or boarders widened, as did the distance between the household and the rest of society. Physical privacy became more important, and it became more acceptable for individual family members to pursue their own happiness.

Throughout most of the pre-industrial period, the household was the central protective unit of society. Children either were trained for their future occupations in their own homes or were employed in someone else's household. As the economic functions of the household moved to the shop or factory in the late eighteenth and nineteenth centuries, the household, no longer an economic focal point or an undifferentiated part of neighborhood activities, increasingly became a haven or escape from the outside world. Children growing up in fifteenth-century England were expected and encouraged to interact closely with many adults besides their parents, but by the eighteenth and nineteenth centuries, they had come to rely more and more upon each other and their parents for their emotional needs.

The families that migrated to the New World, especially the Puritans,

brought with them the ideal of a close and loving family, and although the economic functions of the American household were altered in the nineteenth century, the overall change was less dramatic than it had been in Western Europe. Thus, although the relationship between parents and children has not remained constant in America during the last three hundred years, the extent of the changes is probably less than it was in Western Europe.

Changing perceptions and treatment of children

We usually assume that an innate characteristic of human beings is the close and immediate attachment between the newborn child and its parents, especially its mother. Because abandonment or abuse of children seems to defy such beliefs, we are baffled by reports of widespread parental abuse of children. A look at the past may provide a different perspective on the present.

According to some scholars, maternal indifference to infants may have been typical of the Middle Ages. Aries says there is evidence that in the sixteenth and seventeenth centuries parents showed little affection for their children, and Edward Shorter argues that this indifference was probably typical among the ordinary people of Western Europe, even in the eighteenth and nineteenth centuries. The death of young children seems to have been accepted casually, and although overt infanticide was frowned upon, allowing children to die was sometimes encouraged, or at least tolerated. For example, in Western Europe it was common for mothers to leave infants at foundling hospitals or with rural wet nurses, both of which resulted in high mortality

rates. Whether these practices were typically the result of economic desperation, the difficulty of raising an out-of-wedlock child, or lack of attachment to an infant is not clear, but the fact that many well-to-do married women casually chose to give their infants to wet nurses, despite the greater mortality risks, suggests that the reasons were not always economic difficulty or fear of social stigma.

While the practice of overt infanticide and child abandonment may have been relatively widespread in parts of Western Europe, it does not seem to have been prevalent in either England or America. Indeed, authorities in both those countries in the sixteenth and seventeenth centuries prosecuted infanticide cases more vigorously than other forms of murder, and the practice of leaving infants with wet nurses went out of fashion in England by the end of the eighteenth century.

By the eighteenth century in Western Europe, parents were expressing more interest in their children and more affection for them, and by the nineteenth century, observers were beginning to criticize parents for being too child-centered. Nevertheless, parents were still not prevented from abusing their own children, as long as it did not result in death. Because the parent-child relationship was regarded as sacred and beyond State intervention, it was not until the late nineteenth century that reformers in England were able to persuade lawmakers to pass legislation to protect children from abusive parents. Ironically, efforts to prevent cruelty to animals preceded those to accomplish the same ends for children by nearly a half century.

Some of the earliest studies of colonial America suggested that at

> Given the recent concern about the "epidemic" of adolescent pregnancies, we might expect more attention to be given to the attitudes of our forebears towards teenage parents.

that time childhood was viewed as a distinct stage: children, these historians said, were expected to think and behave pretty much as adults from an early age. Although a few recent scholars of the colonial American family have supported this view, others have questioned it, pointing out that New England Puritans were well aware that children had different abilities and temperaments and believed that childrearing should be molded to those individual differences.

While young children in colonial America probably were not seen as miniature adults, they *were* thought to be more capable intellectually at a young age than their counterparts generally are today. The Puritans believed that because it was essential for salvation, children should be taught to read the Bible as soon as possible. Indeed, the notion that children could and should learn to read as soon as they could talk was so commonly accepted by educators that they did not think it necessary to justify it in their writings. The infant school movement of the late 1820s reinforced this assumption until it was challenged by Amariah Brigham, a prominent physician who claimed that early intellectual training seriously and permanently weakened growing minds and could lead to insanity later in life.

When the kindergarten movement became popular in the United States, in the 1860s and 70s, intellectual activities such as reading were deliberately avoided. Such examples are a clear indication of how the socialization of children is dependent on our perceptions of children, and one might even speculate that as we become increasingly willing to incorporate the latest scientific and medical findings into our care of the young, shifts in childrearing practices will increase in frequency.

Youth

Not only young children were perceived and treated differently in the past. Although there is little agreement among scholars either about when "adolescence" came to be viewed as a distinct stage or about the importance of education in the lives of nineteenth-century youths, many family historians have offered their perspectives on these topics. Surprisingly little, however, has been done to explore changes in teenage sexuality, pregnancy, and childbearing. Given the recent concern about the "epidemic" of adolescent pregnancies, we might expect more attention to be given to the attitudes of our forebears towards teenage parents.

Because of the stringent seventeenth-century prohibitions against premarital sexual relations and the low percentage of early teenage marriages, teenage pregnancy seems not to have been a problem in colonial New England. Early Americans were more concerned about pre-marital sexual relations, in general, than about whether teenage or adult women were involved. Not until the late nineteenth and early twentieth centuries did society clearly differentiate between teenage and adult sexual behavior, with a more negative attitude towards the former.

Only in the post-World War II period has the issue of teenage pregnancy and childbearing become a major public concern. But although the rates of teenage pregnancy and childbearing peaked in the late 1950s, the greatest attention to this phenomenon came during the late 1970s and early 80s. The controversy over abortion, the great increase in out-of-wedlock births to adolescents, and the growing concern about the long-term disadvantages of early childbearing to the young mother and her child have made this issue more important today than fifty years ago.

Parent-child relations

Historically, the primary responsibility for the rearing of young children belonged almost exclusively to the parents, especially the father. It was not until the late nineteenth and early twentieth centuries that the State was willing to remove a young child from direct supervision of negligent or abusive parents. Even so, in order to reduce welfare costs to the rest of the community, a destitute family in early America, incapable of supporting its own members, was sometimes broken up and the children placed in other households.

During the eighteenth and nineteenth centuries the mother's role in the upbringing of children was enhanced: women became the primary providers of care and affection; and as men's church memberships declined, women also became responsible for the catechizing and educating of young children, even though they often were less literate than men. While childrearing manuals continued to acknowledge the importance of the father, they also recognized that the mother had become the major figure in the care of the young.

Throughout much of Western history, as long as children remained in the home, parents exercised considerable control over them, even to the extent of arranging their marriages and influencing their career choices. Children were expected to be obedient and to contribute to the well-being of the family. And, perhaps more in Western Europe than in America, children were often expected to turn over almost all of their earnings directly to the parents—sometimes even after they had left home.

By the late eighteenth or early nineteenth century some of this control had eroded, and the rights of children as individuals were increasingly recognized and acknowledged. Interestingly, the development of children's rights has proceeded so rapidly and so far that we may now be in the midst of a backlash, as efforts are being made to re-establish parental responsibility in areas such as the reproductive behavior of minor children.

Clearly there have been major changes in the way our society treats children; but it would be very difficult for many of us to agree on the costs and benefits of those trends—whether from the viewpoint of the child, the parents, or society. While many applaud the increasing individualism and freedom of children within the family, others lament the loss of family responsibility and discipline. A historical analysis of parents and children cannot settle such disputes, but it can provide us with a better appreciation of the flexibility and resilience of the family as an institution for raising the young.

This essay was adapted from a longer version, "Historical Perspectives on the Development of the Family and Parent-Child Interactions," in *Parenting Across the Life Span: Biosocial Dimensions,* Jane B. Lancaster, Jeanne Altmann, Alice S. Rossi, and Lonie Sherrod, eds. (New York: Aldine 1987).

Textbook

Description Opinion

Business Text

Book Review Advisory Report

Family Narratives

Narrative Description Biography

Reading Selection 1
Textbook

Before You Begin

1. Following is an article from the field of anthropology. What is the task of an anthropologist?

2. If you wanted to describe customs of your country in order to help others understand an important aspect of your culture, what would you describe? Would it be your culture's religious practices? Would it be how people in your country handle their money? Would it be how the elderly are treated in your society? The way the culture treats visitors? Something else?

"The Sacred 'Rac'" is adapted from an introductory social anthropology textbook written for students in the United States. The article describes the customs of a tribe of people studied by the Indian anthropologist Chandra Thapar. Read the passage and answer the questions that follow. Your teacher may want you to do the Vocabulary from Context exercise on page 314 before you begin.

The Sacred "Rac"

Patricia Hughes

1 An Indian anthropologist, Chandra Thapar, made a study of foreign cultures which had customs similar to those of his native land. One culture in particular fascinated him because it reveres one animal as sacred, much as the people in India revere the cow. The things he discovered might interest you since you will be studying India as part of this course.

2 The tribe Dr. Thapar studied is called the Asu and is found on the American continent north of the Tarahumara of Mexico. Though it seems to be a highly developed society of its type, it has an overwhelming preoccupation with the care and feeding of the rac—an animal much like a bull in size, strength and temperament. In the Asu tribe, it is almost a social obligation to

"The Sacred 'Rac'" by Patricia Hughes, in *Focusing on Global Poverty and Development* by Jayne C. Millar (Washington, D.C.: Overseas Development Council).

own at least one if not more racs. People not possessing at least one are held in low esteem by the community because they are too poor to maintain one of these beasts properly. Some members of the tribe, to display their wealth and social prestige, even own herds of racs.

3   Unfortunately the rac breed is not very healthy and usually does not live more than five to seven years. Each family invests large sums of money each year to keep its rac healthy and shod, for it has a tendency to throw its shoes often. There are rac specialists in each community, perhaps more than one if the community is particularly wealthy. These specialists, however, due to the long period of ritual training they must undergo and to the difficulty of obtaining the right selection of charms to treat the rac, demand costly offerings whenever a family must treat an ailing rac.

4   At the age of sixteen in many Asu communities, many youths undergo a puberty rite in which the rac figures prominently. Youths must petition a high priest in a grand temple. They are then initiated into the ceremonies that surround the care of the rac and are permitted to keep a rac.

5   Although the rac may be used as a beast of burden, it has many habits which would be considered by other cultures as detrimental to the life of the society. In the first place the rac breed is increasing at a very rapid rate and the Asu tribe has given no thought to curbing the rac population. As a consequence, the Asu must build more and more paths for the rac to travel on since its delicate health and its love of racing other racs at high speeds necessitate that special areas be set aside for its use. The cost of smoothing the earth is too costly for any one individual to undertake; so it has become a community project, and each member of the tribe must pay an annual tax to build new paths and maintain the old. There are so many paths needed that some people move their homes because the rac paths must be as straight as possible to keep the animal from injuring itself. Dr. Thapar also noted that unlike the cow, which many people in his country hold sacred, the excrement of the rac cannot be used as either fuel or fertilizer. On the contrary, its excrement is exceptionally foul and totally useless. Worst of all, the rac is prone to rampages in which it runs down anything in its path, much like stampeding cattle. Estimates are that the rac kills thousands of the Asu in a year.

6   Despite the high cost of its upkeep, the damage it does to the land, and its habit of destructive rampages, the Asu still regard it as being essential to the survival of their culture.

Comprehension

Answer the following questions. Your teacher may want you to answer orally, in writing, or by underlining appropriate portions of the text. True/False items are indicated by a T / F preceding the statement.

1. What society reveres the rac? _____

    _____

2. Where is the tribe located? _____

3. T / F   People who don't own racs are not respected in the Asu community.

4. Why does it cost so much to have a rac specialist treat an ailing rac? _____

    _____

5. T / F   An Asu must pass through a special ceremony before being permitted to keep a rac.

6. How is the rac helpful to the Asu? _____

_____

7. What effects does the size of the rac population have on the life of the Asu? _____

_____

8. T / F   Rac excrement can be used as fuel or as fertilizer.

9. According to the author, what is the worst characteristic of the rac? _____

10. T / F   The Asu feel that their culture cannot survive without the rac.

11. What is *rac* spelled backward? _____

Drawing Inferences

What is the author's attitude toward the rac? Why does she choose to present her opinion using this story about the Asu society?

Discussion/Composition

1. Is the rac essential to the survival of the Asu society? Of your society? What effects is the rac having on your society? Do people in your society revere the rac as much as the Asu do?

2. Describe some aspects of your culture from the point of view of an anthropologist.

3. In her essay "Who Can Tell My Story?" Jacqueline Woodson, an African American writer, speaks about people outside her home culture writing without true knowledge and insight.

> We want the chance to tell our own stories, to tell them honestly and openly. We don't want publishers to say, "Well, we already published a book about that," and then find that it was a book that did not speak the truth about us but rather told someone on the outside's idea of who we are.

Is it possible for "outsiders" to write with understanding about a culture? How do you feel when people on the outside write about your culture?

4. Can there be a scientific description of human behavior? The author of "The Sacred 'Rac'" constructed a culture she called the Asu. Many modern-day anthropologists believe that all cultural descriptions are really inventions—creations of the writer—and that the line between scientific and literary writing is not clear. Anthropological writing, they believe, is a place where art and science come together. Do you believe that studying human cultures is an art or a science or both?

Vocabulary from Context

Use the context provided and your knowledge of stems and affixes* to determine the meanings of the italicized words. Write a definition, synonym, or description of each of the italicized vocabulary items in the space provided.

1. _____ Alex has had trouble studying for the final examination because he has been *preoccupied* with happy thoughts of his summer vacation.

2. _____ Alice's dog is gentle and friendly; unfortunately, my dog doesn't have such a pleasant *temperament.*

3. _____ Peter wants to be a lawyer because he feels it is a very *prestigious* occupation, and he has always wanted to hold a high position in society.

4. _____ Do you know a doctor who has experience *treating* children?

5. _____ Instead of complaining to me that you're *ailing,* you should see a doctor to find out what's wrong with you.

6. _____ Many people believe that only primitive societies have a special ceremony to celebrate the time when a child becomes an adult; however, anthropologists say that advanced cultures also have *puberty rites.*

7. _____ The criminal was to be killed at dawn, but he *petitioned* the president to save him and his request was granted.

8. _____ Doctors believe that smoking cigarettes is *detrimental* to your health. They also *regard* drinking alcohol as harmful.

9. _____

*For a list of all stems and affixes taught in *Reader's Choice,* see the Appendix.

Reading Selection 2
Business Text

Before You Begin

1. What have been the most important world events of your life?

2. Who are the famous people who have influenced your thinking?

3. What would you say are the most important characteristics of people your age?

4. What are the important differences between you and people older than you?

5. What are the important differences between you and people younger than you?

Have you heard the phrase "generation gap"? It refers to differences between people of different ages. People are shaped by their times. The times in which we grow up influence the way we think about things and the way we make important decisions. Recently, businesses have begun to notice problems caused, at least in part, by miscommunication between workers of different generations.

Overview

The book *Generations at Work,* was written to help businesses deal with cross-generational conflict in the workplace. Skim* the following adaptation from the book and take a few minutes to study table 1 on page 318. Then answer the following questions.

1. What are the four generations that the book discusses?

   _____

2. What are some of the important events in each generation?

   _____

   _____

3. Which generation do you belong to?

   _____

Now read the excerpt carefully to decide if you agree or disagree with the authors' description of the generations and of the crisis in the workplace. Your teacher may want you to do Vocabulary from Context exercise 1 on pages 321–23 before you begin.

---

*For an introduction to skimming, see Unit 1.

The Cross-Generational Workplace

Introduction

1   Today's workforce is unique. Never before have there been a workforce and workplace so diverse in so many ways. The mix of race, gender, ethnicity, and generation in today's workplace is stunning. Generational diversity and the problems it presents are the focus of this book. There is a growing awareness that the gulf of misunderstanding and resentment between older, not so old, and younger employees in the workplace is growing. It is a rift that will not heal itself or just go away, as so many organizations hope. It is a problem based in economics, demographics, and worldviews that must be confronted to be solved.

2   In today's business environment there is a growing sense of individual and generational enmity. "Us" versus "Them" attitudes are easy to comprehend—and sympathize with. It is easy to see why the "Us's" are often generational groupings. Oldsters holding fast to their positions of power are increasingly pitted against youngsters hungering for their own advancement and security.

3   The legions of ancient Rome were composed of ten cohorts each: cohesive units of 300 to 600 men who trained, ate, slept, fought, won, lost, lived, and died together. Their strength was their ability to think, act, and react as a unit. Though each cohort was composed of individuals, training and experience equipped them to behave as if of a single mind when called into battle. Social demographers, students of the effects of population on society, use the term *cohort* to refer to people born in the same general time span who share key life experiences—from setting out to school for the first time to entering the workforce or university or marriage or middle age or dotage at the same time.

How Generations Differ

4   In addition to the coincidence of birth, a generation is also defined by common preferences, attitudes, and experiences; a generational cohort is a product of its times and tastes. Those times encompass a wide range of circumstances—economic, political, and social. The prosperity or scarcity of the society at the time that a generation is growing up shapes their general confidence in life—or lack thereof. Their first job, their career choices, their sense of what is possible in work—all are determined in part by the economies they grow up in. Leaders and heroes are also important—national and international figures who define the values of the times. And then there are a generation's defining moments: events that capture the attention and emotions of thousands—if not millions—of individuals at a formative stage of their lives. An old saying holds that "people resemble their times more than their parents." This is the tempo of the times, and both the individuals and the cohort acquire defining rhythms almost without being aware of it—the first headlines to inspire and awe, to horrify and thrill; the music that plays in the background of their lives as they grow up, fall in love, fall out of love.

5   The three generations that occupy today's workplace and the fourth generation that is entering it are clearly defined by all these criteria. Their differences can be a source of creative strength and opportunity or a source of stress and conflict. Understanding generational differences is critical to making them work *for* the organization and not against it. It is critical to creating harmony, mutual respect, and joint effort instead of suspicion, mistrust, and isolation.

6   The four cohorts that characterize the modern workplace can be identified by their dates of birth. While generalizations are always dangerous (including this one), the following are the groups vying for power and position in most companies.

7   • **The Veterans (1922–1943).** Those born prior to World War II and those whose memories and influences are associated with that event. They are characterized by civic pride, loyalty, respect for authority. In the workplace, this group is primarily men; gender roles are stereotypical, with most of the women occupying traditional roles of teacher, nurse, and secretary. In their day, corporate men wore white shirts and ties to work and

Adapted from *Generations at Work: Managing the Clash of Veterans, Boomers, Xers, and Nexters in Your Workplace* by Ron Zemke, Claire Raines, and Bob Filipczak (New York: AMACON, 1999).

arrived and departed with their hats on. They are traditionalists, and while they have seen a lot of change, they are not typically happy with it. Today, they attend more symphonies than rock concerts, watch more plays than play in pick-up softball games, and eat more steak than tofu.

8 • **The Baby Boomers (1943–1960).** Those born during or after World War II and raised in an era of extreme optimism, opportunity, and progress. They are the civil rights generation, the protesters working for empowerment and individual rights, leaders in the sexual revolution. They work 60-hour weeks and engage in community projects and international causes. This is the generation shaped by the Vietnam War, environmental activism, and general prosperity. They are optimistic and confident that they can get things done, and they are used to getting their way.

9 • **Generation Xers (1960–1980).** Those born just before or during the Vietnam War and those raised in the emerging world economy anchored by the U.S. and Japan. They are technologically adept, clever, and resourceful and more interested in new software than comfortable offices. They are comfortable with change; after all, they have changed cities, homes, and parents all their lives. They are, indeed, the new change masters. They are very clear about the meaning of balance in their lives: Work is work and play is play; they work to live, not live to work.

10 • **Generation Nexters (1980–present).** Those born of the Baby Boomers and early Xers and into the current high-tech, neo-optimistic time. Their parents have sacrificed to provide them with the best educational and recreational experiences. They are programmed on a nonstop schedule—school, music lessons, soccer and swimming, dancing lessons. They are technologically competent; indeed, they do not know a world without computers, cable TV, digital video and audio. They have relaxed attitudes toward gender stereotyping, racial and sexual categorizing, and the nature of time and space. They are comfortable on the Internet and used to instant connections.

11 Note that the generations overlap at their endpoints. There are no hard lines between generations. It is important to keep in mind the dangers of

stereotyping and overgeneralization. To say that most Boomers like Elvis and the Beatles and that the Nexters prefer the Spice Girls and Alanis Morissette does not imply that Veterans and Xers cannot appreciate these musicians. But the specific affections of a generation's formative years *do* bind them together in important ways. Table 1 provides a summary of the important characteristics of the generations.

To learn more about stereotypes, see "The Stereotype of Stereotypes," pages 116–17.

12 There have always been multiple generations working in companies, but in traditional organizations, age groups were segregated from each other by rigid hierarchy and tradition. In today's post-industrial, information-centered work world, social and physical separations are no longer barriers to generational mixing. This means that, more than ever before, successful organizations will need people who understand and are able to work with people from different generations.

The Challenge

13 These four generations—Veterans, Boomers, Xers, and Nexters—have different points of view about work and preferred ways of managing and being managed, idiosyncratic styles, and unique ways of viewing such work-world issues as quality, service, and, well . . . just showing up for work.

14 Managing this collection of ages, faces, values, and views is an increasingly difficult duty. For one thing, few people are able to understand their own generation in context. Canadian pop-culture observer Marshall McLuhan is reported to have observed, "We don't know who discovered water, but it probably wasn't a fish." Whether the citation is correct or not, the attitude is. It is difficult to look at one's own life as part of history. We each feel too unique and important to be merely a statistic. According to William Strauss and Neil Howe, authors of *Generations*, "people of all ages feel a

TABLE 1. Key Characteristics of the Generations

Generation	The Veterans	The Baby Boomers	Generation Xers	The Nexters
Also known as . . .	Traditionalists Seniors The Silent 　Generation	Boomers	Xers Twenty-Somethings Thirteeners Baby Busters Post-Boomers	Millennials Generation Y Generation 2001 Nintendo 　Generation Generation Net Internet Generation
Birth Years	1922–1943	1943–1960	1960–1980	1980–present
Defining Events and Trends	Patriotism Families The Great 　Depression World War II New Deal Korean War Golden Age of 　Radio Silver screen Rise of labor unions	Prosperity Children in the 　spotlight Television Suburbia Assassinations Vietnam Civil Rights 　movement Cold War Women's liberation The Space Race	Watergate, Nixon 　resigns Latchkey kids Stagflation Single-parent homes MTV AIDS Computers *Challenger* disaster Fall of the Berlin 　Wall Wall Street frenzy Persian Gulf Glastnost, 　Perestroika	Computers Schoolyard violence Oklahoma City 　bombing *It Takes a Village* TV talk shows Multiculturalism Girls' movement Mark McGwire and 　Sammy Sosa
Visible Members	Harry Belafonte George Bush Jimmy Carter Geraldine Ferraro Phil Donahue Sidney Poitier Lee Iacocca Gloria Steinem John Glenn	George W. Bush Bill Clinton Hillary Clinton David Letterman Oprah Winfrey Jane Pauley Bill Gates Rush Limbaugh P. J. O'Rourke Mick Jagger	George 　Stephanopolous Douglas Coupland Kurt Cobain Jewel Brad Pitt Michael Jordan Matt Groening Neil Stephenson Michael Dell Adam Werback Meredith Bagby	Kerri Strug Macaulay Culkin Chelsea Clinton Tara Lipinski LeAnn Rimes
Music of Their Early Years	Swing Big Band Glenn Miller Duke Ellington Benny Goodman Tommy Dorsey Bing Crosby Kate Smith Ella Fitzgerald Frank Sinatra	Rock 'n' roll Acid rock Elvis Beatles Rolling Stones Grateful Dead Beach Boys Jimi Hendrix Janis Joplin Bob Dylan Supremes Temptations	Disco Rap Reggae Elton John Bruce Springsteen Tina Turner Bon Jovi Michael Jackson Guns 'n' Roses U2 Prince	Alternative Rap SKA Remix Jewel Puff Daddy Alanis Morissette Toni Braxton Will Smith Savage Garden Spice Girls Hanson Garth Brooks Backstreet Boys 'NSync

disconnection with history. Many have difficulty placing their own thought and actions, even their own lives, in any larger story." It is diversity management at its most challenging. Frustrated managers can be heard to be asking the questions that have come to characterize the modern workplace:

15 • How can I get my older employees to sit down and discuss projects with my younger ones when they can't even share a cup of coffee without snarling at each other—or even agree on what a cup of workplace coffee *is*?

16 • How can I convince my young employees to listen to their older counterparts when they don't see anything relevant in the older employees' experiences? And when my oldsters insist on communicating like World War II generals?

17 • Some of my most valuable people are only 35

and *they* have laid down the law: forty-hour work-weeks—period! Meanwhile, my boss is breathing down my neck to produce, produce, produce. *And,* our competition has mandatory overtime!

18 • A customer just called. He said one of my sales reps—a new, young, technological hotshot—just told him, "Look, this is obviously the best system out there. If you're too damn dumb to realize it, maybe I should be talking to someone else." Now what do I do?

19 • A brand-new, young, intelligent MBA who I said we should hire wandered into the second day of a training session two hours late. When the instructor challenged him, he gave one of those looks and said, "My people have a different time sense than yours. Get used to it." And the boss was there! Now what do I do?

Comprehension

Answer the following questions according to your understanding of the authors' point of view. Your teacher may want you to do this exercise orally, in writing, or by underlining appropriate portions of the text. True/False items are indicated by T / F preceding the statement.

1. Why do the authors claim that today's workforce is unique? _____

_____

2. T / F   Problems between generations will heal themselves.

3. What are some of the important forces that shape generations? _____

_____

4. T / F   As they acquire their own values, children pay more attention to their friends than to their parents.

5. T / F   Of the four generations, the Veterans are the most likely to favor traditional roles for women.

6. T / F   The war that most shaped Boomer attitudes was World War II.

7. T / F   Xers have experienced so much change in their lives that they no longer master change.

8. T / F   Nexters are the youngest of the generations.

9. T / F   You can often tell which generation someone is from by the music he or she listens to.

10. T / F   Most people are unaware of their own place in history.

Critical Reading

1. Each of the statements below is a generalization that describes a characteristic of one of the generations discussed in the selection you just read. For each statement, decide which generation best fits the generalization. Put a *V* (Veteran), *B* (Boomer), *X* (Xer), or *N* (Nexter) in the space provided and be prepared to defend your choices with excerpts from the book.

   a. _____ believes that men make the best bosses

   b. _____ prefers Bon Jovi to the Spice Girls

   c. _____ has always been online

   d. _____ considers JFK a role model

   Discuss your answers with a classmate. Can you think of other factors in addition to one's generation that would contribute to the accuracy of these generalizations? For example, what role might gender, race, or native culture play? Does it matter where you grew up or what your native language is?

2. According to *Generations at Work,* we are all shaped by the events, visible members, and music of our time. Return to table 1 and circle all the items mentioned anywhere in the table that have influenced who you are, regardless of your generation. Add events, people, and music to the table that you think would need to be included if it were to accurately reflect the major influences in your life.

   a. How many circles do you have for each column? Does the number of circles confirm the authors' analysis of the generations? (That is, if you are an Xer, do you have the most circles in the Xer column?)

   b. Discuss the events, people, and music that you added to the table with classmates. Do your additions reflect national or international influences?

   c. What changes would have to be made to this table if it were to be used in your country/culture?

Discussion/Composition

1. According to the authors, managers can adapt their management style to match the expectations and preferences of different generations. Below are some of the recommendations they make for each of the four generations discussed. For each of the statements, indicate whether you agree (A) or disagree (D) with the recommendation based on your personal experience with members of the four generations.

   Veterans

   a. _____ Use clear pronunciation and good grammar. Include "please" and "thank you" and avoid words that have sexual references.

   b. _____ Messages that emphasize family, home, and patriotism will get the best response.

   c. _____ Dress formally—coat and tie for men, conservative suits (skirts) for women.

Boomers

d. _____ They like to take on lost causes. Tell them that they will be the one to make a difference in the new project.

e. _____ Watch for the "I know all that" attitude. They are used to being in charge. If you need to correct them, do it gently.

f. _____ Respect them, but do not call them "sir" or "ma'am."

Xers

g. _____ They like multitasking; give them several projects to handle at once.

h. _____ They want freedom to do the work at their own pace and in their own way. Use a style of management that will not be seen as tightly controlling.

i. _____ Because they grew up without their parents' attention, they want positive feedback on their work. Give them a lot of support, but do not say things you do not believe.

Nexters

j. _____ They respond well to bosses who seem like their parents.

k. _____ They have more experience dealing with technology than with people; give them specific advice for handling office politics.

l. _____ They like working in groups. Organize jobs so that they have opportunities to work together in a team.

Discuss your responses with a classmate and compare your impressions. Decide if you would recommend this book for employers. Make a list of positive and negative qualities, and write a brief book review that would be appropriate for publication in your local newspaper.

2. Develop a list of questions and interview two members of each generation about their work experiences. Using insights you have gained from *Generations at Work* and the work you have done with it, discover their work habits and attitudes. Do the people you talk to fit the categories in this book? Use what you have learned to prepare advice for employers similar to that provided by the authors of the book. Your teacher may want you to do this in pairs or small groups, orally, or in writing.

Vocabulary from Context

Exercise 1

Both the ideas and the vocabulary in the following passage are taken from Generations at Work. *Use the context provided to determine the meanings of the italicized words. Write a definition, synonym, or description of each of the italicized vocabulary items in the space provided.*

1. _____ Today's workplace is *unique* in history. Never before have we seen people working together who represent such different backgrounds and experiences.

2. _____ This *diversity* of age, race, gender, and work style makes it very difficult to organize and run a company.

3. _____ As a result, companies are looking for individuals who can *manage* a wide range of employees effectively. Increasingly, managers are discovering that age differences among workers are a cause for concern.

4. _____ This has been an important *realization.*

5. _____ When one employee is young enough to be the son or daughter of another, there are usually problems that come from these *generational* differences. The difficulty is learning how to manage these employees so that the work gets done and differences of opinion about how to do the work do not become open battles.

6. _____ These management difficulties and *challenges* have led some experts to study intergenerational differences for an understanding of problems in the workplace. What they have discovered is interesting and may provide ways of improving working conditions in companies that employ individuals from different generations.

7. _____ The first thing to realize, they say, is that differences of opinion about the importance of work and how to get work done are not a *coincidence.* That is, it is not an accident that young employees will be different from older employees. In fact, if employers do not pay attention to these differences, it is possible that anger will build up between people and lead to difficulties in the company.

8. _____ *Resentment* between members of different generations, if not attended to, can lead to extreme anger and unhappiness and even

9. _____ lasting *enmity* if people are not careful. That individuals from different generations should come to view each other as if they were from different sides of warring countries should not be surprising.

10. _____ It is natural for individuals from the same generation to form *alliances,* to come together for protection. Different generations represent different experiences in life, and these lead naturally to different opinions about oneself and one's approaches to work.

11. _____ If you were raised in a time of plenty, when products were readily available and relatively inexpensive, you would believe that *prosperity* is natural and expectable.

12. _____ If, on the other hand, you were raised in a time of *scarcity,* you would always be careful not to waste things for fear you would not have enough. You would resent people who seem to believe that problems will always solve themselves.

13. _____ Such *optimism* in the face of difficulties would be a source of irritation and unhappiness between you and them. It is difficult, in such circumstances, to achieve a happy, agreeable atmosphere in the workplace.

14. _____ *Harmony* among workers is difficult to achieve in any situation but is more difficult when employees come from different generations.

Exercise 2

This exercise is designed to give you additional clues to determine the meanings of unfamiliar vocabulary items in context. In the paragraph indicated by the number in parentheses, find the word that best fits the meaning given. Your teacher may want to read these aloud as you quickly scan* the paragraph to find the answer.

1. (1) Which word means *surprising; amazing*?

2. (4) Which word means *include*?

3. (4) Which word means *important in forming a person's personality*?

4. (9) Which word means *skilled*?

Exercise 3

This exercise should be done after you have read "The Cross-Generational Workplace." The exercise is designed to give you practice using context clues to determine the meaning of unfamiliar vocabulary. Give a definition, synonym, or description of each of the words and phrases below. The number in parentheses indicates the paragraph in which the word or phrase can be found. Your teacher may want you to do these orally or in writing.

1. (1) gulf _____

2. (1) rift _____

3. (3) social demographers _____

4. (3) cohort _____

5. (3) dotage _____

6. (19) challenge _____

---

*For an introduction to scanning, see Unit 1.

Dictionary Study

Many words have more than one meaning. When you use a dictionary to discover the meaning of an unfamiliar word or phrase, you need to use the context to determine which definition is appropriate. The sentences below are based on "The Cross-Generational Workplace." Use the portions of the dictionary provided to select the best definition for each of the italicized words or phrases. Write the letter of the definition in the space provided.

_____ 1. Oldsters holding on to their positions of power are increasingly *pitted against* youngsters hungering for their own advancement and security.

    a. to set up in opposition to; to create a situation in which the goals of one person or group are directly contrary to the goals of another person or group

    b. to mark surface with small holes; to cause small indentations to form in the outside part of something

    c. to put somebody or something into a deep hole; to place or bury someone or something in an opening carved out of the ground

_____ 2. Boomers work 60-hour work weeks and are engaged in community projects and international *causes*.

    a. what makes something happen; the person or circumstance that is responsible for a certain result • *the cause of all the uproar*

    b. reason; grounds for doing or feeling something • *no cause for complaint*

    c. principle; an idea that people believe in and work for

_____ 3. Gen Xers were raised in the world economy *anchored* by the U.S. and Japan.

    a. to hold in place in the water by an anchor

    b. to secure firmly

    c. to narrate or coordinate a news broadcast

Figurative Language and Idioms

In the paragraph indicated by the number in parentheses, find the word or phrase that best fits the meaning given. Your teacher may want to read these aloud as you quickly scan the paragraph to find the answer.

1. (1) Which word means *faced; met head on; dealt with*?

2. (2) Which phrase means *desiring greatly; wanting*?

3. (4) Which word means *those things one likes more than other possible choices*?

4. (17) What phrase means *made the rules; told someone else how things must be done*?

5. (17) What phrase means *putting pressure on me to do something; standing right behind me to make sure I am reaching my goals*?

Reading Selections 3A–3C
Family Narratives

The three selections that follow present accounts of family life written retrospectively by adults. "An Attack on the Family" describes a British family in Greece between the world wars; "The Circuit" tells of growing up in southern California among farmworkers. "Fish Cheeks" portrays the contradictory emotions of a girl with feet in two cultures.

Selection 3A

Before You Begin

1. What is it like to be the youngest child in a family?

2. Below is a picture of a scorpion. What would be the reaction of your family if a child were to bring one home as a pet?

The following selection is taken from Gerald Durrell's book *My Family and Other Animals,* written from the point of view of the youngest child. The book is an account of the year, during Durrell's childhood, that his family spent on the Greek island of Corfu. As the title indicates, the book is not an ordinary autobiography. In this selection, the author's habit of collecting strange and wonderful animal life throws the house into complete confusion.

Read the selection to get a general understanding of the story; then do the exercises that follow. Your teacher may want you to do Vocabulary from Context exercise 1 on pages 330–31 before you begin reading.

An Attack on the Family

Gerald Durrell

I grew very fond of the scorpions in the garden wall. I found them to be pleasant, unassuming creatures with, on the whole, the most charming habits. Provided you did nothing silly or clumsy (like putting your hand on one), the scorpions treated you with respect, their one desire being to get away and hide as quickly as possible. They must have found me rather a trial, for I was always ripping sections of the plaster away so that I could watch them, or capturing them and making them walk about in jam-jars so that I could see the way their feet moved. By means of my sudden and unexpected assaults on the wall I discovered quite a bit about the scorpions.

2   By crouching under the wall at night with a torch, I managed to catch some brief glimpses

Adapted from *My Family and Other Animals* by Gerald Durrell (New York: Viking).

of the scorpions' wonderful courtship dances. I saw them standing, claws joined, their bodies raised to the skies, their tails lovingly intertwined; I saw them waltzing slowly in circles, claw in claw. But my view of these performances was all too short, for almost as soon as I switched on the torch the partners would stop, pause for a moment, and then, seeing that I was not going to extinguish the light, they would turn round and walk firmly away, claw in claw, side by side. They were definitely beasts that believed in keeping themselves *to* themselves. If I could have kept a colony in captivity I would probably have been able to see the whole of the courtship, but the family had forbidden scorpions in the house, despite my arguments in favour of them.

3   Then one day I found a fat female scorpion in the wall, wearing what at first glance appeared to be a pale brown fur coat. Closer inspection proved that this strange garment was made up of a mass of tiny babies clinging to the mother's back. I was enraptured by this family, and I made up my mind to smuggle them into the house and up to my bedroom so that I might keep them and watch them grow up. With infinite care I manoeuvred the mother and family into a matchbox, and then hurried to the villa. It was rather unfortunate that just as I entered the door lunch should be served; however, I placed the matchbox carefully on the mantelpiece in the drawing-room, so that the scorpions could get plenty of air, and made my way to the dining-room and joined the family for the meal. Dawdling over my food, feeding Roger under the table and listening to the family arguing, I completely forgot about my exciting new captures. At last Larry, having finished, brought the cigarettes from the drawing-room, and lying back in his chair he put one in his mouth and picked up the matchbox he had brought. Unaware of my impending doom I watched him interestedly as, still talking glibly, he opened the matchbox.

4   Now, I maintain to this day that the female scorpion meant no harm. She was agitated and annoyed at being shut up in a matchbox for so long, and so she seized the first opportunity to escape. She hoisted herself out of the box with great rapidity, her babies clinging on desperately, and scuttled on to the back of Larry's hand. There, not quite certain what to do next, she paused, her sting curved up at the ready. Larry, feeling the movement of her claws, glanced down to see what it was, and from that moment things got increasingly confused.

5   He uttered a roar of fright that made Lugaretzia drop a plate and brought Roger out from beneath the table, barking wildly. With a flick of his hand he sent the unfortunate scorpion flying down the table, and she landed midway between Margo and Leslie, scattering babies like confetti as she thumped on the cloth. Thoroughly enraged at this treatment, the creature sped towards Leslie, her sting quivering with anger. Leslie leapt to his feet, overturning his chair, and flicked out desperately with his napkin, sending the scorpion rolling across the cloth towards Margo, who promptly let out a scream that any railway engine would have been proud to produce. Mother, completely bewildered by this sudden and rapid change from peace to chaos, put on her glasses and peered down the table to see what was causing the pandemonium, and at that moment Margo, in a vain attempt to stop the scorpion's advance, hurled a glass of water at it. The shower

missed the animal completely, but successfully drenched Mother, who, not being able to stand cold water, promptly lost her breath and sat gasping at the end of the table, unable even to protest. The scorpion had now gone to ground under Leslie's plate, while her babies swarmed wildly all over the table. Roger, mystified by the panic, but determined to do his share, ran round and round the room, barking hysterically.

6   "It's that bloody boy again . . ." bellowed Larry.

"Look out! Look out! They're coming!" screamed Margo.

"All we need is a book," roared Leslie; "don't panic, hit 'em with a book."

"What on earth's the *matter* with you all?" Mother kept asking, wiping her glasses.

"It's that bloody boy . . . he'll kill the lot of us . . . Look at the table . . . knee deep in scorpions . . ."

"Quick . . . quick . . . do something . . . Look out, look out!"

"Stop screeching and get a book, for God's sake . . . You're worse than the dog . . . Shut *up*, Roger."

"By the Grace of God I wasn't bitten . . ."

"Look out . . . there's another one . . . Quick . . . quick . . ."

"Oh, shut up and get me a book or something . . ."

"But *how* did the scorpions get on the table, dear?"

"That bloody boy . . . Every matchbox in the house is a deathtrap . . ."

"Look out, it's coming towards me . . . Quick, quick, do something . . ."

"Hit it with your knife . . . *your knife* . . . Go on, hit it . . ."

7   Since no one had bothered to explain things to him, Roger was under the mistaken impression that the family were being attacked, and that it was his duty to defend them. As Lugaretzia was the only stranger in the room, he came to the logical conclusion that she must be the responsible party, so he bit her in the ankle. This did not help matters very much.

8   By the time a certain amount of order had been restored, all the baby scorpions had hidden themselves under various plates and bits of cutlery. Eventually, after impassioned pleas on my part, backed up by Mother, Leslie's suggestion that the whole lot be killed was defeated. While the family, still simmering with rage and fright, retired to the drawing-room, I spent half an hour collecting the babies, picking them up in a teaspoon, and returning them to their mother's back. Then I carried them outside on a saucer and, with the utmost reluctance, released them on the garden wall. Roger and I went and spent the afternoon on the hillside, for I felt it would be wise to allow the family to have a siesta before seeing them again.

Comprehension

Exercise 1

Answer the following questions. Your teacher may want you to answer the questions orally, in writing, or by underlining appropriate portions of the text. True/False items are indicated by a T / F preceding the statement. In many cases you will have to use your own judgment because the answer is not specifically given in the passage.

1. T / F   Scorpions are not dangerous.

2. T / F   The author likes scorpions.

3. Why wasn't the author able to observe the whole courtship dance? _____
_____

4. T / F   The author knew that his family would not allow scorpions in the house.

5. How did the mother scorpion carry her babies? _____

6. T / F   The author caught the scorpion family in a jam-jar.

7. When was the scorpion family discovered? _____
_____

8. Why did Margo throw water on Mother? _____
_____

9 T / F   The author tried to kill the scorpions with a book.

10. T / F   The author felt that the scorpions were attacking his family.

11. T / F   Mother supported the author in his attempt to save the scorpions.

12. How were the scorpions removed from the house? _____
_____

13. T / F   The author stayed outside for the rest of the day because he didn't want to see the family until everyone had rested.

Exercise 2

To answer the following questions you will have to make decisions about the story based on careful reading. Many questions do not have clear-cut answers; you will have to decide what you think the best answer is. Be prepared to defend your choices with portions of the text.

1. Who is Roger? _____

2. Who is Lugaretzia? _____

3. How many people are in the Durrell family? _____ Name them and indi-

cate if they are male or female. _____

_____

4. Who keeps yelling for a book? _____

5. Who says that every matchbox in the house is a death-trap? _____

6. Who is "screeching"? _____

7. Who says, "But *how* did the scorpions get on the table, dear?" _____

8. Who is the youngest member of the family? _____

9. In your opinion, who seems the most confused? _____

Discussion/Composition

Can you describe an incident from your childhood in which one of the children in your family threw the household into confusion?

Vocabulary from Context

Exercise 1

Use the context provided to determine the meanings of the italicized words. Write a definition, synonym, or description of each of the italicized vocabulary items in the space provided.

1. _____ Because the light frightened the scorpions away, I wasn't able to observe them for very long. However, by appearing suddenly with my electric torch, I was able to get brief *glimpses* of their behavior.

2. _____ I was completely *enraptured* with the scorpion family. My happiness at finding them was so great that I decided I would keep them in my room for closer study.

3. _____ The members of the family were so angry that I decided to stay away from the house until dinner. Their *rage* truly frightened me.

4. _____ Because she had not seen the scorpions, Mother was completely *bewildered* by the sudden confusion.

5. _____ I begged the family not to kill the scorpions, and they finally listened to my *pleas*.

6. _____ Mr. and Mrs. Firth had a long *courtship*. They dated for nine years before they got married.

7. _____ He *crouched* down to look under the table for his shoes.

8. _____ After the scorpion affair the whole family tried *in vain* to get me to stop collecting animals and insects. They should have known that I wouldn't stop collecting just because of one little scare.

Exercise 2

This exercise is designed to give you additional clues to determine the meanings of unfamiliar vocabulary items in context. In the paragraph of "An Attack on the Family" indicated by the number in parentheses, find the word or phrase, that best fits the meaning given. Your teacher may want to read these aloud as you quickly scan* the paragraph to find the answer.

1. (1) Which word means *a bother; an annoyance; a problem*?

2. (3) Which word in the third sentence means *bring in secretly*?

3. (3) Which word at the end of the paragraph means *fate; future problems*?

4. (5) Which two words in the middle of the paragraph mean *confusion*?

5. (8) Which word in the first sentence means *peace and quiet; organization*?

Exercise 3

This exercise should be done after you have finished reading "An Attack on the Family." The exercise is designed to give you practice using context clues to guess the meaning of unfamiliar vocabulary. Give a definition, synonym, or description of each of the words below. Your teacher may want you to do these orally or in writing.

1. assaults (last sentence, paragraph 1) _____

2. clinging (second sentence, paragraph 3) _____

3. manoeuvred (middle, paragraph 3) _____

4. maintain (paragraph 4) _____

5. hoisted (paragraph 4) _____

6. scuttled (paragraph 4) _____

7. peered (middle, paragraph 5) _____

8. hurled (bottom, paragraph 5) _____

9. drenched (bottom, paragraph 5) _____

10. swarmed (bottom, paragraph 5) _____

11. screeching (middle, paragraph 6) _____

12. reluctance (bottom, paragraph 8) _____

_____

*For an introduction to scanning, see Unit 1.

"The Circuit," written by Francisco Jiménez, is included in the book *Growing up Chicana/o,* a collection of stories by Mexican-American authors. The foreword to the book is written by Rudolfo Anaya, one of the most respected Chicano writers in the United States. His book *Bless Me, Ultima* is considered a classic portrayal of cultural and individual identity. Read the following excerpt from Anaya's foreword to *Growing up Chicana/o* and answer the questions that follow before moving on to the story.

Foreword

[excerpt]

Rudolfo Anaya

Growing up is one of the universal themes in literature. It is during the childhood years that our values are formed by family and community. It is also a time when we acquire many of the basic skills we will use later in life. For the child or the teenager, growing up is a series of new experiences, emotions, relationships, and the awareness of sexuality. Everything about growing up is more intense and heartfelt.

Writers often need to describe the world of their childhood. We believe that by writing about growing up we can give meaning to those tumultuous years. That is how I felt when I wrote my first novel, *Bless Me, Ultima.* It was important to capture in a story the swirl of emotions and experiences that shaped my growing-up years.

Our growing-up stories provide a history of our past, and in so doing they illuminate the present. *The Adventures of Huckleberry Finn* and *Tom Sawyer* are classics not only because of the wonderful characters but because they provide a history of the times and thus inform us of the world of the author.

It is important for each generation to read the growing-up stories of previous generations, and thus acquire the touchstone by which to chart a course for the future. Each one of us remembers the stories, written or in the oral tradition, that affected us as children. Those stories fired our imagination, filled us with wonder, and allowed us to understand our place in the world. Those stories also taught us that each one of us is a storyteller, each one of us is a creative human being.

From *Growing Up Chicana/o: An Anthology,* edited by Tiffany Ana López (New York: William Morrow, 1993).

Comprehension

Answer the following questions according to your understanding of the author's point of view. True/false items are indicated by a T / F preceding the statement.

1. Anaya says that growing up is a universal theme in literature. Can you name growing-up stories of authors important to you? _____

   _____

2. T / F   Childhood provides an important time of learning about who you are and who your people are.

3. T / F   Authors use their skill in writing to understand experiences from their childhoods.

4. T / F   *The Adventures of Huckleberry Finn* and *Tom Sawyer* are important literary pieces that provide insight into the times during which they were written.

5. T / F   Growing-up stories can be used by young people in making life decisions.

1. Where do you call home? Have you lived there long?

2. In your culture, at what age do people first get jobs? How old were you when you got your first job?

3. When you were a child, did you ever change schools?

4. Have you ever attended a school in a language different from the language you speak with your family?

Francisco Jiménez is an author, educator, and editor. His short story "The Circuit" tells of growing up in the fields of southern California as the child of hardworking migrant laborers—farmworkers who followed the harvest in search of work. The story is told from Jiménez's point of view as a child. He says of the story:

> It is a collection of recollections of my past growing up as a child in a migrant setting. Some of these were written in the form of a journal when I was an undergraduate at Santa Clara, and I wrote them because I wanted to keep in touch with my family roots. I did not want to forget that experience because it is what motivated me to work hard in acquiring my education. To be more philosophical, it was the reflection of that experience that gave meaning to my profession.

Read the story just for enjoyment. (We *will* be asking you questions, but we trust they won't ruin your enjoyment!) Try to get a general understanding of the events that Jiménez tells us about and of the feelings that surround them. Don't worry about unfamiliar words. Keep reading to appreciate the story as a whole. Your teacher may want you to do Vocabulary from Context exercise 1 on pages 340–41 before you begin.

The Circuit

Francisco Jiménez

1 It was that time of year again. Ito, the strawberry sharecropper, did not smile. It was natural. The peak of the strawberry season was over and the last few days the workers, most of them braceros, were not picking as many boxes as they had during the months of June and July.

2 As the last days of August disappeared, so did the number of braceros. Sunday, only one—the best picker—came to work. I liked him. Sometimes we talked during our half-hour lunch break. That is how I found out he was from Jalisco, the same state in Mexico my family was from. That Sunday was the last time I saw him.

3 When the sun had tired and sunk behind the mountains, Ito signaled us that it was time to go home. "Ya esora," he yelled in his broken Spanish. Those were the words I waited for twelve hours a day, every day, seven days a week, week after week. And the thought of not hearing them again saddened me.

4 As we drove home Papá did not say a word. With both hands on the wheel, he stared at the dirt road. My older brother, Roberto, was also silent. He leaned his

From *Cuentos Chicanos: A Short Story Anthology* (Albuquerque: University of New Mexico Press, 1984).

head back and closed his eyes. Once in a while he cleared from his throat the dust that blew in from outside.

5   Yes, it was that time of year. When I opened the front door to the shack, I stopped. Everything we owned was neatly packed in cardboard boxes. Suddenly I felt even more the weight of hours, days, weeks, and months of work. I sat down on a box. The thought of having to move to Fresno and knowing what was in store for me there brought tears to my eyes.

6   That night I could not sleep. I lay in bed thinking about how much I hated this move.

7   A little before five o'clock in the morning, Papá woke everyone up. A few minutes later, the yelling and screaming of my little brothers and sisters, for whom the move was a great adventure, broke the silence of dawn. Shortly, the barking of the dogs accompanied them.

8   While we packed the breakfast dishes, Papá went outside to start the "Carcanchita." That was the name Papá gave his old '38 black Plymouth. He bought it in a used-car lot in Santa Rosa in the winter of 1949. Papá was very proud of his little jalopy. He had a right to be proud of it. He spent a lot of time looking at other cars before buying this one. When he finally chose the "Carcanchita," he checked it thoroughly before driving it out of the car lot. He examined every inch of the car. He listened to the motor, tilting his head from side to side like a parrot, trying to detect any noises that spelled car trouble. After being satisfied with the looks and sounds of the car, Papá then insisted on knowing who the original owner was. He never did find out from the car salesman, but he bought the car anyway. Papá figured the original owner must have been an important man because behind the rear seat of the car he found a blue necktie.

9   Papá parked the car out in front and left the motor running. "Listo, " he yelled. Without saying a word, Roberto and I began to carry the boxes out to the car. Roberto carried the two big boxes and I carried the two smaller ones. Papá then threw the mattress on top of the car roof and tied it with ropes to the front and rear bumpers.

10   Everything was packed except Mamá's pot. It was an old large galvanized pot she had picked up at an army surplus store in Santa María the year I was born. The pot had many dents and nicks, and the more dents and nicks it acquired the more Mamá liked it. "Mi olla," she used to say proudly.

11   I held the front door open as Mamá carefully carried out her pot by both handles, making sure not to spill the cooked beans. When she got to the car, Papá reached out to help her with it. Roberto opened the rear car door and Papá gently placed it on the floor behind the front seat. All of us then climbed in. Papá sighed, wiped the sweat off his forehead with his sleeve, and said wearily: "Es todo."

12   As we drove away, I felt a lump in my throat. I turned around and looked at our little shack for the last time.

13   At sunset we drove into a labor camp near Fresno. Since Papá did not speak English, Mamá asked the camp foreman if he needed any more workers. "We don't need no more," said the foreman, scratching his head. "Check with Sullivan down the road. Can't miss him. He lives in a big white house with a fence around it."

14   When we got there, Mamá walked up to the house. She went through a white gate, past a row of rose bushes, up the stairs to the front door. She rang the doorbell. The porch light went on and a tall husky man came out. They exchanged a few words. After the man went in, Mamá clasped her hands and hurried back to the car. "We have work! Mr. Sullivan said we can stay there the whole season," she said, gasping and pointing to an old garage near the stables.

15   The garage was worn out by the years. It had no windows. The walls, eaten by termites, strained to support the roof full of holes. The dirt floor, populated by earth worms, looked like a gray road map.

16   That night, by the light of a kerosene lamp, we unpacked and cleaned our new home. Roberto swept away the loose dirt, leaving the hard ground. Papá plugged the holes in the walls with old newspapers and tin can tops. Mamá fed my little brothers and sisters. Papá and Roberto then brought in the mattress and placed it in the far corner of the garage. "Mamá, you and the little ones sleep on the mattress. Roberto, Panchito, and I will sleep outside under the trees," Papá said.

17   Early next morning Mr. Sullivan showed us where his crop was, and after breakfast, Papá, Roberto, and I headed for the vineyard to pick.

18   Around nine o'clock the temperature had risen to almost one hundred degrees. I was completely soaked in sweat and my mouth felt as if I had been chewing on a handkerchief. I walked over to the end of the row, picked up the jug of water we had brought, and began drinking. "Don't drink too much; you'll get sick," Roberto shouted. No sooner had he said that than I felt sick to my stomach. I dropped to my knees and let the jug roll off my hands. I remained motionless with my eyes glued on the hot sandy ground. All I could hear was the drone of insects. Slowly I began to recover. I poured water over my face and neck and watched the dirty water run down my arms to the ground.

19   I still felt a little dizzy when we took a break to eat lunch. It was past two o'clock and we sat underneath a large walnut tree that was on the side of the road. While we ate, Papá jotted down the number of boxes we had picked. Roberto drew designs on the ground with a stick. Suddenly I noticed Papá's face turn pale as he looked down the road. "Here comes the school bus," he whispered loudly in alarm. Instinctively, Roberto and I ran and hid in the vineyards. We did not want to get in trouble for not going to school. The neatly dressed boys about my age got off. They carried books under their arms. After they crossed the street, the bus drove away. Roberto and I came out from hiding and joined Papá. "Tienen que tener cuidado," he warned us.

20   After lunch we went back to work. The sun kept beating down. The buzzing insects, the wet sweat, and the hot dry dust made the afternoon seem to last forever. Finally the mountains around the valley reached out and swallowed the sun. Within an hour it was too dark to continue picking. The vines blanketed the grapes, making it difficult to see the bunches. "Vámonos," said Papá, signaling to us that it was time to quit work. Papá then took out a pencil and began to figure out how much we had earned our first day. He wrote down numbers, crossed some out, wrote down some more. "Quince," he murmured.

21   When we arrived home, we took a cold shower underneath a waterhose. We

then sat down to eat dinner around some wooden crates that served as a table. Mamá had cooked a special meal for us. We had rice and tortillas with "carne con chile," my favorite dish.

22   The next morning I could hardly move. My body ached all over. I felt little control over my arms and legs. This feeling went on every morning for days until my muscles finally got used to the work.

23   It was Monday, the first week of November. The grape season was over and I could now go to school. I woke up early that morning and lay in bed, looking at the stars and savoring the thought of not going to work and of starting sixth grade for the first time that year. Since I could not sleep, I decided to get up and join Papá and Roberto at breakfast. I sat at the table across from Roberto, but I kept my head down. I did not want to look up and face him. I knew he was sad. He was not going to school today. He was not going tomorrow, or next week, or next month. He would not go until the cotton season was over, and that was sometime in February. I rubbed my hands together and watched the dry, acid-stained skin fall to the floor in little rolls.

24   When Papá and Roberto left for work, I felt relief. I walked to the top of a small grade next to the shack and watched the "Carcanchita" disappear in the distance in a cloud of dust.

25   Two hours later, around eight o'clock, I stood by the side of the road waiting for school bus number twenty. When it arrived I climbed in. Everyone was busy either talking or yelling. I sat in an empty seat in the back.

26   When the bus stopped in front of the school, I felt very nervous. I looked out the bus window and saw boys and girls carrying books under their arms. I put my hands in my pant pockets and walked to the principal's office. When I entered I heard a woman's voice say: "May I help you?" I was startled. I had not heard English for months. For a few seconds I remained speechless. I looked at the lady who waited for an answer. My first instinct was to answer her in Spanish, but I held back. Finally, after struggling for English words, I managed to tell her that I wanted to enroll in the sixth grade. After answering many questions, I was led to the classroom.

27   Mr. Lema, the sixth grade teacher, greeted me and assigned me a desk. He then introduced me to the class. I was so nervous and scared at that moment when everyone's eyes were on me that I wished I were with Papá and Roberto picking cotton. After taking roll, Mr. Lema gave the class the assignment for the first hour. "The first thing we have to do this morning is finish reading the story we began yesterday," he said enthusiastically. He walked up to me, handed me an English book, and asked me to read. "We are on page 125," he said politely. When I heard this, I felt my blood rush to my head; I felt dizzy. "Would you like to read?" he asked hesitantly. I opened the book to page 125. My mouth was dry. My eyes began to water. I could not begin. "You can read later," Mr. Lema said understandingly.

28   For the rest of the reading period I kept getting angrier and angrier with myself. I should have read, I thought to myself.

29   During recess I went into the restroom and opened my English book to page 125. I began to read in a low voice, pretending I was in class. There were many words I did not know. I closed the book and headed back to the classroom.

30   Mr. Lema was sitting at his desk correcting papers. When I entered he looked up at me and smiled. I felt better. I walked up to him and asked if he could help me with the new words. "Gladly," he said.

31   The rest of the month I spent my lunch hours working on English with Mr. Lema, my best friend at school.

      One Friday during lunch hour Mr. Lema asked me to take a walk with him to the music room. "Do you like music?" he asked me as we entered the building.

32   "Yes, I like corridos," I answered. He then picked up a trumpet, blew on it and handed it to me. The sound gave me goose bumps. I knew that sound. I had heard it in many corridos. "How would you like to learn how to play it?" he asked. He must have read my face because before I could answer, he added; "I'll teach you how to play it during our lunch hours."

33   That day I could hardly wait to get home to tell Papá and Mamá the great news. As I got off the bus, my little brothers and sisters ran up to meet me. They were yelling and screaming. I thought they were happy to see me, but when I opened the door to our shack, I saw that everything we owned was neatly packed in cardboard boxes.

Comprehension

1. Questions 1a–f are intended to remind you of the basic story. Answer them quickly without referring to the story. Check your comprehension with your classmates before you continue with the items that follow. True/False items are indicated by a T / F preceding the statement.

    a. Where does the story take place? What seasons, roughly, does the story cover?

    b. T / F   The author of the story is the oldest boy in the family.

    c. T / F   The family moves from farm to farm seeking work throughout the growing season.

    d. T / F   The author is happy that he does not have to attend school.

    e. T / F   The author enjoys the adventure of traveling from farm to farm.

    f. T / F   The author will finish sixth grade with Mr. Lema.

2. How old do you think Panchito, the author, is at the time of this story? Who are the other members of the family? _____

    _____

3. T / F   Carcanchita is the name of Panchito's older sister.

4. Paragraph 8 tells how Panchito's father acquired his beloved jalopy, and it gives us insight into the father. Check (✓) all of the adjectives that you think describe the father. Be prepared to defend your answers.

_____ a. poor

_____ b. proud

_____ c. intelligent

_____ d. careful

_____ e. clever

5. T / F   The family often moves from place to place.

6. T / F   Everyone in the family is bilingual.

7. Why do Roberto and Panchito hide when they see the school bus coming?

_____

8. Based on this account, which would you rather harvest, strawberries or grapes? _____

9. T / F   Roberto doesn't go to school with Panchito because he prefers to work.

10. T / F   Panchito enjoys school.

11. T / F   Mr. Lema is a kind man.

12. How does Panchito spend his lunch hours? _____

13. What is your impression of Panchito? Check (✔) all of the following that you think apply. Be prepared to defend your answers.

_____ a. friendly

_____ b. helpful

_____ c. loves his parents

_____ d. dislikes working in the fields

_____ e. dislikes school

_____ f. sad

_____ g. happy

_____ h. poor

_____ i. a good student

_____ j. hardworking

_____ k. angry

_____ l. an early riser

_____ m. bilingual

_____ n. observant

Discussion/Composition

1. a. What do you think happened to Panchito and his family after this story ends? How do you think Panchito got to be an author and educator?

   b. If you're curious to know more about how Francisco Jiménez became an author and educator, you might want to research his life and career at the library or on the Web. Your teacher may want you to write a brief biography summarizing what you find.

2. a. In paragraphs 10 and 11, Jiménez gives details about Mamá's cooking pot and how the family packed it when they moved. Why do you think he focuses specifically on the pot as a memory of his childhood? What do we learn about Panchito's family from reading this?

   b. What object from your childhood could you describe that would reveal something about yourself or your family? Write a descriptive essay about that object. Include details that help your readers visualize the object and understand you and your family.

3. If you were going to write a short story about your experiences growing up, what would you describe? Can you identify a particular period of time that was especially intense or tumultuous and that would help others understand what your childhood was like?

4. Write a brief narrative that tells Panchito's story from Mr. Lema's point of view.

Vocabulary from Context

Exercise 1

The vocabulary in the following passage is taken from "The Circuit" and from the foreword to the book that it appears in. Use the context provided to determine the meanings of the italicized words. Write a definition, synonym, or description of each of the italicized vocabulary items in the space provided.

1. _____

2. _____

3. _____

4. _____

Growing up is a topic that authors everywhere in the world want to explore, perhaps because this is one experience shared by everyone. Stories about growing up provide a *universal theme* in literature. All children are sensitive and curious, and they live every experience to the fullest emotional degree; this *intense* approach to life gives the stories of childhood their interest and power. The fact that for people everywhere, growing up is not a calm and orderly experience but a *tumultuous* one, gives authors rich material to work with.

5. _____

6. _____

The literature of Chicanos, citizens of the United States of Mexican heritage, includes many growing-up stories. Childhood stories can be an important source of self-understanding and self-confidence for a community. Communities affirm their cultural heritage and pride through these stories. Chicano author Rudolfo Anaya says that his community can learn about themselves by using the growing-up stories of previous generations as *touchstones,* something against which to check their own experience. Like gold miners who learned about the characteristics of the rocks they had found by rubbing them on a particular kind of stone, people can learn about themselves by referring to the stories of their elders. The stories are also important sources of continuity across the *generations;* when the elders of the culture tell stories to their children and grandchildren, the history of the culture lives on, providing important connections between past, present, and future.

Exercise 2

This exercise is designed to give you additional clues to determine the meanings of unfamiliar words in context. In the paragraph indicated by the number in parentheses, find the word or phrase that best fits the meaning given. Your teacher may want to read these aloud as you quickly scan* the paragraph to find the answer.

1. (1)   What phrase means *an individual who farms land for the owner of property in return for a share of the value of the crop?*

2. (5)   Which word means *a small, crude building?*

3. (8)   Which word means *an old car?*

4. (8)   Which word means *discover?*

5. (8)   Which word means *indicated?*

6. (10)   Which two words mean *marks; scratches; bent places?*

7. (9, 16)   Which word means *the soft part of a bed?*

8. (23)   Which word means *enjoying?*

9. (26)   Which word means *suddenly surprised; shocked?*

10. (26)   What phrase means *kept oneself from doing something; restrained oneself?*

11. (27)   What phrase means *calling the names of the students in the class?*

---

*For an introduction to scanning, see Unit 1.

Exercise 3

This exercise should be done after you have finished reading "The Circuit." The exercise is designed to give you practice using context clues to guess the meaning of unfamiliar vocabulary. In this case, the new vocabulary items are Spanish words within a story written in English. Give a definition, synonym, or description of each of the words and phrases below. The number in parentheses indicates the paragraph in which the word or phrase can be found. Your teacher may want you to do these orally or in writing.

1. (1)   braceros _____

2. (3)   ya esora _____

3. (9)   listo _____

4. (10) mi olla _____

5. (11) es todo _____

6. (19) tienen que tener cuidado _____

7. (20) vámonos _____

8. (20) quince _____

9. (21) carne con chile _____

10. (32) corridos _____

Exercise 4: Descriptive Language

Both Anaya's foreword and Jiménez's story use descriptive language—carefully chosen adjectives, images, and analogies (comparisons of one thing or idea to another)—to communicate intensely felt experiences. Each example of descriptive language below is followed by a list of words, phrases, or sentences. For each item, check all those that have a similar meaning to the italicized phrase. Some items have several correct answers. A number in parentheses indicates the paragraph in the story where these phrases may be found.

1. (foreword) "It was important to capture . . . *the swirl of emotions* . . . that shaped my growing-up years."

   _____ a. confusing mix of feelings

   _____ b. wide variety of feelings

   _____ c. hidden feelings

   _____ d. quickly changing feelings

2. (foreword) "Those stories *fired our imagination.*"

   _____ a. made us hot   _____ d. destroyed our hopes

   _____ b. injured our imaginations   _____ e. encouraged us

   _____ c. inspired our imaginations

3. (12) "As we drove away, I felt *a lump in my throat*."

_____ a. hunger

_____ b. sadness

_____ c. uncertainty

_____ d. anger

_____ e. confusion

4. (15) "The dirt floor, populated by earth worms, looked *like a gray road map*."

_____ a. colorful

_____ b. large

_____ c. exotic

_____ d. as though it had lines across it

_____ e. as if it were made of paper

5. (18) "My mouth felt *as if I had been chewing on a handkerchief*."

_____ a. dry

_____ b. clean

_____ c. fresh

_____ d. bad

_____ e. as if I had just eaten

6. (20) *"The mountains around the valley reached out and swallowed the sun."*

_____ a. The sun went down behind the mountains.

_____ b. The glare of the sun blocked out the view of the mountains.

_____ c. The moon became visible.

_____ d. It got darker.

7. (20) *"The vines blanketed the grapes,* making it difficult to see the bunches."

_____ a. The farmers put a cover over the grapes.

_____ b. The grapes shone in the light.

_____ c. The grapes couldn't be seen anymore.

_____ d. The vines covered the grapes.

Vocabulary Review

Complete the paragraphs below using the following words. Use each word only once.

mattress	theme	generations	jalopy	shack
universal	dents	spells	nicks	migrant

One important _____ of Francisco Jiménez's story "The Circuit" is that a family can be poor in terms of what they own but rich in terms of love. Jiménez illustrates this idea with the story of a Chicano family of _____ farmworkers, but it is a _____ truth no matter what culture you look at.

Panchito's family was extremely poor by one definition. Instead of living in a comfortable house, they often slept in a small _____ with a dirt floor. They didn't own any furniture, just one _____ that Mamá and the little children slept on. They could pack everything else they owned, including Mamá's old pot, with its _____ and _____, inside their old _____ when it was time for them to move from one farm to the next.

This family didn't have many possessions, but they had something many other families don't have. The parents and the children clearly loved each other. The two _____ worked together, cooperating to earn money for the family and to take care of the daily tasks of living. The way they treated each other shows their love and mutual respect.

Growing up, moving between cultures, traveling in foreign countries—all these experiences require us to meet new people and discover ways in which we are similar and different. For children of immigrants, this process of discovery occurs on at least two levels: they must discover how they, personally, fit into their home country, and they must also learn how their parents' culture and the dominant culture relate to each other. In the following story, "Fish Cheeks," author Amy Tan tells about an evening in her own life when she was put in the position of discovering things about herself and her culture.

Amy Tan was born in California in 1952, the daughter of Chinese immigrants to the United States. She is the author of essays, children's books, and novels, including *The Joy Luck Club,* which has been made into a movie. As you read Tan's story about a special dinner party her mother gave, try to understand the feelings not only of the author but of her mother and her guests as well. Don't worry about unfamiliar words. Keep reading to appreciate the story as a whole.

Before You Begin   All people have times when they feel like they belong and times when they feel different than others.

1. Have you ever wished you looked different or belonged to a different culture? Have you ever felt rejected because of who you are or who your family is?

2. Do you remember a time when you were embarrassed by your family? When you wished your family were more like the families of your friends?

Fish Cheeks

1   I fell in love with the minister's son the winter I turned fourteen. He was not Chinese, but as white as Mary in the manger. For Christmas I prayed for this blond-haired boy, Robert, and a slim new American nose.

2   When I found out that my parents had invited the minister's family over for Christmas Eve dinner, I cried. What would Robert think of our shabby Chinese Christmas? What would he think of our noisy Chinese relatives who lacked proper American manners? What terrible disappointment would he feel upon seeing not a roasted turkey and sweet potatoes but Chinese food?

3   On Christmas Eve I saw that my mother had outdone herself in creating a strange menu. She was pulling black veins out of the backs of fleshy prawns. The kitchen was littered with appalling mounds of raw food: A slimy rock cod with bulging eyes that pleaded not to be thrown into a pan of hot oil. Tofu, which looked like stacked wedges of rubbery white sponges. A bowl soaking dried fungus back to life. A plate of squid, their backs crisscrossed with knife markings so they resembled bicycle tires.

4   And then they arrived—the minister's family and all my relatives in a clamor of doorbells and rumpled Christmas packages. Robert grunted hello, and I pretended he was not worthy of existence.

5   Dinner threw me deeper into despair. My relatives licked the ends of their chopsticks and reached across the table, dipping them into the dozen or so plates of food. Robert and his family waited patiently for platters to be passed to them. My relatives murmured with pleasure when my mother brought out the whole steamed fish. Robert grimaced. Then my father poked his chopsticks just below the fish eye and plucked out the soft meat. "Amy, your favorite," he said offering me the tender fish cheek. I wanted to disappear.

6   At the end of the meal my father leaned back and belched loudly, thanking my mother for her fine cooking. "It's a polite Chinese custom to show you are satisfied," explained my father to our astonished guests. Robert was looking down at his plate with a reddened face. The minister managed to muster up a quiet burp. I was stunned into silence for the rest of the night.

7   After everyone had gone, my mother said to me, "You want to be the same as American girls on the outside." She handed me an early gift. It was a miniskirt in beige tweed. "But inside you must always be Chinese. You must be proud you are different. Your only shame is to have shame."

8   And even though I didn't agree with her then, I knew that she understood how much I had suffered during the evening's dinner. It wasn't until many years later— long after I had gotten over my crush on Robert—that I was able to fully appreciate her lesson and the true purpose behind our particular menu. For Christmas Eve that year, she had chosen all my favorite foods.

Comprehension

Indicate if each of the statements below is true (T) or false (F) according to your understanding of the story.

1. T / F   Amy wished she looked less Chinese.

2. T / F   Amy invited Robert to dinner.

3. T / F   Amy helped her mother plan the menu for the dinner.

4. T / F   Amy was excited to show Robert some things about Chinese culture.

5. T / F   Amy was embarrassed by the dinner.

6. T / F   Amy likes Chinese food.

7. T / F   Amy talked to Robert a lot during the Christmas dinner.

8. T / F   Robert enjoyed the dinner.

9. T / F   The way to show appreciation for a fine meal is different in the U.S. and China.

10. T / F   The minister tried to compliment the cook.

11. T / F   Amy's mother didn't want her to dress like a typical American girl.

12. T / F   Amy's mother didn't know how Amy felt at the dinner.

Discussion/Composition

1. What do you think Robert was feeling during the dinner? Could he and Amy have been having similar feelings? At this dinner, who do you think felt more different, Amy or Robert?

2. Amy's mother prepared a very elaborate, traditional Chinese dinner for this party. Why did she choose this particular menu?

3. The differences that trouble Amy in this story are primarily cultural differences. Do feelings like Amy's happen to teenagers whose culture is the same as the culture of the larger community in which they live?

4. What kinds of differences make teenagers embarrassed? Do the same things embarrass adults?

5. In what ways do the following indicate Amy's mother's love and wisdom?

    a. She gave Amy a tweed miniskirt for Christmas.

    b. She prepared all of Amy's favorite dishes for the meal.

    c. She said to Amy, "Your only shame is to have shame."

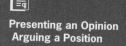
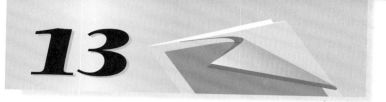

Longer Reading
Psychology

This unit addresses issues of obedience to authority. Before you begin the longer reading in this unit, you will need to complete the Attitude Questionnaire and discuss The Question of Obedience. These selections will provide an introduction to the longer reading, "The Milgram Experiment."

—————————— **Attitude Questionnaire** ——————————

In the following questionnaire you are asked to predict your behavior in particular situations and to predict the behaviors of others. Specifically, you are asked to indicate three things.

1. What you, yourself, would do in the situations. Indicate your opinion on the scale marked *S* (for self).

2. What you think would be the reactions of people from your native culture. Indicate this opinion on the scale marked *C* (for native culture).

3. What you think would be the reactions of people in the United States. Indicate this opinion on the scale marked *U* (for U.S. native).

Example | The following item was marked by a college student from Japan.

You are a department head in a company that has very strict rules concerning punctuality. One of your most talented and productive employees is habitually late for work in the mornings. Company policy is to reduce latecomers' wages. Do you obey the company rule?

Definitely Yes ⟵——————⟶ Definitely No

S   ___ ___ ✓ ___ ___ ___
C   ✓ ___ ___ ___ ___ ___
U   ___ ___ ___ ___ ___ ✓

Explanation

The checks on the scale indicate that the student believes that there is some difference between her and her fellow citizens and that there is substantial difference between her and U.S. natives. She indicates that she would probably follow the company rule, while she thinks that most of the people from her native culture would definitely follow the rule and that most U.S. natives would definitely not follow the rule.

In the questionnaire that follows you will be asked to respond to a number of items such as the one preceding. Remember, there are no right answers. What matters is your honest opinion.

After you have responded to all of the items, your teacher may want you to discuss your answers in small groups.

---

1. You travel on business a great deal with all expenses paid by your company. On one trip a waiter offers to leave the space blank on your receipt so that you can fill in whatever amount you wish. Do you accept the offer?

Definitely Yes ←——→ Definitely No

S ___ ___ ___ ___ ___ ___ ___
C ___ ___ ___ ___ ___ ___ ___
U ___ ___ ___ ___ ___ ___ ___

2. You have been attending a course regularly. An acquaintance, who rarely comes to class, asks for help with the take-home exam. Do you agree to help?

Definitely Yes ←——→ Definitely No

S ___ ___ ___ ___ ___ ___ ___
C ___ ___ ___ ___ ___ ___ ___
U ___ ___ ___ ___ ___ ___ ___

3. The police ask you for information about a friend who has strong political views. Do you give it to them?

Definitely Yes ←——→ Definitely No

S ___ ___ ___ ___ ___ ___ ___
C ___ ___ ___ ___ ___ ___ ___
U ___ ___ ___ ___ ___ ___ ___

4. You are in love with a person who is a devout follower of a different religion. What do you do?

	Continue to see the person, hoping your differences in religion will not matter.	Change your religion.	Attempt to change the religion of your lover.	End the relationship.
S	___	___	___	___
C	___	___	___	___
U	___	___	___	___

5. You are the manager of a grocery store. You notice a woman stealing food. She is an acquaintance whom you know to be the unemployed single mother of three small children. What do you do?

	Report her to the police.	Speak to her privately; allow her to replace the food.	Ignore the situation.	Secretly pay for the food she took.
S	___	___	___	___
C	___	___	___	___
U	___	___	___	___

6. In a high-level meeting with all of the bosses in your company, a superior takes credit for work of a colleague who is not present. Do you correct the information?

Definitely Yes ←——→ Definitely No

S ___ ___ ___ ___ ___ ___ ___
C ___ ___ ___ ___ ___ ___ ___
U ___ ___ ___ ___ ___ ___ ___

7. The police have captured a man who they say is a dangerous criminal and whom they hope to convict of a series of violent crimes. You have been brought in to see if he is the same person who robbed you recently in the park. He is not the man who robbed you, but the police are pressing you to testify against him. Do you identify him as the robber?

Definitely Yes ←——→ Definitely No

S ___ ___ ___ ___ ___ ___ ___
C ___ ___ ___ ___ ___ ___ ___
U ___ ___ ___ ___ ___ ___ ___

8. Your boss is about to fire a woman for a mistake that you know she did not make. You think the woman is not a very good employee. Do you correct your boss?

Definitely Yes ←——————→ Definitely No

S   ____ ____ ____ ____ ____ ____ ____

C   ____ ____ ____ ____ ____ ____ ____

U   ____ ____ ____ ____ ____ ____ ____

9. You discover that your brother is selling important information to a foreign power. What do you do?

Report him to the police.	Try to convince him to stop.	Ignore the situation.
S ____	____	____
C ____	____	____
U ____	____	____

10. Your company is about to sign an extremely important contract. Your boss asks you to not mention a production problem you have been trying to solve because knowledge of the problem might cause the client to go to a different company. In a meeting with the client you are asked if there are any production problems. Do you tell the truth?

Definitely Yes ←——————→ Definitely No

S   ____ ____ ____ ____ ____ ____ ____

C   ____ ____ ____ ____ ____ ____ ____

U   ____ ____ ____ ____ ____ ____ ____

11. Your boss is having marital difficulties with her husband. She decides to take a weekend vacation with another man. She instructs you to tell her husband that she is at a business meeting. Do you follow her instructions?

Definitely Yes ←——————→ Definitely No

S   ____ ____ ____ ____ ____ ____ ____

C   ____ ____ ____ ____ ____ ____ ____

U   ____ ____ ____ ____ ____ ____ ____

12. You work for a large firm that owns many apartment buildings. You have been instructed to evict all tenants who are behind in their rent. Mr. and Mrs. Jones are hardworking people who have always paid on time. They have five children to support. They have both just lost their jobs and are unable to pay the rent. Do you evict them?

Definitely Yes ←——————→ Definitely No

S   ____ ____ ____ ____ ____ ____ ____

C   ____ ____ ____ ____ ____ ____ ____

U   ____ ____ ____ ____ ____ ____ ____

13. You are taking a college psychology class. The professor asks you to participate in an experiment that requires you to lie to your friends. Do you do as you are told?

Definitely Yes ←——————→ Definitely No

S   ____ ____ ____ ____ ____ ____ ____

C   ____ ____ ____ ____ ____ ____ ____

U   ____ ____ ____ ____ ____ ____ ____

Examine your answers to the questionnaire. Did you tend to see yourself as agreeing more with citizens of your native culture or with citizens of the U.S.? Do you see yourself as a "member of the group" or as an "individualist"? Did your answers differ markedly from those of other members of your class? What kinds of evidence did people give to support their points of view?

The Question of Obedience

The preceding questionnaire and the longer reading in the next section raise the question of obedience to authority. There are times when we must follow the orders of people in authority and times when we must follow our own consciences. Use the items below to guide your discussion of this conflict between authority and conscience.

1. The following individuals are authority figures in most cultures. Indicate the extent to which they should be obeyed. Compare your responses to those of others in your class.

   Most Obedience ←——→ Least Obedience

   a. employer   ___ ___ ___ ___ ___ ___

   b. police officer   ___ ___ ___ ___ ___ ___

   c. friend   ___ ___ ___ ___ ___ ___

   d. grandmother   ___ ___ ___ ___ ___ ___

   e. mother   ___ ___ ___ ___ ___ ___

   f. teacher   ___ ___ ___ ___ ___ ___

   g. judge   ___ ___ ___ ___ ___ ___

   h. father   ___ ___ ___ ___ ___ ___

   i. military officer ___ ___ ___ ___ ___ ___

   j. religious leader ___ ___ ___ ___ ___ ___

   k. grandfather   ___ ___ ___ ___ ___ ___

2. T / F   Authority figures should be obeyed even when they order you to do something you disagree with.

3. What do you mean when you use the word *obedience*?

   a. Are there situations when one should unquestioningly obey an authority? List occasions when this is true.

   _____

   _____

   b. Can you obey someone without doing *exactly* what that person tells you to do? _____

   c. Are there times when children should not obey their elders? _____

   _____

The Milgram Experiment

Psychological experiments can have unexpected consequences. According to the *Atlantic* online:

> In the fall of 1958 Theodore Kaczynski, a brilliant but vulnerable boy of sixteen, entered Harvard College. There he encountered a prevailing intellectual atmosphere of antitechnological despair. There, also, he was deceived into subjecting himself to a series of purposely brutalizing psychological experiments that may have confirmed his still-forming belief in the evil of science.

Thirty years later he was arrested as "the Unabomber," an antitechnology terrorist who over the course of seventeen years sent bombs to people involved in science and technology.

The experiments that Kaczynski was exposed to were precursors of the famous psychological experiments conducted by Yale psychologist Stanley Milgram. During the 1960s Milgram conducted a study to determine the extent to which ordinary people would obey clearly immoral orders. The results were disturbing and led Milgram to conclude that "ordinary people, simply doing their jobs, and without any hostility on their part, can become agents in a terrible destructive process."

The article that follows summarizes the experiment conducted by Milgram. Your teacher may want you to do Vocabulary from Context exercise 1 on page 360 before you begin reading. Read the first eight paragraphs to understand the design of the experiment and then answer the questions that follow. Your teacher may want you to discuss your answers before continuing with the reading.

THE MILGRAM EXPERIMENT

Ronald E. Smith, Irwin G. Sarason, and Barbara Sarason

1 After World War II the Nuremberg war trials were conducted in order to try Nazi war criminals for the atrocities they had committed. In many instances the defense offered by those on trial was that they had "only followed orders." During the Vietnam War American soldiers accused of committing atrocities in Vietnam gave basically the same explanation for their actions.

2 Most of us reject justifications based on "obedience to authority" as mere rationalizations, secure in our convictions that we, if placed in the same situation, would behave differently. However, the results of a series of ingenious and controversial investigations performed in the 1960s by psychologist Stanley Milgram suggest that perhaps we should not be so sure of ourselves.

3 Milgram wanted to determine the extent to which people would obey an experimenter's commands to administer painful electric shocks to another person. Pretend for a moment that you are a subject in one of his studies. Here is what would happen. On arriving at a university laboratory in response to a classified ad offering volunteers $4 for one hour's participation in an experiment on memory, you meet another subject, a pleasant, middle-aged man with whom you chat while awaiting the arrival of the experimenter. When the experimenter arrives, dressed

---

Quote from the *Atlantic* online, June 2000.
Ronald E. Smith, Irwin G. Sarason, and Barbara R. Sarason, "Blind Obedience to Authority" (pp. 19–22 sans table, figure, and quotes by Milgram) from *Psychology: The Frontiers of Behavior* by Ronald E. Smith, Irwin G. Sarason, and Barbara R. Sarason (New York: Harper and Row).

in a laboratory coat, he pays you and then informs you and the other person that one of you will be the subject in the experiment and that the other will serve as his assistant. You are chosen by lot to be the assistant, but in reality you are the subject.

4   The experimenter explains that the study is concerned with the effects of punishment on learning. Accompanied by you, the "subject" is conducted into a room and strapped into a chair, and a large electrode is attached to his wrist. He is told that he is to learn a list of word pairs and that whenever he makes an error he will receive electric shocks of increasing intensity. On hearing this, the "subject" responds, "When I was at the West Haven V.A. Hospital a few years ago, they detected a slight heart condition. Nothing serious, but are these shocks dangerous?" The experimenter replies in an unconcerned manner that although the shocks may be painful, they will cause no permanent tissue damage.

5   You and the experimenter then proceed to an adjoining room connected by an intercom so that the "subject's" responses can be heard. You are seated in front of an apparatus with 30 toggle switches ranging from 15 volts to 450 volts. (See Figure 1.) Your task is to administer the learning task to the "subject." Whenever he gives an incorrect answer, you must give him an electric shock, starting at the lowest level (15 volts) and increasing the level by 15 volts each time. You are given a sample shock of 45 volts and find it moderately painful.

6   What you are unaware of at this point is that you are in a carefully contrived situation. The learner is actually an actor who receives no shock at all, and the responses you hear over the intercom are tape-recorded so that they will be exactly the same for each "assistant." The experimenter's actions are also carefully programmed.

7   As the experiment proceeds, the learner makes error after error. You increase the shock level steadily until he is clearly experiencing pain. The tape-recorded responses are programmed to correspond to the shock intensities as follows:

75 volts	Ugh!
90 volts	Ugh!
105 volts	Ugh! *(louder)*
120 volts	Ugh! Hey, *this* really hurts.
135 volts	Ugh!!
150 volts	Ugh!!! Experimenter! That's all. Get me out of here. I told you I had heart trouble. My heart's starting to bother me now. Get me out of here. I told you I had heart trouble. My heart's starting to bother me. I refuse to go on. Let me out.
165 volts	Ugh! Let me out. *(shouting)*
180 volts	Ugh! I can't stand the pain. Let me out of here! *(shouting)*
195 volts	Ugh! Let me out of here. Let me out of here. My heart's bothering me. Let me out of here! You have no right to keep me here! Let me out! Let me out of here! My heart's bothering me. Let me out! Let me out!
210 volts	Ugh!! Experimenter! *Get* me out of here. I've had enough. I won't be in the experiment any more.
225 volts	Ugh!
240 volts	Ugh!
255 volts	Ugh! Get me *out* of here.

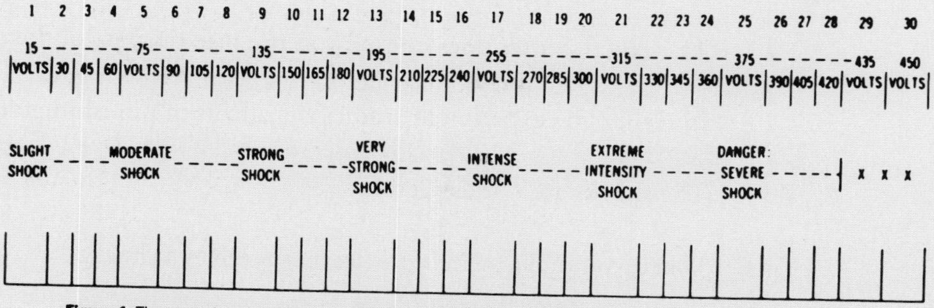

Figure 1 The control panel of the shocking apparatus used in the Milgram research. Copyright © 1974 by Stanley Milgram. Reprinted by permission of Harper & Row, Publishers, Inc.

270 volts   *(Agonized scream).* Let me out of here. Let me out of here. Let me out of here. Let me out. Do you hear? Let me out of here.

285 volts   *(Agonized scream).*

300 volts   *(Agonized scream).* I absolutely refuse to answer any more. Get me out of here. You can't hold me here. Get me out. Get me out of here.

315 volts   *(Intensely agonized scream). I told you I refuse to answer.* I'm no longer part of this experiment.

330 volts   *(Intense and prolonged agonized scream).* Let me out of here. Let me out of here. My heart's bothering me. Let me out, I tell you. *(Hysterically)* Let me out of here. Let me out of here. You have no right to hold me here. Let me out! Let me out! Let me out of here! Let me out! Let me out!

345 volts   *(At 345 volts and thereafter, there was only silence.)*[1]

8   But supposing you express unwillingness at some point to continue shocking the learner? In that event the experimenter, sitting at a nearby desk, would respond in one of the following ways:

"Please continue" or "Please go on."

"The experiment requires that you continue."

"It is absolutely essential that you continue."

"You have no other choice. You must go on."

---

[1] Stanley Milgram, *Obedience to Authority* (New York: Harper and Row, 1974).

Comprehension

Exercise 1

Pretend you have volunteered to participate in Milgram's experiment as you answer the following questions. True/False items are indicated by a T/F preceding the statement.

1. T / F   The person you first meet at the laboratory is the experimenter.

2. T / F   You have an equal chance of being the person giving the shocks (the assistant) or the person receiving the shocks (the learner).

3. T / F   You are told you will be the assistant.

4. T / F   The experimenter does not tell you the true purpose of the experiment.

5. T / F   In reality, the experiment studies the effects of punishment on learning.

6. T / F   The shocks are not dangerous.

7. T / F   When you pull a switch, the learner receives a shock.

8. T / F   Some learners make more mistakes than others.

9. T / F   If you say that you do not want to continue, the experimenter stops the experiment.

10. Why is *subject* in quotation marks in paragraphs 4 and 5? _____

_____

11. If you were a participant in this experiment, at what point would you stop administering "shocks"? _____

_____

12. What results would you predict for the experiment?

   a. Do you think most people would continue pulling the switches? How long do you think most people would continue?

   _____

   b. Do you think there would be different results depending on the subject's age, education, nationality, sex?

   _____

Now, read the rest of the article, and answer the questions that follow.

9   Having now experienced the Milgram situation at least in your imagination, how long do you think you would continue to administer shocks? Most of our students maintain that they would not go beyond 105 volts before refusing to continue the experiment. A panel of psychiatrists predicted before the experiment that perhaps only 1 percent of the subjects would proceed to the 450-volt level.

10   In fact, however, the "shock" produced by the results of this study was much more startling than the simulated shocks in the experiment. Forty men ranging in age from 20 to 50 and representing a cross section of the population, participated in the investigation. The maximum shock levels they administered are shown in Table 1. Nearly two-thirds of them administered the 450-volt maximum shock, and the average maximum shock they administered was 368 volts.

Table 1 Maximum shock levels administered by subjects in the Milgram experiment.

Shock level	Verbal designation and voltage level	Number of subjects giving each maximum shock level
	Slight Shock	
1	15	
2	30	
3	45	
4	60	
	Moderate Shock	
5	75	1
6	90	
7	105	
8	120	
	Strong Shock	
9	135	
10	150	6
11	165	
12	180	1
	Very Strong Shock	
13	195	
14	210	
15	225	
16	240	
	Intense Shock	
17	255	
18	270	2
19	285	
20	300	1
	Extreme-Intensity Shock	
21	315	1
22	330	1
23	345	
24	360	
	Danger: Severe Shock	
25	375	1
26	390	
27	405	
28	420	
	XXX	
29	435	
30	450	26
	Average maximum shock level	368 volts
	Percentage of obedient subjects	65.0%

Copyright © 1974 by Stanley Milgram. Reprinted by permission of Harper & Row, Publishers. Inc.

11   Virtually all the people who administered high levels of shock exhibited extreme discomfort, anxiety, and distress. Most verbally refused to continue on one or more occasions. But continue they did when ordered to do so by the experimenter, who assured them that what happened in the experiment was his responsibility.

12   By contriving a situation with many real-life elements, Milgram succeeded in demonstrating that a high percentage of "normal" people will obey an authority

figure even when the destructive effects of their obedience are obvious. The conclusions that he draws from his work are chilling indeed:

13   A commonly offered explanation is that those who shocked the victim at the most severe level were monsters, the sadistic fringe of society. But if one considers that almost two-thirds of the participants fall into the category of "obedient" subjects, and that they represented ordinary people drawn from working, managerial, and professional classes, the argument becomes very shaky. . . . After witnessing hundreds of ordinary people submit to the authority in our own experiments, I must conclude that [Hannah] Arendt's conception of the *banality of evil* comes closer to the truth than one might dare imagine. The ordinary person who shocked the victim did so out of a sense of obligation—a conception of his duties as a subject—and not from any peculiarly aggressive tendencies.

14   This is, perhaps, the most fundamental lesson of our study: ordinary people, simply doing their jobs, and without any particular hostility on their part, can become agents in a terrible destructive process. Moreover, even when the destructive effects of their work become patently clear, and they are asked to carry out actions incompatible with fundamental standards of morality, relatively few people have the resources needed to resist authority. A variety of inhibitions against disobeying authority come into play and successfully keep the person in his place. (Milgram, 1974, pp. 5–6)[2]

15   Milgram's method of investigation also generated shock waves among psychologists. Many questioned whether it was ethical to expose subjects without warning to experiments that were likely to generate considerable stress and that might conceivably have lasting negative effects on them. But supporters of Milgram's work argue that adequate precautions were taken to protect participants. There was an extensive debriefing at the conclusion of the experiment, and participants were informed that they had not actually shocked anyone. They had a friendly meeting with the unharmed "subject." The purpose of the experiment was explained to them, and they were assured that their behavior in the situation was perfectly normal. Further, supporters argue, the great societal importance of the problem being investigated justified the methods the experimenters used. Finally, they cite follow-up questionnaire data collected by Milgram from his subjects after they received a complete report of the purposes and results. Eighty-four percent of the subjects stated that they were glad to have been in the experiment (and several spontaneously noted that their participation had made them more tolerant of others or otherwise changed them in desirable ways). Fifteen percent expressed neutral feelings, and only 1.3 percent stated that they were sorry to have participated.

16   The controversy over the ethics of Milgram's research has raged for decades. In combination with other controversial issues, it has prompted a deep and abiding concern for protecting the welfare of subjects in psychological research. Because of such concerns, it is most unlikely that Milgram's research could be conducted today.

---

[2]Stanley Milgram, *Obedience to Authority* (New York: Harper and Row, 1974).

Exercise 2

Answer the following questions. Your teacher may want you to do this exercise orally, in writing, or by underlining appropriate portions of the text. True/False items are indicated by a T / F preceding the statement. Some items may not have a single correct answer.

1. What was the purpose of Milgram's experiment? _____

   _____

2. T / F   Most of the subjects continued to shock the learners when the shock level reached the danger level.

3. T / F   The subjects appeared to enjoy the opportunity to hurt other people.

4. T / F   The people who shocked the learners at the most severe level were mentally disturbed or in other ways antisocial.

5. T / F   Today we are far more sophisticated than we were in the 1960s, and therefore we do not have to worry about people submitting to an immoral authority.

6. T / F   Most professionals, schoolteachers for example, are incapable of inflicting pain on others while following a superior's orders.

7. The authors state that the subjects were visibly shaken by the experience and that many refused to continue. Why *did* they continue if it was so painful for the learner and so upsetting for them? Why didn't they just refuse to go on?

   _____

   _____

8. Follow-up studies indicated that the subjects' opinions of the experiment were generally positive.

   a. T / F   These positive evaluations could be attributed to the subjects' respect for the experimenter, and their obedience to his authority.

   b. T / F   The results of the experiment should cause us to doubt the validity of the follow-up study.

9. T / F   If Stanley Milgram participated in such an experiment, he would probably agree to push the shocks above the comfort level.

Vocabulary from Context

Exercise 1

Use the context provided to determine the meanings of the italicized words. Write a definition, synonym, or description of each of the italicized vocabulary items in the space provided.

1. _____ Many people, when forced to justify poor behavior, come up with *rationalizations* that seem convincing but are really just excuses.

2. _____ The experiment was cleverly organized to appear as if it were real, but in fact it was merely a *simulation* in which all of the participants were actors.

3. _____ Extraordinary evil is very frightening, but when it appears as if evil has a common, everyday quality about it, its *banality* is even more frightening.

4. _____ Scientists cannot agree on the value of the Milgram study. Heated debate and angry disagreement have surrounded the *controversial* research ever since the first experiment was completed.

5. _____ We are all comforted by the thought that society is governed by a system of moral principles and human values. It is, in fact, our confidence in the *ethical* nature of the common person that gives us peace of mind.

Exercise 2

This exercise is designed to give you additional clues to determine the meanings of unfamiliar words in context. In the paragraph indicated by the number in parentheses, find the word that best fits the meaning given. Your teacher may want to read these aloud as you quickly scan* the paragraph to find the answer.

1. (1)   Which word means *extremely wicked or cruel acts*?

2. (2)   Which word means *very clever*?

3. (3)   Which word means *give*?

4. (3)   Which word means *person studied in an experiment*?

5. (6)   Which word means *constructed; designed*?

6. (11) Which word means *almost*?

7. (13) Which word means *cruel; experiencing pleasure from others' suffering*?

8. (15) Which word means *a session provided to give information to an experimental subject after the experiment*?

---

*For an introduction to scanning, see Unit 1.

Figurative Language and Idioms

In the paragraph indicated by the number in parentheses, find the phrase that best fits the meaning given. Your teacher may want to read these aloud as you quickly scan the paragraph to find the answer.

1. (3) What phrase means *by chance; at random*?

2. (10) What phrase means *a wide variety*?

3. (12) What word means *frightening*?

4. (13) What phrase means *the edge of normal society*?

5. (16) What phrase means *has occurred energetically and violently*?

Discussion/Composition

1. What is the correct balance between individual conscience and one's obedience to authority? How do we protect ourselves against evil leaders and immoral authority figures?

2. Some scientists argue that experiments such as this violate basic human rights of the subjects because they deceive the participants. Others claim that the deception is justified because of the importance of the findings. What do you think?

   a. In what ways are the subjects deceived?

   b. What might be the negative effects upon the subjects of having participated in the study? Recall that "the Unabomber" took part in similarly disturbing experiments. Do you think the negative effects could be so severe that they could create someone like "the Unabomber?"

   c. What is the importance of this sort of study? What do you know now about society that you did not know before reading the article?

14

Longer Reading
Suspense

Before You Begin   1. Is it possible to rob a bank and not commit a crime?

2. Why would someone want to rob a bank? Money of course. But is that the only reason?

Read "The Dusty Drawer" carefully. It is a special kind of mystery story that raises some interesting questions about human nature and about the difference between breaking the law and doing something that is wrong.

Your teacher may want you to do the Vocabulary from Context exercise on pages 377–78 and the Dictionary Study on page 379 before you begin reading. In addition, after you have read the first eleven paragraphs, you may want to do the first four items of the Figurative Language and Idioms exercise on pages 378–79.

The Dusty Drawer

Harry Miles Muheim

1   Norman Logan paid for his apple pie and coffee, then carried his tray toward the front of the cafeteria. From a distance, he recognized the back of William Tritt's large head. The tables near Tritt were empty, and Logan had no desire to eat with him, but they had some unfinished business that Logan wanted to clear up. He stopped at Tritt's table and asked, "Do you mind if I join you?"

2   Tritt looked up as he always looked up from inside his teller's cage in the bank across the street. He acted like a servant—like a precise butler that Logan used to see in movies—but behind the film of obsequiousness was an attitude of vast superiority that always set Logan on edge.

3   "Why, yes, Mr. Logan. Do sit down. Only please, I must ask you not to mention that two hundred dollars again."

"Well, we'll see about that," said Logan, pulling out a chair and seating himself. "Rather late for lunch, isn't it?"

"Oh, I've had lunch," Tritt said. "This is just a snack." He cut a large piece of

---

"The Dusty Drawer" by Harry Miles Muheim, from *Alfred Hitchcock Presents a Month of Mystery* (New York: Random House).

roast beef from the slab in front of him and thrust it into his mouth. "I don't believe I've seen you all summer," he added, chewing the meat.

4   "I took a job upstate," Logan said. "We were trying to stop some kind of blight in the apple orchards."

"Is that so?" Tritt looked like a concerned bloodhound.

"I wanted to do some research out West," Logan went on, "but I couldn't get any money from the university."

"You'll be back for the new term, won't you?"

5   "Oh, yes," Logan said with a sigh, "we begin again tomorrow." He thought for a moment of the freshman faces that would be looking up at him in the lecture room. A bunch of high-strung, mechanical New York City kids, pushed by their parents into his botany class. They were brick-bound people who had no interest in growing things, and Logan sometimes felt sad that in five years of teaching he had communicated to only a few of them his own delight with his subject.

6   "My, one certainly gets a long vacation in the teaching profession," Tritt said. "June through September."

"I suppose," Logan said. "Only trouble is that you don't make enough to do anything in all the spare time."

Tritt laughed a little, controlled laugh and continued chewing. Logan began to eat the pie. It had the drab, neutral flavor of all cafeteria pies.

"Mr. Tritt," he said after a long silence.

"Yes?"

"When are you going to give me back my two hundred dollars?"

7   "Oh, come now, Mr. Logan. We had this all out ten months ago. We went over it with Mr. Pinkson and the bank examiners and everyone. I did *not* steal two hundred dollars from you."

"You did, and you know it."

"Frankly, I'd rather not hear any more about it."

"Mr. Tritt, I had three hundred and twenty-four dollars in my hand that day. I'd just cashed some bonds. I know how much I had."

"The matter has been all cleared up," Tritt said coldly.

8   "Not for me, it hasn't. When you entered the amount in my checking account, it was for one hundred and twenty-four, not three hundred twenty-four."

9   Tritt put down his fork and carefully folded his hands. "I've heard you tell that story a thousand times, sir. My cash balanced when you came back and complained."

"Sure it balanced," Logan exploded. "You saw your mistake when Pinkson asked you to check the cash. So you took my two hundred out of the drawer. No wonder it balanced!"

Tritt laid a restraining hand on Logan's arm. "Mr. Logan, I'm going a long, long way in the bank. I simply can't afford to make mistakes."

10   "You also can't afford to admit it when you do make one!"

"Oh, come now," said Tritt, as though he were speaking to a child. "Do you think I'd jeopardize my entire career for two hundred dollars?"

"You didn't jeopardize your career," Logan snapped. "You knew you could get away with it. And you took my money to cover your error."

11   Tritt sat calmly and smiled a smug smile at Logan. "Well, that's your version, Mr. Logan. But I do wish you'd quit annoying me with your fairy tale." Leaving half his meat untouched, Tritt stood up and put on his hat. Then he came around the table and stood looming over Logan. "I will say, however, from a purely hypothetical point of view, that if I *had* stolen your money and then staked my reputation on the lie that I hadn't, the worst thing I could possibly do would be to return the money to you. I think you'd agree with that."

"I'll get you, Tritt," said Logan, sitting back in the chair. "I can't stand to be had."

"I know, I know. You've been saying that for ten months, too. Good-by, now."

12   Tritt walked out of the cafeteria. Norman Logan sat there motionless watching the big teller cross the street and enter the bank. He felt no rage—only an increased sense of futility. Slowly, he finished his coffee.

A few minutes later, Logan entered the bank. Down in the safe-deposit vaults, he raised the lid of his long metal box and took out three twenty-five dollar bonds. With a sigh, he began to fill them out for cashing. They would cover his government insurance premium for the year. In July, too, he'd taken three bonds from the box, when his father had overspent his pension money. And earlier in the summer, Logan had cashed some more of them, after slamming into a truck and damaging his Plymouth. Almost every month there was some reason to cash bonds, and Logan reflected that he hadn't bought one since his Navy days. There just wasn't enough money in botany.

13   With the bonds in his hand, he climbed the narrow flight of stairs to the street floor, then walked past the long row of tellers' cages to the rear of the bank. Here he opened an iron gate in a low marble fence and entered the green-carpeted area of the manager and assistant manager. The manager's desk was right inside the gate, and Mr. Pinkson looked up as Logan came in. He smiled, looking over the top of the glasses pinched on his nose.

14   "Good afternoon, Mr. Logan." Pinkson's quick eyes went to the bonds; and then, with the professional neutrality of a branch manager, right back up to Logan's thin face. "If you'll just sit down, I'll buzz Mr. Tritt."

"Mr. Tritt?" said Logan, surprised.

"Yes. He's been moved up to the first cage now."

Pinkson indicated a large, heavy table set far over against the side wall in back of his desk, and Logan sat in a chair next to it.

"Have a good summer?" The little man had revolved in his squeaky executive's chair to face Logan.

"Not bad, thanks."

"Did you get out of the city?"

"Yes, I had a job upstate. I always work during my vacations."

15   Mr. Pinkson let out a controlled chuckle, a suitable reply when he wasn't sure whether or not the customer was trying to be funny. Then he revolved again; his head bobbed down, and he was back at his figures.

Logan put the bonds on the clean desk blotter and looked over at Tritt's cage. It was at the end of the row of cages, with a door opening directly into the manager's area. Tritt was talking on the telephone inside, and for a long, unpleasant minute Logan watched the self-assured face through the greenish glass. "I'll get him yet," Logan thought. But he didn't see how. Tritt had been standing firmly shielded behind his lie for nearly a year now, and Norman Logan didn't seem to know enough about vengeance to get him.

16   Restive, Logan sat back and tipped the chair onto its hind legs. He picked in-effectually at a gravy stain on his coat; then his eye was attracted to a drawer, hid-den under the overhang of the tabletop. It was a difficult thing to see, for it had no handle, and its face was outlined by only a thin black crack in the dark-stained wood. Logan could see faintly the two putty-filled holes that marked the place where the handle had once been. Curious, he rocked forward a little and slipped his fingernails into the crack along the bottom of the drawer. He pulled gently, and the drawer slid smoothly and silently from the table.

17   The inside was a dirty, cluttered mess. Little mounds of grayish mold had formed on the furniture glue along the joints. A film of dust on the bottom covered the bits of faded yellow paper and rusted paper clips that were scattered about. Logan rocked the chair back farther, and the drawer came far out to reveal a delicate spider web. The spider was dead and flaky, resting on an old page from a desk cal-endar. The single calendar sheet read October 2, 1936. Logan pushed the drawer softly back into the table, wondering if it had actually remained closed since Alf Landon was running against Roosevelt.

18   The door of Tritt's cage clicked open, and he came out, carrying a large yellow form. William Tritt moved smoothly across the carpet, holding his body erect.

"Why, hello, Mr. Logan," he said. "I'm sorry for the delay. The main office called me. I can't hang up on them, you know."

"I know," Logan said.

The teller smiled as he lowered himself into the chair opposite Logan. Logan slid the bonds across the table.

19   "It's nice to see you again," Tritt said pleasantly as he opened his fountain pen. "Preparing for the new semester, I suppose?" There was no indication of their meeting across the street. Logan said nothing in reply, so Tritt went to work, re-ferring rapidly to the form for the amount to be paid on each bond. "Well, that comes to sixty-seven dollars and twenty-five cents," he said, finishing the addition quickly.

Logan filled out a deposit slip. "Will you put it in my checking account, please?" He handed his passbook across the table. "And will you please enter the right amount?"

20   "Certainly, Mr. Logan," Tritt said, smiling indulgently. Logan watched care-fully as Tritt made the entry. Then the teller walked rapidly back to his cage, while Logan, feeling somehow compelled to do so, took another glance into the dusty drawer. He kept thinking about the drawer as he got on a bus and rode up to the university. It had surprised him to stumble upon a dirty, forgotten place like that in a bank that was always so tidy.

21   Back in the biology department, Logan sat down at his desk, planning to pre-pare some roll sheets for his new classes. He stayed there for a long time without

moving. The September sun went low behind the New Jersey Palisades, but he did not prepare the sheets, for the unused drawer stayed unaccountably in his mind.

Suddenly he sat forward in his chair. In a surprising flash of creative thought, he had seen how he could make use of the drawer. He wasn't conscious of having tried to develop a plan. The entire plan simply burst upon him all at once, and with such clarity and precision that he hardly felt any responsibility for it. He would rob the bank and pin the robbery on Tritt. That would take care of Tritt . . .

22   In the weeks that followed, Norman Logan remained surprisingly calm about his plan. Each time he went step by step over the mechanics of the robbery, it seemed more gemlike and more workable. He made his first move the day he got his November pay check.

Down on Fifty-first Street, Logan went into a novelty-and-trick store and bought a cigarette case. It was made of a dark, steel-blue plastic, and it looked like a trim thirty-eight automatic. When the trigger was pressed, a section of the top of the gun flipped upon a hinge, revealing the cigarettes inside the handle.

23   With this in his pocket, Logan took a bus way down to the lower part of Second Avenue and entered a grimy little shop displaying pistols and rifles in the window. The small shopkeeper shuffled forward, and Logan asked to see a thirty-eight.

"Can't sell you a thing until I see your permit," the man said. "The Sullivan Law."

"Oh, I don't want to buy a weapon," Logan explained. He took out his plastic gun. "I just want to see if the real thing looks like mine here."

24   The little man laughed a cackle laugh and brought up a thirty-eight from beneath the counter, placing it next to Logan's. "So you'll just be fooling around, eh?"

"That's right," said Logan, looking at the guns. They were almost identical.

"Oh, they look enough alike," said the man. "But lemme give you a tip. Put some Scotch tape over that lid to keep it down. Friend of mine was using one of those things, mister. He'd just polished off a stick-up when he pulled the trigger and the lid flopped open. Well, he tried to offer the victim a cigarette, but the victim hauled off and beat the hell out of him."

"Thanks," Logan said with a smile. "I'll remember that."

"Here, you can put some Scotch tape on right now."

25   Logan walked over to the Lexington Avenue line and rode uptown on the subway. It was five minutes to three when he got to the bank. The old, gray-uniformed guard touched his cap as Logan came through the door. The stand-up desks were crowded, so it was natural enough for Logan to go through the little iron gate and cross to the table with the drawer. Mr. Pinkson and the new assistant manager had already left; their desks were clear. As Logan sat down, Tritt stuck his head out the door of his cage.

"More bonds, Mr. Logan?" he asked.

"No," said Logan. "Just a deposit."

26   Tritt closed the door and bent over his work. Logan took out his wallet, removed the pay check, then looked carefully the length of the bank. No one was looking in his direction. As he put the wallet back into his inside coat pocket, he withdrew the slim plastic gun and eased open the drawer. He dropped the gun in,

shut the drawer, deposited the check, and went home to his apartment. In spite of the Sullivan Law, he was on his way.

27   Twice during November he used the table with the drawer. Each time he checked on the gun. It had not been moved. By the time he deposited his December check, Logan was completely certain that nobody ever looked in there. On the nineteenth of the month, he decided to take the big step.

28   Next morning, after his ten-o'clock class, Logan walked six blocks through the snow down the hill to the bank. He took four bonds out of his safe-deposit box and filled them out for cashing. The soothing sound of recorded Christmas carols floated down from the main floor.

29   Upstairs, he seated himself at the heavy table to wait for Tritt. Pinkson had nodded and returned to his figuring; the nervous assistant manager was not around. The carols were quite loud here, and Logan smiled at this unexpected advantage. He placed the bonds squarely on the blotter. Then he slipped open the drawer, took out the gun with his left hand, and held it below the table.

30   Tritt was coming toward him, carrying his bond chart. They said hello, and Tritt sat down and went to work. He totaled the sum twice and said carefully, still looking at the figures, "Well, Mr. Logan, that comes to eighty-three fifty."

"I'll want something in addition to the eighty-three fifty," said Logan, leaning forward and speaking in an even voice.

"What's that?" asked Tritt.

"Ten thousand dollars in twenty-dollar bills."

Tritt's pink face smiled. He started to look up into Logan's face, but his eyes froze on the muzzle of the gun poking over the edge of the table. He did not notice the Scotch tape.

"Now just go to your cage and get the money," Logan said.

31   It was William Tritt's first experience with anything like this. "Mr. Logan. Come now, Mr. Logan . . ." He swallowed and tried to start again, but his self-assurance had deserted him. He turned toward Pinkson's back.

"Look at me," snapped Logan.

Tritt turned back. "Mr. Logan, you don't know what you're doing."

"Keep still."

"Couldn't we give you a loan or perhaps a—"

32   "Listen to me, Tritt." Logan's voice was just strong enough to carry above "The First Noel." He was amazed at how authoritative he sounded. "Bring the money in a bag. Place it on the table here."

Tritt started to object, but Logan raised the gun slightly, and the last resistance drained from Tritt's body.

"All right, all right. I'll get it." As Tritt moved erratically toward his cage, Logan dropped the gun back into the drawer and closed it. Tritt shut the door of the cage, and his head disappeared below the frosted part of the glass. Immediately, Mr. Pinkson's telephone buzzed, and he picked it up. Logan watched his back, and after a few seconds, Pinkson's body stiffened. Logan sighed, knowing then that he would not get the money on this try.

33   Nothing happened for several seconds; then suddenly the little old guard came rushing around the corner of the cages, his big pistol drawn and wobbling as he tried to hold it on Logan.

"Okay, Okay. Stay there! Put your hands up, now!"

Logan raised his hands, and the guard turned to Pinkson with a half-surprised face. "Okay, Mr. Pinkson. Okay, I've got him covered now."

34   Pinkson got up as Tritt came out of the cage. Behind the one gun, the three men came slowly toward Logan.

"Careful, Louie, he's armed," Tritt warned the guard.

"May I ask what this is all about?" Logan said, his hands held high.

"Mr. Logan," said Pinkson, "I'm sorry about this, but Mr. Tritt here tells me that—"

"That you tried to rob me of ten thousand dollars," said Tritt, his voice choppy. "I—I *what?*"

"You just attempted an armed robbery of this bank," Tritt said slowly. "Don't try to deny it."

35   Logan's face became the face of a man so completely incredulous that he cannot speak. He remembered not to overplay it, though. First he simply laughed at Tritt. Then he lowered his hands, regardless of the guard's gun, and stood up, the calm, indignant faculty member.

"All I can say, Mr. Tritt, is that I do deny it."

"Goodness," said Pinkson.

"Better take his gun, Louie," Tritt ordered the guard.

The guard stepped gingerly forward to Logan and frisked him, movie style. "Hasn't got a gun, Mr. Tritt," he said.

36   "Of course he's got a gun," snapped Tritt. He pushed the guard aside. "It's right in his coat." Tritt jammed his hand into Logan's left coat pocket and flailed it about. "It's not in that pocket," he said after a moment.

"It's not in any pocket," Logan said. "I don't have one."

37   "You do. You *do* have a gun. I saw it," Tritt answered, beginning to sound like a child in an argument. He spun Logan around and pulled the coat off him with a jerk. The sleeves turned inside out. Eagerly, the teller pulled the side pockets out,

checked the inside pocket and the breast pocket, then ran his hands over the entire garment, crumpling it. "The—the gun's not in his coat," he said finally.

"It's not in his pants," the guard added.

38   Tritt stepped over to the table quickly. "It's around here somewhere," he said. "We were sitting right here." He stood directly in front of the closed drawer, and his hands began to move meaninglessly over the tabletop. He picked up the neat stack of deposit slips, put them down again, then looked under the desk blotter, as though it could have concealed a gun.

39   Logan knew he had to stop this. "Is there any place I can remove the rest of my clothes?" he asked loudly, slipping the suspenders from his shoulders. Several depositors had gathered on the other side of the marble fence to watch, and Mr. Pinkson had had enough.

40   "Oh, no, no," he said, almost shouting. "That won't be necessary, Mr. Logan. Louie said you were unarmed. Now, Louie, put *your* gun away, and for goodness' sake, request the customers to please move on."

"But Mr. Pinkson, you must believe me," Tritt said, coming over to the manager. "This man held a gun on me and—"

"It's hard to know what to believe," said Pinkson. "But no money was stolen, and I don't see how we can embarrass Mr. Logan further with this matter. Please, Mr. Logan, do pull up your suspenders."

41   It was a shattering moment for the teller—the first time his word had ever been doubted at the bank.

"But sir, I insist that this man—"

"I must ask you to return to your cage now, Mr. Tritt," Pinkson said, badly agitated. Tritt obeyed.

The manager helped Logan put on his coat, then steered him over to his desk. "This is all a terrible mistake, Mr. Logan. Please do sit down now, please." The friendly little man was breathing heavily. "Now, I just want you to know that if you should press this complaint, it—it would go awfully bad for us down in the main office downtown, and I—"

42   "Please don't get excited, Mr. Pinkson," Logan said with a smile. "I'm not going to make any complaint." Logan passed the whole thing off casually. Mr. Tritt imagined he saw a gun, that's all. It was simply one of those aberrations that perfectly normal people get occasionally. Now, could Mr. Pinkson finish cashing his bonds? The manager paid him the eighty-three fifty, continuing to apologize.

Logan left the bank and walked through the soft snowfall, whistling a Christmas carol. He'd handled himself perfectly.

43   In the weeks that followed, Logan continued to do business with Tritt, just as though nothing had happened. The teller tried to remain aloof and calm, but added sums incorrectly, and his hands shook. One day late in January, Tritt stood up halfway through a transaction, his body trembling, "Excuse me, Mr. Logan," he murmured, and rushed off into the corridor behind the cages. Pinkson followed him, and Logan took advantage of the moment to check on the gun. It lay untouched in the drawer. Then Pinkson came back alone. "I'm awfully sorry to delay you again, sir," he said. "Mr. Tritt doesn't feel too well."

44   "Did he imagine he saw another gun?" Logan asked quietly.

    "No. He just upsets easily now. Ever since that incident with you last month, he's been like a cat on a hot stove."

    "I've noticed he's changed."

    "He's lost that old, calm banking touch, Mr. Logan. And of course, he's in constant fear of a new hallucination."

    "I'm sorry to hear that," Logan said, looking genuinely concerned. "It's very sad when a person loses his grip."

45   "It's particularly disappointing to me," the manager said sadly. "I brought Tritt into the bank myself, you see. Had him earmarked for a big spot downtown someday. Fine man. Intelligent, steady, accurate—why he's been right down the line on everything. But now—now he's—well, I *do* hope he gets over this."

46   "I can understand how you feel," Logan said sympathetically. He smiled inside at the precision of his planning. William Tritt had been undermined just enough— not only in Pinkson's mind but in his own.

47   On the tenth of March, Norman Logan acted again. When Tritt was seated across from him, Logan said, "Well, here we go again, Mr. Tritt." Tritt's head came up, and once more he was looking into the barrel of the toy automatic. He did not try to speak. "Now go get the ten thousand," ordered Logan. "And this time, do it."

48   Without objecting, the teller moved quickly to his cage. Logan slipped the gun back into the drawer; then he picked up his brief case and stood it near the edge of the table. Pinkson's telephone didn't buzz, and the guard remained out of sight. After a few minutes, Tritt came out of the cage, carrying a small cloth bag.

49   "All right, continue with the bonds," Logan said. "The bag goes on the table between us." Logan shifted forward and opened the bag, keeping the money out of sight behind the brief case. The clean new bills were wrapped in thousand-dollar units, each package bound with a bright yellow strip of paper. Logan counted through one package, and, with Tritt looking right at him, he placed the package of money carefully in the brief case.

50   "There," he said. "Now finish with the bonds." Tritt finished filling out the form and got Logan's signature. He was not as flustered as Logan had thought he'd be. "Now listen, Tritt," Logan went on, "My getaway is all set, of course, but if you give any signal before I'm out of the bank, I'll put a bullet into you—right here." Logan pointed to the bridge of his own nose. "Please don't think I'd hesitate to do it. Now get back to your cage."

51   Tritt returned to the cage. While his back was turned, Logan slipped the bag of money from his brief case and dropped it into the drawer, next to the gun. He eased the drawer into the table, took the brief case, and walked out of the bank.

    Outside, he stood directly in front of the entrance, as though he were waiting for a bus. After just a few seconds, the burglar alarm went off with a tremendous electrical shriek, and the old guard came running out of the door after him.

    He was followed immediately by Pinkson, the assistant manager, and Tritt.

52   "Well, gentlemen," said Logan, his hands raised again in front of the guard's gun, "here we are again, eh?"

A crowd was gathering, and Pinkson sent the assistant to turn off the alarm. "Come, let's all go inside," he said. "I don't want any fuss out here."

It was the same kind of scene they'd played before, only now Logan—the twice-wronged citizen—was irate, and now ten thousand dollars was missing from William Tritt's cage. Tritt was calm, though.

53   "I was ready for him this time," he said proudly to Pinkson. "I marked ten thousand worth of twenties. My initial is on the band. The money's in his brief case."

"Oh, for Heaven's sake, Tritt," Logan shouted suddenly, "who ever heard of making a getaway by waiting for a bus. I don't know what your game is, but—"

"Never mind my game," said Tritt. "Let's just take a look in your brief case."

54   He wrenched it from Logan's hand, clicked the lock, and turned the brief case upside down. A group of corrected examination books fell out. That was all.

"See?" said Logan. "Not a cent."

The guard put away his gun as Pinkson began to pick up the scattered books.

55   Tritt wheeled, threw the brief case against the wall, and grabbed Logan by the lapels. "But I gave you the money. I did. I did!" His face was pasty gray, and his voice was high. "You put it in the brief case. I saw you. I *saw* you do it!" He began to shake Logan in a kind of final attempt to shake the ten thousand dollars out of him.

Pinkson straightened up with the exam books and said, "For goodness' sake, Mr. Tritt. Stop it. Stop it."

Tritt stopped shaking Logan, then turned wildly to Pinkson. "You don't believe me!" he shouted. "You don't believe me!"

"It's not a question of—"

56   "I'll find that money. I'll show you who's lying." He rushed over to the big table and swept it completely clear with one wave of his heavy arm. The slips fluttered to the floor, and the inkwell broke, splattering black ink over the carpet. Tritt pulled the table in a wild, crashing arc across the green carpet, smashing it into Pinkson's desk. Logan saw the dusty drawer come open about a half-inch.

57   The big man dropped clumsily to his knees and began to pound on the carpet with his flattened hands as he kept muttering, "It's around here someplace—a cloth bag." He grabbed a corner of the carpet and flipped it back with a grunt. It made a puff of dust and revealed only a large triangle of empty, dirty floor. A dozen people had gathered outside the marble fence by now, and all the tellers were peering through the glass panes of the cages at Tritt.

58   "I'll find it! I'll find it!" he shouted. A film of sweat was on his forehead as he stood up, turned, and advanced again toward the table. The slightly opened drawer was in plain sight in front of him, but everyone's eyes were fixed on Tritt, and Tritt did not see the drawer under the overhang of the table.

Logan turned quickly to Pinkson and whispered, "He may be dangerous, Mr. Pinkson. You've got to calm him." He grabbed Pinkson by the arm and pushed him backward several feet, so that the manager came to rest on the edge of the table, directly over the drawer. The exam books were still in his hand.

59   "Mr. Tritt, you must stop this!" Mr. Pinkson said.

"Get out of my way, Pinkson," said Tritt, coming right at him, breathing like a bull. "You believe him, but I'll show you. I'll find it!" He placed his hands on Pinkson's shoulders. "Now get away, you fool."

"I won't take that from anyone," snapped Pinkson. He slapped Tritt's face with a loud, stinging blow. The teller stopped, stunned, and suddenly began to cry.

"Mr. Pinkson. Mr. Pinkson, you've *got* to trust me."

Pinkson was immediately ashamed of what he had done. "I'm sorry, my boy. I shouldn't have done that."

60   "I tell you he held a gun on me again. A real gun—it's not my imagination."

"But why didn't you call Louie?" Pinkson said. "That's the rule, you know."

"I wanted to catch him myself. He—he made such a fool of me last time."

"But that business last time was hallucination," said Pinkson, looking over at Logan. Logan nodded.

"It's no hallucination when ten thousand dollars is missing," Tritt shouted.

"That's precisely where the confusion arises in my mind," Mr. Pinkson said slowly. "We'll get it straight, but in the meantime, I must order your arrest, Mr. Tritt."

61   Logan came and stood next to Pinkson, and they both looked sympathetically at the teller as he walked slowly, still sobbing, back to the cage.

"I'm just sick about it," Pinkson said.

"I think you'll find he's not legally competent," said Logan, putting a comforting thought into Pinkson's head.

"Perhaps not."

62   Logan showed his concern by helping to clean up the mess that Tritt had made. He and the assistant manager placed the table back into its position against the far wall, Logan shoving the dusty drawer firmly closed with his fingertips as they lifted it.

Norman Logan returned to the bank late the next day. He sat at the table to make a deposit, and he felt a pleasantly victorious sensation surge through him as he slipped the gun and the ten thousand dollars out of the drawer and into his overcoat pocket. As he walked out the front door past the guard, he met Mr. Pinkson, who was rushing in.

63   "Terrible. Terrible," the little man said without even pausing to say hello.

"What's that?" Logan asked calmly.

"I've just been talking to the doctors at Bellevue about Tritt," Pinkson said. "He seems all right, and they've released him. Unfortunately, he can answer every question except 'Where's the money?'" "Logan held firmly to the money in his pocket and continued to extend his sympathies."

Back at his apartment, Logan borrowed a portable typewriter from the man upstairs. Then he sat down and wrote a note:

> *Dear Mr. Pinkson:*
> *I'm returning the money. I'm so sorry. I guess I didn't know what I was doing. I guess I haven't known for some time.*

After looking up Tritt's initials on an old deposit slip, he forged a small tidy *W.T.* to the note.

64   Logan wiped his fingerprints from the bills and wrapped them, along with the note, in a neat package. For one delicious moment he considered how nice it would be to hang on to the money. He could resign from the university, go out West, and continue his research on his own. But that wasn't part of the plan, and the plan was working too well to tamper with it now. Logan drove to the post office nearest Tritt's apartment and mailed the money to Pinkson at the bank.

65   In the morning, Mr. Pinkson telephoned Logan at the university. "Well, it's all cleared up," he said, relieved but sad. "Tritt returned the money, so the bank is not going to press charges. Needless to say, we're dropping Tritt. He not only denies having taken the money, he also denies having returned it."

"I guess he just doesn't know what he's doing," Logan said.

66   "Yes. That's what he said in the note. Anyway, Mr. Logan, I—I just wanted to call and apologize for the trouble we've caused you."

"Oh, it was no trouble for me," Logan replied, smiling.

"And you've been very helpful, too," Pinkson added.

"I was glad to be of help," Logan said quietly. "Delighted, in fact."

They said good-by then, and Logan walked across the hall to begin his ten o'clock botany lecture.

Comprehension

1. Before you can appreciate a suspense story, you must understand the characters involved. Below is a list of physical and personality characteristics. Put a *T* next to those that describe Tritt and an *L* next to those that describe Logan. Some adjectives may describe both men. Be prepared to defend your choices with portions of the text.

_____ a. large   _____ d. ambitious   _____ g. greedy   _____ j. clever

_____ b. stubborn   _____ e. thin   _____ h. careless

_____ c. dishonest   _____ f. careful   _____ i. self-assured

2. The most important factor in enjoying a suspense story is a complete understanding of the plot. The following sentences will tell the story of "The Dusty Drawer" when they are arranged in the correct sequence. Read all of the sentences quickly, and then number the sentences according to the order in which the events occur.

_____ a. Logan writes a note to the bank and forges Tritt's initials, then returns the money by mail.

_____ b. Tritt steals $200 from Logan to cover a mistake he had made while depositing money in Logan's account.

_____ c. Logan learns that Tritt has been fired from his position at the bank.

_____ d. Logan buys a toy gun and hides it in the dusty drawer.

_____ e. Logan gets $10,000 from Tritt and hides it in the drawer.

_____ f. Logan's first attempt to rob the bank causes Tritt to lose his banker's touch.

3. What was Tritt's position in the bank? _____

4. What was Logan's profession? _____

5. T / F   Tritt was considered a valuable employee who would make great progress in the bank if he made no mistakes.

6. Logan believed that Tritt stole the $200 because _____

   _____ a. he needed the money.

   _____ b. he had made an error and didn't want to admit it.

   _____ c. he hated Logan and wanted a safe way to hurt him.

   _____ d. he knew he would not be caught.

7. Logan suspected that $200 had been stolen when _____

   _____ a. he noticed that the wrong amount of money had been deposited in his account by Tritt.

   _____ b. he didn't receive the right amount of cash when his bonds were cashed by Tritt.

   _____ c. he checked his wallet after talking to Tritt.

   _____ d. he returned from his summer vacation, and the money wasn't in his account.

8. T / F   As they were talking in the cafeteria, Tritt admitted to Logan that he had taken the money.

9. Although Tritt denied taking the $200, he did say that _____

   _____ a. Mr. Pinkson might have made a mistake when he counted the money.

   _____ b. he would have told Logan if he had stolen it.

   _____ c. he thought he knew who did.

   _____ d. he certainly wouldn't return the money if he had stolen it.

10. Logan wanted to get even with Tritt because _____

   _____ a. he had difficulty living without that $200.

   _____ b. he hated Tritt.

   _____ c. he did not like to be cheated.

   _____ d. he wanted to prevent Tritt from cheating other people.

11. T / F   Logan made regular trips to the bank.

12. Logan's plan to pin the robbery on Tritt _____

_____ a. had been carefully developed over a period of ten months.

_____ b. developed because he learned that Tritt had been promoted to the first cage.

_____ c. was suggested to him by something that a shop owner told him.

_____ d. came to him suddenly after he found an unused drawer in the bank.

13. T / F   Tritt had received a promotion while Logan was away on summer vacation.

14. T / F   The Sullivan Law prevents the sale of guns unless the customer has a permit.

15. T / F   In order to convince Tritt that the robbery was genuine, Logan bought a .38 caliber pistol.

16. T / F   The shopkeeper of the gun store assumed that Logan was going to attempt a robbery.

17. Logan became convinced the old drawer was never used because _____

_____ a. the handles had been removed before the desk was painted.

_____ b. the rest of the bank was so clean and efficient.

_____ c. the gun was not moved during the time that he watched it.

_____ d. neither Mr. Pinkson nor Mr. Tritt ever mentioned it.

18. The first time Logan tried to rob the bank _____

_____ a. Tritt placed the money in a cloth bag after initialing the packets of bills.

_____ b. Tritt said he would not bring the money from his cage.

_____ c. Tritt signaled Mr. Pinkson from his cage.

_____ d. Tritt thought it was all a joke.

19. T / F   Logan offered to remove all his clothes because he was afraid that Tritt might accidentally find the drawer.

20. In the months following the first robbery attempt, Tritt _____

_____ a. questioned Logan carefully about the robbery whenever he entered the bank.

_____ b. tried to prove that Logan had had a gun.

_____ c. became nervous and easily upset.

_____ d. lost his position in the first cage because of his frequent errors.

21. T / F   The second time Logan attempted the robbery, Tritt brought the money.

22. T / F   When no one was looking, Logan moved the money from the brief case to the drawer.

23. Logan didn't keep the $10,000 because _____

_____ a. the plan was working so well that he didn't want to change it.

_____ b. he was too honest.

_____ c. he was afraid that someone would find the drawer.

_____ d. he knew that crime never benefits anyone.

Discussion/Composition

1. Do you believe that Tritt stole $200 from Logan? On what do you base your opinion? (How did you learn that the money was missing?)

2. What is the nature of the crimes committed in "The Dusty Drawer"? What is the difference between the consequences of Tritt's actions as compared to Logan's? Is there any moral difference between the two men? Is one better than the other?

3. Was Logan justified in doing what he did? How would you defend him? Has he committed a crime? Are there other considerations that should be used to judge his actions besides the question of whether or not he has broken the law?

4. Has justice been served in "The Dusty Drawer"?

5. When do you think this story was written? Compare your experience in banks today with the events in the story. In what ways are they similar and different?

Vocabulary from Context

Both the ideas and the vocabulary in the following sentences are taken from "The Dusty Drawer." Use the context provided to determine the meanings of the italicized words. Your teacher may want you to do this exercise orally or in writing.

1. _____   The man's *obsequious* behavior made everyone nervous. Like a servant, he was always rushing to open doors and perform other small tasks, apologizing unnecessarily for any inconvenience that he might have caused.

2. _____   Although he really did not want to open the mysterious drawer again, his curiosity *compelled* him to take one last look.

3. _____   The shop was dusty and dirty. Everything seemed to be covered with grease. He was very happy to escape that *grimy* place.

4. _____   Logan wanted to hit Tritt in the nose, but he *restrained* himself because he knew that violence would not help him get his money back.

5. _____ Tritt never allowed himself to become angry with customers. Like a parent with spoiled children, he always listened *indulgently* to their complaints.

6. _____ Both men had convincing stories to tell concerning the missing money, but Logan's *version* of what happened was by far more believable.

7. _____ Logan felt that the situation was hopeless, and the *futility* of his efforts bothered him a great deal.

8. _____ Logan finally decided that, although he might not recover the money that had been stolen from him, he would have the pleasure of seeing the thief punished. Soon, Logan could think of little else but *vengeance*.

9. _____ The floor of the grimy little store was covered with paper, boxes, pieces of metal and wood, empty paint cans, and used brushes. The floor was so *cluttered* that Carl had difficulty walking to the door.

10. _____ Tritt was sure that he had seen a pistol, but everyone else felt that the robbery was just a product of Tritt's imagination—the *hallucination* of an overworked man.

11. _____ The banker was *incredulous* when the money did not fall out of the thief's brief case; he couldn't believe that it wasn't there because he had seen him put the bills inside just before leaving the bank.

12. _____ Logan certainly had reason to be *indignant;* twice he had been unjustly accused of trying to rob the bank.

13. _____ After the first time someone tried to rob him, the banker became *flustered* easily, and in his confusion he would make many careless errors.

14. _____ Although he often had the opportunity, Tritt never stole money from a customer. This would have endangered his position at the bank, and he did not want to *jeopardize* his future.

Figurative Language and Idioms

In the second half of the section indicated by the number in parentheses, find the word or phrase that best fits the meaning given. Your teacher may want to read these aloud as you quickly scan* the paragraph to find the answer.

1. (9)   What phrase means *advancing greatly in one's career*?

2. (10) What phrase means *escape without punishment*?

_____

*For an introduction to scanning, see Unit 1.

3. (11) What phrase is used to promise vengeance?

4. (11) What phrase means *not able to tolerate being cheated*?

5. (21) What phrase means *put the blame on someone for something*?

6. (24) What phrase means *completed*?

7. (24) Which word means *a robbery*?

Dictionary Study

Many words have more than one meaning. When you use the dictionary to discover the meaning of an unfamiliar word or phrase, you need to use the context to determine which definition is appropriate. Use the portions of the dictionary provided to select the best definition for each of the italicized words below.

1. Logan *reflected* that all had gone well for him in the bank so far.

2. As he sat waiting for the cashier, Logan *stumbled* across the old drawer.

3. After the first robbery attempt, the cashier began to lose his *grip* on reality.

4. Tritt knew that if he were caught stealing money from the bank, he would lose his position and go to prison, but he *staked* his future on the hope that the manager would believe his version of the robbery.

grip (grip), *n.* [ME.; AS. *gripe*, a clutch, *gripa*, handful < var. of the base of AS. *gripan* (see GRIPE) with a reduced vowel; akin to G. *griff*; some senses < the *v.*], 1. the act of taking firmly and holding fast with the hand, teeth, an instrument, etc.; secure grasp; firm hold. 2. the manner in which this is done. 3. any special manner of clasping hands by which members of a secret or fraternal society identify each other as such. 4. the power of grasping firmly: as, his hand has lost its *grip*. 5. the power of understanding; mental grasp. 6. firm control; mastery: as, in the *grip* of disease, get a *grip* on yourself. 7. a mechanical contrivance for clutching or grasping. 8. the part by which a tool weapon, etc. is grasped in the hand; handle. 9. [prob. < or after D.], a small bag for holding clothes, etc. in traveling; valise. 10. a sudden, intense pain. 11. [Slang], in a motion-picture studio, a stagehand. 12. in *sports*, the manner of holding a bat, club, racket, etc. *v.t.* [GRIPPED or GRIPT (gript), GRIPPING], 1. to take firmly and hold fast with the hand, teeth, an instrument, etc. 2. to give a grip (sense 3) to. 3. to fasten or join firmly (*to*). 4. to get and hold the attention of. 5. to take hold upon; control (the attention, emotions, etc.). *v.i.* to get a grip.
   come to grips, 1. to engage in hand-to-hand fighting. 2. to struggle; try to cope (*with*).

re·flect (ri-flekt′), *v.t.* [ME. *reflecten*; OFr. *reflecter*: L. *reflectere*; *re-*, back + *flectere*, to bend], 1. to bend or throw back, as light, heat, or sound. 2. to give back an image of; mirror or reproduce. 3. to cast or bring back as a consequence (with *on*): as, his deeds *reflect* honor on the nation. 4. [Rare], to fold or turn back. *v.i.* 1. to be bent or thrown back: as, the light *reflected* from the water into his eyes. 2. to bend or throw back light, heat, sound, etc. 3. *a*) to give back an image or likeness. *b*) to be mirrored. 4. to think seriously; contemplate; ponder (with *on* or *upon*). 5. to cast blame or discredit (with *on* or *upon*). —*SYN.* see **consider, think.**

stake (stāk), *n.* [ME.; AS. *staca*; akin to D. *staak*; base as in *stick*], 1. a length of wood or metal pointed at one end for driving into the ground. 2. the post to which a person is tied for execution by burning. 3. execution by burning. 4. a pole or post fitted upright into a socket, as at the edge of a railway flatcar, truck bed, etc., to help hold a load. 5. a truck having a stake body. 6. *often pl.* something, especially money, risked or hazarded, as in a wager, game, or contest: as, the gamblers were playing for high *stakes*. 7. *often pl.* a reward given a winner, as in a race; prize. 8. a race in which a prize is offered. 9. a share or interest, especially a financial one, in property, a person, a business venture, or the like. 10. [Colloq.], a grubstake. *v.t.* [STAKED (stākt), STAKING], 1. to mark the location or boundaries of with or as with stakes, specifically so as to establish a claim (with *out*, etc.). 2. to fasten or support with a stake or stakes. 3. to hitch or tether to a stake. 4. to close (*up* or *in*), shut (*out*), etc. by stakes in the form of a fence or barrier. 5. [influenced by MD. *staken*, to fix, place], to risk or hazard; gamble; bet: as, he *staked* his winnings on the next hand. 6. [Colloq.], to furnish with money or resources, as for a business venture. 7. [Colloq.], to grubstake.
   at stake, being risked or hazarded, or dependent upon the outcome (of something specified or implied).
   pull up stakes, [Colloq.], to change one's place of residence, business, etc.
stake body, a flat truck body having sockets into which stakes may be fitted, as to support railings.
stake·hold·er (stāk′hōl′dĕr), *n.* one who holds money, etc. bet by others and pays it to the winner.

stum·ble (stum′b'l), *v.i.* [STUMBLED (-b'ld), STUMBLING], [ME. *stomblen, stomelen*; prob. < ON. *stumla* (cf. Norw. *stumla*, to stumble in the dark, etc.) < the base seen in *stammer*], 1. to trip or miss one's step in walking, running, etc. 2. to walk or go in an unsteady or awkward manner, as from age, weakness, etc. 3. to speak, act, or proceed in a confused, blundering manner: as, he *stumbled* through his recitation. 4. to fall into sin or error; do wrong. 5. to come by chance; happen: as, I *stumbled* across a clue. *v.t.* to cause to stumble. *n.* 1. the act of stumbling. 2. a blunder, error, or sin.
stumbling block, something that causes stumbling; obstacle, hindrance, or difficulty.

From *Webster's New World Dictionary,* College Edition (New York: World Publishing Company).

Vocabulary Review

Place the appropriate word or phrase from the following list in each of the blanks below. Use each word only once.

indulgent	indignantly	grime	clutter
get away with it	go a long way	compelled	restraint
futile	hallucinations	incredulous	grip
obsequiousness	vengeance	flustered	
reflect	jeopardize	version	

1. Although it is true that a good employee should be respectful and helpful, Harry's extreme _____ makes everyone uncomfortable.

2. Karen is intelligent, hardworking, and honest. She should _____ in her profession.

3. Douglas is well known for his self-_____; it is said that, no matter how angry he becomes, he never allows himself to show it.

4. John becomes _____ easily these days. Merely by asking him a simple question, you can confuse him.

5. My aunt Vera suffers from frequent _____; just last night she thought she saw a pink elephant in a tree.

6. If you don't clean your kitchen regularly, the _____ on the wall above the stove will become too thick to remove with soap and water alone.

7. Debbie knew that the bank officials regularly examined her records. She should have known that she couldn't steal any money and _____ .

8. After he was robbed, Robert ran around madly shouting, "I'll get him, I'll get him!" It was obvious that he could think of nothing but _____ .

9. Arthur's behavior became stranger every day until he seemed to completely lose his _____ on reality.

10. The judge told us not to be impatient; after the other man told his story, we could tell our _____ of what had happened.

11. I have tried for a number of years to get my grandfather to buy a new car, but my attempts have been _____; he just won't part with his old Ford.

12. Although I didn't particularly want to accompany the children to the zoo, my sense of responsibility _____ me to go with them.

13. No matter how often we reminded the children, they never cleaned their room; the _____ in the room became so bad that we couldn't even open the door.

14. Before I make an important decision, I need some time to just sit and _____.

15. As Uncle Andy described the size of the fish he had caught, I became more and more _____. (You just never know when he is telling the truth.)

16. Grandparents are always more _____ of children than parents. For that reason, we always enjoyed our vacations on our grandparents' farm.

17. Angry and insulted because he had been accused of stealing the money, Dean _____ demanded to see his lawyer.

18. Claudia had been working so hard that she decided to take a vacation, even though she knew she might _____ her chances of doing well on the upcoming examination.

Exercise 2

Complete the sentences below with the correct form of the word provided on the left.

1. obsequiousness — Quite apart from any question of the man's honesty, I would not hire him because I dislike his _____ manner.

2. incredulity — The police officer watched _____ as the family proceeded to do their laundry in the public swimming pool.

3. futility — "If wishes were horses, beggars would ride" is an old saying that emphasizes the _____ of dreaming about unrealistic good fortune.

4. vengeful — The man promised the judge that he would not seek _____ against the person who had robbed him.

5. indulgence — Some people believe that modern parents are far too _____ of their children.

6. grimy — No matter how hard we try, we will not be able to remove the _____ from public monuments.

7. jeopardy — Most of us would not _____ our lives without a good reason, but firefighters are in almost constant danger.

Appendix

Below is a list of the stems and affixes that appear in *Reader's Choice*. The number in parentheses indicates the unit in which an item appears.

Prefixes

(5) **a-, an-**   without, lacking, not
(3) **ante-**   before
(5) **bene-**   good
(5) **bi-**   two
(9) **by-**   aside or apart from the common, secondary
(3) **circum-**   around
(1) **com-, con-, col-, cor-, co-**   together, with
(3) **contra-, anti-**   against
(9) **de-**   down from, away
(9) **dia-**   through, across
(9) **epi-**   upon, over, outer
(9) **hyper-**   above, beyond, excessive
(9) **hypo-**   under, beneath, down
(1) **in-, im-, il-, ir-**   in, into, on
(1) **in-, im-, il-, ir-**   not
(3) **inter-**   between
(3) **intro-, intra-**   within
(1) **micro-**   small
(5) **mis-**   wrong
(5) **mono-**   one, alone
(7) **multi-**   many
(7) **peri-**   around
(5) **poly-**   many
(3) **post-**   after
(1) **pre-**   before
(1) **re-, retro-**   back, again
(7) **semi-**   half, partly
(3) **sub-, suc-, suf-, sug-, sup-, sus-**   under
(3) **super-**   above, greater, better
(5) **syn-, sym-, syl-**   with, together
(3) **trans-**   across
(7) **tri-**   three
(7) **ultra-**   beyond, excessive, extreme
(7) **uni-**   one

Stems

(5) **-anthro-, -anthropo-**   human
(5) **-arch-**   first, chief, leader
(7) **-aster-, -astro-, -stellar-**   star
(1) **-audi-, -audit-**   hear
(7) **-auto-**   self
(7) **-bio-**   life
(9) **-capit-**   head, chief

(3) **-ced-**   go, move, yield
(1) **-chron-**   time
(9) **-corp-**   body
(7) **-cycle-**   circle
(9) **-derm-**   skin
(1) **-dic-, -dict-**   say, speak
(3) **-duc-**   lead
(5) **-fact-, -fect-**   make, do
(3) **-flect-**   bend
(5) **-gam-**   marriage
(9) **-geo-**   earth
(1) **-graph-, -gram-**   write, writing
(5) **-hetero-**   different, other
(5) **-homo-**   same
(9) **-hydr-, -hydro-**   water
(1) **-log-, -ology-**   speech, word, study
(5) **-man-, -manu-**   hand
(7) **-mega-**   great, large
(3) **-mit-, -miss-**   send
(5) **-morph-**   form, structure
(7) **-mort-**   death
(5) **-onym-, -nomen-**   name
(9) **-ortho-**   straight, correct
(5) **-pathy-**   feeling, disease
(7) **-phil-**   love
(1) **-phon-**   sound
(9) **-pod-, -ped-**   foot
(3) **-pon-, -pos-**   put, place
(7) **-polis-**   city
(3) **-port-**   carry
(7) **-psych-**   mind
(1) **-scrib-, -script-**   write
(3) **-sequ-, -secut-**   follow
(9) **-son-**   sound
(1) **-spect-**   look at
(3) **-spir-**   breathe
(7) **-soph-**   wise
(3) **-tele-**   far
(5) **-theo-, -the-**   god
(9) **-therm-, -thermo-**   heat
(3) **-ven-, -vene-**   come
(9) **-ver-**   true
(1) **-vid-, -vis-**   see
(3) **-voc-, -vok-**   call

Suffixes

(3) **-able, -ible, -ble**   capable of, fit for
(9) **-ate**   to make
(1) **-er, -or**   one who
(9) **-fy**   to make
(5) **-ic, -al**   relating to, having the nature of
(5) **-ism**   action or practice, theory or doctrine

(1) **-ist**   one who
(7) **-ity**   condition, quality, state of being
(9) **-ize**   to make
(7) **-ness**   condition, quality, state of being
(5) **-oid**   like, resembling
(3) **-ous, -ious, -ose**   full of, having the qualities of
(1) **-tion, -ation**   condition, the act of

Answer Key

The processes involved in arriving at an answer are often more important than the answer itself. It is expected that students will not use the Answer Key until they have completed the exercises and are prepared to defend their answers. If a student's answer does not agree with the Key, it is important for the student to return to the exercise to discover the source of the error. No answer is provided in instances where the students have been asked to express their own opinions or when there is no one best answer.

Unit 1

Discourse Focus: Reading for Different Goals—Web Work

Skimming (page 1)

1. This is the Web site of Cable News Network. This page focuses on technology and computer news.
2. Although all Web sites have advertisements and opportunities for you to spend your hard-earned money, this Web site is primarily for news, not for sales.
3. The center of the page contains a news story of current interest. The columns on either side provide links to other pages and to specific information. You would use these items to learn more about the topics addressed here.
4. Answers will vary.

Scanning (pages 1–3)

1. At the top of the left-hand column, you can click on **MAINPAGE**.
2. It looks as if two options would be the fastest way to find out about the weather in Montreal. In the upper left-hand column, under the **CNN.com** logo, is a list of the main Web pages, one of which is **Weather**. You could click there, or there is another weather link in lower right-hand corner.
3. At the bottom of the left-hand column under **CNN WEB SITES** you can click on **Spanish**.
4. You have several options. You might click on **SPORTS**, just under the **CNN.com** heading in the upper left-hand corner, or you could click on **Sports** CNNSports Illustrated in the right-hand column.

Reading for Thorough Comprehension (pages 3–4)

1. The installation of Internet connections for on-flight use by airline passengers
2. F (It was a Montreal to Toronto flight.)
3. F (No mention of remodeling; merely addition of internet ports)
4. F (Cathay airline is also developing in-air Internet connectivity.)

Critical Reading (page 4)

1. People who travel and people who are addicted to internet use
2. No, this is a news page.
3. F (Like all Web sites, you can find all manner of information here.)
4. Your answer will depend on your tolerance for Internet mail. We find that we get too much unwanted email as it is, and we would not subscribe.
5. a. N   e. N
   b. T   f. To discover how people voted, you
   c. N   would click on *View Results*.
   d. F (but on the Internet it is difficult to distinguish between news and advertisements)

Nonprose Reading: Menu

Scanning (page 5)

1. Probably not; the menu section titled "Assorted Beverages" does not list any alcoholic drinks.
2. Yes; there is a section titled "Sweet Delights" that shows pictures of desserts like pie and ice cream.
3. No. The dishes that mention *buffalo* are chicken meat prepared with a spicy sauce, not buffalo meat.
4. Any of the dishes under Just For Starters. Any of the Select Sides except perhaps the soup (you'd have to ask). All the Breakfast Favorites contain pork except sirloin steak and eggs and chicken-fried steak and eggs. Breakfast Sides with pork are: biscuit and sausage gravy, grilled Canadian bacon, grilled ham slice, bacon or sausage links, and sausage patty. Other items with pork are: bacon-cheddar burger, the club, chicken melt, the Super Bird, Charleston chicken sandwich with bacon and cheese, ham sandwich as part of the sandwich and salad or soup combination.
5. Among Breakfast Sides, meatless items are hashed browns, fresh fruit, bagel and cream cheese, blueberry

muffin, biscuit, toast or English muffin, cereal and eggs. All the sandwiches except the gardenburger include meat. Perhaps the soup of the day would be vegetarian. All dinner items include meat. Any of the Sides would be meatless except perhaps the stuffing (you'd have to ask).

6. Every Breakfast Favorite includes some meat, so if you wanted one without meat, you would have to ask the waitperson if your order could be made without meat.
7. Food that is served alongside main dishes of a meal; food that accompanies the main dishes.
8. Fruit that is in season at the time you are ordering; we don't know exactly what kind of fruit.
9. Yes; the menu says "Breakfast and lunch served 24 hours."
10. No
11. No
12. a. $4.99 + $.99 = $5.98
    b. $4.99 + $1.79 = $6.78
13. We don't know; the menu doesn't say.

Reading for Details (page 6)

1. T
2. T
3. F
4. T
5. F; you would need more money to pay for tax and tip.
6. F
7. F
8. T
9. T

Critical Reading (page 6)

1. Answers will vary.
2. Vegetarians could find something to eat here, but because most of the items contain meat, this restaurant probably wouldn't be their first choice.
3. Answers will vary.
4. The four items are: Original Grand Slam Breakfast, Scram Slam, All-American Slam, and French Slam. They all have at least four different types of food (a lot!). The one served the longest is probably the "Original" Grand Slam Breakfast. A grand slam is a baseball play in which the batter hits a home run when there are runners on all three bases. This scores 4 runs, the most possible in a single play.

Wordy Study: Context Clues

Exercise 1 (page 9)

1. to pounce: to jump
2. to adapt: to adjust to new circumstances
3. egret: a type of bird
4. to inveigh against: to talk loudly against; to attack verbally; to protest
5. to slither: to move like a snake; to slide
6. to pelt: to hit
7. kinesics: the study of body motion
8. gregarious: sociable; friendly
9. ravenous: extremely hungry
10. to salvage: to save

Word Study: Dictionary Use

Exercise 1 (pages 10–11)

1. All spellings and pronunciations are acceptable as long as they correspond to the meaning you intend.
2. a. 2
   b. ·
   c. When you reach the end of a line, you may need to hyphenate long words at a syllable division.
3. a. the second
   b. the first
4. a. across the bottom of the page
   b. Answers will vary.
   c. *be*
5. a. two
   b. two
6. words with related meaning that have been produced from the entry word, for example, *prefixal*
7. before
8. They help you know how, where, or if a word is used.

Exercise 2 (pages 11–12)

1. no
2. five
3. glu*tam*ic
4. paw, for
5. glottises
6. glued
7. gloweringly
8. glossography
9. Benjamin Peter Gloxin
10. French and Greek
11. no
12. four; although synonyms, their meanings are not exactly the same
13. 1714
14. 26,000
15. Answers include such things as the following: definitions; synonyms; parts of speech; pronunciation (syllabification and stress); alternate pronunciations; spelling and alternate spellings; if verb—principal parts; if noun—plural form; usage labels (archaic, obsolete, regional, etc.); origin of word (etymology); derived words; information about famous people; information about geographical places.

Word Study: Stems and Affixes

Exercise 1 (page 15)

1. a. 1   b. 2   c. 3
2. insane, inactive, invisible
3. For example, coworker, coauthor, copilot
4. For example, rework, replay, rewind, relive

Exercise 2 (page 16)

1. inhale: breathe in
2. import: bring in from outside the country; buy from other countries
3. collaborated: worked together
4. informal: casual (not formal)
5. prediction: statement foretelling the future; statement saying what will happen in the future
6. inscriptions: writings, drawings, or marks written on or into some surface
7. preregister: register before classes start
8. reflection: image; likeness
9. dictated: spoke or read (the letter) aloud so that it could be written down

10. graphologist: person who studies handwriting
11. microbiology: the branch of biology that deals with animal or vegetable organisms that can be seen only with a microscope
12. phonograph recordings: records (from: write [record] sound)
13. prescription: written order for medicine
14. chronic: long-lasting; constant; continuous
15. reapplied: applied again
16. recall: remember
17. in retrospect: looking back
18. audiovisual: involving both hearing and sight (such as movies)
19. immoral: not moral; against ethical principles; wrong
20. prenatal: before birth

Exercise 3 (page 17)

1. g	3. c	5. h	7. a
2. d	4. f	6. e	8. b

Paragraph Reading: Main Idea (pages 19–24)

Paragraph 1: d   Paragraph 4: d
Paragraph 2: b   Paragraph 5: c
Paragraph 3: b

Paragraph 6: Contrary to popular opinion, change has always characterized the family.

Paragraph 7: Our ideas about the ancient Mayas are changing; we once thought them to be peaceful but now believe them to have been warlike.

Poem: We seem to appreciate the accomplishments of science more than the miracles of nature.

Unit 2

Selection 1A: Journal Graphic "The Globalization of Tourism"

Comprehension (pages 25–28)

1. F
2. T
3. F
4. It encourages the growth of tourism by making it easier for people to get information about making travel reservations.
5. The United States was the country that earned the most from international tourism.
6. F
7. Europe
8. T
9. F
10. China, which was not even in the top 20 "sources of tourism" when this article was written, is predicted to jump to the fourth largest source of tourists. Also, China will move up from the sixth most popular destination for tourists to the most popular destination for tourists.
11. F
12. F (The map for 2020 does not tell us how many tourists will go from Asia to the East Asia/Pacific region.)

Critical Reading (page 28)

2a. Paragraph 3: It is difficult to decide if the text and the graph agree. The text talks about regions, and the graph talks about countries. According to the text, the top destination will be Europe, followed by East Asia/Pacific, and then the Americas. Although not all countries are listed in the bar graph, adding up countries (on the bar graph) by region makes us think the information in the graph might be consistent with the claims about regions made in the text.

Paragraph 4: Yes and No. The bar chart of top destinations in 2020 shows China at the top. However China *did* appear (in sixth place) on the list of top destinations in 1998.

Selection 1B: Essay "The Politics of Travel"

Comprehension (page 29)

1. T	4. F	7. F	10. F
2. T	5. F	8. F	11. F
3. T	6. F	9. T	12. T

Critical Reading (page 29)

1. Answers will vary, but the author was presumably referring to at least two senses of the term *consumer*. The first is someone who buys things and turns them into commodities (even tourist experiences), often as a result of advertising. The second is the sense of "consuming" or using up our natural resources.

2. Answers will vary. Some of the possible answers include: Politics will effect how people feel about tourism; tourism reveals/makes obvious the dramatic differences between rich and poor, for example, when people from rich nations pay for the experience of living with poor people; tourism can damage or destroy natural or cultural treasures of tourist locations; large-scale travel (for example, by car or train or plane) can damage the Earth's atmosphere and lead to global warming.

Vocabulary from Context

Exercise 1 (pages 32–33)

1. unqualified: definite; complete; absolute; not qualified or limited
2. income: money; earnings
3. ecosystem: the interrelated community of plants and animals and bacteria that make up the Earth
4. fragile: easily damaged or broken; delicate
5. threatens: endangers; puts at risk
6. trekkers: people who take a difficult, laborious trip, especially on foot
7. dilemma: question; problem; situation in which one must choose between unpleasant alternatives
8. profit: income; earnings; monetary gain
9. habitats: places where plants or animals normally live; ecosystems; environments; surroundings
10. survival: continued living; continued existence
11. thrive on: succeed / grow / do very well / prosper with
12. authentic: real; genuine; true

13. cumulative: taken all together, especially over time; collective; total
14. disruptions: troubles; disturbances; interruptions of the normal
15. campaigns: organized, planned actions to bring about a specific result
16. launched: begun; started; introduced; initiated; inaugurated
17. exponents: supporters; advocates; promoters; proponents
18. initiative: action that is the first of its kind; first step; plan; proposal
19. industrialization: the process of organizing something on a large scale as though it were an industry with interchangeable parts

Exercise 2 (page 34)

1. local: resident; native; person from that area
2. culprits: problems; causes of problems
3. monuments: buildings; statues; tombs that keep alive a memory
4. notably: especially; particularly
5. trampling: destroying under foot; flattening; walking on
6. replicas: copies; reproductions
7. awareness: knowledge; consciousness
8. redressed: addressed; fixed; put right; rectified
9. postindustrial: there are two meanings here. The more conventional meaning has to do with economic systems that have replaced manufacturing, based on advanced technology, especially information technology. The author refers to another, related meaning. With the possibility to focus beyond products and profits, the author hopes that a postindustrial system will focus on people and places.

Figurative Language and Idioms (page 34)

1. poses a serious threat
2. appetite for
3. cost-benefit equation
4. salvation lies in
5. breed

Stems and Affixes (page 35)

1. deforestation: cutting down forests
2. herbicides: chemicals used to kill unwanted plants and weeds
3. underpins: supports
   wildlife: plants and animals
4. reservoir: supply; pool; reserve
5. uniform: the same
6. transformed: changed
7. nonprofit: not intended to make a profit; not maintained for financial gain; charitable
   asymmetries: inequalities

Dictionary Study (page 36)

1. vtr 2
2. This is an adjective, not directly listed in the dictionary; the meaning is based on that listed under boom[1], vintr 2
3. n 7

Vocabulary Review (page 37)

1. asymmetry
2. profit
3. inevitable
4. consumer
5. thriving

Selection 1C: Travel Guide "Learning Holidays"

Comprehension (pages 39–40)

1. F
2. F
3. The first Art and Architecture tour and the Language (in Siena, Italy) tour
4. F
5. Tours where you live with and live as traditional people.
6. F
7. Possible answers are the third Art and Architecture tour, the fourth Archaeology tour, the fifth Archaeology tour, and Earthwatch under "Further Information."
8. The first Language and the first and second Living In tours
9. F
10. "Further Information"
11. Answers will vary.

Reading Selection 2: Mystery "The Midnight Visitor"

Comprehension Clues (page 43)

1. T   2. F   3. T   4. T   5. T

Max will not return because he jumped onto a balcony that did not exist.

Selection 3A: Essay "Can English Be Dethroned?"

Comprehension (pages 45–46)

1. T   3. F   5. T   7. T   9. T
2. T   4. F   6. F   8. F   10. T

11. He seems to use these terms with respect to numbers of speakers. Answers to the rest of this question will vary.

Critical Reading (pages 46–47)

1. a. Through a monopoly on education: languages not taught in schools tend to die out because they are not used for official functions. Languages not used outside the home or beyond traditional customs tend to die out.
   b. Answers will vary.
2. The author is referring to a number of relationships. The first is between individual freedom and political power, that is, if one is not free as an individual, one does not have real power within a community. The second is the tie between language and society and economics. If one doesn't have linguistic freedom/power, one is unlikely to have social freedom or economic success. Because the personal freedom to use language is fundamental to other freedoms and power, if one's language is destroyed, it endangers one's standing in the world.
3. Answers will vary.

Vocabulary from Context

Exercise 1 (pages 48–49)

1. trend: tendency; when something moves generally in a particular direction; inclination; pattern; propensity
2. imperialism: the practice of controlling and dominating other nations, for example, through colonialism
3. diplomacy: international relations
4. eliminates: gets rid of; removes; forces out
5. denounce: criticize; accuse; condemn
6. inconspicuous: not noticeable; not immediately obvious; subtle
7. tangible: obvious; actual; able to be touched
8. subtle: not obvious
9. excesses: extremes; lack of moderation
10. deliberate: knowing; intentional; purposeful
11. policy: plan; course of action; strategy
12. intentional: with intent; knowing; purposeful; deliberate
13. initiatives: plans; programs; proposals
14. penetrating: entering into; gaining access to
15. tacit: unspoken; understood; inferred; implicit
16. resistance: opposition; challenge; standing firm against
17. summits: meetings
18. promote: encourage; help; support
19. cope with: deal with; handle; manage
20. colonization: taking complete control of distant territory usually for the purpose of taking advantage of economic resources

Exercise 2 (page 50)

1. don't mind
2. sphere
3. inevitable
4. folklore
5. encroachment
6. extinction

Exercise 3 (page 50)

1. mechanisms: processes; systems
2. embraces: includes; comprises
3. surpasses: is more than; is greater than; exceeds
4. tongues: languages

Figurative Language and Idioms (pages 50–51)

1. has taken root
2. the last word
3. deep-rooted
4. makes a mark
5. hand in glove (Par. 2: hand in hand)
6. broke new ground
7. a concerted strategy
8. make headway
9. at stake

Stems and Affixes (page 51)

1. to have a monopoly: to have control; to dominate
2. globalization: the process by which things that were once local are becoming worldwide
3. unavoidable: cannot be avoided; inevitable

4. underpin: underlie; support; form the foundation for
5. transnational: across nations; international
6. biennially: every two years
7. subnational: within a nation; smaller than a nation
8. linguicide: killing a language
   ethnocide: killing/destroying a culture
   deculturation: destroying a culture; ethnocide
   semi-official: not completely official; a policy that is not completely stated but is systematic and known

Vocabulary Review (page 52)

1. excess
2. subtly
3. monopoly
4. inevitable

Selection 3B: Journal Graphic
"Winners and Losers"

Getting Oriented (page 53)

1. Linguistic densities, the density of languages spoken in a geographical area
2. They are similar, but not the same. In the pie chart, these colors represent different continents. The use of color on both graphics is similar in the sense that the highest density color on the map is used to represent the continent with the highest distribution of languages. On both graphics, the ordering of the colors is the same from highest to lowest.
3. Some languages are essentially tied for a particular rank. A better title might be "The World's Top Languages by Number of Speakers" or "The Ten Top Rankings of Languages by Number of Speakers."

Skimming and Scanning (page 56)

1. Answers to Before You Begin are: 1. 3%; 2. The Asia-Pacific region, particularly New Guinea; 3. 100,000; 4. 10; 5. The text and the graph disagree. Paragraph 3 lists Chinese, English, Hindi, Spanish, Russian, Arabic, Portuguese, and French. The graph lists English, Mandarin Chinese, Hindi (with Urdu), Spanish, Russian, Arabic, and Bengali.
2. F
3. New Guinea (Irian Jaya and Papua New Guinea)
4. Africa
5. F
6. T
7. F
8. T
9. Nearly extinct: spoken by only 12 people at most; seriously endangered: more widely used but not being passed down to children; endangered: languages spoken by some children but fewer and fewer.

Critical Reading (page 56)

1. The text notes that the numbers vary depending on the method of counting. One difference between the text and the graph may be that the bar graph lists both first and second language speakers. Also, in counting, the graph

combines speakers of Malay and Indonesian. Can you think of other possible reasons why the two sources may differ? Do you have complete confidence in the people who write and edit technical articles?

2. The kinds of government policies that can affect language survival include whether the languages are taught in schools, whether they are designated "official" languages, and whether their use is encouraged in the public sphere, e.g., on ballots, in newspapers, in courts.

3. This question calls for personal opinion; answers will vary.

Selection 3C: International Agency Report "6,000 Languages: An Embattled Heritage"

Skimming (page 57)

1. The major causes listed are the rise in nation states and industrialization/scientific progress. Because national unity became tied to linguistic homogeneity, governments have tried to eliminate minority languages. Industrialization and global communication have made language diversity seem inefficient.

2. If we were all monolingual, our brains might lose some of their linguistic abilities. Also, the loss of linguistic history is the loss of human history. Finally, the loss of languages means the loss of cultures and ways of seeing the world.

Critical Reading (page 57)

This question calls for personal opinion; answers will vary.

Unit 3

Nonprose Reading: Newspaper Advertisements

Overview (page 59)

1. Help Wanted, Help Wanted Over 18, Business Opportunities, Internships, Child-care, Tutoring
2. Furnished Apartments, Unfurnished Apartments, Shared Housing
3. Shared Housing and Rooms
4. Parking
5. Internships (Also some Volunteer positions are similar to Internships.)

Comprehension (page 62)

1. SAT Tutors Needed; Teacher/Tutors ESL; High School Freshman Needs
2. Smart, Energetic, Creative; Teacher and Assistant; Seattle Athletic Club
3. Restaurant-Summer Job; SAT Tutors Needed; Summer Job in Seattle; Summer Job Food Processing; Trekleader; Student Intern
4. Telemarketer/Appointment Setter; Wanted! Part-Time Telemarketer; Part-Time Receptionist
5. Answers will vary with respect to qualifications; you do not have to be a perfect student.
6. F
7. No, it is a volunteer position that doesn't pay.
8. F

9. T
10. $425, New Building; 1-1/2 blocks to UW; From $260–$280; Large Bedroom, Furnished; Summer Rentals
11. We wouldn't; 10 bedrooms and "cool roommates" doesn't sound quiet to us.
12. Probably 0 BLOCKS to UW
13. Female Roommate Wanted (the second one). If you think she would be willing to share with a male, you could also tell her about Share 3 Bedroom; you might also tell her about some of the ads under Rooms.
14. Yes at www.thedaily.edu

Critical Reading (page 62)

1. We wouldn't. Whenever we read "this offer is going fast," we're suspicious. But you may be more curious than we are.
2. It seems to be the opportunity to buy the millionaire maker's information and other tapes. Often this kind of advertiser becomes a millionaire by selling useless tapes. We wouldn't answer this one either.
3. We wouldn't; it seems you would need some real experience to lead others on an adventure.
4. This question calls for personal opinion; answers will vary.

Web Activity (page 63)

1. 835, 845
2. 360
3. Often these are ads from people who are looking for relationships. Obviously you don't know these people; you don't know whether what they say is true or whether they are dangerous people.
4. a. $6.00
   b. No
   c. Friday
5. Your ad depends on the kind of roommate you want.

Word Study: Stems and Affixes

Exercise 1 (pages 66–67)

1. c   2. a   3. b   4. c   5. c
6. telephone: an instrument that reproduces sound that comes from far away (*tele:* far; *phon:* sound) telegram: a written message sent far away (*tele:* far; *gram:* written) television: an instrument that produces a picture of something that is far away (*tele:* far)
7. when he or she wants to take a picture of something far away
8. support: to hold up physically or emotionally (*sup:* under; *port:* carry)
9. Interstate commerce is business between different states. Intrastate commerce is business within one state.
10. aqueduct: a structure built to carry (lead) water from one place to another
11. He is going bald; his hairline is moving back.
12. *post meridiem*
13. *Sub* means under or below. *Scribe* means write.
    a. Before telephone agreements, when people subscribed to a magazine, they would sign an agreement to buy the magazine for a certain period of time. They would

write their name at the *bottom* of a contractual agreement.

b. To subscribe to a theory means to believe it or support it (figuratively, you sign your name in support of that theory).

Exercise 2 (pages 67–68)

1. to the contrary: against (this belief)
2. postpone: delay; put forward to a later time
3. supervisor: boss
4. remit: send back
5. superscript: symbol that is immediately above and to the right of another symbol
6. antibiotics: chemical substances that kill bacteria and other small organisms
7. transported: carried (from one place to another)
8. inexcusable: not acceptable; very bad; unpardonable
9. interaction: actions between two or more people
10. transmit: send
11. reconvene: meet (come together) again
12. revoked: called back
13. flexible: able to bend without breaking
14. portable: lightweight; capable of being carried
15. circumnavigate: sail around
16. imposed: placed (the tax) upon

Exercise 3 (pages 68–69)

1. b   3. a   5. e   7. d   9. a   11. c
2. d   4. c   6. b   8. e   10. f

Word Study: Dictionary Use (pages 70–71)

1. a. 1. adjective
      2. weak; exhausted
   b. 1. noun
      2. break
2. consecutively
3. a and c
4. b
5. a
6. a

7. a
8. a. runner: 8
   b. runway: 6
   c. runes: 1
9. b
10. b
11. ruralist
12. a. 2
    b. 1

Sentence Study: Comprehension (pages 75–77)

1. c   3. b   5. a   7. c   9. c
2. b   4. d   6. d   8. a

Paragraph Reading: Main Idea (pages 78–84)

Paragraph 1: c   Paragraph 3: d   Paragraph 5: c
Paragraph 2: d   Paragraph 4: a

Paragraph 6: A summit is a meeting between leaders of enemy Great Powers trying to reach agreements in order to avoid future conflict.

Paragraph 7: Recognizing that you have choices about what you do will make you feel better.

Poem: Our photo albums show our lives as we want to believe they are.

Discourse Focus: Reading for Different Goals—Web Work

GetAways.com (pages 85–87)

1. Yes. Possibilities include the following:
   a. The icon for flights at the top of the page
   b. Need help planning your trip?
   c. **Customer Service**
   d. Enter info for your next trip, . . .
2. At the top of the page, the icon for lodging
3. You enter your city and St. Louis. For the three of us, the home cities are Denver, Detroit, and Seattle, so the pairs would be
   a. Denver/St. Louis
   b. Detroit/St. Louis
   c. Seattle/St. Louis
4. a. We would try Air Travel, **At the airport**.
   b. The most likely place to find information about storing baggage at the airport would be **At the airport**.
   c. You could check under **On the plane**, but in general, we do not tip pilots.
5. This question calls for personal opinion; answers will vary.

MapIt.com (page 87)

1. a. Highway 64 runs between the St. Louis Science Center and Forest Park. It would probably be hard to find a place to cross the highway. This map does not show a scale so it would be hard to judge distances, but looks like the museums in Forest Park would all be quite far away from your hotel area. In general, we would find this to be too far to walk unless we had a lot of time and it was a nice day.
   b. Public Transportation
   c. Click on Museums.
2. Construction update and perhaps Driving Directions
3. Either My Maps & Routes or Directions FROM this address.
4. Restaurants
5. **Help** or **Customer Service**

The Expressionist Museum (page 89)

1. Yes, there is a section on artist biographies.
2. **Artists' Biographies**
3. **Tours & Lectures**

ArtLive (page 89)

1. a. Yes
   b. T
   c. **Online Resources**
2. a. It doesn't say.
   b. 1890 or 1891
   c. Under articles, on page 91, click on **Text about "The Starry Night"**
   d. Yes, *Vincent: A Complete Portrait.*

3. <u>Early Work, Arles, Saint-Rémy</u>, and
   <u>Auvers-sur-Oise</u>
4. F
5. F
6. N
7. T
8. If you click on Support ArtLive, you will get information on becoming a patron of the ArtLive Web site. Advantage: as a member of the site you will get a lot of email and information. Disadvantage: as a member of the site you will get a lot of email and information. You will also, almost assuredly, be asked to contribute money to the site.

Starry Night Gallery (page 93)

1. F (He is an enthusiastic amateur.)
2. F
3. F
4. T
5. T
6. We liked it, but none of us bookmarked it; we figured we could find it easily enough if we need the information, and right now we have too many sites bookmarked.
7. We would cite **ArtLive** because it provides more authoritative coverage of the artist. We have more confidence in *The Bulfinch Guide* than in the webmaster of **Starry Night Gallery**, who says he is on "shaky ground."

Unit 4

Selection 1A: Reference Book
"The Creative Spirit"

Comprehension (page 97)

1. Pressures that inhibit creativity: surveillance, evaluation, rewards, competition, over-control, restricting choice, pressure
2. T
3. T
4. F
5. Reader's choice
6. T
7. F
8. T
9. T

Critical Reading (page 101)

1. F (They will learn, but we will not know what they learned.)
2. F (Merely by living and engaging in activity we are learning all the time; what we are learning, and whether it is what the teacher wants us to learn—that is another matter.)
3. This is open to debate.
4. Reader's choice
5. Reader's choice

Vocabulary from Context (pages 102–3)

1. creativity: ability to use the imagination to develop original ideas
2. toddlers: children who are just learning to walk
3. risk-taking: inclined to try new things, sometimes without proper care or preparation
4. inhibit: to stop something from continuing or developing; constrain; hold back; restrict
5. restricting: holding back; making difficult to accomplish; inhibiting
6. savor: to enjoy; to make something last because of the enjoyment
7. intrinsic: natural; essential
8. peers: age-mates; individuals who are of the same approximate age
9. engrossed: completely absorbed in something; totally involved
10. flow: unconscious and easy involvement in an activity
11. rhythms: regular habits; comfortable tendency and routine
12. compulsions: strong feelings of being required to do something
13. surveillance: excessive observation; constant watching
14. to hover: to stay close by; to be overly protective
15. excessive: more than necessary; too much
16. competition: activity aimed at someone doing better than someone else; contest organized to see who is best
17. desperate: urgent, anxious desire to accomplish something
18. aversion: dislike of something
19. proclivities: inclinations; tendencies

Figurative Language and Idioms (page 103)

1. A creative "urge" is a desire to try something new. Being observed makes us want to avoid being seen, that is, not to take risks.
2. A good thing. They favor activities that give children the opportunity to forget about time and other pressures.

Selection 1C: Newspaper Article
"Parents Seeking Cool Classroom for Son"

Comprehension (pages 107–8)

1. He is unable to walk due to an auto accident in infancy.
2. His body is unable to control its temperature.
3. Above 78 degrees.
4. The district provided a transparent air-conditioned cubicle for Raul. The box was placed within the classroom.
5. F
6. F
7. His parents believe that the cubicle is too restrictive. Raul is unable to interact normally with his classmates and teacher.
8. This item is intended for discussion.
9. F (We know from paragraph 13 that the school district has already air-conditioned its high schools.)

10. T or F. You might answer true if you believe the statements of school district personnel. You might answer false if you believe that the school board could find funds if it wished to do so.

11. Based on the information in paragraph 13, the cost might be about $5,700.

12. T or F. You might answer true if you believe that the school board made the decision to air-condition high school classrooms based on the ability of the younger students to handle heat. You might answer false if you believe the decision was made for other reasons.

13. We could not think of any alternatives. Can you?

14–17. These questions are intended for discussion.

Vocabulary from Context

Exercise 1 (page 109)

1. resume: start again
2. transparent: clear; capable of being seen through
3. alternatives: different choices; different possibilities
4. persuade: convince
5. restrictive: limiting; confining

Exercise 2 (page 109)

1. swelter
2. peering
3. cubicle
4. paraplegic
5. environment
6. dismayed
7. jealousy
8. discrimination

Reading Selection 2: Newspaper Questionnaire "How Do You Handle Everyday Stress?"

Vocabulary Review (page 114)

demand

Reading Selection 3: Science Reporting "The Stereotype of Stereotypes"

Comprehension

Exercise 1 (pages 116–17)

1. F
2. T
3. F
4. T
5. T
6. T
7. T
8. F
9. F

Exercise 2 (page 117)

1. P
2. N
3. N
4. N
5. P
6. P

Vocabulary from Context

Exercise 1 (page 119)

1. prejudices: negative feelings before the facts are known; preconceived ideas; biases
2. biased: prejudiced
3. bigotry: prejudice; intolerance
4. stigmatize: mark someone as not normal or standard
5. exploit: treat unfairly; take advantage of; misuse
6. unjustified: having no justification; mistaken; wrong; incorrect; invalid; untrue
7. erroneous: mistaken; wrong; incorrect; invalid; untrue
8. tendency: when something moves generally in a particular direction; inclination; propensity
9. propensity: tendency; inclination
10. abet: help; aid; support
11. confront: face up to; meet head on; deal with
12. animosities: negative feelings
13. traits: characteristics; qualities
14. subtlety: looking for the less obvious; making fine distinctions

Exercise 2 (page 120)

1. to enhance
2. probes
3. delineating
4. keener
5. to marshal
6. punctuality
7. deadlines
8. neglects to ask
9. a wide array

Exercise 3 (page 120)

1. dwellings: houses; homes; residences
2. (in the) realm: (in the) area; (in the) field; (on the) topic; (on the) subject
3. employ: use
4. invalid: untrue; false; unproven; unsupported
5. encase: surround; include; enclose
6. counteract: act against; work against; counterbalance; neutralize; offset; undo an effect with opposing action
7. crucial: important; necessary; vital; critical; fundamental
8. tagged: identified; selected; labeled
9. tardiness: lateness; not being on time; missing deadlines
10. distort: make inaccurate; misrepresent; cloud; twist

Figurative Language and Idioms (page 121)

1. fall short of
2. to give (stereotypes) their due
3. gained (particular) favor
4. conflict resolution
5. bridge-building

Dictionary Study (page 121)

1. punch^2 n 2
2. boast^1 vtr 2 or 3
3. vtr 4
4. vtr 3
5. vintr

Vocabulary Review (page 122)

1. accuracy
2. justified
3. animosity
4. trait
5. deadlines

Unit 5

Word Study: Context Clues

Exercise 1 (pages 127–28)

1. hazy: not clear
2. to anticipate: to guess in advance; to think of ahead of time; to foresee
3. massive: large; heavy; clumsy
4. vague: not specific; not clear; imprecise
5. to appease: to satisfy
6. to provoke: to cause
7. to manifest: to show; to demonstrate
8. toll: total; count; extent of loss
9. wretched: poor; terrible; miserable
10. mammoth: large

Exercise 2 (page 128)

diminutive: very small; tiny
notable: noteworthy; remarkable; extraordinary; significant
hover: to remain (to hang suspended or flutter) in the air near one place
unique: one of a kind; exceptional
ornithology: the study of birds

Word Study: Stems and Affixes

Exercise 1 (pages 130–31)

1. a	3. c	5. d	7. d	9. c	11. d
2. d	4. a	6. b	8. b	10. c	

12. Originally, *manufacture* meant to make by hand (*manu:* hand; *fact:* make). Now products that are manufactured are often made by machine. Originally, *manuscripts* were books written by hand (*manu:* hand; *script:* write). Today, a manuscript is a document that is either handwritten or typed; it is a document in prepublication form.

Exercise 2 (page 131)

1. beneficial: good (for)
2. mislaying: misplacing; putting in a place that is later forgotten
3. bilingual: speaks two languages
4. misbehave: behave badly; act the wrong way
5. anonymous: nameless; not named; without giving their name

Exercise 3 (page 132)

1. e	3. c	5. d	7. b	9. d	11. e
2. f	4. b	6. a	8. f	10. c	12. a

Sentence Study: Comprehension (pages 133–35)

1. d	3. c	5. b	7. a	9. a
2. c	4. d	6. c	8. b	

Paragraph Reading: Restatement and Inference (pages 137–39)

Paragraph 1: b, d, e
Paragraph 2: b, d, e
Paragraph 3: a, d, e
Paragraph 4: b, d, e
Paragraph 5: a, b, e

Discourse Focus: Careful Reading/Drawing Inferences (pages 140–43)

1. "Class Day": The museum authorities knew the communication was not an authentic one because of the manner of expressing the dates of the Pharaoh's reign. All B.C. dates are expressed in the reverse manner from A.D. dates. Thus, for example, Moses lived from 1571 to 1451 B.C. and Tutankhamen reigned from 1358 to 1350 B.C.
2. "Ruth's Birthday": Her bill smelled of the perfume she'd spilled on her purse.
3. "The Ex-Wife Murder": Rogers could not have known that his ex-wife had been shot unless he had guilty knowledge of the crime. The maid did not say why she had been taken to the hospital, yet Roger's first words on entering it were "Who shot her?"
4. Case #463: Fordney knew that the dog had not bitten Miss Marshall because he found no teeth marks in the dress. She later confessed to inflicting the wound herself with a fork in the hope of collecting damages from Mrs. McGuire.

Unit 6

Selection 1A: Newspaper Advertisement "Smoking in Public: Live and Let Live"

Recognizing a Point of View (pages 145–47)

1. a, b, d (Note: you might also have checked *c*. It can be argued that in their attempt to portray smokers as just like everyone else, the advertiser wants us to like smokers.)
2. a, d
3. a, b, c, d

Evaluating a Point of View (page 147)

1. b, c

Selection 1B: Magazine Exposé "America's New Merchants of Death"

Comprehension (page 151)

1. T
2. T
3. They replace those who have quit smoking or have died. Also, people are unlikely to begin smoking if they don't start when they are young.

4. T
5. Africa, Asia, Europe, South America, North America.
6. F
7. advertising nontobacco products and services named after cigarette brands
8. T
9. It associates smoking with fitness (health).
10. F
11. Young people around the world are interested in what is supposed to be a glamorous and wealthy U.S. lifestyle. If U.S. cigarettes can be associated with this lifestyle, the cigarette companies hope that young people will want to smoke their cigarettes.
12. F
13. The biggest market, with the most money to be made by cigarette companies, is China. It is a dream come true.
14. F
15. The U.S. government has threatened to impose tariffs against imports from countries that place restrictions on U.S. cigarettes.
16. Write to the President of the United States.

Vocabulary from Context

Exercise 1 (pages 152–54)

1. merchants: salespeople; buyers and sellers of things for profit; traders
2. promote: encourage; advertise; push
3. overseas: in other countries; outside the U.S.
4. appeal: attract; make attractive to
5. lured: strongly attracted; drawn
6. habit: a behavior you can't stop; addiction
7. addiction: habit; uncontrollable use of a harmful substance
8. succumb: give in to; are attracted by; yield to
9. deny: declare untrue; say it is false
10. devastating: destructive; ruining; very terrible
11. stockholders: those who own part of (stock in) a corporation
12. abroad: overseas; in other countries; outside the U.S.
13. ban: stop; get rid of completely; disallow the use of; prohibit; forbid; exclude
14. curtail: make less; reduce; curb
15. curbed: curtailed; controlled; reduced
16. violate: go against; fail to show respect for; break; disregard
17. spirit: meaning; purpose; idea; significance; sense; intent
18. insidious: harmful, but not obviously so; harmful, but appealing; harmful, but taking a long time to show its effects; sneaky
19. sponsor: pay for the cost of in return for advertising time/space; support
20. brands: company names; kinds
21. logo: a picture or design associated with a product, such as a camel for Camel cigarettes
22. pervasive: all around; everywhere; throughout every part; common
23. outrage: act causing injury; act that violates accepted behavior; mistreatment; therefore, acts that cause anger
24. barriers: actions that stop movement or action; actions that keep people and things out

25. retaliated: taken counter action; responded; given in return; countered; reciprocated
26. tariffs: charges; price charge; money charged by governments on imported products; duties
27. punitive: punishing; retaliatory
28. soaring: increasing at a great rate
29. booming: very high; developing rapidly; very strong; prospering; thriving; flourishing

Exercise 2 (page 154)

1. leaflet
2. original
3. classic
4. disregard
5. ally
6. prospects
7. fitness
8. theme

Exercise 3 (pages 154–55)

1. passersby: people who are passing/walking by
2. giveaways: free gifts
3. frequented: regularly visited
4. domestic: national; within the country (U.S.)
5. growth industry: an industry that is expected to continue growing rapidly
6. timetable: schedule showing when things will be done

Figurative Language and Idioms (page 155)

1. kick their habit
2. begin as cobwebs end up as steel cables
3. sea of denim
4. joined forces
5. at the end of the rainbow
6. pave the way

Stems and Affixes (page 155)

1. c
2. d
3. e
4. a
5. f
6. b

Dictionary Study (page 156)

1. vt 1a or d
2. vt 3a
3. vt 3a
4. n 10

Vocabulary Review (page 156)

1. exported
2. sophisticated
3. invasion
4. addiction
5. devastating
6. machines
7. insidious

Reading Selection 2: Magazine Article "Conjugal Prep"

Comprehension (pages 158–59)

1. F
2. T
3. housing, insurance, and child care
4. T
5. nine weeks; ten years
6. renting an apartment, having a baby, paying medical and other bills
7. a mother-in-law moves in, death, imprisonment
8. Some have found the experience "chastening to their real-life marital plans"
9. This question is intended for discussion.
10. This question is intended for discussion.

Vocabulary from Context (pages 160–61)

1. mock: not real; imitation; false
2. to drown out: to cover (up) a sound
3. to giggle: to laugh nervously
4. adjustment: a change (made in order to fit a new situation)
5. to expose: to allow to be seen or experienced
6. nitty-gritty: basic; fundamental
7. trials and tribulations: problems
8. to strain: to weaken by force; to put pressure on
9. alimony: money paid to a former wife or husband
10. unsettling: disturbing
11. to endorse: to give support or approval

Reading Selection 3: Science Reporting "Gene Mapping May Foster Discrimination"

Skimming and Scanning (page 163)

1. The genetic code that determines such physical characteristics as hair and eye color and other personal characteristics
2. Discrimination in the areas of job opportunities and health insurance

Comprehension

Exercise 1 (page 166)

1. T
2. T
3. T
4. T (if the CNN poll is representative of all Americans)
5. F
6. T

Exercise 2 (page 166)

1. T
2. T
3. T
4. T
5. T
6. Thousands
7. Complete reports can be found on line at: **www.sciencemag.org** and **www.nature.com**.

Critical Reading (page 167)

2. a. Paul Recer is the reporter who wrote "Gene Mapping May Foster Discrimination."
   b. Bill Frist is a Republican senator from Tennessee, and a physician.
   c. Olympia Snowe is a Republican senator from Maine.
   d. Tom Daschle is a Democratic senator from South Dakota.
   Recer writes newspaper stories that may influence public opinion; Frist, Snowe, and Daschle make laws concerning the use of medical research.

Vocabulary from Context (pages 168–69)

1. genetics: a branch of biology dealing with heredity; the study of how characteristics are passed from parents to child
2. predictive genetics: relating to the future; saying what will happen biologically in the future
3. chronic: long term; lasting over a long period of time
4. mutations: variations; changes in the normal state of things
5. predisposition: tendency; inclination; likelihood of occurring
6. promote: to give a better job
7. insurance: protection against possible harm; an arrangement by which a company gives individuals financial protection against harm or disease
8. workers' compensation: money paid to a worker for injury suffered on the job or for illness resulting from work
9. discrimination: unfair treatment of people usually because of their race, religion, physical handicap, or other condition
10. genome: the complete picture of genetic information about an individual
11. prohibit: to forbid or prevent somebody from doing something
12. dismissing: sending someone away; firing someone from his or her job
13. eliminate: to do away with; to remove completely

Unit 7

Nonprose Reading: Poetry

Comprehension (page 174)

"Living Tenderly": a turtle
1. rounded
2. a short snake
3. F
4. T
5. F

"Southbound on the Freeway": a highway with motorists and a police car
1. The tourist is parked in the air.
2. They are made of metal and glass.
   a. Their feet are round.
   b. They have four eyes; the two in back are red.
3. the road on which they travel
4. a. They have a fifth turning red eye on top.
   b. The others go slowly when it is around.
5. a large roadway

"By Morning": snow
1. fresh, daintily, airily
2. transparent
3. a covering
4. They become like fumbling sheep.
5. snow

Word Study: Context Clues

Exercise 1 (pages 175–76)

1. attributes: qualities; talents; abilities
2. to confer: to grant; to give to
3. plump: fat; chubby
4. pedantic: bookish; boring; giving attention to small, unimportant, scholarly details
5. aloof: above; apart from
6. to refrain: to hold back; to control oneself
7. ineffectual: not effective; not producing the intended effect
8. marigolds: a (type of) flower
9. drab: uninteresting; dull; cheerless; lacking in color or brightness
10. skin/cortex/membrane: outside cover of a body or organ; boundary

Exercise 2 (pages 176–77)

babbling: meaningless sounds that babies make before they learn to talk

sequence: related group; series; the coming of one thing after another

hearing-impaired: deaf; having problems hearing

myth: untruth; an untrue story or belief

Word Study: Stems and Affixes

Exercise 1 (pages 179–80)

1. b   3. d   5. b   7. c
2. c   4. d   6. b   8. a

9. An astronaut is a person who sails (travels) to the stars (outer space). (*astro:* star)
10. All the clothes look the same.
11. birth rate

Exercise 2 (page 180)

1. biographies: life histories
2. triplets: three children born at a single birth
3. multimillionaire: person who is worth many millions of dollars
4. metropolitan: a population area consisting of a central city and smaller surrounding communities
5. semiprivate: partly, but not completely private; a room with more than one person
6. multivolume: several-volume; consisting of more than one book
7. peripheral: (vision) away from the center, at the sides; having good peripheral vision means having the ability to see things on either side
8. semiprecious: of lesser value; semiprecious stones have lesser value than "precious stones"
9. mortal wound: injury that causes death
10. periodontist: dentist concerned with diseases of the bone and tissue around the teeth
11. popularity: the state or quality of being popular; being liked by the general population

Exercise 3 (page 181)

1. f   4. d   7. c   10. e   13. a   16. b
2. e   5. c   8. a   11. d   14. f   17. e
3. a   6. b   9. f   12. b   15. d   18. c

Sentence Study: Restatement and Inference (pages 183–85)

1. c, e   3. b, e   5. b, d   7. b, c   9. a, c, d
2. b, c, e   4. b, c   6. d   8. b, d, e   10. b, e

Paragraph Analysis: Reading for Full Understanding (pages 188–97)

Paragraph 1
1. a   3. a   5. a
2. d   4. c   6. d

Paragraph 2
1. a   3. a   5. b   7. a
2. b   4. d   6. c

Paragragh 3
1. d   3. a   5. b   7. a
2. d   4. c   6. b   8. a

Paragraph 4
1. c   3. c   5. c   7. c
2. b   4. a   6. a

Paragraph 5
1. d   2. a   3. d   4. a

Discourse Focus: Prediction (pages 199–201)

There are no single correct responses to the items in this exercise. Students should work interactively: interacting with each other and the text in order to form predictions, then reading to see if these are confirmed. The answers, therefore, are available by further reading.

3. While there is no single correct answer, *a* and *d* are the most likely. The inset suggests that the author will *begin* by reviewing the current troubled state of calculus instruction.
4.–5. These questions require a personal response.
6. This paragraph presents calculus instruction in a negative light: calculus is described as a *barrier;* students have *no choice* but to take it; calculus brings back *painful memories.* This very *general* introductory description might lead us to expect that the author will go on to describe *specific* aspects of the current state of calculus instruction.
7. This question is intended for discussion.
8. The final, transition sentence of the previous paragraph states that "participants brought worthwhile suggestions." One might expect that suggestions for change will follow.
9. This question requires a personal response.
10. This question is intended for discussion.
11. This question requires a personal response.
12. The rest of the article discusses suggestions for change

and issues involved in implementing that change. Suggestions for change include utilizing the potential of handheld calculators to eliminate routine problems, thus concentrating on the central ideas of calculus. Other suggestions are to reinforce the important role of approximation and to streamline courses by eliminating much specialized material. In terms of implementation, issues discussed are the need for change in high school math curricula, for new textbooks, and for smaller university calculus classes.

Unit 8

Selection 1A: Magazine Graphic "Six Billion . . . and Counting"

Comprehension

Exercise 1 (page 204)

1. a. 2
   b. 4 (the text in Graphic 1 mentions a "prediction" for world population in 2200, so some may say Graphic 1 is a possible answer)
   c. 1 (if you include the paragraphs), 2, 3, and 4
   d. 3
   e. 1

Exercise 2 (pages 204–7)

Graphic 1
1. F   3. T   5. F
2. T   4. F   6. b
7. An increased burden on food and water supplies; a burden on the habitat of endangered species
8. F

Graphic 2
9. T
10. F
11. Africa
12. Europe = b, North America = c, Africa = a
13. F
14. T

Graphic 3
15. A city of at least 10 million people
16. This information doesn't appear in the graphics. Our guesses include Tokyo, New York City, Mexico City, and Cairo. What are yours?
17. T

Graphic 4
18. F
19. The lines are broken to show these numbers are projections, predictions about the future. There are two different lines to show two different projections that have been made, one in 1992 and one later, when the article was written.
20. There are many different generalizations that can be made. For example: World population grew only slightly from the year 0 to 1500. World population did not start to increase dramatically until around 1800. World popu-

lation skyrocketed in the 20th century. The rate of population growth accelerated after 1700. It took the world until 1804 to reach the one billion population mark. It took about 125 years for the world's population to go from 1 billion to 2 billion but only about 30 years to go from 2 billion to 3 billion and 15 years to go from 3 billion to 4 billion.

Critical Reading (page 207)

1. Since 1987, the world's fertility rate has decreased because of increased education and use of family planning. The mortality rate has risen because of the spread of AIDS. These rates might change in the future for a number of reasons such as changes in education levels, availability of birth control, government policies, wars, famines, medical advances, etc.
2. The predictions in this article are for a smaller world population than people in the 1970s predicted. The world's growth rate at the time of this article was 1.3%, not the 2% of the 1970s. According to this article, even the highest prediction for 2100 is well below 12 billion.

Selection 1B: News Magazine "The World Turns Gray"

Overview (page 209)

1. The proportion of elderly people in the world is increasing, and this may create serious problems for many countries.
2. Answers will vary. Information about specific countries can be found in the text and on the map and accompanying graphics.
3. Looking at the map would be the fastest way to get information about Western Europe.
4. According to the "Map key," the different colors represent differences in the fertility rate and projected population growth/decline in the various countries.
5. a. One represents the proportion of people in the world age 14 and under at different times in the past and future. The other represents the proportion of the world's population age 60 or older at different times.
   b. When the lines cross (between 2040 and 2050), the proportion of older people in the world will be greater than the proportion of younger people.
6. a. The percentage of people 14 and younger and the percentage of people 60 and older
   b. No. In the bar charts on the right side of the map, the colors refer to different years.

Comprehension (pages 212–14)

1. F   2. T   3. T
4. Because a large proportion of people in those countries are still in their childbearing years and because life expectancy has risen
5. People over 60 are becoming a greater proportion of the world's population than they were in the past, and young people are becoming a smaller proportion.
6. F
7. It's very costly to support the growing number of elderly,

and there will be fewer workers to support retired elderly people. Also, markets will shrink, limiting economic growth.

8. Raise taxes on workers. Cut benefits to the elderly. Borrow money from another country.
9. F
10. F
11. Out-migration is people moving out of a country to live elsewhere. Outmigration ages a nation as it is mainly younger people who leave. It also leaves fewer younger people to take care of older people.
12. T
13. F
14. Between 2040 and 2050
15. Any country in orange on the map has a population that will decline by 2050; any country in green on the map has a relatively high birthrate.
16. France
17. T
18. T
19. Italy
20. Italy, France, Germany
21. T

Critical Reading (page 214)

1. Before their populations aged, developed countries had time to build up resources/wealth to support an aging population. Poor countries, unfortunately, did not.
2. *Replacement fertility rate* means the number of children each woman would need to bear in order to keep the size of the population unchanged. (That number is 2.1.) Population decline may not happen because of immigration, a large proportion of women of childbearing age in the country, and/or a decreasing death rate.
3. The footnote under the graph "Developed Countries" lists North America, Japan, Europe, Australia, and New Zealand. Opinions about these terms will vary.
4. No. In the last sentence of the article, he implies that the problems of global aging are not as bad as the problems of too many people on the planet.

Vocabulary from Context

Exercise 1 (page 215)

1. challenge: test; problem; demanding task calling for special effort
2. trend: pattern; tendency; when something moves generally in a particular direction; inclination; propensity
3. fiscal: financial; economic; monetary
4. retirement: stopping work because of age
5. pensions: payments made regularly to a person who has reached a certain age and fulfilled certain requirements of service (for example, having worked for a company for 25 years)
6. pensionable: eligible for; qualified for; entitled to a pension
7. debt: money that is owed
8. ethical: moral; having to do with right and wrong
9. obstacle: something that gets in the way; barrier; hindrance; impediment; obstruction

10. capacity: ability; capability; potential; resources
11. famine: extreme and widespread food shortage; starvation

Exercise 2 (pages 215–16)

1. inevitably
2. thanks to
3. fertility rates
4. dearth
5. feat
6. dire
7. absent
8. divert
9. gap
10. are bound to
11. exuberance
12. ravages

Exercise 3 (page 216)

1. plummeting: rapidly falling; dropping; declining; decreasing
2. strains: difficulties; challenges; stresses; pressures
3. shrink: decrease in size; get smaller; contract
4. escalate: increase
5. diminishing: shrinking; decreasing
6. exceed: go above; surpass; are greater than
7. compounded: increased; made worse; multiplied
8. toils: works hard; labors

Figurative Language and Idioms (pages 216–17)

1. to rack up mountains of debt
2. dental-floss bikinis
3. to make ends meet
4. be called upon

Stems and Affixes (page 217)

1. d   3. h   5. e   7. b   9. f
2. g   4. c   6. i   8. a

Dictionary Study (page 218)

1. prep
2. vtr 2b
3. n 2
4. vtr 1 or 2
5. vtr 1
6. vtr 6a

Vocabulary Review

Exercise 1 (page 219)

S declining   S plummeting   S shrinking
S diminishing   L compounding   L outnumbering
L burgeoning   L escalating   L exceeding
S cutting

Exercise 2 (page 219)

1. absent
2. cut
3. support
4. strain
5. gap

Exercise 3 (page 220)

1. shrinking: declining
2. outnumber: exceed
3. escalating: increasing

4. uses: consumes
5. plummeted: greatly diminished
6. strained: burdened
7. invitation to test himself: challenge
8. worried: preoccupied
9. burgeoning: rapidly increasing
10. birthrate: fertility of a population
11. predictions: projections
12. raise: rear

Reading Selection 2: Magazine Article "Why We Laugh"

Comprehension

Exercise 1 (page 223)

1. T	4. T	7. F	10. T	13. T
2. T	5. F	8. T	11. T	14. F
3. T	6. F	9. T	12. F	

Exercise 2 (pages 223–24)

1. 3 (4)   2. 4   3. 12   4. 8   5. 1   6. 2
(Other answers are possible for these questions.)

Critical Reading

Exercise 1 (page 224)

1. Bergson: essayist
2. Grotjahn: psychiatrist
3. Levine: professor of psychology
4. Plato: philosopher

Exercise 2 (page 224)

1. Freud	3. author	5. author
2. author	4. Grotjahn	6. author

Vocabulary from Context

Exercise 1 (pages 225–26)

1. anxiety: uneasiness; worry; nervousness, tension
2. to resent: to feel displeasure; to feel injured or offended
3. conscious: aware; knowing what one is doing and why
4. tension: nervousness; anxiety; mental or physical strain
5. to disguise: to hide; to cover up; to make unrecognizable
6. aggressive: attacking; bold; energetic; active
7. butt: the object of joking or criticism; target
8. target: the object of verbal attack or criticism; butt
9. to master: to control; to conquer; to overcome
10. factor: any circumstance or condition that brings about a result; a cause; an element
11. crucial: of extreme importance; decisive; critical; main
12. to suppress: to keep from appearing or being known; to hide; to repress
13. to repress: to prevent unconscious ideas from reaching the level of consciousness; to suppress
14. drive: basic impulse or urge; desire; pressure
15. to discharge: to release; to get rid of; to emit; to relieve oneself of a burden
16. to trigger: to initiate an action; to cause a psychological process to begin
17. cue: a stimulus that triggers a behavior; a trigger

18. crisis: an emergency; a crucial or decisive situation whose outcome decides whether possible bad consequences will follow
19. guilty: having done wrong; feeling responsible for wrongdoing
20. integral: essential; basic; necessary for completeness

Exercise 2 (pages 226–27)

1. to intersperse: to put among things; to interrupt
   to avert: to avoid; to miss; to prevent
2. to inhibit: to suppress; to hide
3. foible: weakness; fault; minor flaw in character
4. to ogle: to keep looking at with fondness or desire
   dowdy: not neat or fashionable

Vocabulary Review (page 227)

1. cue	3. resent	5. aggression
2. trigger	4. conscious	

Reading Selection 3: Short Story "The Lottery"

Comprehension

Exercise 1 (pages 234–35)

1. T	3. F	5. F	7. T	9. T
2. F	4. T	6. F	8. F	

Exercise 2 (page 235)

1. T	3. T	5. T	7. F
2. F	4. T	6. F	

Drawing Inferences (page 235)

1. Answers might include such things as the following:
   People were nervous.
   Tessie didn't want to win the lottery.
2. Answers might include such things as the following:
   Normal Lottery
   a. The whole village was present.
   b. Tessie's arrival was good-humored.
   c. Mr. Summers conducted square dances, teen clubs, and the lottery.
   d. The slips of paper and the initial ritual of the lottery seemed typical.
   Strange Lottery
   a. Piles of rocks were prepared.
   b. People hesitated to volunteer to hold the box.
   c. Some villages had already stopped having a lottery.
   d. Mr. Warner considered such villages barbaric.
   e. A girl whispered: "I hope it's not Nancy."
   f. Tessie didn't want to win; she wanted to include her married children in the second drawing.
   Double Meaning
   a. There was no place to leave the box during the year.
   b. The Watson boy blinked his eyes "nervously."
   c. There were continual references to tension, nervousness, and humorless grins.
   d. Mrs. Dunbar said to "get ready to run tell Dad."
3. They had to take part so that everyone would be responsible, so that everyone would have to take part next year.

4. Mr. Warner felt that giving up the lottery would bring bad luck and would be uncivilized. He represents the older, more conservative members of a society who resist change.
5. Tessie wanted more people to be included in the final drawing so that her chances of "winning" would be reduced.
6. *Changes in the Lottery*
   a. The original paraphernalia had been lost.
   b. The box had changed.
   c. Slips of paper had replaced wooden chips.
   d. There used to be a recital and ritual salute.
   Unchanged Elements of the Lottery
   a. The list of names was checked in the same way.
   b. The black box was made with wood from the original box.
   c. There were two drawings and the result of the lottery had remained the same.

Vocabulary from Context

Exercise 1 (page 236)

1. ritual: any formal, customary observance or procedure; ceremony; rite
2. paraphernalia: equipment; any collection of things used in some activity
3. drawing: a lottery; the act of choosing a winner in a lottery
4. gravely: seriously; soberly; somberly; solemnly
5. soberly: seriously; gravely; solemnly; sedately
6. murmur: a low, indistinct, continuous sound
7. to discard: to throw away, abandon, or get rid of something that is no longer useful
8. to disengage: to release oneself; to get loose; to leave

Exercise 2 (pages 236–37)

1. boisterous   3. gossip   5. interminably
2. reprimands   4. fussing

Exercise 3 (page 237)

1. to devote: to give
2. stirred up: moved; shook; displaced
3. to fade off: to slowly disappear or end; to die out
4. shabbier: older; more broken down; worn out; showing more wear
5. to lapse: to fall away; to slip from memory; to return to former ways
6. craned: raised or moved
7. tapped: hit lightly
8. consulted: looked at; checked; referred to; sought information from

Unit 9

Nonprose Reading: Bus Schedule

Exercise 1 (page 240)

1. 20th Avenue
2. The schedule does not list the university; however, if you knew that the university was in downtown Denver, you would know that the bus goes near the university. The bus does go by the museum.
3. "Peak hours" are when the most traffic is on the road: 6–9 A.M. and 4–6 P.M. weekdays. Because the traffic moves more slowly, your ability to get to work on time may depend on this knowledge. Also, it costs more to ride the bus during peak hours.
4. $2.80 (round-trip: 70 cents per adult each way; children 5 or under may ride free)
5. Yes, you must have exact change or use tokens.
6. 573-2288
7. 303-299-6000 or 1-800-366-7433 or 303-299-6039 (for people with hearing or speech impairments)
8. Five cents

Exercise 2 (pages 240–41)

1. Yes   2. T   3. F
4. Yes (on selected trips only)

Exercise 3 (page 241)

1. T
2. All 20th Avenue buses are accessible to wheelchairs.
3. The 8:56 A.M. bus will get you there 40 minutes early. The 9:58 bus will get you there 22 minutes late. You decide which bus to take.
4. The 6:08 P.M. bus
5. None
6. F
7. F
8. F

Word Study: Stems and Affixes

Exercise 1 (page 245)

1. hydroelectric (plant): a plant that uses water power to produce electricity
2. thermometer: an instrument that measures heat and indicates temperature
3. hyperactive: overactive; too active; abnormally active
4. to verify: to make sure it is true; to confirm
5. pedals: the parts of the bicycle moved by the feet to make the wheels turn
6. dehydration: loss of water from the body
7. tripod: a three-legged stand used to hold a camera
8. hypersensitive: overly sensitive; too easily hurt
9. hypodermic: a needle used to inject substances under the skin
10. orthodontics: a type of dentistry concerned with straightening teeth
11. deported: made (him) leave the country
12. per capita: individual; for each person
13. dermatologist: a doctor who treats skin diseases
14. geothermal: heat of the earth
15. bipedal: walked on two feet
16. veracity: truth
17. supersonic: faster than (above) the speed of sound

Exercise 2 (page 246)

1. d	6. e	12. c	18. a
2. a	7. f	13. a	19. c
3. e	8. d	14. d	20. e
4. c	9. b	15. f	21. d
5. b	10. a	16. b	22. b
	11. c	17. e	

Sentence Study: Comprehension (pages 247–49)

1. d	3. a	5. c	7. b	9. b
2. b	4. c	6. a	8. d	

Paragraph Reading: Restatement and Inference (pages 250–52)

Paragraph 1: e

Paragraph 2: a, b, c, d

Paragraph 3: c, d

Paragraph 4: a (c)

Paragraph 5: a, d

Discourse Focus: Careful Reading/Drawing Inferences (pages 253–56)

1. "Murder on Board": Nathan Cohen was held because it would have been impossible for him to have written in small, precise handwriting during a storm that "tossed and rocked" the boat.

2. "Death in the Mountains": It was a dark, starless, moonless night. No animal's eyes shine unless there is a light that can be reflected from them. A human's eyes NEVER shine under any circumstances.

   Wylie could not possibly have seen eyes shining at him in the dark. It was clearly murder.

3. "Case #194": If the newspaper account was correct, Mayer was lying. He could not possibly have been in the water, walked half a mile through ten below zero weather, and then shaken water from his clothes. Had the tragedy happened as he described it, the water on his clothes would have been frozen.

4. "The Break": Before ascertaining the killer's identity we will find out who is the mob leader.

   The leader is not Louis Segal (2). And he is not Anton Kroll or Sam Chapin (3), therefore the leader is Dan Morgan. Dan Morgan (the leader) is not the killer (4). The killer is not Louis Segal (2 and 4) and in (5) we learn Anton Kroll is not the murderer. Hence the man who killed Trooper Burton is Sam Chapin.

Unit 10

Selection 1A: Popular Science "Grains of Hope"

Comprehension (pages 260–62)

1. Answers will vary somewhat for these two charts. Here is one possibility for how the charts might be answered.

TABLE 1.   People and Organizations Who Are "for" GM Crops and the Reasons They Give for Supporting Their Use

Name	Job/Position	Reason for supporting GM crops
Ingo Potrykus	Creator of a GM crop, golden rice	He sees GM crops as a way to improve the health of poor people in the world.
Jimmy Carter	Former U.S. President	He sees GM crops as a way to fight world starvation.
Gordon Conway	Agricultural ecologist at the Rockefeller Foundation	He sees GM crops as a way to feed hungry people.
Monsanto	GM food producer	It makes and sells GM crops for profit.
Bruce Tabashnik	University of Arizona entomologist	GM crops reduce the need for insecticides without making insects resistant.
Dennis Gonsalves	Cornell University plant pathologist	He developed a GM papaya that helped Hawaiian growers.
Rusty Perry	Hawaiian papaya farmer	Using GM papayas helped his crops grow, and customers were pleased with the results.
Florence Wambugu	Kenyan plant scientist	GM crops could provide desperately needed food with less labor and suffering.

TABLE 2.   People and Organizations Who Are "against" GM Crops and the Reasons They Give for Opposing Their Use

Name	Job/Position	Reason for opposing GM crops
European environmentalists and consumer advocacy groups	Varied; some farmers, some consumers, some political activists	They worry about possible bad effects of GM foods related to the environment and consumer issues.
European farmers	Farmers	They fear GM crops might cross-pollinate other crops and are suspicious that the same companies produce both the pesticide chemicals and the plants that need to be resistant to them.

Names that might or might not be circled rather than placed in one or the other chart are Losey, Goldberg, and Mellon. Some might see these people as not clearly for or against GM crops; others might see them as opposed to GM crops because there has not yet been enough research to ensure that they will not have negative effects, such as killing monarch butterflies.

2. Answers will vary. See answer to question 1 for names that some may have circled.

3. Answers will vary. Some other arguments are listed here. The numbers in parentheses show the paragraphs where these arguments are made or implied.

(6) People shouldn't try to change nature.

(8) GM crops are mainly just a way to make money for large corporations like Monsanto.

(13) GM foods might be a source of allergens.

(14) GM foods may pollinate non-GM plants nearby.

(15) GM crops may lead to insects that are resistant to natural insecticides that are now used by organic farmers (endangering organic farming).

(16) GM crops may kill butterflies.

(19) GM crops may lead to the development of stronger, harder-to-kill weeds.

Vocabulary from Context

Exercise 1 (pages 262–63)

1. resistant to: unaffected by; not destroyed by
2. damage: harm; injury; destruction
3. properties: characteristics; traits
4. drought: a long period with no rain
5. starvation: dying from lack of food; famine
6. challenges: problems; tests; demanding tasks calling for special effort
7. suspicious: mistrustful; believing that something is probably bad; harmful; questionable; doubtful; disbelieving; unconvinced; skeptical; dubious
8. risks: dangers; threats; hazards
9. ecosystem: the interrelated community of all living things and their surroundings; environment
10. environment: ecosystem; (in this context: natural) surroundings; natural world
11. pollen: powder- or dustlike substance that allows flowers to reproduce. Some people are allergic to pollen; it makes them cough and sneeze.
12. fertilize: to spread pollen from one plant to another with the result that it will reproduce
13. allergens: substances that cause an allergic reaction. An allergy is a strong sensitivity to something. Allergic reactions can range from coughing and sneezing to death.
14. ruin: destroy; make unusable
15. contaminate: make inferior or impure by mixing with something else; pollute
16. pollute: contaminate; to make impure or unclean
17. poison: a substance that chemically kills or severely hurts plant or animal life; something destructive or harmful
18. ecologists: biologists who study the interrelationship of organisms and their environment; environmentalists; conservationists
19. web: complex pattern; network; maze; shape that a spider weaves
20. benefits: positive results; advantages; improvements
21. monitoring: checking; making sure; ensuring; verifying; confirming; observing

Exercise 2 (page 264)

1. elated
2. properties
3. rot
4. leap forward
5. consumer-advocacy groups
6. critical
7. conserve
8. take advantage of
9. entomologist
10. drifting
11. pathologist
12. (doubly) green revolution
13. drought-ridden land

Exercise 3 (pages 264–65)

1. Frankenfood: monster food; something terrible invented by scientists
2. escalated: increased; grown; expanded
3. protests: speaking against something; complaints; objections; public meetings called so people can argue strongly against something; demonstrations
4. insect pests: insects that destroy plants; a destructive or troublesome insect
5. projected: predicted; expected; anticipated
6. proponents: supporters; those who argue in favor
7. alarmed: worried; concerned; troubled
8. transgenic contaminants: genetic material from another plant (making the seeds impure)
9. weeds: undesirable plants, particularly those that crowd out crops

Stems and Affixes (page 265)

1. d 2. a 3. b 4. c

Vocabulary Review

Exercise 1 (page 265)

1. escalate
2. proponent
3. consumer advocate

Exercise 2 (page 266)

1. a. resistance
   b. resistant
2. a. ecological
   b. ecologist
3. a. environmentalists
   b. environmental
4. a. polluting
   b. pollution
5. a. allergens or allergies
   b. allergic
6. a. contaminate
   b. contaminants
7. a. Pollen
   b. pollinated

Selection 1B: Magazine Graphic
"The Global Food Fight"

Comprehension

Exercise 1 (page 267)

1. Color is used to indicate a country's attitude toward genetically modified food.
2. They refer to the paragraphs at the top of the page that describe some recent events related to the controversy over GM food.
3. The percentage of the nation's diet made up of grains

Exercise 2 (page 270)

1. Britain, France
2. Argentina, China
3. N; We don't know this from reading this article.
4. N; The article does not give information about this.
5. U.S., Canada, Argentina
6. 130 nations signed an agreement putting some requirements on the shipping and labeling of GM foods.
7. F; Paragraph 9 (Tokyo, 2001) at the top of the page and the Japan paragraph at the bottom of the page reveal that people in Japan hold varying positions on GM food.
8. T
9. N or F; We don't know, but mad cow disease is a neurological disorder that destroys the brains of cows and people.

Critical Reading (page 270)

1. It's possible that a country's diet, for example, and its reliance on grain will affect its position on GM foods. Answers about what, if any, relationship might be suggested by this map will vary.
2. Countries generally favoring GM crops are producers of GM foods, countries where grain is a high proportion of the diet, and countries with large populations to feed. Countries most opposed to GM foods are in Europe, do not have diets with a high proportion of grain, and are not identified as GM food producers. They also have had problems with the safety of their foods.
3. Answers will vary.
4. Answers will vary. Possible sources of information could be found using search engines on the Web, magazine indexes at libraries, or library catalogs. Other sources of information might be organizations supporting or opposing GM foods. To decide if the information is reliable, one would have to evaluate aspects such as the author of the information, the date of the information, the quality of any research reported, and the publisher of the information.

Vocabulary from Context

Exercise 1 (page 271)

1. Paragraph 1: block, banned, blockade, logjam
   Paragraph 3: freeze
   Paragraph 5: bans
   Paragraph 6: prohibits

2. Paragraph 7: approves
   Paragraph 8: receptive
   Paragraph 9: promoting
3. Brazil: alienating
   Britain: alarmed
   France: hostility
4. France: tainted food
   Japan: food-poisoning

Exercise 2 (page 272)

1. wary: cautious; mistrustful
2. reap: get; gain; collect; obtain
3. eager: enthusiastic; excited; anxious
4. alienating: making angry; putting off; pushing/turning away
5. alarmed: worried; concerned; bothered; upset

Vocabulary Review (page 272)

1. promote
2. prohibiting

Reading Selection 2: Poetry

Comprehension: "How to Eat a Poem" / "Unfolding Bud" (page 274)

1. a. Reading a poem is like eating because, to enjoy a poem, you bite into it; you make a poem part of you and it nourishes you. You "ingest" the poem: you pick it up, examine it closely, enjoy it, and put it inside you. You can enjoy every part of it; every part provides nourishment.
   b. The author is urging us to "get our hands dirty," to really experience and ingest the poem, to touch all parts of it.
   c. There is nothing to throw away; no part of a poem is left uneaten.
   d. Eating fruit is messier than eating bread, but it can be sweeter. Similarly, reading poetry can require taking more chances, making more guesses, but it too can be very satisfying.
   e. This question is intended for discussion.
2. a. Like a water-lily bud, a poem can appear at first to be closed. As we read, we open the bud, revealing the many wonderful things inside.
   b. We expect a bud to reveal a rich inner self: we forget that poems, too, reveal different colors and dimensions upon reading.
3. Both points of view suggest that one needs to examine poems closely, to fully appreciate them. Many differences might be mentioned. Among them is the fact that Merriam stresses the sensuous joy of consuming poetry, while Koriyama stresses the contemplation of beauty.

Comprehension: "This is Just to Say" (page 275)

1. People who don't like the poem mention such things as the fact that it lacks poetic rhyme and rhythm, is not on a lofty topic, and it contains everyday language. People who

like the poem tend to enjoy its haiku-like format, its references to nature, and the simplicity of the presentation.

2. Although the note says, "forgive me," this is not primarily an apology. The writer does not seem to fear serious punishment.

3. Most readers agree that there is a degree of intimacy between the writer and the receiver of this note. They appear to live together. Students have suggested the following relationships between the two: spouses, lovers, child and parent, siblings. This may be considered a love letter.

4. The note may have been written to ask forgiveness, but the expression of intimacy and caring seems to be its primary purpose.

5. This question is intended for discussion.

Comprehension: "in Just-" (page 276)

1. The poem mentions spring weather (mud puddles), children's games (pirates, hop-scotch, jump-rope, marbles), and seasonal salespeople (the balloonman).

2. Eddie, Bill, Betty, and Isabel

3. mudluscious: the wonderful feeling of playing in the mud

4. You can argue either that the poem evokes a happy springtime or suggests a sadder or more sinister theme. To argue for a joyful poem you can point to the use of words like *mudluscious* and *puddle-wonderful,* and to the joyful games of the children. A sadder theme is suggested by the description of the physical handicap of the balloonman who is referred to as *old* and *lame.* The balloonman is also described as *queer* and *goat-footed* (like the devil). If we change the title from "in Just-" to *injust,* it suggests that some injustice has or will occur. Is our view of the balloonman unjust, or will he perpetrate an injustice upon the children?

5. This question is intended for discussion.

Comprehension: "Spring and Fall: To a Young Child" (pages 277–78)

1. a. Can you with your fresh thoughts care for leaves like the things of man?
   b. Neither the mouth nor the heart had expressed what heart heard of, ghost guessed.

2. *Goldengrove:* The initial capital letter indicates that this is the name of an imaginary place where a group of trees have turned golden during the fall season.
   unleaving: The trees are losing their leaves.
   wanwood: Wan is a colorless, sick color. The term suggests colorless, dead stems and branches.
   leafmeal: In this context, meal refers to any substance with a powdered, grainy quality, e.g., corn meal. Leafmeal suggests a ground substance made of leaves. The leafmeal also apparently contains colorless, dead stems and branches.

3. Margaret is grieving for herself: like all living things she, too, will one day die.

Reading Selection 3: Short Story "The Chaser"

Comprehension (pages 281–82)

1. F
2. F
3. a glove-cleaner or a life-cleaner
4. poison
5. T
6. She is sociable, fond of parties, and not interested in Alan.
7. Diana will want nothing but solitude and Alan; she will be jealous; Alan will be her sole interest in life; she will want to know all that he does; she will forgive him anything but will never divorce him.
8. T
9. The first drink is the love potion; the unpleasant "taste" is the fact that Diana will be so possessive; the chaser will be the poison (the glove-cleaner).
10. People who bought the love potion always came back for the $5,000 mixture.

Drawing Inferences (page 282)

1. Alan thinks the old man is describing love. The old man knows he is describing a terrible situation.
2. Alan thinks it is wonderful that his wife will never divorce him. The old man knows that some day Alan may want his wife to give him a divorce and she will refuse.
3. Alan thinks customers come back, as they do to any store, because they have found something there before that they needed; they come back of their own free will. The old man knows that if he "obliges" his customers with the love potion, they *must* come back.
4. Alan thinks the old man means goodbye. The old man means, "until I see you again"; he knows that Alan will return.

Vocabulary from Context

Exercise 1 (page 283)

1. poison: a substance, usually a drug, causing death or severe injury
2. imperceptible: not able to be perceived; unnoticeable
3. sufficient: enough
4. confidential: trusting; entrusted with private or secret matters
5. to oblige: to satisfy, please, help someone; to do a favor for; to perform a service
6. solitude: to be alone; isolation
7. jealous: demanding exclusive loyalty; resentfully suspicious of competitors; envious; distrustful; suspicious

Exercise 2 (page 283)

1. dim	3. apprehensively	5. sirens
2. stock	4. oblige	6. grounds

Exercise 3 (page 284)

1. peered: looked at closely and searchingly in order to see more clearly

2. potion: a drink, especially a medicine or poison
3. slip a little: make a mistake; fall into error; be unfaithful to his wife
4. dear: expensive
5. better off: wealthier; richer

Unit 11

Nonprose Reading: Road Map

Introduction

Exercise 1 (pages 285–86)

2. a. G-45, L-10
3. Centennial Boulevard and 28th Avenue
4. a. Bowling Green is about 25 miles/40 kilometers from the KY/TN border.
    b. Route 31W is a Federal highway while route 65 is an Interstate highway.
        [*All* Interstate highways are multilane, divided, controlled access roads. In contrast, Federal highways have widely varying characteristics. For instance, although some Federal highways are divided, 31W is not.]
5. 63 miles (101 kilometers)

Exercise 2 (pages 286–87)

1. e   3. a   5. d
2. b   4. c   6. c

Map Reading

Exercise 1 (page 287)

1. T   3. T   5. T   7. T   9. T   11. F
2. F   4. T   6. T   8. F   10. T

Exercise 2 (pages 287–88)

1. yes; 50 miles per hour/80 kilometers per hour
2. Answers might include such routes as the following:
    31W or 65 → 101 → 259 → 70
    or (31W) → 65 → 70
    You can spend the night at the Park.
3. Answers might include such routes as the following:
    56 (E. E. State Park) → 40 →
                           → 70 → 96 → 266
    231 (C. L. State Park) → 40 or 41 (Nashville)

Word Study: Context Clues

Exercise 1 (page 292)

1. precariously: dangerously; uncertainly
2. to trudge: to walk tiredly, slowly
3. turmoil: confusion
4. grooming: personal cleaning; the act of making neat and tidy
5. matrimony: marriage
6. probe: a long slender instrument used for delicate exploration
7. to convene: to call together; to start
8. to ingest: to eat; to take inside

9. autocratic: dictatorial; undemocratic; tyrannical; domineering
10. limnology: freshwater biology

Exercise 2 (page 293)

genetic/genes: referring to biological inheritance; the elements by which parents biologically transmit characteristics to their children

rearing/reared: referring to the process of raising children, bringing them up. In this article nurture (child rearing) is contrasted to nature (genetics).

findings: discoveries; conclusions

shatter: disprove; destroy

primacy: being first in importance; supremacy

heredity: the biological process of passing on characteristics from parent to child

nurture: the act of raising, rearing; all the environmental factors that affect individuals as distinguished from their nature or heredity

Sentence Study: Restatement and Inference (pages 294–97)

1. d   5. c   9. b
2. a, b   6. a, c   10. a, d
3. a, b, c, e   7. b, c, d, e
4. a   8. d, e

Paragraph Analysis: Reading for Full Understanding (pages 298–304)

Paragraph 1		Paragraph 4	
1. a	4. c	1. b	3. c
2. b	5. c	2. c	4. b
3. a			

Paragraph 2		Paragraph 5	
1. c	3. b	1. c	4. a
2. b	4. d	2. d	5. a
		3. b	6. c

Paragraph 3
1. b   4. b
2. c   5. d
3. c

Discourse Focus: Prediction (pages 305–7)

There are no single correct responses to the items in this exercise. Students should work interactively: interacting with each other and the text in order to form predictions, then reading to see if these are confirmed. The answers, therefore, are available by further reading.

1. This article is about changes in the family. You might expect to read about changes in such things as the size of families, the roles of family members, the role of families in society, or even the definition of the family. There are many other possible responses.

2.–3. These questions require a personal response.
4. b, d, i

5.–6. There are many possible answers. Based on the mention of family members and the reference to definition, you might have listed such things as the roles of family members, the definition of the family, perhaps the size of the family.

7. Because the opening sentence discusses changes in the historical view of family size and definition, you might expect to find historical data that speaks to these issues.
8. This question requires a personal response.
9. b, d, e, g, h, i, j

Unit 12

Reading Selection 1: Textbook "The Sacred 'Rac'"

Comprehension (pages 312–13)

1. the Asu
2. They live on the American continent north of the Tarahumara of Mexico.
3. T
4. The cost is so high because of the long period of training the specialist must undergo and the difficulty of obtaining the right selection of magic charms.
5. T
6. It may be used as a beast of burden.
7. The Asu must build more paths for the rac; the Asu must pay high taxes; some Asu must move their homes.
8. F
9. The rac kills thousands of the Asu a year.
10. T
11. car

Drawing Inferences (page 313)

She feels that individuals and societies are foolish to sacrifice so much for cars. People often notice problems of other cultures more easily than those of their own culture. The author hopes that people in the United States will be able to examine the effect of the car on their society more realistically if they do not realize immediately that they are reading about themselves.

Vocabulary from Context (page 314)

1. preoccupied: absorbed in one's thoughts; unable to concentrate
2. temperament: disposition; emotional or psychological characteristics; frame of mind
3. prestigious: admired; important; distinguished; of a high rank
4. to treat: to give medical care to
5. ailing: sick
6. puberty rites: ceremonies that mark adulthood
7. to petition: to make a formal request; to ask; to beg
8. detrimental: damaging; harmful; injurious
9. to regard: to consider or think of as being something

Reading Selection 2: Business Text "The Cross-Generational Workplace"

Comprehension (page 319)

1. Because of the diversity in terms of age, race, gender, ethnicity
2. F

3. Economy; political and social circumstances
4. T
5. T
6. F (The Vietnam War had a greater direct influence.)
7. F
8. T
9. T
10. T

Critical Reading (page 320)

1. a. V   b. X   c. N   d. B

Vocabulary from Context

Exercise 1 (pages 321–23)

1. unique: one of a kind
2. diversity: variety; difference, usually concerning race, religion, or another characteristic
3. manage: direct; control; take responsibility for
4. realization: understanding; insight; discovery
5. generational: of or characteristic of the same age; this term is sometimes used to describe traits of people who were born about the same time
6. challenges: difficulties; tests of ability
7. coincidence: something that happens by accident, by chance, without planning
8. resentment: anger; unhappiness that stays with a person
9. enmity: anger; prolonged hatred
10. alliances: groups with common interests; close relationships
11. prosperity: good fortune; wealth
12. scarcity: insufficient supply; not enough of something
13. optimism: tendency to expect the best; confidence in the future
14. harmony: agreement; happiness; feelings of good will and cooperation

Exercise 2 (page 323)

1. stunning
2. encompass
3. formative
4. adept

Exercise 3 (page 323)

1. gulf: distance; difference
2. rift: gap; break; disagreement; distance
3. social demographers: people who study human populations, especially patterns of birth, death, distribution, etc.
4. cohort: a group of people united by common interests or characteristics
5. dotage: old age (The term refers to mental decline.)
6. challenged: confronted; questioned

Dictionary Study (page 324)

1. pitted against: definition a
2. causes: definition c
3. anchored: definition b

Figurative Language and Idioms (page 325)

1. confronted
2. hungering for
3. preferences
4. laid down the law
5. breathing down my neck

Selection 3A: Family Narrative
"An Attack on the Family"

Comprehension

Exercise 1 (page 329)

1. F
2. T
3. When he switched on the torch, they would walk away. Also, the family would not allow him to bring scorpions into the house to study.
4. T
5. The babies clung to the mother's back.
6. F
7. when Larry went to light a match after dinner
8. Margo was trying to throw water on the scorpions but missed.
9. F
10. F
11. T
12. The author carried them outside on a saucer.
13. T

Exercise 2 (pages 329–30)

1. Roger is a dog.
2. Lugaretzia is not a member of the family; she is probably a servant.
3. five: Mother (f), Larry (m), author (m), Leslie (m), Margo (f)
4. Leslie
5. Larry
6. Margo
7. Mother
8. the author
9. This question is intended for discussion.

Vocabulary from Context

Exercise 1 (pages 330–31)

1. glimpses: brief, quick views; passing looks
2. enraptured (with/by): fascinated; enchanted; entranced; filled with pleasure
3. rage: extreme anger
4. bewildered: confused
5. plea: a request; appeal; statement of begging
6. courtship: the process or period of time during which one person attempts to win the love of another
7. to crouch: to bow low with the arms and legs drawn close to the body; to bend low; to squat
8. in vain: without effect; fruitlessly

Exercise 2 (page 331)

1. trial   4. chaos, pandemonium
2. to smuggle   5. order
3. doom

Exercise 3 (page 331)

1. assaults: attacks; invasions
2. clinging: holding on to
3. manoeuvred: managed or planned skillfully; manipulated; moved
4. maintain: argue; affirm; declare to be true
5. hoisted: pulled; lifted
6. scuttled: ran or moved quickly, as away from danger
7. peered: looked closely and searchingly, as in order to see more clearly
8. hurled: threw
9. drenched: made wet all over; saturated with water
10. swarmed: moved around in large numbers; completely covered something
11. screeching: screaming
12. reluctance: hesitation; unwillingness; a feeling of not wanting to do something

Selection 3B: Family Narrative
"The Circuit"

Comprehension (page 333)

1. Answers will vary.
2. T   4. T
3. T   5. T

Comprehension (pages 338–39)

1. a. California (near Fresno). Summer and fall.
   b. F   d. F   f. F
   c. T   e. F
2. Panchito is about 11 years old. His family consists of his father and mother, his older brother Roberto, himself, and little brothers and sisters.
3. F
4. Answers will vary.
5. T
6. F
7. The family would get in trouble for not having the boys attend school. The boys might be forced to go to school and not be able to work to help the family.
8. Panchito describes picking grapes as worse than picking strawberries.
9. F
10. T
11. T
12. At lunchtime, Panchito studied English with Mr. Lema.
13. Answers will vary.

Vocabulary from Context

Exercise 1 (pages 340–41)

1. universal: shared by everyone in the world; common to all
2. themes: topics

3. intense: strong; powerful; emotional
4. tumultuous: not calm or orderly; disorderly; stormy
5. touchstone: a test used to identify something; from mining—a hard black stone that was used to test for gold or silver by rubbing other stones on it
6. generations: groups of people of approximately the same age

Exercise 2 (page 341)

1. sharecropper
2. shack
3. jalopy
4. detect
5. spelled
6. dents, nicks
7. mattress
8. savoring
9. startled
10. held back
11. taking roll

Exercise 3 (page 342)

1. braceros: Mexican farm workers
2. ya esora: Now is the time (to stop working).
3. listo: ready
4. mi olla: my pot
5. es todo: That's all.
6. tienen que tener cuidado: You have to be careful.
7. vámonos: Let's go (home).
8. quince: fifteen (a small amount of money)
9. carne con chile: chile with meat
10. corridos: a type of Mexican music

Exercise 4 (pages 342–43)

1. a, b, d
2. c, e
3. b
4. d
5. a, d
6. a, d
7. c, d

Vocabulary Review (page 344)

1. theme
2. migrant
3. universal
4. shack
5. mattress
6. nicks or dents
7. nicks or dents
8. jalopy
9. generations

Selection 3C: Family Narrative "Fish Cheeks"

Comprehension (page 346)

1. T   3. F   5. T   7. F   9. T   11. F
2. F   4. F   6. T   8. F   10. T   12. F

Unit 13

Longer Reading: Psychology "The Milgram Experiment"

Comprehension

Exercise 1 (pages 355–56)

1. F   4. T   7. F
2. F   5. F   8. F
3. T   6. T   9. F
10. The quotation marks around "subject" indicate that the man strapped into the chair is not the real sub-ject. The real subject is the person who administers the shocks.
11.–12. These items are intended to provoke discussion. There is no single correct answer.

Exercise 2 (page 359)

1. Milgram wanted to determine the extent to which people would obey an experimenter's commands to administer painful electric shocks to another person.
2. T
3. F
4. F
5. This item is intended for discussion.
6. F
7. The answer depends on your view of human nature. You might agree with Milgram, who believed that few people have the resources needed to resist authority. On the other hand, you might believe that people are sadistic and that they want to hurt other people.
8. a. T or F. You might answer true if you believe that the subjects were simply obedient and gave positive evaluations. On the other hand, you might answer false if you believe that the subjects rated the experiment positive for another reason—if, for example, they felt that they learned something.
   b. T or F. Your answer might be either true or false depending on your answer to 8a. If obedient subjects merely continued to respond obediently to the follow-up study, the answers would not reflect their true feelings.
9. T or F. You might answer true if you consider Stanley Milgram to be an ordinary person subject to the same pressures as the rest of us. On the other hand, you might answer false if you consider Milgram to have special knowledge about the experiment that he authored.

Vocabulary from Context

Exercise 1 (page 360)

1. rationalizations: excuses; explanations that are based on logical reasoning, but are essentially false
2. simulation: imitation; artificial situation created to resemble a real situation
3. banality: commonness; ordinariness
4. controversial: full of controversy; causing argument or disagreement
5. ethical: having ethics; acting according to moral principles or beliefs

Exercise 2 (page 360)

1. atrocities
2. ingenious
3. administer
4. subject
5. contrived
6. virtually
7. sadistic
8. debriefing

Figurative Language and Idioms (page 361)

1. "by lot"
2. "a cross section"
3. "chilling"
4. "fringe of society"
5. "has raged"

**Longer Reading: Suspense
"The Dusty Drawer"**

Comprehension (pages 374–77)

1. The answers to this question depend on the reader's perception of people and events. Students can potentially defend Tritt and/or Logan as answers to all items except a and e (we know from paragraphs 1, 12, and 57 that Tritt is a large man).
2. b, d, f, e, a, c
3. Tritt was a teller.
4. Logan was a professor of botany at a local university.

5. T	10. c	15. F	20. c
6. b	11. T	16. T	21. T
7. a	12. d	17. c	22. T
8. F	13. T	18. c	23. a
9. d	14. T	19. T	

Vocabulary from Context (pages 377–78)

1. obsequious: being excessively willing to serve or obey; extremely submissive; acting like a servant
2. to compel: to force
3. grimy: extremely dirty and greasy
4. to restrain: to hold back; to control
5. indulgently: patiently; kindly
6. version: an account showing a particular point of view; a particular form or variation of something
7. futility: uselessness; hopelessness
8. vengeance: injuring someone in return for an injury that person has caused you; the return of one injury for another
9. cluttered: messy; confused, disorganized; filled with junk
10. hallucination: a product of the imagination; the apparent perception of sights, sounds, etc., that are not actually present
11. incredulous: unbelieving; doubtful; unwilling or unable to believe; skeptical
12. indignant: angry; scornful, especially when one has been improperly or unjustly treated
13. flustered: upset; confused; nervous
14. to jeopardize: to endanger; to put into danger

Figurative Language and Idioms (pages 378–79)

1. "going a long, long way"
2. "get away with it"
3. "I'll get you"
4. "I can't stand to be had"
5. "pin (the robbery) on"
6. "polished off"
7. "a stick-up"

Dictionary Study (page 379)

1. to reflect: (*v.i.* 4.) to think seriously; contemplate; ponder (with *on* or *upon*) Note: the answer is misleading. Many people would consider *reflect* in this sentence to be a transitive verb. However, there is not an appropriate definition in the dictionary entry under *v.t.* An example of *reflect* used in an obviously intransitive sense is the following: After hearing that he had lost his job, John just sat for several minutes and *reflected*.
2. to stumble: (*v.i.* 5.) to come by chance; happen: as, I *stumbled* across a clue.
3. grip: (*n.* 5.) the power of understanding; mental grasp or (*n.* 6.) firm control; mastery
4. to stake: (*v.t.* 5.) to risk or hazard; gamble; bet: as, he *staked* his winnings on the next hand.

Vocabulary Review

Exercise 1 (pages 380–81)

1. obsequiousness	10. version
2. go a long way	11. futile
3. restraint	12. compelled
4. flustered	13. clutter
5. hallucinations	14. reflect
6. grime	15. incredulous
7. get away with it	16. indulgent
8. vengeance	17. indignantly
9. grip	18. jeopardize

Exercise 2 (page 381)

1. obsequious	5. indulgent
2. incredulously	6. grime
3. futility	7. jeopardize
4. vengeance	

Grateful acknowledgment is made to the following authors, publishers, and journals for permission to reprint previously published materials.

Bill Adler Books Inc. for Foreword by Rudolfo Anaya for *Growing Up Chicana/o: An Anthology,* edited by Tiffany Ann López (New York: William Morrow, 1993). Copyright © 1993 by Rudolfo Anaya.

Aldine de Gruyter for "The Changing Family." Reprinted with permission from Jane B. Lancaster, Jeanne Altmann, Alice S. Rossi, Lonnie R. Sherrod. *Parenting Across the Life Span: Biosocial Dimensions.* (New York: Aldine de Gruyter). Copyright © 1987 Social Science Research Council.

American Automobile Association for material from Kentucky/Tennessee Road Map. ©AAA reproduced by permission.

American Management Association for material from *Generations at Work.* Reprinted from *Generations at Work* by Ron Zemke, Claire Raines and Bob Filipczak Copyright © 1999 by Performance Research Associates, Claire Raines and Bob Filipczak. Reprinted by permission of the publisher, AMACOM, a division of American Management Association International, New York, NY. All rights reserved. <http://www.amacombooks.org>.

The Estate of Robert Arthur for "The Midnight Visitor" from *Mystery and More Mystery* by Robert Arthur. Copyright © 1939 and renewed 1967 by Robert Arthur.

Associated Press for "Gene Mapping May Foster Discrimination" by Paul Recer, *Ann Arbor News,* February 12, 2001. "The Human Genome" from the *Seattle Post Intelligencer,* February 12, 2001. "Parents Seeking Cool Classroom for Son," from the *Denver Post, August 5, 1981.* Reprinted with permission of The Associated Press.

David Brooks for text on the paintings of Vincent Van Gogh displayed in the Starry Night site.

Christian Science Monitor for "Unfolding Bud." This article first appeared in *The Christian Science Monitor* on July 3, 1957 and is reproduced with permission. Copyright © 1957 The Christian Science Monitor. All rights reserved. Online at csmonitor.com.

CNN.com for link to January 23, 2001 Web site. © Copyright 2001 Cable News Network LP, LLC.

The Daily, University of Washington, for classified ads, vol. 106, no. 137, (May 20, 1999), and for screen shot of classified Web site for November 28, 2001.

Denny's for the menu, © 1998.

Sandra Dijkstra Literary Agency for "Fish Cheeks" by Amy Tan. Copyright © 1987 by Amy Tan. First appeared in *Seventeen Magazine.* Digitalized with permission of the author and the Sandra Dijkstra Literary Agency.

Farrar, Straus and Giroux, Inc., and Brandt and Brandt for "The Lottery" from *The Lottery and Other Stories* by Shirley Jackson. Copyright © 1948, 1949 by Shirley Jackson. Copyright renewed 1976, 1977 by Laurence Hyman, Barry Hyman, Mrs. Sarah Webster and Mrs. Joanne Schnurer. Reprinted by permission of Farrar, Straus and Giroux, LLC.

Features and News Service for adaption of "How Do You Handle Everyday Stress?" by Dr. Sylvil Marquit and Marilyn Lane.

Harcourt, Inc., for excerpt from *American Civics* by William H. Hartley and William S. Vincent, copyright © 1974 by Harcourt, Inc., reprinted by permission of the publisher. And for "Fueled" by Marcie Hans from *Serve Me a Slice of Moon,* copyright © 1965 by Marcie Hans and renewed 1993 by Ernestine Hans, reprinted by permission of Harcourt, Inc.

Mark Hardin for text in Vincent van Gogh displayed on the Art-Live site.

HarperCollins for table, figure, and excerpt from *Obedience to Authority* by Stanley Milgram, copyright © 1974 by Stanley Milgram. Reprinted by permission of HarperCollins Publishers, Inc.

Houghton Mifflin Company for material from *The American Heritage Dictionary of the English Language.* Copyright © 1969, 1970, 1971, 1973, 1975, 1976, Houghton Mifflin Company. Reprinted by permission from *The American Heritage Dictionary of the English Language.* And for material from *The American Heritage College Dictionary, Third Edition.* Copyright © 2000 by Houghton Mifflin Company. Adapted and reproduced by permission from *The American Heritage College Dictionary, Third Edition.*

King Features Syndicate for "Sally Forth" and "Between Friends" cartoons. Reprinted with special permission of King Features Syndicate.

Ladies Home Journal for "Why We Laugh" by Janet Spencer, *Ladies Home Journal,* November 1974.

Library of Congress Prints and Photographs Division for photograph of a painting of Galileo.

Liveright Publishing Corp. for "in Just-". Copyright 1923, 1951, © 1991 by the Trustees for the E. E. Cummings Trust. Copyright © 1976 by George James Firmage, from *Complete Poems: 1904–1962* by E. E. Cummings, edited by George J. Firmage. Used by permission of Liveright Publishing Corporation.

Harold Matson, Co., Inc., for "The Chaser." Originally appeared in the New Yorker 1940, © 1951 by John Collier. Renewed 1978 by the Estate of John Collier. Reprinted by permission of the Harold Matson Co., Inc.

Merriam-Webster, Inc. for dictionary entries for "book," "draw," "skirt," "spot," from *Merriam-Webster's Collegiate Dictionary,* Springfield, Mass.

Harry Miles Muheim for "The Dusty Drawer" by Harry Miles Muheim. Copyright © 1969 by Harry Miles Muheim. Published in *Alfred Hitchcock Presents a Month of Mystery* © 1969 by Random House Inc. Reprinted by permission of the author.

The Nation for "The Politics of Travel" by David Nicholson-Lord. Reprinted with permission from the October 6, 1997 issue of *The Nation.*

New Directions Publishing Corporation and Carcanet Press Limited for "This is Just to Say" by William Carlos Williams from *Collected Poems: 1909–1939, Volume 1,* copyright © 1938 by New Directions Publishing Corp. Reprinted by permission of New Directions Publishing Corp. and Carcanet Press Limited.

New York Times for "Major Personality Study Finds that Traits Are Mostly Inherited" by Daniel Goleman, December 2, 1986. Copyright © 1986 by the New York Times Co. Reprinted by permission.

Newsweek for adaptions from "Conjugal Prep," copyright © 1975 by Newsweek, Inc. All rights reserved.

Opera Mundi, Inc., for "Class Day," "Ruth's Birthday," "The Ex-Wife Murder," "Case 463," "Murder on Board," "Death in the Mountains," "Case #194," and "The Break" from *Minute Mysteries* by Austin Ripley.

Overseas Development Council for material from "The Sacred Rac" by Patricia Hughes, in *Focusing on Global Poverty and Development* by Jayne C. Millar (Washington, D.C.: Overseas Development Council, 1974), pp. 357–58. Reprinted with permission.

Penguin Putnam for material from *The Creative Spirit* by Dan Goleman and Paul Kauffman, and Michael Ray, copyright © 1992 by Alvin H. Perlmutter, Inc. Used by permission of Dutton, a division of Penguin Putnam Inc.

Reader's Digest for "America's New Merchants of Death" by William Ecenbarger. Reprinted with permission from the April 1993 Reader's Digest. Copyright © 1993 by The Reader's Digest Assn., Inc.

Regional Transportation District, Denver, Colorado, for the Denver Bus Schedule.

Marian Reiner for "How to Eat a Poem" from *Jamboree: Rhymes for All Times* by Eve Merriam. Copyright © 1962, 1964, 1966, 1973, 1984 by Eve Merriam. All rights reserved. Reprinted by permission of Marian Reiner for the author.

Science News for excerpts from the following articles: "The Troubled State of Calculus," April 5, 1986, "Babies Sound Off: The Power of Babble," June 28, 1986, "When Science and Beliefs Collide," Bruce Bower, June 29, 1996, and "Math Fears Subtract from Memory, Learning," June 30, 2001. Reprinted with permission from *Science News,* the weekly newsmagazine of science, copyright 1986, 1996, and 2001 by Science Service Inc.

Pete Sickman-Garner for select illustrations and cover illustration.

May Swenson for the following poems: "By Morning," "Living Tenderly," and "Southbound on the Freeway," by May Swenson. Used by permission of the author from *Poems to Solve,* copyright © 1966 by May Swenson.

Time, Inc., for material from the following articles: "Grains of Hope," 7/31/00; "How to Make Golden Rice," 7/31/00; "Global Food Fight," 7/31/00; and "Six Billion and Counting," 10/18/99. Copyright 1999 and 2000, Time, Inc. Reprinted by permission.

TODTRI Book Publishers for material adapted from the dust jacket of *Hummingbirds: A Portrait of the Animal World* by Hal H. Wyss, © 1999.